THE PAST IS
BEFORE US

THE PAST IS BEFORE US

Feminism in Action since the 1960s

SHEILA ROWBOTHAM

BEACON PRESS   BOSTON

Beacon Press
25 Beacon Street
Boston, Massachusetts 02108

Beacon Press books
are published under the auspices of
the Unitarian Universalist Association of Congregations.

Published by agreement with Penguin Books Ltd

98 97 96 95 94 93 92 91   8 7 6 5 4 3 2 1

Library of Congress Cataloging-in-Publication Data

Rowbotham, Sheila.
    The past is before us: feminism in action since the 1960s /
Sheila Rowbotham.
        p.   cm.
    Reprint. Originally published: Pandora Press, 1989.
    Includes bibliographical references and index.
    ISBN 0-8070-6759-8
    1. Feminism — Great Britain. 2. Women — Great Britain — Social
conditions. I. Title.
HQ1597.R69   1991
305.42'0941 — dc20   90-26157
                                                         CIP

THE PAST IS BEFORE US

Feminism in Action since the 1960s

SHEILA ROWBOTHAM

BEACON PRESS   BOSTON

Beacon Press
25 Beacon Street
Boston, Massachusetts 02108

Beacon Press books
are published under the auspices of
the Unitarian Universalist Association of Congregations.
Published by agreement with Penguin Books Ltd

98 97 96 95 94 93 92 91   8 7 6 5 4 3 2 1

Library of Congress Cataloging-in-Publication Data

Rowbotham, Sheila.
    The past is before us: feminism in action since the 1960s /
Sheila Rowbotham.
        p.   cm.
    Reprint. Originally published: Pandora Press, 1989.
    Includes bibliographical references and index.
    ISBN 0-8070-6759-8
    1. Feminism—Great Britain. 2. Women—Great Britain—Social
conditions. I. Title.
HQ1597.R69   1991
305.42′0941—dc20   90-26157
                                                    CIP

Contents

Acknowledgements

Thanks to Sally Alexander, Ros Baxendall, Veronica Beechey, Caroline Bond, Chris Huxley, Charlene Gannagé, Roberta Hamilton, Hermione Harris, Kathy Jones, Radha Kumar, Marina Lewycka, Jill Liddington, Meg Luxton, Ruth Milkman, Heather Jon Maroney, Jean McCrindle, the late Jill Norris, Sue O'Sullivan, Janet Rée, Sue Sharpe, Hilary Wainwright and Rochelle Wortis for their encouragement and help. I owe special thanks to Marsha Rowe, who made detailed criticisms of the manuscript and valuable editorial suggestions, and to Lynne Segal, who spent many hours discussing problems, hearing my woes, lending me material, commenting on the chapters and convincing me it was worthwhile. Thanks also to Margaret Donovan and the Typing Pool Co-op, who typed the manuscript and commented on the text.

I am grateful to the Women's Studies Department of the University of Amsterdam, who employed me as their Visiting Professor between 1981 and 1983 and enabled me to present the first drafts of some of these chapters as lectures. I am also indebted to the students and teachers of the following institutions, where I was invited to give lectures based on themes in the book. In the USA: Barnard College, New York; the University of Madison, Wisconsin; Occidental College, Los Angeles; the University of Southern California; and San Diego State University. In Canada: the Universities of York, Queens, Trent, Western Ontario, and Halifax, Nova Scotia. In Britain: Goldsmiths' College, London; the Central and North London Polytechnics; the University of York; and Northern College, Barnsley. I also gave talks to the London Socialist Feminist Conference in 1984, *Marxism Today*'s 1986 Women Alive conference, and the Fundación Pablo Iglesias in Madrid. The work would have been considerably lonelier without the interest of all these people.

Finally, thanks to Neil Middleton and Geraldine Cooke for their patience in waiting so long for completion, and to Annie Pike for her scrupulous editing and challenging inspiration.

Copyright Acknowledgements

The author and publishers wish to thank the following for permission to reproduce or quote from poems and songs:

Astra: 'mother and daughter' (from *Back You Come, Mother Dear*, Virago, London, 1986). Sharon Barba: 'A Cycle of Women' (from Laura Chester and Sharon Barba, eds., *Rising Tides: Twentieth Century American Women Poets*, Washington Square Press, New York, 1973). Alison Fell: 'For Ivan Aged 9' (from Alison Fell *et al.*, *Licking the Bed Clean: Five Feminist Poets*, published by the authors, London, 1978): 'Rannoch Moor' (from *Kisses for Mayakovsky*, Virago, London, 1984). Jeremy Hunter Henderson: 'Thoughts of an Onion'. Sandra Kerr: 'The Maintenance Engineer' (copyright © Sandra Kerr, 1974). Stef Pixner: 'The pain that I find in dust and disorder' (from *Sawdust and White Spirit*, Virago, London, 1985). Peggy Seeger: 'I'm Gonna Be an Engineer' (copyright © Peggy Seeger, 1972). Pat V. T. West: 'intimations of a sweet past never had' (*Enough*, 3, Bristol, 1971).

Every effort has been made to trace the copyright holders of poems reproduced or quoted from in this book, but in some cases this has not proved possible. The author and publishers therefore wish to thank the authors or copyright holders of any such material which is included without acknowledgement above.

Introduction

'The past is before us' is a backwards-way-round kind of expression. We tend to assume the past is securely behind us as we head towards the future. Yet on second thoughts it makes sense. The past has gone by and is already evident for scrutiny. It is after all the future which is behind us. For, with all our gazing and peering, we cannot see what is not yet. We can only surmise and prophesy.

The expression has lodged in my brain ever since I heard a talk given by Nicolas Krasso at Hackney Young Socialists about twenty years ago. He was speaking on existentialism and illustrated a point with a Buddhist saying, 'The past is before us, the future's behind us.' Now, while it is true that the past can be seen, *how* it is seen obviously depends on who is looking. Clearly the 'I' who is writing this account of ideas in the women's movement in Britain is a person with certain biases and preconceptions. For instance, I do not think it is sufficient to concern ourselves with one form of subordination. I see the liberation of women as inseparable from the creation of a society which is not structured on oppression and competition, though this is not to trust in the ideal future to deliver freedom without autonomous struggle in the here and now. I am a socialist feminist – although I do not conceive of socialism as a fixed set of dogma but as a process of political creating formed from the movement of people against inequality, injustice and humiliation.

The manner in which I have assembled and interpreted the material from books, journals, magazines, internal papers, leaflets, which are the sources for this book, has been influenced not only by my politics but by my situation as a participant in the first women's liberation groups which formed in Britain. My assessment of what is significant is inevitably influenced by the tracks along which I travelled subsequently.

I can remember thinking in the early 1970s, when I was writing *Women, Resistance and Revolution*, that if you were part of history you could write a full account. In retrospect this appears naive. For, however much material you collect and read, you are going to select. In ordering chaos to create shape and structure, we inevitably ignore and exclude. To remember is an advantage because it gives an understanding of the context in which ideas and actions developed. But memory can also play tricks with perspective, because you are distanced from some lines of argument and embroiled still in others.

It is never very clear quite when history begins. The movement for women's liberation which emerged in the late 1970s is not simply in the past and cannot be perceived only as history. It is also part of politics. So, like any other feminist, I have my axes to grind. Consequently, I have not attempted to write a history of the movement, which would have entailed a deeper search, for example into how groups formed and the internal problems of organization they faced. Instead I have confined myself to an account of ideas and assumptions generated around the family, housework, control of fertility, caring for children, and work. I have also described how feminists have approached the state, touched on the contradictory actions and ideas about images of femininity, and outlined some forms of women's collective action which question a politics focused exclusively on gender.

In the period I cover, from the stirrings of consciousness in the late 1960s, which led to the first women's liberation conference early in 1970, through to the mid-1980s, there have been changes both in form and content. Writing of the American movement in the late 1970s, Sara Evans observed:

> As the women's movement dispersed, splintered, formed and re-formed, its importance lay less and less with the specific groups who initiated it and more with the kind of response it made possible. . . The experiences which had provoked and formed a feminist consciousness in the first place re-created themselves not only beyond the new left, but beyond the middle class as well.[1]

This process was to become evident in Britain also. During the 1970s small groups appeared in most large towns, loosely connected by the national conferences. The movement was sufficiently concerted to back national campaigns, for example on abortion. The range of political disagreement was considerable but the situation was fluid and differences did not lead to large schisms until the late 1970s. Though tendencies appeared – anarchist feminist, radical feminist, revolutionary feminist, socialist feminist – attempts to characterize the development of ideas exclusively

within these frameworks over-simplifies, and marginalizes women
who identified with none of the labels.

Now, in the 1980s, there is no longer a single women's liberation
movement. The context in which ideas have developed is more
diffuse. I do not see this as a cause for nostalgia, movements after
all move. So, while any sense of a collective checking back is now
more fragmented, the influences are much wider.[2]

Rather than writing an internal political history of sects and
schisms, I have tried to depict different viewpoints by relating
how specific groups of women have approached issues they faced in
their own lives. So references to feminist tendencies and to women's
groups in left political parties are kept to a minimum.

While this is an assessment of thought in the British women's
movement, national boundaries cannot contain the movement of
feminist ideas. Influences have travelled from North America and
Europe. Now there is a growing interaction with women in the Third
World, which has been documented in the magazine *Outwrite* and
increasingly in *Spare Rib*. I have not attempted to trace all these
currents but have concentrated primarily on the movement within
Britain. I have however quoted feminists from other countries who
influenced debates or whose observations appear to me to unlock
problems which are stumbling blocks within the arguments in
Britain.

At the risk of missing some vital theoretical text, I have extended
the scope of enquiry beyond the mounting piles of women's studies
volumes. As a writer of books, I am all too aware of their limits.
After all, it is not entirely a matter of chance who writes, how books
are marketed and who reads them. Moreover, the thought of a social
movement is not packaged neatly between two covers. It is always
tricky to assess the relationship between what is said or written by
the visible figures in the movement, which may well be in books,
and the turbulent dissemination of the ephemeral in which the
concepts of people who are not nationally known but remembered
locally are more likely to find an outlet.[3] The record of women's
liberation is being recreated already through books, so I have sought
to balance these sources by drawing equally on leaflets, magazines,
letters, internal papers. For, along with snatches of poetry and
memories of conversation, they express understandings as much as
sociological tomes do. Anyone who has been an active participant
in politics knows people do not all sit solemnly reading a book and
then march off to make strategies and programmes. There is a less

conscious process of political thinking in a movement, untidy for historians to be sure, but fascinating nonetheless.

Already it requires some effort to validate ephemeral evidence, since the more distanced theorizing of concepts is authorized within the prevailing structure of knowledge. Here we come upon a tension, for women's liberation has been engaged in gaining admittance to the male-dominated culture *and* contesting its framework. Both endeavours are vital but they are hard to balance. In its origins the women's movement of the early 1970s combated the existing hierarchies of thought. The women's studies courses which emerged out of argument and struggle have now begun to grow into a little knowledge industry of their own. At the risk of biting the hand that feeds, it is not sufficient to produce for an academic milieu, for this does not engage with the power relations involved in the ranking of certain forms of knowledge and understanding.

Intellectual contemplation does require some distancing from life and politics. But the total separation of a bookish world diminishes understanding of the ideas and projects generated by a popular movement for radical change. The theory of the academy has been linked with privilege in Britain and it imposes criteria and priorities on thought and subject and subject matter. The ideal would be a kind of to-and-fro movement between engagement and rumination. But neither the structures of intellectual institutions nor the pressures of everyday politics are conducive to such a solution.

Still, the attempt to render an account of the range of ideas and assumptions which have stirred so many women and turned so many lives around compels, despite the complexities in the telling. The effort of women's liberation to change society has contributed to the redefining of the scope of necessary radical change. It has shifted the terrain of politics and, I believe, has intimated the shape of what could be.

A feature of the movement which has brought both strength and deep confusion has been that the preoccupations of many women involved in it have not been only with changing external social arrangements. Women's liberation has also sought to change conceptions and experience of what it is to be a woman and a man. So throughout the political discourse there are other dialogues, psychological, spiritual, existential. The implications of such explorations in rebellion are uncharted and sometimes emotionally painful in their consequences. There is no knowing where they might lead. Because the ways are unknown and the strains considerable, it is not surprising that some of the women who found themselves left exposed as political pioneers drew back, or that women have sometimes turned on one another wrathfully for supposed desertions when change took longer than hope. There are severe psychological costs in both pitting yourself against existing forms of relationship and dissolving aspects of identity.

On the other hand, a vital resilience is gained within a movement that so valiantly combats the existing definitions of politics and seeks their transcendence. I hope I have transmitted an inkling of these startling adventures in the mundane by chronicling, as assiduously as I am able, conceptions generated by activity to transform everyday living.

I have not attempted to detail theories of culture which have also been a crucial part of the feminist offensive. There are only brief references to anthropological, psychological, sociological, legal, educational and aesthetic debates. This is not because I dismiss the value of this work but because it seems to me that others far better equipped than I are writing about these ideas. I have also restrained my pen in respect of my own trade, history.

What follows, then, elaborates on what might be summed up as the nitty-gritty of conceptualizing. It is written in the belief that there is a great deal to be learned by turning our minds to the obvious. For it is often what seems most apparent which goes unrecorded and is forgotten. Movements for radical change face considerable odds and can do with remembering themselves from one decade to the next.

THE PAST IS
BEFORE US

PART ONE

The Family and Housework

1

Hanging Out Nappies in the Moonlight

The women's liberation movement erupted in the late 1960s in a literature of complaint which focused on the experiences of the family – both in the sense of life in the household and with kin. In the early years of the movement, confinement in the family, dependence and lack of identity were common themes in articles which appeared in magazines like *Shrew*, the London Women's Liberation Workshop journal.

At the first Women's Liberation Conference, held in Oxford early in 1970, members of one of the initial women's liberation consciousness-raising groups, which had grown out of a one o'clock club, the Peckham Rye Group, gave a paper which protested against the meaning of being all day with a family. They exploded angrily against the sense of confinement: 'Our window on the world is looked through with our hands in the sink and we've begun to *hate that sink and all it implies – so begins our consciousness.*'[1] The woman's identity merged with home and family:

. . .the 'family' as it is experienced, is the woman and the children *in* the home, the flat or the room and the man who comes and goes . . . In the house the woman is *in the family* and the two are disturbingly synonymous.[2]

In the writing of the early years there is a struggle to assert a separate identity and challenge the house as a fantasy of happiness. Michelene Wandor wrote in *Spare Rib* of

. . .overwhelming pressures which are the reality behind the vision of 'happily ever after' . . . The emotional focus of this dream is the woman, caught in a million gossamer threads, lightly woven into the finest and most delicate mantle of suffocation. Love and the woman's place are in the home.[3]

Feminist writing in the early 1970s argued that love and marriage offered an impossible promise, a fantasy of fixed union and mutuality. Women's actual situation in the family was perceived to be at variance with the ideal. The pursuit of the ideal, 'the myth', was seen as women's undoing. It was a crucial element in the other side of the coin, women's dependence, financial and emotional, in the family.[4] For instance, the authors of the Peckham Rye paper on the family described the woman caught 'like a pet mouse in its cage spinning round on its exercise wheel, unable to get off'.[5]

When Suzanne Gail contributed 'The Housewife' to a collection of essays about work in the mid-Sixties it had not been customary to see these 'little circular activities'[6] as labour. Yet the accounts testify to the peculiar strains of an activity in which the effort to overtake oneself is so consuming: 'Housework is a worm eating at one's ideas. Like a fever dream it goes on and on until you desperately hope that it can be achieved at one blow.'[7] The effort to plan becomes the attempt to eliminate: 'When the housework was still new, I used to take a little pleasure in finding ways of doing the jobs quicker and better. . . Now I am simply bent on eliminating as many tasks as possible,' wrote Suzanne Gail.[8] And Mary Michaels observed:

> how the women put out their washing
> late in the evening
> as if it will ripen
> in secret
> like blackberries
> with the dew.[9]

There was a mundane material reality behind the mystery, the effort to plan amidst an incalculable accumulation of variables. Emmy Smith found that after working in an office, motherhood did not come naturally. Keeping the flat in which she and her two children and husband lived was impossible: 'I would get so behind with the ironing that pillow-cases in the bottom of my ironing bag gathered mildew. Surely I was the only housewife to be hanging out nappies in the moonlight?'[10]

Combining housework with caring for children meant it was necessary to balance material tasks with relating. These early accounts describe the strain of trying to keep a grip on the routine while being ready to respond to a child's needs. Suzanne Gail explained:

> I used to get very tense while making sure Carl was not getting into trouble. I have overcome this by freezing the surface of my mind from thoughts altogether, leaving it swimming aimlessly so that it can be called into action by an alarming sound. This is a further loosening of concentration, and one that has to be practised for a distressingly large part of the day, often leaving me too empty for real concentration when the chance comes.[11]

The passing of time brought a sense of emptiness:

> Housework, lone work, all work, don't work
> thoughts of an onion dripping tears
> 23 – a loving wife
> 43 – and what is life?
> Thoughts of that onion dripping years.[12]

Women puzzled in isolation about their lack of purpose, about merging into an unacknowledged activity which was both consuming and dissolving. Housework had become socially invisible and disregarded, yet it was still woman's assumed domestic destiny. It took a tremendous effort to challenge the force of the prevailing assumption that this should be what the majority of women wanted. Emmy Smith said:

> I thought of myself as being very peculiar because I could not fit myself into the pattern. Every week I took in one of the cosy women's magazines and read the hints and recipes hoping that something would rub off.[13]

Well, the 'peculiar' women found one another. They began to wonder together and felt less peculiar. The relief released an extraordinary energy. Dissatisfaction was not a personal inadequacy. There was something wrong with this domestic destiny which there seemed to be a conspiracy of family and media to foist upon women as inevitable. Michelene Wandor tried to situate the feeling of discontent in the imbalance of power and the division of work. Complaint thus shifted towards a recognition of the need for change:

If anything is to change we must examine the signs: no irritation or discontent should be ignored, however small. We need to be as honestly critical as we can about our own families, whether we're parents or children or both. We must realize that our failure is not that of individuals.[14]

This process of critical, collective self-examination could develop through the consciousness-raising group. The group enabled women to remember their childhoods with new meanings. It meant that a personal relationship in a particular family assumed a social dimension. Dependence and loss of identity were not just the experience of individuals, they were occurring because of a specific social arrangement in a historical family. Apparently trivial incidents found a wider philosophical connection.

The consciousness-raising group had origins in popular religious movements and had appeared in the US Black movement in the early 1960s. The organizational form proved to be well suited as a means of conveying the dissatisfaction expressed in the first stages of women's liberation. It built on an area of experience in women's upbringing in which there was already confidence – the ability to examine relationships. It transferred this familiar personal culture into politics – unfamiliar to most of the young women who became involved. In the process it introduced a different way of conceiving needs and writing about politics. This was one of the sources for the concept 'the personal is political'.

Every woman who joined a consciousness-raising group became engaged in constructing a biography and in examining those elements in personal life which overlapped with the experiences of other women. Initially, a persistent question was why sexual love between men and women, or the bearing and rearing of children, seemed to eclipse autonomous identity in, as Lee Comer put it, 'a forgetting of who they might have been'.[15] There was a sustained puzzling over the habit of acceptance, the sense of emotional numbness, of being merely an 'extension' of the man.[16]

Men in this early literature are not portrayed as bad, or as overtly controlling and dominating. They are, rather, absent, or emotionally incapable of comprehending the pain and frustration felt by the women, which became particularly acute when they were at home with the first child. One woman described how in her work in the make-up department at the BBC 'I trotted round in my blue overall, maximum cleavage displayed, trying to be efficient but never so that I wasn't attractive'. When she met her future husband she felt he was someone she could love and respect: '. . . if he liked me I would have a better picture of myself.'[17] The inadequacy of such a borrowed identity became evident with motherhood:

> The crunch came after the baby was born. Waves of boredom, apathy and aimlessness descended, together with overwhelming guilt about the feelings. There were positive feelings too, of pride and love and creativity, but somehow they were drowned by the knowledge that now my life revolved solely round pleasing people, my husband, my son, even my mother-in-law, by being a good wife and mother, an efficient home-maker. Out of this I was supposed to blossom as a fulfilled person and I couldn't. . .[18]

Dissatisfaction with family life was not of course peculiar to young women in the 1970s. It was the social expectation which changed. An assumption of freedom appeared among middle-class women, many of whom were among the first generation to go into higher education, and was also expressed by lower-middle-class and some upper-working-class women. A woman from Glasgow, married to an electrician and with a couple of children under two, commented:

> Ben is a good husband and father, in that he does not go out a great deal by himself, and helps me with the children in the evening. We used to get on well together, but since I had the children things have changed. A feeling of impotence began to pervade my life after they were born. . . which seems to be a paradox, considering the sense of potency and fulfilment motherhood is said to bring women. In fact thinking about that contradiction has often made me hark back to the clichés and attitudes I most hate. 'Can I truly be a woman if I do not feel — such and such?' I do love my children, but then again I often find myself standing outside watching them and my husband and myself 'being a family'.[19]

It was not that every woman suddenly became unhappy, but that significant numbers of women felt entitled to a destiny which was not simply domestic. The conviction that options should be available began to be a means of legitimizing frustration with the gap between the domestic ideal and the family as it was experienced. There was in this early writing a recognition that at some level this was not simply a matter of economic power, or even of the material transformation of how work was distributed. There was a problem in how we perceived ourselves as women. A writer in *Shrew* in 1970 described this:

My husband has accepted a fairer division of the housework fairly happily. More difficult have been my own attempts to stop acting out the role of a wife. In many situations I react automatically, such as smoothing over difficulties, by being sympathetic and helpful when my husband is irritated or has lost something, by giving way in discussions and by seeking advice or reassuring unnecessarily.[20]

There was from the start a tension between seeking social explanations of personal feelings and relations in the family, and thus pushing for specific material changes, and a psychological probing of habits of subordination present within our consciousness as feminine people. This could be a most creative tension which pressed on the existing boundaries of the very concept of 'politics'. But it is not easy to maintain such an ambiguity in a political movement. Politics tends to move towards clarification. As 'demands' appear they tend to shed contradictory perceptions.

Demands were less vulnerable when they could be legitimized by the more extreme instances of inequality between men and women in the family. The conventions of politics were reconstituted. Complaint shifted gear into indictment, which could not be dismissed as psychological petulance.

My husband wanted to dominate me completely. He was very fussy about the house, always criticizing my housekeeping.

He gave me a black eye and a burst lip when I was expecting my first baby and when I went into labour he went on about the ironing needing doing.

He was never in, always at the pub. He thought if you had a roof over your head and food to eat that was all you needed. I felt trapped, didn't know who to talk to.[21]

The existence of coercive and brutal control was evident. The creation of refuges for battered women was an organizational innovation which enabled this personal experience of subordination to find a social expression. Women who were the dependent victims of male violence were able to reject explanations which stressed failures in their individual personalities. The Women's Aid Centre was an alternative space in which women could cast off the victim's memories and reach out to a new personality: 'The refuge gives you time to think and get organized.'[22]

This alternative shelter meant that the direct and coercive control experienced by many women in relation to men could be expressed.

Women from a Women's Aid Centre described how they were expected to stagger mealtimes to suit the man's convenience – regardless of whether they knew when the men were coming back. In some cases women were not allowed out by their husbands – even to do the shopping. Beatings were the punishment for failure or defiance.[23] The specific accounts of violence contributed to an attempt to understand the family and marriage in the context of power and powerlessness. In a paper given at a London Women's Liberation Conference in 1977, 'You're Either Someone's Daughter or You're Someone's Wife', family bonds were presented as relationships which contributed to such extremes of control and passivity:

> All the women had been kept in the place which was decided for them by their husbands. They were held back from trying anything. The first time they took any initiative was when they got themselves out of their dreadful situation and into the refuges. And this requires a very great initiative. . .
> They couldn't think of their own needs when every thought and action had to be watched so as not to provoke a beating. They now have the opportunity to realize they are not odd, ill or deviant women. They can question the institution of marriage, where before they would have been faced with a total lack of approval and support from a society which upholds marriage as the ideal state in the face of many, many instances of its blatant failure.[24]

An attempt to understand the ambiguity in relations between men and women, and to explore the economic, social and psychological factors that contributed to dependence and control in the family, was displaced by a much starker portrayal which symbolically polarized relations between men and women. Instead of actual relationships between human beings, inherently evil and inherently good forces confronted each other. Implicitly, violence in the family was presented as the reality behind the false ideal. The slogan 'Rape, like charity, begins at home',[25] could be interpreted to mean that violation and vulnerability could occur in the family – or it could be taken as the determining aspect of the family. The political consequences of these differing interpretations are significant. The emphasis on the family simply as a site of violence, violation and subordination pessimistically assumes it is impossible for a man and woman to live together without the man being a brute and the woman a victim and a liar. This led some women to see women

together without men as the solution. But this did not relate to
the predicament of women still in heterosexual relations. Indeed,
it tended to mean that to be a 'real' feminist was to live differently
from most women.

This was not to go completely unchallenged among feminists.
In 1980 Bea Campbell commented on the silence which had
fallen about sexual relationships between men and women. The
assertion of sexuality between women had become confused with
an equation of heterosexual relations with a betrayal of feminism.
Sex in the family became a new taboo. 'The effect was to reduce
the mainstream of the movement to dumb insubordination in the
sex war, leaving heterosexual struggle to the individual initiatives
of women more or less on their own.'[26] She went on to argue that
this had meant 'There has been little space for a feminist erotica
which could represent heterosexuality as both erotic and an arena
of contradiction and contestation.'[27]

Some feminist women articulated their choice to remain within
contradictory relations which involved men and children. For
instance, Nell Myers, Annie Mitchell, Adah Kay and Valerie
Charlton argued in the late 1970s that it was too simple to assume
that the 'transition to new forms of relating can only take the form
of moving out.'[28] They acknowledged love and affection along with
'intermittent rage and frustration'[29] and desire for other sexual
relationships.

'Moving out' of a heterosexual family still begged the question of
how to bring up children and earn enough to support them. This
was hard for a single parent, while alternative groupings of adults
meant new problems. Clearly, a family consisting of two women and
children or a communal household of adults and children is going to
be the site of contradictory passions as well. It can be illuminating
to shift the pattern of contradiction, but it is clearly illusory to
imagine relationships without contradiction. 'Entanglements, webs,
traps, unexpected connections and inescapable links'[30] face women
who can envisage change, and even as that ppossibility is glimpsed,
they become acutely aware of the power of habits handed on and
reinforced.

The conviction that the women's liberation movement was about a
'transition to new forms of relating'[31] was assumed with considerable
certainty in the 1970s. In the 1980s this utopian drive has faltered,
become more self-questioning, but it still lingers. An element in
feminism is thus very much about making a break, as if will and

striving can by sheer force of effort create new human matter – as in the slogan 'I am a woman giving birth to myself'. Yet all movements, however radical, are also within existing society and the human participants have lived or do live within networks of relationships and carry memories of the inherited 'entanglements' of our kin. The women's liberation movement's continuing dialectic has been the attempt to understand as well as to change existing relations in the family.

One of the most passionate relationships in modern feminist writing is that between mothers and daughters. There have been many descriptions by daughters of both the yearning for separation from mothers and the desire for reconciliation with them. Some of the memories rebel against the symbiotic closeness and a masochistic inheritance from mother to daughter. The daughter in Astra's poem 'Mother and Daughter' ironically echoes her mother's life:

> mascot of the domicile
> > smothered
> > devoured
> > obliterated
> eventually the daughter fled
> into marriage
> with a male duplicate
> of mum.[32]

'Dear Mother' in an early issue of *Shrew* maintained, 'My mother is not my oppressor, rather you are only a vehicle for teaching me my worthlessness.'[33] Mothers are blamed for conveying acceptance and subordination. They keep part of the harsh truth from daughters:

> My mother said a gentleman was a man who walked on the outside when accompanying a lady and raised his hat in greeting. My office had a fair sprinkling of gentlemen. Some of them would be called male chauvinists nowadays.[34]

The conforming mother hands over her daughter to the husband and is confronted by a rebellion:

> 'No way, mother am I going up for auction
> Tapping out a foxtrot with my silver-plated toes
> Papering the walls while the dance-hall Johnnies
> Trip around ripping my best silk hose.'[35]

As for these men's mothers, they are guardians at the gate of slavery and dependence:

> I've met your mother and know just what you want of me.
> Dinner in the oven and washing on the line.[36]

This suppression is not simply overt. Cathy Kerr argued a mother might

> . . .unconsciously try and prevent daughters from obtaining independence by teaching one lesson with their tongue and a totally different lesson by their body language and their lifestyle and thus confuse their dependants into immobility.[37]

The mother is not only the curber of freedom, she is also a victim. Are we simply to relive the masochism and misery of our mothers?

> On many occasions during my childhood I saw my mother being beaten by my father. The more drunken he became the more vicious the attack, the less housekeeping there was. So my mother worked 8 till 5 and some evenings in our local factory. Chicken processing was its grand title: for her it was standing all day, no stools, handling frozen chickens and crying at night with arthritis in her knuckles. My childhood revenge to her beatings was, 'When I'm big enough I'll beat you up,' and I did. The heavy poker across his head frightened him sufficiently not to do it again.[38]

The courage of the young girl was not sufficient to embolden her own maternity. Theoretically she understood the social forces which trapped her own mother, as a working-class woman. Yet understanding did not quell her own guilt and panic:

> The factory set-up is not so easy to change. After 40 years, 15 in the same factory, my mum has nothing but ill-health to show for it. With such experiences I believed I understood the often used term 'double oppression'. But a few weeks ago I gave birth to Sam. Our living conditions are good. I really don't have any worries, but found myself getting blinding headaches when he cried, feeling that it was my fault, that I wasn't caring for him properly.[39]

Mothers have been burdened with a heavy responsibility in feminist writing. But this has not been the only mining of the density of the mother–child relation. Antagonism, the desperate shaking off of our mothers within, has been accompanied by a loving evocation of echoes, smells, memories of softness and warmth, of the mother's imposing vastness:

> I viewed the world,
> Then three-quarters of the way up my mother's legs.[40]

There are recollections of being fetched from school, bread and Marmite, and bubbles in the bath, of playfulness amidst intimations of an adult's sadness.[41] There is too a sense of loss as intimacy is replaced by criticism. This has been particularly painful for working-class daughters, it seems. Sheena Adams in 'Just an Ordinary Woman' describes her early childhood love of her mother:

> First smell was of baking
> Saturday ritual, sister out playing
> She and me and warmth
> A timeless bustle
> – she was magic my mum.[42]

But as she grew older she came to despise her mother's poverty and lack of education. She looked with contempt now at the 'Grey gloves on trips to town to hide work-worn hands'.[43] Her mother became an embarrassment and the mother within her a source of fear: 'They will see through me – see my mother in me.'[44]

Sheena Adams, though, does not simply move out on her mother, she wants to understand her mother's background and meet her on new terms. She remembers the educational prizes her mother won and her grandfather's refusal to let her stay on at school, the restrictions of working as a domestic servant and the scaling down of aspiration which accompanied it – adapting, 'learning not to expect too much'.[45] Sheena Adams appreciates her mother's tolerance: '. . .she accepted my comings and goings'.[46]

Several of the women Jean McCrindle and I interviewed for *Dutiful Daughters* had been hostile to their mother's severity and preoccupation with housework, then, when they had children themselves, came to realize what it must have been like trying to cope with large families without much money.[47] It is clearly an over-simplification to assume that particular patterns of family relations appear by class or ethnic group, but there are obvious

reasons why many working-class women found the struggle for
material survival emotionally consuming and that children bore
the strain. 'Kay' wrote in *Socialist Worker* in 1974:

> I remember the cold most of all. . .Mother would cut a piece of
> old lino and put it inside the shoes but the snow would still come
> through . . .It must have been far worse for my mother than I ever
> realized. Sometimes she would get into terrible rages, we soon learnt
> to recognize the look on her face and keep out of her way. Now, years
> later, I can understand the pressures and anxieties of a single-parent
> family.[48]

Ann Whitehead suggests too that the apparent severity of some
mothers, which was seen by the 'daughters' she interviewed in
Herefordshire as repression, could be a form of protection after
all:

> Mothers and daughters do not have the same values and the mother
> may damp down her daughter's demands rather than support them. It
> has been suggested to me that this does not have to be seen as the act
> of a woman who resents freedom which she does not have, but that
> older women may be more aware of the quite serious consequences
> for women if they do not toe the line.[49]

Dissatisfaction with an overweening universalism has led to an
exploration of difference. For instance, Jewish feminists have looked
at the mixture of guilt and annoyance in the heritage of being both
the 'Chosen People' and a persecuted people, and at the social factors
behind the stereotype of the 'Jewish Mother'. There was the lack of
geographical and political roots, and when families emigrated there
was the responsibility for survival. Time and greater prosperity did
not destroy the anxiety, it made it inappropriate: 'The classic saying
on the one hand "Eat, eat" and on the other "You're too fat". Good
and plentiful food signified survival, security and success – but today
so does thinness.'[50]

From the mid-1970s lesbian feminists began to write about the
difficulty of communicating their lesbianism to their mothers. Julia
Wright worried about how to tell her mother, 'a very working-class
woman. . . She isn't a liberal woman generally'.[51] Julia described
how her mother began to respond in a positive way whenever the
subject came up. Gradually she began to refer to her daughter
as gay and joke with her about it. Their relationship changed.

Before, it had not been very straightforward or warm: 'We never joked together, couldn't relax with each other. Now it's changing we have begun talking.'[52]

While the writing on mothers has been considerable, feminist mothers have not written so much about their daughters. Is there silence because the relationship is trouble-free or because there is too much tension in it? The tension has been more explicit in relation to boy children. For some women the contradictory experience of mothering boys has been the source of such pain that they have rejected sons. There is also the feminist version of the proud mum, though: 'I brought my sons up to respect women as equal and valuable human beings and to do their share of household chores.'[53] Alison Fell's poem 'For Ivan aged 9' expresses ambivalence about aspects of her son's masculinity but also love and delight in both his childhood and his masculine difference:

> He
> is a small battlefield of loyalties
> sturdy
> still the night lies heavy on his chest
> beasties bang on his doors
> he fears his heart may stop
>
> He blushes when I sing sweetly
> hurls his barrel self at my
> arms open wide then draws back
> remembering
>
> Already he
> yearns for past idylls
> mother and father united
> two beloveds in a double bed
> under a single roof
>
> He
> passes hours
> rosy-faced over flashing
> river-fish, kicks his
> feet like a crazy lamb and
> sings up the spring sun
>
> He
> tools precision pictures spiked

with armaments, thrills to
the sharp technologies of war

I fear for you unreasonably
I fear the day these wars or
others dry your wells and
lay you waste

You who already have strength
to comfort,
bathe me in your laughter
O moonface of innocence.[54]

Fathers, by and large, were kept at bay in feminist literature
in the 1970s. Then in 1983 Ursula Owen edited a collection of
essays by women, *Fathers*. The authors wrote of ideal fathers,
of domineering fathers and of absent fathers. Ursula Owen said
that many of the contributors found it the most difficult subject
to write about. There was no idiom apart from fiction for the
daughter portraying the father.[55] Sara Maitland also claimed that
women rarely murdered fathers.[56] She saw daughters as locked in
a struggle with the internalized power of their fathers:

> I am my father's daughter. I cannot love myself unless I love him. I
> am a woman. I cannot be free while I am a daughter possessed by
> the Father inside my head.
> He was just a man, I tell myself. He was a man whom I loved, as
> it happens. He was my father; he was the most influential person in
> my life. He was a man who introduced me into a male-dominated
> world.[57]

Elaine Feinstein still felt that she was under her father's protection:

> . . .a voice in my own heart pointing up my anxieties in contemptuous
> Yiddish phrases. The *why worry?* of my childhood which would serve
> me so well now.
> And my prayer?
> It is to make me bolder.[58]

When I wrote of my father in a consciousness-raising group in
the late 1970s it was a struggle and a great relief, as if I had
reached and passed some little-known boundary stone. But it was
only to find new boundaries in a strange terrain in which I

frequently lose my bearings. Still, it felt like a crossing-point, the power to define and depict your own father. Feminism appears a round-about way to reach your own father. Yet it seems a journey few women can deny.

Gail Lewis describes in *Truth, Dare or Promise* what is hard to discuss, the racism of her white mother towards her black father and the reassessment of this under pressure from her daughters: '. . .it involved a re-evaluation of her understanding of the dynamics of her life with Dad.' Their arguments would be riddled with race/sex tensions: 'He truly believed women were there just to serve their men, and when not out at work to wait at home for the man.'[59] Gail Lewis struggles to understand her parents' 'competitions for superiority or domination. Him calling on his maleness, she on her whiteness. And there *was* a kind of excitement in it so long as it wasn't violent or demeaning.'[60]

It is so hard to both understand and detach ourselves from the passions of our parents. Fay Weldon writes of this wrestling for separation with sympathetic irony:

> She has been crying. It is not easy thus to change the patterns of the past: to forgo the reassuring pleasures of servitude, to face the unknown. Don't think it doesn't hurt. The first sea animals crawling up onto dry land must have had an agonizing time; struggling for breath, burning in the primaeval sun.[61]

What is amazing is how easy we thought it would be in the early years of women's liberation to change identity and relationships. We were like lovers at the onset of an affair, filled with energy. We looked out so surely. We saw what should be done with such clarity. 'Change the toys,' we said. 'Change the books.' 'Change the names.' 'Change the family.' 'Let there be no fathers, several fathers.' 'All share child care.' 'Mothers only.' 'No jealousy, no fear.'[62] Then followed a long unravelling:

> Though each remembers little of it
> and some remember nothing at all
> resting in crazy houses
> from the long spin of history
> drinking the grief of their sex
> eating it in bitter pills
> muttering in kitchens
> telling their daughters the story

of a sleeping princess;
but knowing it takes more than a man's kiss
to wake one so bent on sleeping her life away.[63]

Amidst the unravelling feminists began to wonder whether the
family was simply the site of 'sex roles', the place where girls learned
to be girls and boys to be boys in the simple sense we had imagined
at first with an input–output model of human consciousness.
For surely the complexity of reflection in so many meetings,
the rethinking of our own consciousness, the re-interpretation
of our own childhoods, the observation of our own children
suggested people were not such *tabulae rasae*, to be injected or
even constructed with the ideology of the day?

A new feminist psychological literature suggested that femininity
and masculinity are not only a series of behaviours we are taught
but also integral parts of human personality which we form partly
through the different ways each sex experiences mothering and
fathering.[64] Many women turned to therapy and psychoanalysis in
an effort to understand these contradictory perceptions.[65] Sheila
Ernst and Lucy Goodison in their book on self-help therapy, *In
Our Own Hands*, argued that it was not just a matter of raising
consciousness but of bringing to the surface repressed feelings,
exploring the unconscious factors which made it hard to change
our feelings and relationships. They said:

> As women we had been brought up to be submissive and supportive to
> others, to be seductive, manipulative and passive. We have rarely been
> encouraged to decide what we want and to go for it openly, to be angry,
> powerful, demanding; nor to value our own needs as equal to other
> people's, especially those of men and children. Unconscious feelings
> formed by our childhood conditioning would continue to sabotage our
> conscious choices for liberation.[66]

Sally Alexander and Barbara Taylor observed, 'The ropes which
bind women are the hardest to cut, because they are woven with
so many of our own desires.'[67]

The turn to therapy and psychoanalysis as a means of comprehending the complexity of sexual desire and identity in the family
made it easier to understand why it was more difficult to change
need, fantasy, habit and desire than we had imagined.[68] It may
be that some psychoanalytic patterns appear as fixed because
they change more slowly than the outer forms and framework of

society.[69] Perhaps a critical consciousness is forged in incongruence and the emergence of a women's liberation movement is part of such a contradictory historical process.

As early as 1972 Juliet Mitchell outlined a psychoanalytic tension which illuminates the feminist exploration of the family: '. . .in manifold disguises in our all-important "unreason" we utter the same language. Within this each of us demands to be a person like any other.'[70] At the same time, she argues, we all want to be unique. Quoting Octave Mannoni, she says that women's demand for equality concealed the demand 'to be recognized in their uniqueness as women, and for each woman to be recognized in her oneness, as herself – as the woman she feels herself to be and not as men wish to see her'.[71] Mannoni compared this to the shift in the Black movement from a universalist demand for equality to an insistence on uniqueness. Juliet Mitchell observed, 'Women have been seen to be women before they have been recognized as people (that is racism, sexism) the demand now is to be people in order to be women.'[72]

Over time, as feminism became stronger, women of differing classes, colours, cultures, sexual preferences have stressed their uniqueness along with the desire for equal connection expressed in sisterhood. It could be taken as feminism's ideal impetus for transforming the family: the recognition of equality and the recognition of difference. This is the utopian desire behind complaint, the cataloguing of control, and the compulsive returns to be reconciled. Trying to make ideal families in the real world is a much more confused business, of course. Nor is it easy to dwell on the emotional intensity of nuance and intimacy that we experience in our personal world and translate such 'knowing' into the public sphere of politics. Yet women's liberation has been very much about the re-ordering of private and public, personal and political. Without this, great depths of women's material lives and relations are denied any social significance.

While a powerful formative influence on women's liberation was dissatisfaction with life and relations in the family, the women's movement was never decisively anti-family in a simple way. Anna Coote and Beatrix Campbell observed in *Sweet Freedom* in 1982:

> Of course it would be easier to develop a clear political analysis of family life if it were altogether a bad thing. We could then call for the abolition of the family, and perhaps join with those radical feminists

who prescribe a separatist life-style as the only correct way. But for the majority of women, this would be rather less appealing than the calls of Conservative politicians to restore traditional values and strengthen the family. For there are ways in which the family can be a source of care, affection, strength and security, as much as it can be a source of physical violence, psychic oppression and social control.[73]

While feminists protested against the prevailing division of labour between the sexes, they also recognized that there were aspects of women's life in the family which, transposed into the external sphere, could expand into new social relationships. It was the imbalance of domestic and public life that was wrong. In innumerable consciousness-raising groups women began to ask why the division of labour was there. Feminist enquiry about the family thus moved away from identification and reflection, through all the radiating strands of kin, away from the clustering of households and the entanglements of subjectivity. It sought to situate the family within society, to get the lay-out of household, street, area, country, world. Feminists were not content with a definition of the family simply as personal relationships – even though the impetus to understand these has been a continuing source of renewal for the politics of women's liberation. From the early days of the movement, the concern has been to understand the *interconnections* of family and society. As an American feminist anthropologist, Rayna Rapp, has put it, 'The family's boundaries are always decomposing and recomposing in continuous interaction with larger domains.'[74]

But how is communication within the personal sphere to travel into these larger domains? And how can a language of social concepts meet the nuanced conversation of parents and lovers? The women's liberation movement has not solved this enormous dilemma but it has shown a persistent radical vigour in moving between the two polarities. We have had pressing material reasons to bridge the gulf.

2

Larger Domains

The subjective description of life in the home and the mulling over of family relationships have been punctuated by a series of 'whys'. If the ideal happy family was a myth which did not tally with women's household accounts in Britain in the 1970s, what were the forces which had brought the myth into being, and whose interests did it serve?

An early emphasis was the impact of commerce upon the woman's activity in the house and upon her conception of herself. Recognition that the family and personal life were becoming important targets for the mass marketing of domestic and fashion goods indicated that there were economic interests behind the reproduction of media images of the family, the housewife, motherhood, beauty.[1] Ros Delmar summed up this argument:

> The pressures to buy are directed mainly at women, and are expressed through an ideology which reinforces the home and the individual household. What is being hawked is not so much a product but a whole life-style. The individual family with its individual kitchen, its individual TV, washing machine, is an ideal environment for capitalist marketing which aims at getting the maximum of its products sold. The women who are held captive hate and resent them. But that doesn't prevent them being held out as an ideal to which other women can only aspire. In capitalism's fantasy of itself as an 'affluent' society, woman remains in her 'proper' place chained between the kitchen and the bedroom.[2]

During the 1970s, however, the impact of capitalist society on women's position in the family was discussed in the women's movement most extensively in terms of work, relations and values. The family as a place of work, and the division of labour which placed the onus of housework on women as a sex, gave rise to a great body of feminist theory.[3] The theorizing in turn raised a whole series of questions. How did it come about? Had it always been so? How had other societies solved the problem of producing goods, bearing children and caring for dependants?[4] These enquiries took off into the 'large domains' of history and anthropology. Feminist searchers did not always return with clear answers – but the generation of such questions revealed how extensively male-defined priorities had ordered intellectual definitions.

One proposition of the women's movement was that women's special responsibility for caring for children has been economically and socially necessary to capitalism. It was argued that while the division of labour preceded capitalism, it also contributed to the way in which capital exploited human beings' capacity to labour. In modern capitalism the family conveyed values which transmitted the dominant assumptions of capitalist society. There was a convergence of interest between employers, the capitalist state and men in the family. Women could be a source of cheap labour kept in reserve in the family. Their unpaid labour in the home saved the state from providing resources for reproduction. Men benefited from women's domestic work and acquired an interest in women being lower paid.[5]

Over-simplifications in this approach soon became apparent. Feminists observed that there was contradictory historical evidence. There have been periods, for example in the mid-nineteenth century, when some working-class men and women have regarded their family life as a means of *protection* from the larger domain of the new factory system.[6]

A critique based on contemporary conditions has also emerged. Black women have pointed out that an account of the family as mechanically reproducing the dominant values of capitalism is far too simple. Thus, a family of Afro-Caribbean people could consolidate in the face of attacks from the police on the black community. Asian women have to resist traditional forms of male power in the family, yet are critical of the assumption that the 'modern' way of capitalism is a good alternative. They point out that the British state's immigration policies have broken up their families rather than consolidating them. Black feminists have shown how imperialism is one of the larger domains acting on the form of human relations in the family.[7] So while one group of women were protesting that relations in the family oppressed women, others were concerned because imperialism and racism could break up family life. The North London Women Against Racism and Fascism group observed, 'Clearly for black people family life is a luxury they are not entitled to.'[8] This was an over-generalization, but it points to the inadequacy of theories which assume all women are affected in the same way by the same social forces in capitalism. The growth of welfare has been discussed at length by feminists. It too has been seen to have a contradictory effect on women's position in the family. The taking over of many of the activities which were carried out in the household, including education and healing, has undermined the status of the housewife. On the other hand the existing division of labour was taken for granted in the creation of the welfare state. The system of benefits and social welfare assumed that women were still at home caring for children full time. The movement of women into paid work on a more continuous basis and the reduction of family size contradict this assumption. How the need to earn a living affects women's position in the family has been extensively discussed by feminists. It is a significant change in the structure of capitalist society. Even the economic crisis of the early '80s produced not a decisive move back into the home but a growth of low-paid work. Meanwhile the attack on state services amid rhetoric about family and community has simply served to increase the burden of labour carried by women, especially working-class and black women with children or other dependants.[9]

It is apparent that in studying the interaction between 'the larger domain' and the family we are again confronted with incongruence. Irene Bruegel argued that capitalism had taken over, destroyed and reinforced the family: 'The relationship of capitalism to the family is contradictory: it tends both to destroy it and maintain it.'[10] It is always difficult to examine contradictory social tendencies and easier to impose a coherent line of analysis. In the short term, the coherent line can gain more immediate political support because it appears to have greater clarity. In the second half of the 1970s there was a tendency to equate relationships in the family with those at work and in the state, and to equate the man with the oppressive employer. These observations contained partial truths which have to be offset by the other aspects of life and relationships in the family. Few people, however unhappy in their families, would prefer to live on a factory assembly line. Few women must give birth while mentally noting that they are performing an economic function for capital. Violence and power are not the only features of relations between men and women, and values we encounter in specific families are contradictory. Nor of course do women live with men for purely economic reasons, though the reality of women's material and psychological dependence is apparent.

Ironically, the logic of this vision of the family as part of the continuum of capitalist oppression was to place a stronger emphasis on the state as an alternative – for example, the demand of wages for housework. Yet there was plenty of evidence that while many women found dependence on a man restrictive and demeaning, dependence on the state was felt to be more degrading. For instance, a woman on Social Security described her feeling of insult when she was interviewed about her claim and was asked about cohabitation:

> . . .they asked me if I was paid for having sex with him, and these were their exact words. The question to me was saying I was a prostitute, and I told them this too, but they denied this and they said I was misinterpreting what they had said. I put it to them that I didn't think they had any right to ask this question and I know of nobody else only a prostitute who is paid for having sex from a man. I have nothing at all against prostitutes but when they have to fall to this level, then there is something drastically wrong somewhere.[12]

Alison Langan pointed out that dependence on the state was a grim alternative:

> Living on Social Security is being despised. It means bread and scraps and hand-me-down clothes. It is dreading Christmas, avoiding toy-shops with your child. It's being isolated. It's going to bed at 8 p.m. so you don't have to put the fire on.[13]

A woman at the Claimants' Union Conference on women and unemployment put it graphically in the early 1970s: 'The State's worse than a jealous husband.'[14] There is this tension in a great deal of feminist writing on the family. Women are caught between the devil and the deep blue sea of dependence on the man or dependence on the state.

Views on men's role have diverged. Were they the helpless pawns of capital, locked willy nilly into domination, or were they responsible for women's subordination in the family? The first view, which was put forward in some Marxist writing on the family, tended to reduce the potential of human beings to act. It presented relations between men and women as determined by capital. The second, a radical feminist perspective, reflected the optimistic assumptions of American liberal thought. Change of circumstance was possible by a pure effort of will. While the first immerses the individual in the structure of capitalism, the second detaches the individual from the web of social and economic constraints which make choice difficult. The radical feminist approach had the salutary effect of asserting the need for individual men and women to take action to change their lives in the here and now – instead of simply demanding equal pay or campaigning for different laws, or waiting with the vague hope that 'revolution' would alter the position of women in the family. But when it met obstacles it had no strategic retreat for a new offensive, only a repetition of moralistic denunciation.

In 1971, in *Women's Estate*, Juliet Mitchell pointed to an interesting tension within Western liberal political thinking. Every member of a family is meant to be an individual with rights, and yet the family as an ideal is presented as a unity: 'It is almost as though the family has got smaller and smaller in order to make itself "one", in a desperate struggle against the disparity of its members in the outside world.'[15]

The notion of the individual with rights is bound up with economic independence. While this model fits a male wage-earner or two wage-earners, male and female, there are immediate problems if the woman is caring for children and thus dependent on a man, or even if the woman is working for less money doing part-time work. Over and over again feminists have found themselves returning to this problem of dependence. In 1982, in the collection of articles, *What is to be done about the Family?*, Fran Bennett described this as walking 'the tightrope'.[16] Feminists were advocating financial independence for women, and yet trying not to penalize women who were dependent upon men. There could be differences of interest between women dependent on a male breadwinner's wage and women, concerned to raise their own pay, who questioned the assumption that a man needs higher earnings. It was also not sufficient to view each woman as an equivalent atom seeking to maximize her earning power. The realities of care were interacting bonds.

The liberal tradition of thought which feminism has inherited has been much stronger on the individual's right to equality. When difficulties about the necessary dependence of women caring for children made the concept of individual rights problematic, the response was to graft state responsibility on to the theory of individual rights. But this assumed that the state treated people equally regardless of class and race. The Marxist approach has traditionally stressed the need for women to become wage-earners. From the late nineteenth century, socialists argued for the professionalization of aspects of family care. The care of young children and the elderly in state institutions could ensure independence for women wage-earners. The incompleteness of such a solution became evident in practice. People's relationships and needs proved to be more complex. Another strand in Marxist thought has made the family curiously immaterial. It has floated around as a detached cultural superstructure.[17]

When the women's liberation movement emerged in the late 1960s there was criticism of both the liberal feminist and the Marxist approach to women's emancipation. The growth of state welfare and its inadequacy, the conflict for women between earning a wage and still caring for children became apparent. As the family did indeed 'make itself one', contradictory forces of a most material kind converged on the single mother. Denise Riley described these in 1975. As a single mother she faced

> . . .an interlocking mesh of housing, employment, wages, nursery provision; a mesh which is quite merciless in its consistency and confronts us at every twist we make. We live in a society which founds itself on the assumption of the bourgeois family where there is one wage-earner and one domestic caretaker and administrator of consumption, and these two divide by gender.[18]

Modern feminism has confronted a contradictory social predicament in which neither the liberal nor the state socialist solutions work. Moreover, even in the last two decades there have been rapid changes in the structure of capitalism. Feminist critiques of the early Seventies no longer fit the situation of the 1980s.

The ideas in the women's liberation movement arose with the intention of understanding how and why dissatisfaction existed among women. In the early years there was fluidity. Ideas were checked and corrected by new experiences. But over time the ideas have tended to become split from women's experience, or they have been generalized from the limited experience of specific groups of women or they have expressed partial truths. When you are in a hurry for reformation you can overlook reservations along the way. Revision in politics tends to take on a pejorative meaning. But space to include feelings which question prevailing understandings makes for a more resilient political process. The capacity to revise has to be asserted repeatedly when the scope has narrowed. Otherwise an ideological model becomes a self-justifying system which is then projected back on to women's perceptions and culture as a universal quintessence.

Since the late 1970s this has been a cause of vexation and confusion. Criticism has come from several sources. For example, Kum-Kum Bhavnani pointed out:

> As Black women we are often 'invisible'. Many of us have felt that the white-dominated women's liberation movement in Britain has made very little attempt to take on issues which relate to *our* experience. To talk of the 'oppression' within the family denies, unless it is qualified, our lack of rights even to live with our spouses and our children, who are usually extremely important in providing support and encouragement for our struggles outside the home, like workplace campaigns, fighting against the 'sus' laws and so on. To be 'against marriage' without qualification, ignores the fact that immigration laws and the State can stop us from marrying the men we want to marry – and this process is further made legitimate by crude and inaccurate stereotypes of 'arranged marriages' for women of South Asian origin.[19]

There was not only the problem of generalization which ignored the complex pulls of black women's social existence, where imperialism's legacy met the exploitation of capitalism. A more general question was raised about how theory was being formed. Four feminist mothers, Nell Myers, Annie Mitchell, Adah Kay and Valerie Charlton, put it this way in the socialist feminist journal *Red Rag*:

> We worry that at the moment, what is identified as 'Movement theory' is miles away from the reality experienced by so many of us. . .
> . . .Theory which is incomplete can emerge as tyrannical, something which can in itself be a form of oppression reducing complex issues to manageable struggles. . .
> . . .We feel that incomplete theory has created among feminists a hierarchical pyramid – it hasn't been built to plan or design, but has arisen inevitably from the course of the movement's development. It is a pyramid which places at the top, as the most evolved of us, the woman who has worked her way free of attachments to men and children, or the woman who has remained free of those attachments. We are not denigrating that freedom; we have a lot to learn from women who are

exploring it. But we feel dislocated, worried and sometimes threatened, because extolling the desirability of such freedoms means that we are ignoring the oppression of children and the love of many women for many men.[20]

They were not, however, against theorizing in itself:

> If there is value in process and change, then we should be constantly wary and sceptical of fairly casual assumptions and conclusions which pass for theory. If we are frustrated or fail to connect with such 'theory' then we owe it to ourselves to try uncovering our unease and dissatisfaction.[21]

Feminists have not only struggled to theorize and examine ideas about the family in relation to experience. The most direct expression of dissatisfaction with existing circumstances in the family has been the continuing action many women have taken to change their own lives. Anna Coote and Beatrix Campbell described this resistance in *Sweet Freedom*:

> Since the late 1960s many women have tried – individually and collectively – to break out of the conventional mould of family life. They have waged guerrilla warfare over the housework. They have 'nagged' and 'scolded' to get men to change their habits. They have fought for their own space within the household. They have 'reversed roles', leaving their husbands with the kids while they go out to work. They have lived communally with other men and women. They have set up networks of 'women's houses' in towns and cities throughout the country. All this has been intrinsic to feminist politics since the birth of the women's liberation movement.[22]

Some have set off with great funds of cheery optimism, embarking on a new life-style with little idea of quite what they were getting into. Lesbian women who formed a bisexual commune in the early 1970s reported in an early lesbian feminist publication *Lesbians Come Together*:

> After about a week we decided to share all our clothes; these we moved into one big cupboard. We pooled our money for food, Tampax, toilet rolls and cat-food. Around the same time a women's awareness group was started. . . Tears, traumas, temper, were spent talking, crying, confessing; barriers came down with painful crashes. Egos took an incredible battering; usually just as we had reached a point where

honesty reigned, someone would say something to show how wrong we had been. Because it was not always possible (for us in the collective) to be in one room all the time, we decided that if two or more of us got together and talked then anything said should be repeated to whoever was missing. This helped us to fight couples and factions.[23]

It was arduous, this freedom. Individuality suffered from the emphasis upon the new collective unity which was to replace the family. Many of these new growths proved too forced. They collapsed under the emotion they disregarded. Such systematic ego-battering could in the long term drive people into a retreat which was as absolute as their initial desire for transformation had been.

A more considered approach to changing the form in which a group of adults and children might live together was expressed by a woman from a large communal house in Scotland, Laurieston Hall. In the mid-1970s ten adults and eight children lived there. The house was bought by a group of the residents and survived by providing a centre for radical meeting and holidays:

> The life-style for us isn't an objective we can or can't achieve. It's a process. What we do, how we do it, what we think is worked out not in meetings, but through issues and incidents. It's a daily, often painful, collision between theory and practice. Hopefully it's a dialectic – going somewhere.[24]

Expediency in the form of a crisis over child care or lack of money tended to turn people back on the resources of the past. Household labour was equally divided at Laurieston, but still the women saw the needs of the children as the most urgent priority in distress or illness and the men tussled over the finances. They discovered amidst the 'collisions' of theory and practice that emotional patterns are more deeply set than external arrangements. 'It took us a week to realize that 'a commune' wasn't a panacea for anything, and about a year of trouble to begin to understand why.'[25]

You have to have a lot of time and energy to fuel such a total alternative. One woman with teenage children told Anna Coote and Beatrix Campbell, 'We once tried to share a house with another couple; but you know it's hard enough to work out a relationship with one man – this was almost like being married to three people at once.'[26] There has consequently been a wide range of variation in women's strategies for freedom. Less dramatic and self-consciously 'political' than the creation of alternative households, they are nonetheless signs of a resolve to seek alternative ways to live. In 1971 an interviewer in the London Women's Liberation Workshop journal *Shrew* asked a woman from a half-way house, who had been involved in the occupation of Fulham Town Hall, how she would like to live:

> What would I do? Maybe a bit of gardening, tootle along. . . Joseph and me'll see each other at weekends. I think it's good for men and women to get away from each other and not be under each other's feet the whole time. Otherwise you just run out of speech.[27]

The desire to 'tootle along' is not conspicuous on political programmes. Nor is much attention paid to the need for fun and sociability. Just getting out can still be a major step for women which arouses male antagonism.

Mira Jones thought living in a flat after a painful divorce would bring a new freedom, 'but coming home to a quiet house with all the kids asleep made me feel lonely'.[28] She started to play darts with friends, joining a women's darts team in Islington and then playing in mixed pairs. The men were resistant initially but yielded. When she was expecting twins she went on playing, leaning on her big belly amidst cracks like, 'You know this is a doubles match, not trebles, don't you?'[29] When women picketed the Blackpool Conference for the Working Men's Clubs and Institute Union in 1980 for the right to equal membership, the 'cracks' were less good-natured: 'Get back and cook your old man's dinner. . .' 'Get back to your bairns. . .' 'You've never cooked a decent dinner in your lives.'[30]

Venturing into the larger domains can get you into trouble. Also, for many women it is not freely chosen but a desperate escape. Sharda Patel writes:

> Sick of being beaten,
> With bruises blue and green,
> I dressed the kids and packed my bags,
> And quit the bloody scene.[31]

She describes the confusion of the hectic women's refuge with affectionate irony:

> First of all it's easy
> But it gets harder by the day,

Everyone is different
They do things different ways.[32]

But even the temporary alternative of the refuge, along with other forms of provision – nurseries, toy libraries, community laundries, and so on – which enable women to extend beyond the family by developing social networks, require resources. The individual expression of needs for alternatives and extensions to the family consequently raises the issue of women's access to social resources. From the late 1970s socialist feminists have been concerned about how to create an economy in which resources would be reallocated and different relationships would be possible. This has involved thinking about how to overcome the gap between self-help, even mutual self-help, action and the creation of social policies which would engage with women's daily realities. In the course of this there has been a search for alternative values and guiding principles for action. Beatrix Campbell and Val Charlton wrote in 'Work to Rule' in *Red Rag*,

> We have tried being independent without children, we have used nurseries, even instituted non-sexist ones. Fought hard to remove sexual divisions in the home. Turned ourselves inside out in efforts to shed ideologies of the family, monogamy, jealousy, romantic love and dependence.
> Implicit in all our strivings of the last years has been an adaptation to the world of work, rather than the adaptation of that world to one that allows time for children, leisure, politics. . .
> . . .What are the demands about work which would assimilate domestic experience? What kinds of demands, or ways of thinking about demands, would express the concrete and complex reality of most women, which includes waged work and domestic life and children?[33]

The changes women need in the personal relationships of the family involve altering the prevailing division of spheres between the sexes. Domestic grievance can thus lead to a call for change in economic organization and in politics. However, articulating needs as demands removes them from the specific social contexts in which they are experienced. Women's liberation has engaged with this tension. So the struggle to remain in touch with, yet get beyond, personal experience has been part of a movement combining assertion of the everyday needs of women's social existence with the attempt to develop thinking and strategies that challenge male-defined politics.

The practice of the women's liberation movement has shown that the family is part of material life and affects our consciousness as much as what happens at work or in school, in a law court or in parliament. The 'Why Be a Wife?' Campaign in the late 1970s, for example, challenged legal dependence, the allocation of domestic work, private responsibility for child care, and the isolation of couples. It was an attempt to project the needs women experienced in families into a wider political context of law, economics and social provision. Angela Weir and Elizabeth Wilson wrote:

> Many of us cling to marriage and family life because the family is the only place where our society allows us to experience deeply felt, loving relationships, the only place where we can bring up our children and give them the care they need. What the 'Why Be a Wife?' Campaign is arguing is that love and the care of children should cease to be synonymous with a dependent and unequal status for women.[34]

The assumption of dependence was noted in social policy. Katherine Gieve pointed out, '. . .it affects pensions, taxes, student grants, unemployment, sickness and supplementary benefits. . .'[35] She argued that there was not a 'general solution' to this state of affairs: 'We will have to work out the answers in the context of particular campaigns.'[36]

At the time this working-out could be observed in, for instance, the Family Allowance campaign and in the struggles of women claimants, as well as in the 'Why Be a Wife?' Campaign itself. These campaigns stimulated many discussions about how to safeguard what women valued in the family while seeking better circumstances. In the 1970s the predominant complaint was that the family situation of women consumed their aspirations for freedom. Even amidst the critiques, however, there was a recognition that the family met many needs and that domestic values could be transformed. Rose Ades argued in 1976: 'We need to take the emotions of warmth, care and involvement, now warped and confined in the family, into the rest of our lives.'[37]

An interesting argument which suggests why women's complaint in the family has assumed a radical form of expression in modern capitalism was put forward by the German feminist Ulrike Prokop in 'Production and the Context of Women's Daily Life'. She suggested

that the circumstances of the modern family in capitalism both raised expectations of care and made them unrealizable except at the expense of the woman's individual sense of identity: 'The contradiction between dealing with human beings as more than mere cogs in a work process and at the same time denying our own needs and desires is the central contradiction in women's oppression.'[38] Thus women's immediate rebellion against the mystique of ideal mothering and the exhaustion of actual mothering – sometimes combined with a paid job – in a society which ignores this activity, and is structured as if women's domestic work did not exist, could express a most radical impulse for change in society as a whole. So, without idealizing women's role in the family, it has been possible to see women's dissatisfaction with family life as a *potential* for imagining how society could be better. The implication is that the purpose of life is not to produce: the purpose of production is to make life possible.

Anna Coote took an important step in expressing this aspiration as a questioning of the way socialists prioritized economic and social aims:

> Instead of asking 'How do we achieve full employment?' or 'How do we achieve workers' control of industry?' we ask: *'How do we want to care for our children?'* . . . When we work out what we want, we work out how to pay for it, and how to organize the industrial and social life of the country in order to implement the kind of child care and education that we really need.[39]

Anna Coote then crystallized over a decade of complaint, observation and argument about unmet needs in the family into six guiding principles for the making of policy:

1 Family policy should be designed to enable equal parenthood and equal opportunities, to break down rather than reinforce the artificial division of labour between women and men.
2 Family policy should be built on freedom of choice, which means people should be free to choose whether to have children or not, and whether to live alone, as couples, with friends or relations, without suffering social disadvantage.
3 Family policy should recognize that children are our most precious resource and that everyone has an obligation towards them, whether parents themselves or not.

4 Family policy should be based on maintaining and expanding the social wage and community control.
5 Family policy should recognize the rights and needs of individuals within families.
6 Family policy should recognize the additional financial pressure on families with dependent children and restore and protect the resources of these families.[40]

Policy proposals are convenient ways of summing up needs, demands, campaigns, agitation. After all, large meetings of mothers and toddlers find it difficult to squash into the corridors of power. And there are no doubt these days gentlemen of the left as well as of the right who are relieved to see a feminist policy document trundling along on a messenger's trolley, rather than enormous gangs of the needers in person, scattering Wispas and Wotsits in their wake. Policy can move into established institutions. It can contest, win support, gain adherents and be accepted in part or as a whole. It is clearly vital in providing an arena where feminist arguments can challenge the male-defined scope of 'politics'. But policy – feminist or otherwise – is liable to lose contact with experience in all its complexity. It is also inclined to censor the imagination.[41] The women's liberation movement has necessarily been involved in the formulation of policy, but it also encourages women to risk glimpses of alternative futures in which freedom and community could find a new balance.

One brave soul in *Women's Voice* in 1976 launched off on the subject of what could be put in the place of the existing family.

What would be simpler than communal laundries; huge restaurants where we all take it in turns to cook food and everyone gets on with it together; entertainment made by the people for the people; pubs where the kids can come in as well; dormitories where they can sleep with lots of other kids instead of shut off in their own rooms; a community where to be single isn't seen as a stigma; where just because you're married it doesn't mean you can't have other friends; where you don't have to be economically dependent on one man; hostels where people can live together naturally without fear of moral retribution; where sex becomes a mutual pleasure and not a further means of exploitation and fear.

If this seems too simple just think – I'll bet there's a few people reading this article who'd love to go out tonight but can't get a baby-sitter. They can send men to the moon, but *you* can't get out

to the pictures. But if your kid was sleeping in a communal neighbourhood dormitory being looked after by a qualified nurse. . .[42]

At this point a mystery person pops out of the paper's production process to observe wryly, '(one of the unstigmatized single people I suppose)'.[43]

The vision is indeed over-simple. The desire for privacy, the fact of jealousy and the mounting decibels of noise in communal dormitories are blithely disregarded. But the courage to express aspiration through describing utopia is of great value because it gets people talking in fundamental terms about what they would like. In 1978 Eve Lyn wrote in 'Bits and Pieces from a Shattered Mind' of her ideal family:

> My own experience of families is that they're (mostly) very destructive. I wouldn't live in one. Couldn't, in fact, as a lesbian. What I want is a different much better family: that gives me warmth, some security, and doesn't imprison me, where women don't police each other; that doesn't crush children, that doesn't neglect old people (or use them as childminders). . .where men are not powerful father figures with all the money; where sexuality is freely chosen. What's wrong with calling that a family? Even if it's very different from anything we've got now?. . .
> . . .I want an unoppressive, an expansive family, children perhaps, *and* independence. What I'll actually get in my lifetime is very different. I know that. But that doesn't stop me wanting. . .[44]

The contrast between the two visions is interesting. This account disregards completely propositions for alternative institutional arrangements. It is not concerned with *how* things could happen, but it is explicit about the values sought from the new relationships and it makes the transformation of our ways of relating to one another a central political concern. It is also of course again too simple. Possession and authority are not to be dealt with so lightly. But its strength is in its refusal to stop 'wanting'. The resolve to talk about wanting and relating has given women's liberation life and renewal, amidst all the conflicts and disillusion of political struggle. The creation of a collective space to express need, aspiration and desire is a major achievement and has to be recognized and protected as a resource, for it is all too easy to smother and crush the capacity to imagine.

Feminists have struggled with the problem of how to ground utopias without denying them. Nell Myers, Annie Mitchell, Adah

Kay and Valerie Charlton noted that our imagination of transformation is rooted in our pasts and our presents:

> . . .We need to know more about the alternatives in practical terms to the blood-tie family, possible now, which can cope with non-exclusivity in sexual relations, the concept of the 'central relationship' in a person's life and the concept of the sexual relationship as the primary one and new forms of emotional involvement not burdened by guilt or jealousy.[45]

But these writers are wary of the consequences of trying to change simply by an effort of will. The early years of women's liberation left many scars on women and on men who tried to live as they thought they should. What of the gap between the rhetoric and 'oughts' and the contradictory pull of our desires? It has been very hard for feminists to face this head on because it is admitting vulnerability and confusion while engaged in conflict, which is hardly politic. But the 'Four Sisters' are women of dogged courage and they plug on:

> . . .such explorations need to be grounded not in moralizing, but in the awareness of the problems of transforming our lives now, under capitalism, as feminists in a variety of ways, with men alone, with children, with other women. A tolerance of the different struggles we are all engaged in and an understanding of the gap between the present theory and its implications is what we need.[46]

3

Dusting Her Life Away

It may seem to be stating the obvious to say that housework is work. This is after all no secret to many housewives, exhausted by eight o'clock at night. Nor is it exactly a new discovery. Songs about housework being an unending toil are part of the folk tradition. In the nineteenth-century American 'Housewife's Lament' the poor woman finally dies and is buried in the dirt she spent her life combating.[1] 'Dust to dust' has a special meaning for houseworkers and cleaners. There is inherent within the labour a certain humility about the transience of human effort. Pamela Greenwood mused upon this in a letter to *Spare Rib* in 1974: 'Dust the great enemy is always with us. No matter what great technical aids are brought to bear against it, the dust remains long after we are gone.'[2]

Circumstances can be known and not known. They can be known by the people who experience them, but not 'acknowledged', not part of official knowledge to be taught in colleges and schools or read about in 'serious' economic or social studies. Margaret Benston's 'The Political Economy of Women's Liberation', originally published in Canada in 1969, was an important breakthrough because she saw that the family was not simply a unit of consumption but a place where work was being done.[3] Of course it made sense when this obvious material fact of life was stated. Very quickly, though, came the question: if housework was work and the housewife a worker, where were her unions, her banners, her strikes? There has in fact been a long tradition of housewives' organization but when women's liberation emerged we were not aware of this.

Peggy Morton, also from Canada, raised an awkward point in May 1970 in her article 'Woman's Work is Never Done'. What strategy followed from recognizing housework as production?[4] How could housewives organize effectively? As Lee Comer wrote in *Wedlocked Women*, 'There is no other occupation which is comparable.'[5]

I can remember sitting in many a meeting in the early 1970s pondering the problem. The more we pondered the more complexities opened out. It was evident these workers were not as other workers. Most housewives did not make things any more. But they were not the same as service workers who were employed as wage-earners in capitalism. They exchanged their services for a kind of protection in a manner which resembled the feudal relation of lord and serf. Were housewives serfs or even slaves? My mother would remonstrate ironically, 'O slave live for ever.' But to characterize women's domestic situation in terms of slavery or serfdom was clearly to over-state the toiling aspect to a ludicrous degree. Few women could be found who saw their domestic lives as unmitigated oppression. Nor could it be imagined that all those cheerfully smiling young brides were on the threshold of a destiny as galley-slaves. So the equation with slavery would not do. Indeed, it was somewhat insulting to women who had been housewives for many years to tell them they were merely dupes of a slave-owner. Domestic labour was not then simply to be equated with other unwaged exchanges of services.

This still left the question of whether remnants of older forms of production for use could be detected in housework, making it a different kind of labour from that involved in the production of goods or in the provision of services on the cash nexus. The relationship between a man and a woman differed from that between employer and an employee. There was a bond relationship in the case of marriage, a bond formalized in a contract. The bond was *both* one of mutual interdependence and of appropriation of services by the man. It carried the potential of *both* a relationship of co-operative exchange and a relationship of dominance of one over another.

Yet housework was clearly not separate from life in capitalist society. To view it in isolation from the wider material reality was to present it falsely as a self-sustaining economy. Advertising, the media, the kind of housing available, the class and race factors involved in who had access to housing, the design of the environment, all these affected the conditions of housework and the consciousness of women at home. Nor was it the case by the early 1970s that many women were simply doing housework. They were often combining housework with jobs for money and using any extra income to buy domestic consumer goods. The conditions of the man's job affected housework too. This involved not only his income but also the physical nature of his work and the degree of mental stress involved. Domestic labour was not set apart from the economic and social organization of life as a whole.

The two questions had therefore to be taken together. What kind of work was housework and how did it connect to other forms of labour in capitalism? Wiping the floor with theory, women's liberation brought domestic labour into the political zone. For those of us who were socialists, going through Marx and Engels with a toothcomb revealed undeniable blind spots. Housewives' labour seemed to have been on the whole forgotten, written off in a few phrases. There was scant regard in Marxist orthodoxy for the woes of the poor woman buried in dirt. So we had to burrow in theoretical lumber rooms for a few contradictory sentences, stirring up dusty old terms like 'productive', 'unproductive', 'use value' and 'exchange value', to see if they could be stretched into shape.

All this searching on our part was not simply prompted by dogmatic myopia. Marx's understanding of the historical process through which human beings had acted to maintain their lives and make future life possible was clearly not relevant only for one sex. Marxism's recognition of the significance of understanding how changes in the organization of material existence and relations between people contributed to the possibilities of radical transformation was seen by many feminists as vital to our quest for liberation.

We started our enquiries at the point where many women found themselves in the 1970s, both doing housework and employed for wages. What was the relationship between the two kinds of labour? Why was it assumed that women did housework? Had housework changed over time? If it had, why could it not change some more and be divided between the sexes? Why then could work for wages not also be altered? Did you have to abolish capitalism to change housework? Could there be capitalism without housewives? Would domestic labour be transformed if capitalism were to be replaced by socialism? It appeared that in existing forms of socialism this had not been the case. Could it be, then, that we required a different kind of socialism? It was amazing how extensive were the questions which came from such an apparently humdrum matter as housework. You start off with a mop and bucket in the kitchen and end up reorganizing the world in ways that most gentlemen philosophers had not even deigned to imagine.[6]

Some of the questions that arose from what was to be named later 'the domestic labour debate' paralleled the awkward questions which developments in capitalist society were presenting for socialist economic thought. For instance, Marx had observed how the workers poured their energy and creativity into the formation of capital, only to bring into being a monster of greater force which then extracted from them their life's energies with renewed vigour. When they acted to end this exploitation, they could reappropriate the power which they and their forebears had forfeited and enable it to be used by society as a whole. But, in modern times, in order for capitalist production to continue there had to be many people administering and looking after other people rather than making things themselves. These activities did not fit into the description of the direct exploitation of labour, which Marx had seen as the key to understanding the capitalist economy. The problem of how to characterize administrative and service work in the public sector was somewhat akin to that of locating unpaid domestic labour in the economic system. Both were significant to the continuation of the economy even though they could not be understood in the same terms as the direct exploitation of a factory worker.

There was another parallel dilemma, which was a difficulty not only in Marxist thinking but in sociological theory in a wider sense. How could the situation of the housewife at once involve a personal connection between individuals and a relationship which existed in society as a whole? Was this arrangement simply a private agreement, or the coercion of an individual woman by an individual man? Or was it a capitalist scheme to organize the maintenance of workers and future workers in the most cost-effective manner? Were human beings then trapped in a system, with subjectivity an illusion? Why did women consent to the appropriation of their domestic activity by husband, employer and society? Under what circumstances did women rebel? In what sense did they accept their lot if the relationship was seen as simply oppressive? How indeed could you measure what the woman put into housework and who benefited, when there was no payment in wages but only a tacit obligation of maintenance through marriage or, even less securely, through cohabitation?

It is interesting to consider why there was such a rebellion about domestic labour in women's liberation from the late 1960s. Initially the answer appeared self-evident – it was unpleasant work which oppressed women. The American feminist Pat Mainardi observed in her early and influential pamphlet *The Politics of Housework* that men's upbringing made them quite clear about 'the essential fact of housework right from the very beginning – which is that it stinks'.[7] The contemporary women's liberation movement challenged the prevailing division of labour between the sexes not because of a concern with abstract theory for its own sake, but because, to a significant number of young women, it had come to be seen as unjust and soul-destroying. If the man went out to earn money, Michelene Wandor pointed out, he could always invoke his breadwinner role to evade domestic labour and child care: 'He can refuse to get up in the middle of the night to feed the baby, refuse to do his or anyone else's washing or cooking on the grounds that he needs to conserve his energy for his own "work".'[8]

But why did women only perceive this to be oppressive in certain circumstances? If a change in consciousness had arisen then changes in society must have occurred. Housework was not part of an unchanging and static backdrop but part of the process of transformation.

Housework, for most women, had been reduced in social significance by the growth of state welfare, the development of consumer durables and the increasing tendency of 'products' rather than home-produced goods to be consumed. Even though the hours of labour were still long, the craft pride in housewifery possible for a countrywoman of moderate means in our grandmothers' generation, for instance, had been undermined and assailed. Housework too had clearly been affected by changes in the employment of both working-class and middle-class women and by the decline of domestic service. In this social context housework was felt to be oppressive by the young educated middle class, who were unlikely to have domestic help, yet had been reared to expect intellectual and occupational equality. Their work outside the home was moreover comparable to men's, inequality often taking the form of lack of access to higher positions. Within the working class, however, the persistence of arduous manual work makes the comparison more problematic.

It is often the case that radical discontent develops not among the most oppressed but among people who have been able to conceive of better possibilities than society allows. And so it was in the emergence of women's liberation. The women who questioned first were those whose education and aspirations enabled them to imagine there could be some alternative.

Out of the ferment of questions emerged two basic strategies for changing housework. The first aimed to give housewives a power equivalent to workers outside the home, which it was felt could be secured by the payment of money by the state – wages for housework. The second involved change in the division of labour between men and women. It relied partly on a change of consciousness among men manifested in their individual relationships with women. But it was also evident that with the best will in the world it was not possible for many men to transform the situation merely by a change of heart. Paid work was geared to a male breadwinner. Shiftwork, overtime and heavy manual labour limited men's participation at home. Women's upbringing also gave domestic work deep psychological meanings for them which could not simply be discarded at will. This second strategy for changing housework thus involved arguing for extensive change in how production was organized. It also involved making more traditional socialist demands on the resources controlled by the state to lift some of the burden of housework and child care. Public laundries, community restaurants and nurseries were called for.

The theoretical strength of this second strategy was that it always connected housework to paid employment. In Rosalind Davis's words in 1973, 'We have to deal with and oppose an oppression with multiple aspects.' The point was 'to inter-relate the struggles, not to emphasize one'.[9] But in the political short term the interconnecting vision is less effective in debate. It is too long-winded and qualified to carry the day in conflicts. The arguments of the 'Wages for Housework' group thus took the offensive, and those who saw women's position in the home in relation to the organization of production on the cash nexus tended be forced on to the defensive.

'Wages for Housework' was also a convenient slogan for the more widely held conviction in women's liberation that society should put more value on women's contribution. For instance, Priscilla Allen claimed in 1973:

> Wages for housework offers independence and the dignity that comes from a recognition of one's efforts. It offers a choice of occupation for one's energies, a freedom to leave housework, to enter into a social, instead of privatized existence (however fancy the prison of the home might have been). It offers women the chance to relate to other people on a fully human level, not as doormat, sacrificing angel or cannibalizing matriarch. And immediately it offers women the sisterhood of waging a struggle.[10]

The Wages for Housework Campaign thus shared with early women's liberation thinking an emphasis on how material change affected consciousness. This was part of a wider shift, the legacy of the left of the 1960s, away from the emphasis on socialism as a series of gains, things acquired, or even just material conditions improved, and towards an interest in the transformation of consciousness and relations of power. Supporters of Wages for Housework pointed out that the strategy of sharing housework advocated by their feminist opponents depended on persuading men to change. They maintained instead that the demand for money would increase women's power to fight for themselves. Not only the fact of 'wages' but the struggle for the reform would affect the consciousness of women. However, this symbolic expression of dignity and independence through the wage also represented a theoretical narrowing.

Implicit in the opposition to Wages for Housework was always an awareness of the complex interconnections of economic activity and love and power in the family, and of their implications in capitalism. There was also a rejection of the over-simple notion of women's consciousness on which the wage campaign was based. By extracting 'independence' from the sexual and emotional context in which women work in the family, by assuming 'value' was simply to be equated with cash and power with wages, the arguments of Wages for Housework distorted women's circumstances in the family.

The interconnecting vision was rarely explicitly stated. It was more likely to be implicitly assumed. A graphic exception is Sandra Kerr's humorous song 'The Maintenance Engineer', in which both men and women battle through to a recognition of mutual class and sex dignity. The woman expresses her consciousness of power not as a detached individual but in relation to the man and within a wider web of social relationships:

One Friday night it happened some years after we were wed,
When my old man came in from work as usual I said
'Your tea is on the table, clean clothes are on the rack,
Your bath'll soon be ready, I'll come and scrub your back.'
He kissed me very tenderly, and said 'I tell you flat,
The service I give my machine ain't half as good as that!'

Refrain
I said 'I'm not your little woman, your sweetheart or your dear
I'm a wage-slave without wages, I'm a maintenance engineer.'

So then we got to talking, I told him how I felt,
How I keep him running just as smooth as some conveyor belt,
For after all it's I'm the one provides the power supply,
(He goes just like the clappers on my steak and kidney pie).
His fittings are all shining 'cos I keep 'em nice and clean
And he tells me his machine tool is the best I've ever seen. . .

The terms of my employment would make your hair turn grey,
I have to be on call you see for twenty-four hours a day.
I quite enjoy the perks though when I'm working through the night,
For I get job satisfaction, well he does then I might.
If I keep up full production I shall have a kid or two,
For some future boss to have another labour force to screw!

The truth began to dawn then how I keep him fit and trim
So the boss can make a nice fat profit out of me and him.
And as a solid union man he got in quite a rage
To think that we're both working hard and getting one man's wage.
I said 'And what about the part-time packing job I do?
That's three men that I work for love, my boss, your boss and you!'

He looked a little sheepish and he said 'As from today
The lads and me will see what we can do on equal pay.
Would you like a housewives' union? Do you think you should be paid
As a cook and as a cleaner, as a nurse and as a maid?'
I said 'Don't jump the gun, love, if you did your share at home,
Perhaps I'd have some time to fight some battles of my own.

'I've heard you tell me how you'll pull the bosses down;
You'll never do it, brother, while you're bossing me around,
Till women join the struggle – married, single, white and black,
You're fighting with a blindfold and one hand behind your back.'
The message has got over for he's realized at last
That power to the sisters must mean power to the class.[11]

In the 'domestic labour debate' of the 1970s the interconnection between material existence and consciousness was rarely put so neatly or so wittily. But there were plenty of arguments about the problems in *implementing* the assumption that housework could be given social value by a cash allowance from the state. For if it could be implied that persuading the men with whom we were intimate to change was utopian, how was it to be so easy to change men with state power? There was also a persistent confusion about housework and child care. Clearing up after children could merge with household labour. But there were differences between demanding payments for housework not involving children and demanding money from the state for caring for children. Adults could be expected to maintain themselves; children could not. Some provision existed already in the form of Family Allowances, later Child Benefit. The importance of increasing this cash payment for children was accepted by all feminists but confusion arose in the early 1970s campaign to retain these Family Allowances. Some women's liberation groups argued for the cash benefit to be paid to whoever was mainly responsible for the child – in a minority of cases this was men. Others, including the Wages for Housework group, saw it as payment to women. Wages for Housework also persistently elided payment for housework with the principle of paying towards the upbringing of children.[12] This ignored the fact that housework can be fitted in with a job, while child care is harder to combine. A similar point could be made about the care of sick and elderly dependants, which makes paid employment impossible in ways in which domestic labour alone does not.[13]

Supporters of Wages for Housework were somewhat unclear about quite who was paying and how they could be persuaded. The Power of Women Collective said in 1974, 'We demand that employers and their governments pay us for the work we do free. We want money of our own.'[14] This implied that the state was simply the expression of employers' interests. It conveniently overlooked the fact that the state's resources came from large numbers of other people. They may have lacked power to decide how these resources were used, but they were contributors nonetheless.

Caroline Freeman put a common criticism that the demand obscured the consequences of state involvement:

> Once we make the state our employer, the state will do the policing. A wage is a lever which keeps the worker at work. If we want wages for housework, we must accept that it would be tied to doing *housework*.[15]

Angela Phillips voiced some other common objections in 1976:

> . . . should we pay for women to stay home in the very isolation that we have been campaigning to abolish, or should we fight for

better child-care facilities, encourage communal living and shared housework, press for more part-time work for both parents and try and free ourselves to participate fully in the political and social life of the community?. . .

. . .I personally would not feel happy about subsidizing a childless woman so that she can service her husband (let him service himself) and I am insulted by the suggestion that sex is work which I need to be paid for.[16]

The women's movement was faced with the strategic dilemma of how to recognize that women's responsibility for domestic labour was unequal and unfair without reducing the circumstances of domestic life to a transaction which could be rationalized as a purely economic affair by adding a price tag. Jill Tweedie, for example, struggled with her doubts about the proposal:

> If you find that you feel as deeply uneasy and dismayed as I did when I first heard the arguments for wages for housework, ask yourself why. What is it about the idea of wages that is so unsettling, even obnoxious? I cannot presume to answer for you. My own answer? I do not want to think about the anger I actually feel about 'women's work'. I do not trust myself not to direct it at my husband and children in lieu of taking action. My only way of accepting that work is either to ignore it, shut off my brain and try to do it like a robot, or pretend to myself that I do it for love and therefore am good.
>
> What do I feel? The horrid resentment of the mind bred to slavery and faced with freedom. Wages for Housework? Let them eat cake![17]

The initial strength of women's liberation had been the openness with which women described their perception of oppression. Clearly these descriptions tended to be socially limited, but they were not simply generated by radical ideology. Wages for Housework, in contrast, formulated an interpretation of Marxism which reduced all aspects of human relationships in capitalism to the factory.[18] It certainly stimulated argument but it bypassed many of the specifics of housework which were described in the personal testimonies. Many of these subjective accounts in the early women's liberation literature dwelt on the dissatisfying character of housework and its effects on consciousness. Pamela Greenwood's complaint in *Spare Rib* was that 'everything one does is *undone* by the end of the day'.[19] This was also a common refrain of the women interviewed

in Ann Oakley's study, *The Sociology of Housework*.[20] The seeking of identity through self-abnegation produces 'the underlying feeling of emptiness' which Betty Friedan described in *The Feminine Mystique*.[21] There was thus evidently oppression which was not just about the lack of material things, but about a material activity which seemed to negate itself. Personal accounts often mention the illusion of freedom and control over one's time along with the hopeless effort of taking time back.[22]

The other oppressive feature of housework which is intimately connected with female identity is the struggle to keep up with other women's expectations. In *Dutiful Daughters* an elderly woman married to a Scottish agricultural labourer described how when she was first married neighbours would come round at half past five in the morning to see why her washing was not under way. When she was pregnant a friend came to stay and told her how to defeat her tyrants:

> 'No, Maggie, you're not half fly enough!' I asked, 'What do you mean?' 'Aye,' she says, 'wash it on a Sunday night and then put it out,' she says, 'like a fairy.'[23]

A young woman in London, Linda Peffer, told of coercive monitoring as a working-class housewife with small children:

> You couldn't go out, and if you went out, most of the women I went round to see, well, they were the same. I found that out, it was really funny, a lot of them used to clean all up before I got there, and I done the same before they got there. If we'd have had the courage, I think we could have helped each other out a lot, if only we could have admitted it. It come out when I got a bit stronger, and actually confessed what a mess it was in, and gradually I found out that loads of women were like it, and we all pretended to be all right when we met each other, because we just couldn't confess that we were really in a right state at home.[24]

A young middle-class mother writing in the London women's liberation newsletter *Shrew* in 1971 explained the same syndrome:

> A housewife regarded as 'the woman behind the man' feels a great need to assert her own impact with other people, so housebound women compete with each other and invent their own symbols of achievement.[25]

Alienation from housework was the strongest element in the subjective descriptions. These were formulated in reaction against the shallow optimism of the media, which had presented the domestic domain as at last under the control of the housewife through technology, do-it-yourself and a generally improved standard of living. Michelene Wandor did argue, however, that the home was the woman's space, where, although cut off from power in the wider society, she could achieve some control by organizing the mechanics of the household. The woman was thus expressing a contradiction in seeking as a 'houseworker' to control her working environment by sacrificing herself as a human being.[26] In Ann Whitehead's interpretation of household space a decade later, however, the woman's autonomy was even less evident:

> . . . women's individual activities take place in collective areas of the house, but where space allows there is often a designated area for husbands' hobbies or activities – workshop, den, greenhouse.[27]

Housework is not just a matter of the individual household. The circumstances of domestic work are shaped by wider political and economic forces. The emphasis of the new women's movement on choice and need made it prepared to be critical of apparent material improvements in terms of their consequences for human relationships and the organization of everyday life. There appears to have been little notion in Labour's post-war planning that people themselves might want to exercise choice over how council estates were built and designed, shopping areas developed or schools and hospitals organized.[28] In the 1970s women's liberation groups often got involved in community struggles about the democratic control of the allocation of social resources. Both exponents of community politics and the women's liberation movement were opposed to the tendency on the left in the early 1970s to be concerned primarily with economic struggles at work. Feminists emphasized the subordination of women in the family. Some argued that power relations in the domestic sphere explained the inferior position of women in the labour force and in the economy as a whole.[29]

In 1970 Christine Delphy's 'L'Ennemi principal' maintained that two different ways of producing co-exist in capitalism: the industrial mode which produces goods, and the family mode in which domestic services, child-rearing and certain other goods are produced. In the first, the owner of capital extracts the power to

labour from the worker. In the second, men use women in the family in a similar manner. This form of exploitation is specific to women.[30]

In *Woman's Consciousness, Man's World* I adapted the Marxist concept of a subordinate mode of production existing within the dominant mode. It was important to assert somehow the specific nature of women's subordination.[31] The problem was, however, that this tended to suggest a static structure in which the actual interaction between domestic activity in the household and the capitalist economy as a whole disappeared. I thus tried to describe domestic work as under constant pressure from the wage system, as being in the process of being devoured, yet also as sustaining capitalism.[32]

Christine Delphy's work took the concept of separate modes in another direction. She argued that women are a class and that marriage was the universal institution of the oppression of women. In thus separating the material situation of women from that of men she identified a theoretically distinct form of oppression, 'patriarchy', existing in capitalism.[33] This certainly made the point that women's subordination could not automatically be solved by ending class exploitation. But it artificially divided men's and women's social reality and led logically to absurdity: children, the sick and the elderly turned into exploiters of the woman.

In contrast, the general course of socialist feminist thinking in the women's movement stressed the interrelationship of women's domestic lives with the economic organization of capitalist society. There was also an increasing awareness of the inadequacies of theories which, in Olivia Harris's words tried 'to squeeze sexual divisions into the pre-existing categories of political economy'.[34] One of the most fruitful outcomes of the sometimes rather scholastic 'domestic labour debate' was a recognition among feminists of the need to develop a radical political economy which could recognize the significance of women's unpaid activity and present alternative proposals for the resourcing and organization of this work in response to women's needs.

By the early 1980s discussion of domestic labour had shifted towards a recognition that a major structural change had occurred. In Anne Phillips's words:

The full-time housewife is increasingly rare. Most women are wage earners, combining housework, child care and jobs in what is known as the

'double shift'. There have been major changes in the working patterns
of women, most of them as yet unnoticed in socialist debate.[35]

Socialist feminists looked up from the pages of *Capital* and outside
at the world around them. It was becoming increasingly evident that
the interconnection of home and work was not a theoretical but a
practical problem. In a book based on interviews with women about
how they combined their dual roles, Sue Sharpe called this 'double
identity'.[36]

During the 1970s a change in assumptions had occurred. Women
at home contrived to feel guilty for not going out to work, whereas
in the previous decade they had felt bad about neglecting their
families – combining full-time employment with care for a family was
arduous and exhausting. But in the 'male' world many women began
to wonder: was there any alternative? In 1983 Susan Himmelweit
observed that the argument in the 1970s had 'concentrated on the
similarities between wage work and housework'. In an illuminating
article, 'Production Rules OK? – Waged Work and the Family', she
shifted the terrain to examine the *differences* between waged work
and housework. This made it possible to grasp both the negative
aspects of housework and the positive elements which made women
uneasy about reducing the activity to cash. The positive aspects were
not idealized as in a conservative utopia but taken as potential for a
vision of an alternative approach to work as a whole.[37]

The integration of domestic activity with the forms of human
labour on the cash nexus thus enabled feminists to begin investing
the endeavour to maintain and reproduce our lives with socially
different meanings from those attached to the prevailing profit
motive in capitalism. Thus the political question raised by changes
in capitalist society – why it should be women who did all the
housework – has led to a glimpse of another future. For while the
social arrangements surrounding domestic labour are perceived as
oppressive, the activities themselves are often more useful to human
beings than many of the labours which make profits and are paid
for directly. If we ask how social activities contribute to wellbeing
we can begin to transcend the narrow concept of economics that
capitalism foists upon us. A similar insight can be gained from
feminist anthropological and economic studies of countries where
capitalism is not as developed as it is in the North. The use of time
and energies in the maintenance and production of life can be seen
clearly in the lives of Third World women. For example, Maureen

Mackintosh points out how in Senegal domestic labour is a much more taxing endeavour than in Britain.

> Although the content of. . . domestic labour is the same in the Sen-egalese example and in Britain (cooking, cleaning, child care) the technical production processes involved are of course very different. The time taken for each task, and the heaviness of the labour involved, are much greater in the Senegalese village, and the products of this labour cannot be replaced by products bought on the market. The result is that a household without a woman in good health and strength cannot survive. A really viable household in this village society requires more than one woman able to take on the full burden of the domestic tasks. This is not so in Britain today.[38]

Examples like these show more clearly that the time spent by human beings on domestic activities is a social resource than can be seen in an industrialized economy like Britain where such work has a more hidden aspect. The economic significance of labour-intensive tasks in the Third World enables us more easily to connect social inequality to the question, how is the workload divided? Studies of economic change have begun to trace how women juggle home-time, market work and leisure.[39] These suggest that economic development which does not subordinate women has to take into account specific activities. This approach has relevance in turn for a critique of the capitalist economy. The exploitative nature of waged work is not the only problem that requires change. Control over the allocation of tasks and time is equally important. As Elizabeth Jelin observes in a study of women and the urban labour market, '. . ."employment" should be seen as part of a broader concept, that of "economic activity" which also includes domestic tasks'.[40]

The political complaint about housework has thus had an extremely creative effect as a stimulus to rethinking what is meant by economic life and the direction changes might take. But it is all very well to be theoretically far-ranging and to envisage utopia, but what of all those women still unhappily doing the housework? Pat V. T. West's poem 'intimations of a sweet past never had' returns us to the individual's sense of emptiness:

> . . .ironing she sweeps hurt haven'ts
> from edge to approximate edge
> listening to led zeppelin speaking
> of a sweet past she never would have

a loss she would forever have to live with.[41]

The individual voices continue to testify to the repetitious labour which in poor conditions embitters the very soul. For instance, in *Dutiful Daughters* Barbara Marsh contrasted her life in a two-room flat with a husband and four children in Hackney, London, with her youth in Jamaica. Even a sweet past cannot compensate for the labour of the present which her husband cannot comprehend:

> He believe that I am really troublesome and I make all the trouble. For instance he come to tell me about the mice coming up here now, he will tell me it's because I don't keep the floor tidy and thus. I say 'Yes I call the mice outside' – I really get cross you know – I say, 'Yes I send out the garden to tell the mice to come upstairs, there's plenty things on the floor in here.' I do, because it's not my fault the mice are in here, in these rotten old houses. . .
> . . .You are always doing one work three or four times. You can't finish your work in this house with the ruddy mice. . . They are highly educated – they pass the mousetrap, the food is in there and they don't pay it any mind. They won't go near the trap, they won't bite, and they see the poison and they look at it and say something to themself. They must watch Tom and Jerry, they do.[42]

The desire to change how housework is divided and done continues to work its way through society. This is not the kind of demand which can be put conveniently to some central decision-making body and then enforced. It is, rather, part of the extension of the concept of politics into everyday relationships which has been such a marked feature of the women's liberation movement. In the last two decades many homes have been the site of a guerrilla warfare whose heroines are largely unsung. 'History' knows only of exceptions recorded by chance:

> . . . 4 o'clock Friday afternoon
> Mrs Mable went on strike,
> Pedalling off on her bike
> Whistling a marching tune
> Leaving a note signed Ms Mable
> On the empty kitchen table.[43]

Wendy Whitfield began traditionally, agitating with her husband in the time-honoured way of wives:

After the usual nagging, the disguised and undisguised gibes, I decided on an all-out fight. All or nothing. I went on strike. I announced that from now on I would do only *my* shopping, cooking and cleaning. I would not clean up, nor would I keep doing the incessant tidying, writing lists, washing and returning milk bottles, putting away the dishes that he left to drain instead of drying them, defrosting the fridge or cleaning the cooker, clearing away the coffee cups or writing to his relatives. In short I would do not more than a man would do.[44]

Dave gave way and they eventually agreed to take turns. But he developed a last-ditch stand. He refused to do the toilets. Wendy compromised. She observed that it was not just a battle with her husband in which constant vigilance was necessary it was also a question of reassessing her own attitudes:

Was it really necessary to keep dusting and cleaning? Wasn't it enough to wait until it really looked untidy? Together we had to work out a common definition of 'dirty' and 'untidy'.[45]

The planning and co-ordination exercised by an individual house-worker is hard to divide. Also, this aspect of the work is a skill that is taken for granted and barely acknowledged even by the woman herself. Wendy Whitfield noted ruefully:

When it came to washing Dave worked to rule. He never realized the need of tackling the dirty socks under the bed, or the occasional washing, like curtains and dressing gowns. I resorted to noticing them for him by popping them into the linen basket at the last moment. Tiresome though it is to do his thinking for him, he's beginning to get the message, and is starting to develop a little professional pride. Similarly he pretended not to understand the process of sorting out colours. After a few of my pale things had been ruined, I had to start teaching him. *He* never minded if his handkerchiefs were the colour of his Levis.[46]

Descriptions of sharing housework are often accompanied by confessions of anxiety – one of those more dubious inheritances of womanhood. Reflecting on this legacy, Stef Pixner wrote:

The pain that I find
in dust and disorder
she carries on her back
like bread.[47]

The process of dividing housework brings to the surface the ways in which learning domestic skills was for many women an implicit part of learning how to be a woman. 'It takes tremendous courage to admit even to oneself that life is meaningless and stagnant, how much more courage to discuss it openly and try and fight it,' wrote an early contributor to *Shrew*.[48] But the disentangling of identity from the activity is even harder. The conscious transmission of domestic skills requires detaching oneself from each aspect. Jenefer Coates described this bringing to consciousness of tacit knowing – craft knowhow:

> Teaching people, for instance, to buy food, to recognize signs of good and bad quality – is an exhausting process because it demands rationalizing and articulating a mass of perceptions that one is unaccustomed to talk about.[49]

Anja Bostock, describing how, left with three children, she struggled to mend the lavatory seat, reflected on differences she believed existed in how women and men approached work:

> There are no woman-type jobs and man-type jobs. There is a typical female attitude to work, which consists in minimizing any direct enjoyment that can be got out of it and emphasizing the indirect satisfaction to be derived from its usefulness; and a typical male attitude, which plays up the gratuitous pleasure ('creativity') for all it's worth and shies away from the secondary ancillary aspect. Both sexes are capable of either attitude, and both attitudes are incomplete.[50]

Once the assertion is made that a particular form of human activity is not inevitably connected with women as a sex, it opens the way to rethinking domestic work not just in terms of economics but as part of our wider culture.

The consciousness-raising groups provided an initial means of sharing and re-working experiences. There have been other forms of organization which have extended and developed women's informal domestic networks.[51] In the mid-1970s some women organized a food co-op on the Lincoln Estate in Bow, London. It was partly a matter of getting food cheaper. But a simple division between material life and consciousness would be a distortion. As one of the women said, 'It means more to me than just getting cheap food together, it's the beginning of organizing our lives differently.'[52]

One thing led to another and from the food co-op came a playgroup and a youth club. Women from the estate went on the Women's Day march through East London in 1975. A self-help therapy group was set up. The women began to think about going out more and developed co-operative babysitting, street community associations. They shared the laundry and collecting children. The food co-op began a process of creating community in the wake of the demoralization which had set in after the collapse of the 1969 rent strike against the GLC.[53]

In 1977 a group of women tenants in Pontypridd, South Wales, chained themselves to the town hall railings for twenty-four hours in protest against conditions on their council estate. Electric heating which was far too expensive had been installed without consultation. Barbara Castle described how this conflict over heating was a source of 'learning' and 'awakening':

> It meant re-thinking relationships, questioning roles, disagreeing with family dogma, disapproval, and occasional rejection by neighbours. At the same time it meant new friendships and great support outside the family, all sorts of new experiences, visiting new places, meeting all kinds of different people, beginning to understand what politics is all about, beginning to appreciate what ordinary working people are capable of.[54]

As one of the women tenants said, 'I can't imagine going back to my life before we started this. What did I used to do? I was just a little housewife but suddenly you find you are a person.'[55]

In the long and bitter miners' strike of 1984–5 women emerged as an impressive and inspiring force. They began to get together because of the desperate need to provide for their families. They used informal networks to make contacts and started organizing food kitchens and the distribution of food. In the course of the strike, women began to question their domestic role. As Lorraine Bowler said at the rally in Barnsley in May 1984,

> We are seen to be the domesticated element of a family. This for too many years has been the role expected of us. I have seen change coming for years and the last few weeks has seen it at its best.[56]

Yet all this effort only becomes more than the sum of its parts if it is, however loosely conceived, strategic. Otherwise the individual battles have only private meanings and even the collective changes in relation to other struggles will not be sustained. In *The Politics of Housework* Ellen Malos drew together the interconnecting elements of a strategy which expressed the actions of over a decade in which women have refused to accept 'the division of labour, inside and outside the home, as "natural" '. She called for 'the recognition that jobs done in the home are not necessarily menial and uninteresting in themselves, but that it is the context in which they are carried out that makes them oppressive'.[57] In this spirit Hilary Land pertinently subtitled her paper at a meeting held by the Equal Opportunities Commission in Bradford in 1978, 'Men's Under-achievement in the Home'.[58]

There have also been moves to restore the status of crafts practised by women at home. Rosie Parker has pointed out that the word for embroidery is 'work' yet 'women who embroider at home, instead of regarding their work with pride, refer to it deprecatingly as their occupational therapy. . .'.[59] Beryl Weaver used the craft of embroidery to communicate another destiny:

> I need to fix my memories somehow, and say in a tangible way that housewives are here and alive. . . I was never encouraged to create disturbing images, so my anger comes through in the pretty pictures I was brought up with.[60]

A challenge to the context of housework also involves questioning the prevailing division of the world into public and private spheres. One example is the growing awareness that hazards are not confined to paid work: the home too can be a site of danger – from cleaning chemical or faulty electrical wiring, for instance.[61] It is also a place where resources are consumed. 'Home Sweet Home' is linked into political choices about energy use.

The experience of feminism has been that people do not have to sit back helplessly and wait for some alternative future. Much can be learned from the continuing process of argument over the boundaries of the private and the public. Some of the older models for collectivizing housework have been found to be no longer appropriate. But the women's liberation movement has reasserted the principle of collective responsibility and there has been a series of attempts to claim resources from the state to collectivize private activities done in the home. At present in Britain, however, the government is set on quite a different course, although, under pressure from women, Labour local authorities have begun to create a few new social forms for domestic activities.[62]

Changing housework has led women to question how decisions are made about allocating state resources and how the divisions of public and private, work and home, are created and maintained. Jean Gardiner said in the early 1970s, 'Women's and men's liberation can only finally happen when production is geared to human need and when love and work are joined together.'[63] A decade later Susan Himmelweit was still struggling with the problem of how a new relationship between domestic and wage labour, public and private life, and production and reproduction might be developed.[64] Part of the difficulty was that the theory we inherited crystallized realities that had passed. The feelings of discontent which arose from immediate experience were partial expressions of a changing reality. The theories of transformation have emerged from a social process of practical attempts at change. In Meg Luxton's words, 'Women's politics are like an iceberg. Only the tip shows and it never looks like much. But underneath is a vast mass of women, always moving – usually very slowly.'[65]

Amidst all this movement, Susan Himmelweit points us towards the extraordinary theoretical implications of seeking to change the context in which we do housework:

> . . . we should be attempting to create new relations for all work, in which those of domestic labour and those of wage labour which are more humanizing are blended, perhaps together with new elements as yet unknown, to the exclusion of those which we know to be exploitative and oppressive. . .
>
> . . . we are not just after more women entering into public life and more men taking on private responsibilities. We want to break down the division between the two, but not destroying all aspects of private life. Instead, we want to take the good aspects that we experience of our private lives and spread them around to invade and transform the public arena at the same time as getting public recognition of the political nature of personal relations. . .
>
> . . .Finally, and I think this is the most difficult point to accept, it seems to me that we will not be able to achieve full emancipation of the potential of both sexes without taking on the question of reproduction, and I mean that in the most basic sense of having babies. For all the discussion about why men and women lead such different lives today takes for granted the basic difference between men and women: that women are potential child-bearers while men are not. Visions of a future

society have to take this into account, whether it be by eradicating this difference, as Shulamith Firestone suggested, or. . . by abolishing the social division between productive and reproductive labour. What exactly that would mean is hard to imagine, but it would ensure that the production of things did not have more social importance than the production of people.[66]

There is no doubt about it, with so much theory to be developed and such extensive changes to be made, some of that dusting will just have to wait!

PART TWO

Fertility and Desire

4

Not an Easy Choice

It is well known that women's liberation brought the body into politics, burning bras (so they say) and barracking beauty contests. We did not of course sit down in the late 1960s with an agenda on which someone wrote 'bodies: political implications of'. But in small groups discussion of feelings and relationships turned to how we were regarded by men and by the media and how we experienced our bodies. In the 1960s the insistence on the need for control at the place of work, in education and the community was very strong on the left. The first time I heard the idea transplanted was at a meeting to discuss Juliet Mitchell's article 'The Longest Revolution', which had appeared in the *New Left Review* in 1966. A woman got up and said, 'Women should control their own bodies.' The thought flashed through my head, 'What about the times I want to be out of control?' Twenty years later the thought still hovers. I suppose on the whole, though, I would still want control over when I want to be out of control.

The implications of this connection between mind, body and politics were to prove far-reaching in terms of how feminists saw sexuality, health, the environment, work and culture. Jill Rakusen summed this up in a slogan in 1976 – 'Power over our bodies, power over our lives.'[1] One form of women's oppression in Western capitalism had been the denial of our humanity, so that we have been regarded only as physical beings with bodies but no minds. Earlier strands of feminism tended to assert in opposition to this reduction to biology that women had minds as well as bodies. Contemporary feminism has insisted on contesting the division. How we perceive our bodies in the prevailing culture and in the social circumstances which physically affect us is not unalterable; it is one way in which the personal is political.

In her 1966 article 'Women: The Longest Revolution' Juliet Mitchell made two statements which were to be starting points for feminists applying the idea of control to women's sexuality and fertility. First:

Contraception, which was invented as a rational technique only in the 19th century, was. . .an innovation of world-historic importance. It is only now just beginning to show what immense consequences it could have, in the form of the Pill. For what it means is that at last the mode of reproduction could potentially be transformed. Once childbearing becomes totally voluntary (how much so is it in the West even today?) its significance is fundamentally different. It need no longer be the sole or ultimate vocation of woman: it becomes an option among others. . .

. . .Today there are the technical possibilities for the humanization of the most natural part of human culture – this is what a change in the mode of reproduction could mean.[2]

And her second point:

The fact of overwhelming importance is that easily available contraception threatens to dissociate sexual from reproductive experience – which all contemporary bourgeois ideology tries to make inseparable, as the *raison d'être* of the family.[3]

Juliet Mitchell recognized that the availability of contraception was limited. In many European countries, including Ireland, it was then still illegal. Nor was it possible for most women to have an abortion legally. Nonetheless she was optimistic about the technical potential.

When the first women's liberation groups began to meet in Britain in the late Sixties there were complaints about lack of free access to contraception and abortion. But there was also uneasiness about the forms of contraceptive technology. Monica Sjoo records Bristol Women's Liberation Group in the early 1970s criticizing the contraceptive pill's hormonal interference and the use of Third World women to test the Pill.[4] In 1971 *The Women's Newspaper* emphasized the 'con' in contraception, reporting the recent death from the Pill of a London woman, and documenting the deaths among Puerto Rican women used in trials of the drug.[5] Subsequently the health hazards of the Pill, the coil, the injectable long-term contraceptive Depo-Provera and even the diaphragm were documented extensively in women's liberation writing. Ann Oakley, reviewing the evidence in 1981, remarked ironically in *Subject Woman*, 'The safest and most reliable method of contraception is, as the standard medical joke puts it, an aspirin – between the knees.'[6]

The initial optimism about contraception has waned over the last two decades. Nonetheless, it is true that, with all their defects, the new methods of contraception are more reliable than any earlier means of controlling reproduction. So for the first time it became possible for millions of women to make love with men, knowing that it was unlikely they would conceive.[7] This was an extraordinary change with significant effects on women's consciousness. The next step was a newly confident demand from women for a technology which was not harmful to their bodies. As evidence of the dangers mounted, a hunger for information grew.[8] Feminist magazines like *Spare Rib* pioneered the discussion of contraceptive methods, which by the 1980s were accepted subjects for the mass-market women's magazines. As the coverage became increasingly doom-laden, Jill Rakusen made a plea for balancing the advantages and disadvantages of specific methods – including Depo-Provera. In their zeal to resist being misinformed, she maintained, feminists were failing 'to be rigorous in evaluating and presenting information'.[9] By treating the facts too crudely we were limiting our political understanding, which could lead to the danger of simply crying wolf about every form of contraception without making any estimation of the relative risks, advantages and disadvantages.

Black women were raising another criticism of current contraception: the problem lay not only in the physical dangers of specific methods, but in the social power which decided how the technology was to be used. This was not only the power of men over women, reflected in the institutional hierarchy of the health service. It also involved the power of race and class which sought to determine who should reproduce. Hostility focused particularly on Depo-Provera because this was administered by the medical profession. Black women argued that it tended to be given to women who were seen as 'unreliable' or 'feckless' by doctors, and that such definitions involved race and class prejudices. Further, just as the Pill had been tested in Puerto Rico and Mexico in the 1950s and 1960s, Depo-Provera was tried out by the American drug company Upjohn in Thailand. Knowledge was gained at the expense of Third World women who were not able to resist being treated as human guinea-pigs. The activities of multinational companies were part of the wider imperialist appropriation of the lives and wealth of people in poor countries.[10]

In practice, then, the development of contraceptive technology was to be less transformative than Juliet Mitchell had envisaged;

however, the campaigns for free contraception and abortion which
developed in many countries had tremendous political ramifications.
In the course of the struggle for the freedom to separate sexuality
from giving birth, the abortion campaign involved challenging laws
and the structures and practices of medicine, technology and science.
It led women to examine the inequalities of power that denied
access to knowledge, and the relative values assigned to professional
expertise and subjective experience. The power of the state to
control resources, the values implicit in population policies, the
economic and social consequences of imperialism which enabled the
multinationals to restructure health needs in developing countries
– all were questioned in relation to the demand for contraception
and abortion. So it was not that the existence of the technical
means for controlling reproduction automatically brought change.
It was rather that the possibility of human beings exercising control
revealed the extent to which the unequal organization of society
inhibited choice. To see something as possible and then to be denied
it is more radicalizing than simply bearing apparently irremediable
sufferings.

In 1967 British women gained the right to legal abortion. But
access in practice was circumscribed by the terms of the law, the
views of doctors and the circumstances of the health service.

Contraception and abortion on demand were among the topics discussed by the second Women's Liberation Conference in
Sheffield in June 1970. There were differences in emphasis already.
Toni Gorton, then a member of the Socialist Women groups connected to the Trotskyist International Marxist Group, linked the
demand for control over women's bodies to control over society.
Diane Langford from the Maoist Women's Liberation Front stressed
inequalities of class in access to contraception and abortion. In the
discussion the demand was argued in a wider context of needs for
health clinics, sex education and child care in Britain. Attempts
by the state to use birth control in the regulation of population
in various Asian, African and Latin American countries were also
noted.[11]

In November 1970 this appeal appeared in the London Women's
Liberation Workshop newsletter:

In Liverpool a campaign called the Anti-Abortion Campaign has been
started and they are going to have a public demonstration in Liverpool
on December 12. It is possible this is planned to be a send-off for a

general anti-abortion-law campaign and related to moves in Parliament. Our sisters in Liverpool are proposing a counter-demonstration and they want support from groups throughout the country.[12]

Readers were invited to attend the inaugural meeting of the Abortion and Contraception Campaign, which supported free contraception and a woman's right to choose abortion, and opposed pressure on women to be sterilized against their will.[13] The appeal had been written by Connie Harris, who was active in the trade-union-based National Joint Action Committee for Women's Equal Rights and also connected with the Socialist Women group, which had been involved in initiating the demand.

In the next year the campaign started to take off in the small women's liberation groups which had sprung up around the country. Local groups played it by ear and embarked on wide-ranging activity. By early 1973, for instance, Bolton Women's Liberation Group and the Merseyside and Cambridge Women's Abortion and Contraception campaigns had started free pregnancy testing. York Women's Liberation had started general work on women's health, finding out which doctors were 'helpful', checking out the Family Planning Association and trying to do something about the 'dreadful' VD clinic. Bolton was investigating maternity hospitals and trying to hasten free family planning. The Manchester and Salford groups ran a stall in Salford market with free literature. They also helped Salford's Medical Officer of Health with a cancer prevention scheme.[14]

The immediate response of the small groups was thus to turn outwards on a local basis and take up diverse issues relating to health. They soon noted a snag in this agitation. Women wanted information and practical help but were less keen to stay around discussing the political implications. In Salford they took the literature and did not stop and talk. The South London Women's Centre found women would come for pregnancy tests 'and then disappear'.[15] It was also difficult in the early 1970s to mobilize the disparate groups of women to demonstrate. In 1972 and 1973 the Society for the Protection of the Unborn Child mounted large demonstrations in Liverpool and Manchester. Members of local women's liberation groups made links with people in environmental groups and called counter-demonstrations but turnouts were tiny.[16] By 1975, however, the threat to the existing law from James White's anti-abortion bill had extended the campaign in significant ways.

A new organization, the National Abortion Campaign (NAC) was formed and, along with a smaller feminist organization, a Woman's Right to Choose, and the older Abortion Law Reform Association, began to agitate.[17] Liz Warren urged the women's movement to learn from the thoroughness of Catholic activism. Feminists 'had a lot to learn' in her view and 'not much time to do it'.[18] The point was taken. All over the country feminists went to see their MPs or wrote to them. They lobbied doctors, went on phone-ins and radio programmes. Some did street theatre, others organized a mobile exhibition of photographs.[19]

From 1975 there was also a determined effort to involve the trade-union movement. Here Judith Gray, Judith Hunt, Pat Knight and Dr Berry Beaumont played a crucial role nationally. In this year the TUC Women's Conference passed by a large majority a resolution for abortion on request. A similar motion was passed by the TUC and by the Labour Party Conference.[20] Behind these visible victories there was a great deal of local work. Trade-union branches had discussions on abortion and invited speakers from NAC. Feminists went to local trades councils to argue the case for abortion. At a Hull Labour Party meeting in November 1975 abortion was linked with the issue of accountability, which was subsequently to become an important constitutional issue in the Labour Party. Dr Berry Beaumont from the NAC steering committee spoke, along with a Catholic Labour councillor, Pat McMullan, who said he thought that abortion should be a matter for the consciences of women themselves rather than being decided by MPs in Parliament. A dockers' shop steward, Tony Fee, was in the chair and local union members from the TGWU, ASTMS, NUPE and APEX were present. The meeting passed an unanimous resolution calling for Kevin McNamara, the local MP, to implement the positive Labour conference policy on abortion.[21]

By 1976 20,000 people were marching for abortion rights and in defence of the existing Acts, and in 1978 the TUC march could mobilize 100,000. But the growth of the pro-abortion cause into a mass campaign which involved men and the labour movement was not without tensions. There was, for instance, a rumbling uneasiness that including men in the campaign could lead to abortion being seen as a broad social issue rather than a demand for women's control over their own bodies.[22]

Then there was the question of involvement with Parliament. The links with MPs like Renée Short, Audrey Wise and Jo

Richardson were important in connecting the grass-roots campaign with Parliament. This was vital in the opposition to James White and to Corrie's bill in 1979. But the orientation towards Parliament troubled some socialist women in the libertarian Marxist group Big Flame. In 1975 *Women's Struggle Notes* complained that too much time was being taken up in 'writing letters, lobbying MPs'.[23] They believed that it was more important to 'use the petition to provide a focus for working-class women to organize meetings in workplaces and in communities with women comrades speaking, to have meetings with hospital workers and picket hospitals'.[24]

In addition, non-aligned socialist feminists feared that left groups were going to swallow up the politics of women's liberation.[25] At the NAC conference in 1975 Jane Noble and Ann Scott from Hackney Abortion Campaign pointed out:

> The emphasis yesterday was on working through the unions, which is fair enough. But housework bolsters up capitalism just as much as work outside the home, and Conference has ignored this.[26]

They wanted also to work through 'women's centres, women's groups, housing estates, Social Security offices, clinics, nurseries, community and health centres, bingo halls', as well as trade unions.[27]

It had been the openness to all women of the new movement for women's liberation that had enabled it to grow outside the perimeters of the existing left parties and groups. The abortion campaign was important in bringing these grass-roots community networks into contact with established political structures. But the legitimacy of the former seemed precarious. There was a lack of confidence about attempting this new organizational synthesis.[28] In Hackney and Islington, for instance, women's liberation networks were able to mobilize effectively in the mid-1970s, but success brought its own problems:

> We had big meetings with left-wing Labour MPs. These marked quite a political change in the women's movement from the early direct-action tactics, self-help or consciousness-raising groups. It was strengthening to realize we could hold large public meetings and campaign with loudspeaker vans like a formal political organization. But we found it difficult to carry over the experience of the women's movement in discussing abortion in relation to our personal experience of our sexuality, our relationships, our attitudes to having children or to child care [29]

This dissatisfaction about the way in which the abortion campaign seemed to be losing contact with the personal gave rise to a proposal from a workshop at the NAC conference in 1976 that NAC groups should meet for consciousness-raising sessions. Ruth Petrie and Anna Livingstone explained, 'This grew out of a sense that the fight for abortion had become impersonal – that women felt that they were being talked at about a right that is for other women, not for them.'[30] Thus there was not simply a 'grass-roots versus parliamentary' tension but a problem of how to remain sensitive to personal feeling under the pressure of preparing petitions, persuading trade unions and lobbying MPs, especially when in conflict with tightly organized opposition to abortion.

The difficulty of combining different forms of organization has been raised over and over again during the subsequent decade. At its core has been an anxiety that the 'vital understandings' of the 'connections between personal relations and public political organizations, or of the emotional components of consciousness' should not be disregarded.[31] There was another aspect to the dilemma. It was not clear *how* women came to think of their personal lives as political. Feminists in women's liberation had found political interpretations to explain their experiences as women. But there was no formula for transmitting this reworking of consciousness. To speak of an abortion, even contraception, to a stranger, never mind a group of people or a public meeting was not familiar for most women. In the early 1970s Irish women had spoken of their need for birth control in extraordinary meetings charged with emotion.[32] But it was hard in the Abortion Campaign in Britain. Emotions kept getting lost behind the slogans. Eileen Fairweather commented in 'The Feelings behind the Slogans':

Anyone who has ever petitioned for NAC knows that the person who practically pulls the pen from your hand to jab down a signature is usually a woman – and an older one too – minutes later she's back to tell you of her own experience, the pompous doctor who first humiliated, then refused her, the breakdown after the child she didn't want and, most horrific of all, the tales of quinine and pennyroyal, umbrella spokes and needles.

Yet for every woman like this there are many who simply clam up at the sight of our placards and brusquely walk away. What we seem to forget is that women in their thousands won't come flocking to our demos when so many have never even talked to anyone of their experience. The 'antis' have 'God and right' on their side; we have a legacy of shame, secrecy and often pain which goes so deep you can't even bear to think about it – much less fight *back*.[33]

Despite the stresses and strains of combining a politics which was based on the exploration of feelings with a campaign which sought to externalize the complexity of emotions in a public arena, the capacity to theorize from the immediate and personal observation persisted. Indeed, Ann Scott maintained that working locally for NAC made you realize that, while parliamentary decisions were significant, the case for abortion meant going deeper and contesting consciousness and ideology.[34] As difficulties, resistances and obstacles were encountered, feminists sought to understand the social reasons behind the restriction of abortion rights.

One area of resistance was within the medical profession, manifesting itself most vividly in the hostility women encountered from some doctors. The accounts in women's liberation literature of humiliation and doctors' punitive attitudes towards women seeking abortion had wider implications about the needs of users and the power of professionals in the health service.[35] A London woman who asked her doctor to recommend an abortion in the mid-1970s 'was marched back into the reception room and in front of the patients, the doctor said, "So you want an abortion do you? Well just lie down and open your legs and I'll do it here and now." '[36] Another woman, Marie Arnold, had a long struggle to get an abortion, even though there was a risk the child would be deformed. She was told by a gynaecologist who supported SPUC that as she was sensible, young and healthy there was no reason for her not to bear the child. When she began to cry he told her she would have to wait two more weeks, go into labour and be induced. 'I knew what he meant and I thought, "You bastard. It's barbaric and there must be other methods." '[37] It was evident that a woman's right to control her own body was not simply a matter of the attitudes of individual doctors but involved challenging the social assumptions of the National Health Service. Dr Sheila Abdullah, at the International Women's Day Rally in Trafalgar Square in 1973, asked:

Why was contraception not included in the NHS at its inception? Why have many doctors still never received any formal training in contraception? Yet the time, manner and frequency of conception play a crucial part in the health of a woman and her children.[38]

In the same year, at the anti-abortion rally in Manchester on 25 March, Hilda Bartle reminded nurses on the pro-abortion march of the male domination of the NHS hierarchy. On the whole men were 'the bosses in an industry where the workers are primarily women'.[39] Men not only had the power of rank, but also controlled the way medical skills were conveyed and communicated: 'Isn't it true that the nurse is trained to obedience – and to believe that difference of opinion and initiative amounts to rebellion, and that such rebellion violates not only her "professionalism" but her very femininity?'[40] Thus, while individuals' behaviour was criticized, there was also an attempt to get behind the specific actions and encounters and understand the forces affecting the way people working in the medical profession responded to women. Lesley Doyal pointed out how medical domination of reproductive technology had meant that the potential for control had been appropriated:

> Doctors – and through them the state, the church and even particular sectors of industry – are able to influence issues such as whether or not a woman becomes pregnant, whether she continues an existing pregnancy, or even the conditions under which she will give birth. For women, the development of reproductive technology has therefore been a contradictory process. Technically, it has given more control over their own bodies, but it has increased the capacity of others to exercise control over women's lives.'[41]

There was therefore a snag in Juliet Mitchell's 'technical possibilities for the humanization of the most natural part of human culture'.[42] The social circumstances and power relationships within which a technology was developed affected its nature and application. Feminists asserted that technology was not neutral and that women were denied access to resources which could create a technology that truly served their needs.

The women's movement emerged from a context in which students were questioning the material basis of the education industry and arguing that forms of professional knowledge could be used as a means of coercion. These ideas also appeared in early women's liberation writing. For instance, a contraception and abortion campaign leaflet in 1970 challenged the way money was allotted for research into reproductive technology.[43] In the London Women's Liberation Workshop newsletter in 1971, Caroline Smith appealed for women with specialized knowledge to set up a 'medical and biological group'. But she was careful to add that the 'social aspects' of contraception and abortion should not be usurped by a professional group, even one of feminist women.[44] These political issues were the concern of the movement as a whole. The tension between knowledge based on experience and knowledge as an expertise was discussed from the very early days. Women in a London consciousness-raising group in 1969 argued that learning was not simply a matter of formal education:

> ... it's how people perceive their lives and how they change their lives. We couldn't have an expert come and talk about people's fears about abortion. I don't mean physical fears, I mean emotional fears – which an expert can't allay because it's a question of our own values and experience.[45]

It was harder to argue for an *interaction* between expertise and knowledge based on experience. In the early 1980s Jill Rakusen made a plea for the careful evaluation of specialized information. She said that feminists needed the confidence 'to question and to doubt' without dismissing the contribution of medical science.[46] Feminist suspicion of technology can lead to an idealization of folk methods. There is a real difficulty in being open to unofficial healing methods while recognizing their limitations. The existence of underground knowledge about health and birth control enables us to recognize that women have not been passive victims submitting fatalistically to fertility. But it can also lead to a distortion of history in the pursuit of heroines. For instance, a persistent and popular feminist belief that the persecution of witches was linked to the takeover of medicine by men over-simplifies and distorts both the history of healing and the actual accusations brought against witches.[47]

The process of challenging the nature of modern technology and the social structure of health provision has thrown up several theoretical confusions. One has been about the ways in which the power to control women's fertility has manifested itself. Sometimes this has been presented as a conscious conspiracy against women. Sandra McNeill maintained in the newsletter *Scarlet Woman*, 'Our enemy, whether you consider them as men, or the ruling class, or the State, or all three, are aware of our power of reproduction and are seeking to take it away from us.'[48] It has been apparent, though, that there is not just one prevailing assumption about women's fertility and biological reproductive capacity. Population policies have varied historically. In modern society opposition to 'artificial' birth control, still maintained by the Catholic Church, has been under pressure. Contradictory attitudes are embedded within our health-care system.[49] Not only male power over women but how capitalism structures health care determines the circumstances in which women can obtain abortions. Feminists have given accounts of male doctors as individuals exercising the power to humiliate women – but it is conceded that women in medicine are not exempt from hostility to abortion.

There is also the problem of male power being expressed in direct and indirect relationships. This includes men's actions in individual sexual relations:

> When I got pregnant I had left my diaphragm at home, discussed this with the man I was sleeping with and trusted him to be responsible – that turned out to be a mistake, for although we had sex without penetration, at the last moment he ejaculated between my legs.[50]

Helen Roberts argued, however, that men's control was not just in the immediate encounter but through hegemonic male power in the church, state and medical establishment. Men's assumptions about the world, implicit and unquestioned, assumed a status of objectivity.[51] But the assertion of male power, direct or hegemonic, fails to distinguish between men's differing interests and concerns and to recognize the inequalities among men. For instance, fathers of those Third World women who died in the course of Pill research can hardly be seen as exercising a power equivalent to that of the leaders of state and industry. Further, although male hegemony can be seen to structure decision-making in multinational companies, it is not the only factor which decides whether a drug is to be developed and marketed.

Feminists have also recognized that economic and social forces in capitalism have affected state policy towards biological reproduction.[52] But when generalizations are applied in specific historical instances the difficulties in unravelling the sources and bases of power become evident. Shortly after a speech by Keith Joseph about the need for contraception for 'undesirable' mothers in social classes 4 and 5, Sue Thomas wrote to *Women's Voice* arguing class bias in state policy:

... population control in our society means control by Keith Joseph and his class in their interests. . . Campaigns for control of population lay the blame for poverty and suffering in the world on people who are supposedly 'surplus to requirements' rather than on the system in which production and science are used for the benefit of the few rather than to develop a decent life for all.[53]

It was evident that there were differences in how the fertility of different groups of women was seen. Thus, poor white working-class and most black women were more likely to be categorized as unfit mothers. Black women pointed out how racism could lead to pressure on them to be sterilized or to have abortions. In 1980 the newsletter of the Organization of Women of Asian and African Descent observed that 'abortion has been a double-sided coin'[54] for most black women, even though they opposed the Corrie bill. From the early years of the women's movement black women have insisted on placing control over fertility in specific social and historical contexts.

In the early 1970s the Black Women's Action Committee of the Black Unity and Freedom Party in the USA argued that black women needed to understand

the forms and uses of contraceptives. Not an inch of progress will be made towards the liberation of black people as a whole if the black woman perpetuates the role of breeder, a throwback from slavery which is now under the mis-guidance of the black men.

They were against eugenically based population policies, but distinguished these from '. . .the genuine need for the black woman to reserve the right to control *her* body, to determine when and under what conditions she will bear children'.[56]

Emma Lewis made the connection between the humiliating struggle to get an abortion as a black woman – 'some white man or woman is going to try and make her feel something less than human'[57] – with the pressure for sterilization. She argued that lack of choice about having a child was linked to the power of 'money and profits'. Birth control could not be abstracted from other aspects of women's condition:

To us, as Black women, the right to control our bodies is more than just the right to abortion, if we so decide – it means the right to control our whole lives: no more unhealthy work conditions; we who work must decide what to produce and how to do it; no more managers, no more bosses.[58]

There was a persistent suspicion of the state in women's liberation writing in the 1970s, and a concern to distinguish birth control from population control in Third World countries.[59] But it remained unclear whether it was sufficient simply to stress individual choice. Hilda Bartle maintained that 'if women were given a real choice there would not be a population problem'.[60] The American feminist historian Linda Gordon argued, however, that while we might criticize the imperialist and class-based *politics* of population control, this did not mean that feminists should dismiss the study of the social implications of biological reproduction.[61]

Thus, while the arguments in women's liberation about contraception and abortion have produced slogans emphasizing the individual's right to control, in the more considered discussions these have been qualified by relating the individual's situation to society. This has been most marked in the contributions of black women in capitalist countries and in critiques of population policies towards the Third World. These links have also been made, however, in relation to working-class women's unequal access to abortion. Since the present law gives doctors rather than women the right to choose, and NHS facilities are in any case inadequate, women who cannot afford to pay for a private abortion if necessary are at a disadvantage.[62]

This class effect is even more marked in Ireland where, despite the vigorous efforts of Irish feminists, abortion is almost unobtainable. The 1967 Act does not apply to the North of Ireland, while in the Republic the 1983 'Pro-Life' Referendum made abortion not merely illegal, as before, but unconstitutional. As a result, thousands of Irish women from North and South come to Britain for abortions each year, but this option depends on money, information and support that are less likely to be available to working-class women.[63] The situation has worsened in the Republic since legal proceedings against the Dublin Well Woman Clinic led to court rulings that it was unlawful even to inform someone about where to get an abortion.

Feminists in Britain have meanwhile been criticizing the oppressive features of state services while insisting that women should have a greater degree of access to the resources controlled by the state. However, by the late 1970s this dual approach was coming up against the cuts which were occurring in the NHS.[64] Moreover a strong self-help impulse existed in women's liberation. This had developed partly under the influence of the women's movement in the United States, where books like *Our Bodies Ourselves* had pioneered accessible information on women's health, and women's health centres had been formed on a self-help basis because of the inadequacy of public provision. The emphasis on self-determination and control over our bodies meant that some feminists stressed that services and the exploration of need should be on a self-help basis. The argument for self-help abortion through menstrual extraction has arisen in Britain, though it has not been as influential as arguments for self-help groups as a means of women learning about health needs. The groups have been concerned both with practical matters and with attitudes – for example, the demystification of women's bodies via self-examination. The Essex Road Women's Centre in Islington, London, set up a health group in 1974 which was to be very successful. It

produced literature on women's health, did pregnancy testing, provided a woman doctor for advice sessions, learnt self-examination, took health classes with schoolchildren, collected information on doctors and their treatment of women, provided information on abortion facilities, and more generally, argued for the importance of preventive health care rather than simply curative medicine.[65]

This self-help approach – or perhaps 'mutual aid' is a better term – was prompted by a strong sense that needs were not being met within the existing forms of state health provision. The abortion campaign, however, brought many groups up against the limits of self-help. Just as it linked the grass-roots networks to parliamentary politics and the labour movement, so it also connected the self-help insistence on control and the exploration of needs to the attempt to reshape the NHS. The liaison was to prove a stormy one, though politically fruitful.

By 1976 local women's groups can be seen tussling with these dilemmas. Health groups at Hornsey and Essex Road Women's Centre got involved in the abortion campaign but did not take long to widen their approach into a general critique of the 'control over our lives (and emotions) exercised by the medical profession'. Nonetheless they got involved in defending a local maternity hospital, Liverpool Road.[66] The campaign was unsuccessful and the hospital closed but the women's centre had found itself working with a wide range of local groups to defend a state institution which everyone conceded was far from ideal. West London NAC also moved quite rapidly from arguing for abortion to opposing cuts in the health service.[67] In the same year feminists in Bristol linked the abortion campaign to health workers fighting cuts in the NHS.[68] Nevertheless, tension between the self-help approach and the demand for more state facilities persisted. Lesley Doyal has described how the 'paradox' of state provision presented itself:

> On the one hand, state services can be a source of oppression as the feminist critique has shown, but on the other hand, they do contain elements of considerable value that need to be defended. This is an obvious dilemma, because in criticizing services we can be accused of giving support to those who wish to cut them, and our defence of them can seem contradictory and even hypocritical. The answer, of course, lies in a more sophisticated strategy that involves the defence of services in order to maintain those aspects that we really need, while at the same time campaigning for qualitative changes in those services to meet the real needs of both users and workers.[69]

In the abortion campaign, agitation for day-care abortion centres became an important unifying demand. They combined the recognition of the need for resources to be allocated to abortion while enabling women to have more say in how they were treated. The attempt to get a local clinic was also more immediate than campaigning only in defence of the existing Abortion Act. It indicated a way of improving and extending the Act in practice. NAC news reported in 1976, 'Many NAC groups have taken up the fight for out-patient clinics to be provided in their area.'[70] A woman from West London NAC said that they had heard an out-patient clinic was to open at the New Charing Cross Hospital, but after getting more details from the Community Health Council had realized it would probably be a very limited service because of opposition from one consultant:

> So we are now organizing a really big local campaign to put pressure on the hospital authorities to give us the sort of facilities which women in our area need. We are involving local women by leafleting and speaking around shopping area, workplaces, playgroups and anywhere else we can make contact with women. We are going to approach local organizations like the Trades Unions, the Trades Council and the

Labour Party, who have already given their support to other things NAC has done in the area.[71]

In July 1977 Tower Hamlets day-care centre opened and soon there was a campaign to extend its services to women in Hackney and Newham.

It has to be stressed that there was an organic process connecting the expression of needs, practical struggles, and the theorizing of an approach to the state which was neither dismissive of the advantages of state provision nor content just to demand more of the same. Feminist political assumptions and forms of organizing began to have an impact beyond the women's movement as the attack on public provision accelerated. By the early 1980s Lesley Doyal was observing:

> . . . feminists in the women's health movement are now active partici-
> pants in the defence of the NHS – though it must be said that their
> approach has sometimes brought them into conflict with the more
> orthodox strategies of male-dominated trade unions.[72]

The thwarted possibility of transforming the 'mode of reproduc-tion',[73] in Juliet Mitchell's phrase, had thus had wide political ramifications. The assertion of need, and the criticism of church, legal and state power to determine women's control over fertility, had combined with insistence on women's right to resources controlled by the state. With this political struggle went a resolve to insist that change should be based on women's definition of what they wanted. Ruth Petrie and Anna Livingstone's words in the mid-1970s have significant political echoes for the 1980s. They noted that

> availability of abortion and campaigning for outpatient termination is
> now inextricably related to opposing the cuts and demanding more
> expenditure where we want it. It is crucial, however, to remain specific
> about what we want rather than becoming submerged in defensive
> politics about the NHS.[74]

There was a vision of alternative health needs. Abortion was one focus in a move for the democratization of services. These political concerns were to persist into the next decade as the legacy of struggles in the Seventies. But the extent of the attack on public services in the 1980s made it harder and harder to extend and democratize in practice. Nonetheless, the limited gains of the previous decade increasingly came to be perceived as a right. There was a practical common-sense truth evident in Linda Gordon's observation: '. . . the twists and turns of the rulers of women attempting to adapt their supremacy to new situations help to educate their subjects.'[75]

There were unforeseen emotional complexities in Juliet Mitchell's theoretical recognition that contraceptive technology had the potential to dissociate 'sexual from reproductive experience'. In 1981 Sue O'Sullivan described in *Spare Rib* what it felt like to live through this social process:

> During the late 1950s the hold of traditional sexual morals was breaking down. Sex, divorce, motherhood, the family, youth, were all beginning to be seen as problems. No coherent alternative morality emerged, but the cohesion of the old one was weakening.[76]

It certainly was confusing. In *Truth, Dare or Promise*, a book about girls growing up in the 1950s, I recalled the advice of my friend Joanna who had lived in Trinidad and was 'worldly wise about dating and "how far to go"'.[77] She explained to me when I was thirteen and living in Yorkshire:

> If 'they' tried to kiss you with your mouth open you must keep your teeth tight shut. (Well who could want such sloppy kisses anyway thought I.) And if you lay full length with them on the beach it was a 'sign' you would go all the way. Joanna's moral purpose blurred at the edges. Were you to fend them off or drive them crazy. I ascertained that the aim was to achieve some ideal unity of the two. I couldn't imagine quite how.[78]

In Kilburn, London, Gail Lewis describes

> warehouses behind the laundry, the place where many of us girls received some initiation into the secrets of sexual play. For me such 'experimentation' was often quite a frightening event because the big boys were the same ones who were always calling me 'nigger' or 'sambo' or 'jungle bunny'. My 'going with them' was out of both fear (they threatened us with all sorts of things if we didn't) and, in a funny sort of way, an attempt to fit in, to become one of the gang and get them to stop calling me names.[79]

It was only when she reached her twenties that she could place these childhood encounters in the context of the sexual and racial power of white men over black women. One encounter with a younger black girl was pleasurable, but she was aware it was even less acceptable than 'what we did with the boys'[80] and it haunted her for years. She was only able to overcome the fear and guilt 'when I learned of more and more women, heterosexual and lesbian, who had similar experiences as children'.[81]

Sue O'Sullivan reflects:

> Our lives were changing but were filled with confusion and ambivalence, not the least about sleeping with men and using birth control. . . Women had not defined their own needs, but they were as always terrified of unwanted pregnancies.[82]

She believes that the shift in attitudes contributed to the popularity of the Pill. Changes in consciousness preceded the technology which made sex possible without the fear of pregnancy. Young women were beginning to challenge the assumption that motherhood was women's inevitable destiny – a questioning which coincided with the expansion of educational opportunity.

The break with procreative destiny was described primarily in terms of the rejection of the 'myth' of motherhood, rather than as a means of enabling women to enjoy sexual pleasure. Sex stayed curiously *sotto voce*. It pops up as a side-issue in the abortion propaganda. 'Most people enjoy sexual relationships and recognize the need to control their fertility,' said Sheila Abdullah.[83] 'If you don't have to worry about getting pregnant then you can really enjoy making love,' an early Seventies women's liberation leaflet, called 'True Life Romance', told young girls.[84] Marion Dain and Fran McLean breezily declared, 'As well as female sexuality and the role of the family, abortion raises many other issues which necessitate other concrete struggles.[85]

It was not that feminists in the 1970s were indifferent to sexuality. There were small group discussions, meetings, conferences, enthusiasm for sexual pioneers like Alexandra Kollontai, Stella Browne and Dora Russell. There were frightening American feminists who proposed masturbation in groups. There were therapy groups, co-counselling, books about women's sexual fantasies, articles in *Spare Rib*. But the political connection between sexual pleasure and the campaign for abortion was rarely made in the written material. British feminists found it tremendously difficult to take private desires into the public domain. A movement with the slogan 'the personal is political' failed to incorporate the assertion of sensual delight into the campaign for control over fertility. Why?

There is still a social restraint on women expressing and discussing sexual desires. While women's liberation partially broke this taboo in describing love between women, the sexual feelings of women towards men have proved trickier. Some feminists felt ambivalent about the sexual permissiveness symbolized by the Pill. The separation of sex from procreation relieved many fears and anxieties but it took away some of the protective veneer in relations between young men and women. It made the external trappings of 'respect' unnecessary without enabling people to find a new form of mutual respect. It could expose young women to a more blatant form of sexual exploitation disguised as 'freedom'. This was one of the contradictions which provoked the rebellion of women's liberation, the challenge to a male-defined permission.

One consequence was that women discovered sexual pleasure in lesbian relationships. In the early 1970s the Ilford women's liberation group produced an issue of *Shrew* in which they argued for

the alternative of homosexuality as a form of birth control. . . we could learn more about loving our own bodies and may even undo some of the damage society has done our sexuality and relate sexually with much greater awareness.[86]

This was an early link between the separation of sex from procreation, which modern contraceptive technology made possible, and the social redefinition of lesbianism and homosexuality. It was one aspect of a wider challenge to the assumption that heterosexuality was 'normal' and lesbianism a deviant subculture.

In a paper on 'The Politics of Contraception', presented at the Women's Liberation Conference in 1977, the Women and Science Collective stated:

We believe that society can be changed so that women and men can enjoy their own sexuality and their procreative role. Many women are demanding the right to have complete control of their own fertility and sexuality. This means that through contraception and abortion, abstinence and lesbianism, women will be able to choose for themselves: (a) how many children, if any, they will produce (b) when to produce and (c) what kind of relationship to be in.[87]

It was an orderly vis ion without any messy emotions.

Two years later the National Abortion Campaign paper at the Socialist Feminist conference in March 1979 asserted that both heterosexual and lesbian women were defined by their 'expected role of child-bearing'.[88] Criticism of existing forms of contraception, and of sterilization which was not freely chosen, had to combine with the positive assertion of women's choice of the means and forms of sexual enjoyment, which included celibacy and lesbianism as well as heterosexuality. The writers of the paper had been inspired by the International Campaign for Abortion Rights, in which European women had 'raised these questions of sexuality'.[89] They were puzzled by the silence in the British campaign: 'The right to sexual pleasure is a fundamental issue of women's liberation and yet it is rarely if ever articulated.'[90] They thought the explanation for British feminist reticence might be the restraining influence of the labour movement, whose support women's liberation campaigners for abortion had sought so assiduously:

> These issues are difficult enough to bring up in the women's movement. How can we raise them in the trades union and labour movement? How do we raise these sorts of demands in the health service?[91]

There is probably some truth in the argument that the emphasis on trade-union support – much stronger in Britain than in many other women's liberation movements – influenced the terms in which the call for abortion was presented. Fusty trades council rooms are not the most commodious sites for learned perorations on the multiplicity of female desire. But feminists have raised the most unseemly topics in the most unlikely places; also, the silence existed within the recorded statements of the movement itself.

I think it is more likely to be partly because of an evasion within the women's liberation movement itself. The movement sought to avoid counterposing heterosexuality and lesbianism, but in the process the scope of sexual self-definition narrowed and any discussion of heterosexual pleasure went into defensive retreat.[92] The other factor was simply that, whereas in the earlier birth control and abortion campaigns of the 1920s and 1930s the right to sexual enjoyment was made explicit, latterday campaigners on these issues regarded this as too obvious to explain. This complacency was to weaken the force of the feminist challenge to sexual conservatism.

The conference papers of the late 1970s sound as if they are about an unreal individual rationally choosing sexual options. The personal lives of the women involved in the abortion campaign were more confused, ambiguous, and indeed believable. But yet again the personal and the political had somehow come apart.

This separation did not go unobserved. In the abortion campaign, feminists frequently said they saw abortion as one of a whole range of demands which would enable women to have greater control over fertility. It was enforced motherhood we were against. Indeed, one of the slogans was 'Every child a wanted child'. But women's liberation was no more exempt than any other political movement from contradictory pulls between public assertion and private consensus. Jan O'Malley, who was active in West London NAC in the mid-1970s, pointed this out in *NAC News* in 1976. When she decided to have a third child her feminist friends agreed she must be mad – even though she and the man she lived with were happy looking after their family of two. In an article entitled 'My Child, My Choice' she wrote,

> What a phony choice if the response to choosing the alternative, choosing to have a child, is such horror, bleakness and lack of respect for the decision you have taken.
> My first response was to get apologetic, to feel guilty, but that's crazy – we're not fighting guilt about having an abortion only to replace it with guilt at having children.[93]

The existence of an emotional undertow is an aspect of all politics – and when it comes to the public political expression of human beings' feelings about fertility, sexuality and birth it would be surprising indeed if it could ever be made simple. I certainly believe every woman should be able to choose whether to have a baby. But I have also known moments when I would have preferred not to choose – when the assertion of conscious, responsible will felt onerous rather than a right. But did these moments mean that, like my grandmother, I would spend my life bearing and rearing fourteen children? They did not. Still, there is not complete clarity of need in these matters. Chance and biology still play a part.

An interesting change of tone appears in the writing on abortion by the late 1970s and early 1980s. There was now sufficient confidence to express contradictory feelings and the complexity of choices, both in an existential sense and in relation to social circumstances. Eileen Fairweather quoted Debbie, who wrote to *Spare Rib* about her abortion:

I was stunned by my reaction. I never though I'd want kids and I found I wanted this one. When I got home from hospital and my friends had gone I just rolled about the floor howling, 'I wanted it. I wanted it.'[94]

It is possible for the same woman to have different responses to abortions at various points in her life. And the reactions of different women are diverse. 'Brent Against Corrie Pamphlet Group' published *Mixed Feelings* in 1980. Ten women contributed to the pamphlet, expressing a range of feelings. One woman, Liz, said that she had learned the ambivalence of wants and that choices are tangled, both psychologically and socially:

> The main impression I took away from the clinic was how capable women are of making difficult decisions. I think that ambivalence is an inevitable part of all women's lives in this society. We have to make decisions about all sorts of things, when and whether to have children; if we have them, how much time we give to caring for them and how much we concentrate on other activities.[95]

Contradictions – gaps between desire and social reality, between aspirations and feelings – were thus being raised within the process of political struggle. This was a significant move away from accepting the terms of existing forms of political campaigning. Instead of just arguing on the basis of 'rights' and 'choice', the abortion campaign was saying that people are often confused about what they want. This understanding has wider political implications. Choices are made in a scrambled kind of way. But ultimately every individual has to be the one who decides. However imperfect people's choices might be, another person does not know their feelings, live their life. Liz concluded: '. . . the whole experience showed me how women from all sorts of backgrounds were coping with working through the contradictions that society and our own upbringings impose on us'.[96]

Trusting women to make their own decisions about fertility means also trusting women to comprehend the complexity of this rather new human possibility. Eileen Fairweather argued forcibly that we should not dismiss the ambivalence inherent in this process.[97]

The ethical implications of destroying a foetus have been approached from several angles. One line of argument appeared in a leaflet on abortion and contraception produced by Bristol International Socialism group in the early 1970s: 'We cater for the needs and rights of the child only by building a world which is fit for it to live in.'[98] The concern here is the social circumstances of the reproduction of life. In 'Questions and Answers on Abortion', *Red Weekly*, the newspaper of another Marxist group, maintained that the right to life was relative in the thinking of members of SPUC, some of whom would accept the notion of 'the just war' and approved of capital punishment.[99]

These arguments do not, however, confront the individual's moral dilemma about having or performing a termination. The distinction between a potential human life and a baby has been made often in the National Abortion Campaign. A foetus is 'a potential human being' and still 'part of the woman's body', NAC has argued.[100] Abortion campaigners have argued for better contraception and, if this failed, early abortion. Pro-abortionists have been divided in Britain about whether to support a woman's unlimited right to an abortion or whether to accept a time limit after which abortion would not be legal. NAC came out in support of abortion as the woman's right. Women might seek abortions after twenty weeks with the most compelling reasons – a teenager afraid to tell, a menopausal woman who had not realized she was pregnant, a woman who has just discovered that she is carrying a deformed child. A time-limit on abortion was thus seen as an arbitrary denial of these individual circumstances.[101]

Judy Watson and Rose Knight pointed out also that the 'biological fact' of viability is subject to change and that this affects the moral issue of life or potential life. Advances in medical technology mean a foetus can now survive at an earlier stage than in previous eras. Thhis is clearly a wonderful development for women in danger of losing a wanted child, but it begins to undermine any fixed distinction between foetus and child.[102] It is becoming evident that the distinction cannot be regarded as 'natural'. Human action affects 'viability'.

In fact there was never – even at the height of the campaigning in the mid-1970s – a unified feminist position on abortion. For example, a Christian feminist, Lucy Arnold, wondered in *Spare Rib* in 1976 whether we could be sure that embryonic life does not 'already possess a human individuality or soul' even before it can survive outside the womb.[103] She supported 'A Woman's Right to Choose' because 'such a theory cannot be proven or disproven by scientific means'.[104] There were also feminists who simply opposed abortion on principle. Others disagreed with the slogan 'A Woman's Right to Choose' because they said it was inconsistent with the demand that men should take equal responsibility for contraception and child care. There were also women of 'mixed feelings'. In 1980 Eileen Fairweather presented courageous political arguments for dwelling on the sources of contradiction. In 'The Feelings behind the Slogans' she noted that feminists could support abortion in theory but feel – especially after they had had a child – that the foetus was a human being. It would be ironic to make a feminist politics which trivialized women's emotions:

> The 'potential' human life argument implies that she is merely suffering from feminine fancy and sexist conditioning. It may seem the most 'revolutionary' position, but it is not pro-woman. How can it be, when it denies women's experience?[105]

The question raises a wider political dilemma: how to root a commitment to changing society in the contradictory expression of needs, and at the same time formulate the clear proposals and demands a campaign requires? Eileen Fairweather argued that the feminist struggle for abortion rights has to take into account both that many women feel that the foetus has life and that, regardless of ethics, women who do not want to be pregnant are going to seek abortion by whatever means are available.[106]

Interestingly, feminists in the United States have argued that the foetus is *not* part of the woman's body but that a symbiosis between the two exists. Ros Petchesky, in 'Reproductive Freedom: Beyond "A Woman's Right to Choose"', an article which takes up both ethical and political issues arising from the abortion campaign, observes:

> Recognizing a situation of real conflict between the survival of the foetus and the needs of the woman and those dependent on her, the feminist position says merely that women must decide, because it is their bodies that are involved and because they still have primary responsibility for the care and development of the children.[107]

The campaigns for free contraception and the right to abortion have revealed a whole range of questions about power in society and the relationship between human beings and technology. Kathleen McDonnell, in *Not an Easy Choice*, sums these up:

> With abortion, as with other areas of our reproductive lives, women are at a historical juncture, finding ourselves faced with new and unprecedented choices, choices for which history and our conditioning have ill-prepared us.[108]

5

The Body Politic

There is not a universally accepted feminist case for abortion, though the conviction that women need to decide their own fertility has been the prevailing emphasis of the women's liberation movement. The new social circumstances of reproduction have given rise to needs which are much more complex and ambivalent than the public political demand of the right to an abortion would indicate. In the twenty years which have passed since Juliet Mitchell's 'longest revolution' it has become evident that existing political formulations and concepts are inadequate to express what women want from these new technical possibilities of reproductive control.

Not only do our needs relate to many other tangential factors – thus an abortion is a need in relation to other possibilities – but there is clearly a tension between a politics committed to the exploration of need (which found a form in the consciousness-raising group) and the pursuit of a series of strategic goals which is the function of a campaign. Needs are often ambiguous and contradictory, being both rooted in existing circumstances and seeking an alternative.[1] Consequently the translation of 'needs' into 'demands' tends to uproot them from the social context in which they developed. Demands are more mobile, but, deracinated, they are often incapable of a return to their own contradictory social origins.

Political demands for radical change are often justified by an appeal to 'rights'. The 'right' to abortion has been one of the slogans of the campaign. The problem with the concept of 'rights' is its tendency to remove claims from their historical context. Just as a demand can become cut off from those needs it does not encompass and come to overshadow them, the idea of 'rights' assumes a universal validity. The notion of 'rights' thus legitimizes demands but also invests them with an abstract quality.

The concept of a 'right' to control fertility arises in specific historical circumstances. A right is a historical creature: it is defended as part of the struggle to extend democratic control. The danger comes if we elevate a concept into a universal dogma which cannot be shown to have limits and problems in its conceptualizing. Ros Petchesky highlights a real problem in being complacent about reproductive control as a universal right:

> Some women reversing the prejudice in favour of male children have wanted to only have girl children – and have claimed abortion as a 'right'.
> Should women get an abortion on the grounds that they prefer a different gender (which amniocentesis can now determine)? Such a decision, in my view, would be blatantly sexist, and nobody's claim to 'control over her body' could make it right or compatible with feminist principles.[2]

There is also a political difficulty for feminists in arguing women's right to abortion as absolute or exclusive, because this can be turned back on women to reinforce the view that reproduction is their sphere. There is confusion in feminist views on contraception for a similar reason. It is women's right or equally men's responsibility? These problems are one aspect of the greater dilemma about how to assert the needs of women without strengthening stereotypes and assumptions about fixed, unchanging differences between men and women.

There are also certain limits inherent in the use of the term 'rights'. The tradition of demanding change by the legitimizing of rights asserts that a group's resistance is morally just. It does not necessarily present a means of transforming the society in which injustice is found. Juliet Mitchell has argued that 'rights' demand access for an individual or are the means of barring the access of others.[3] Ros Petchesky states, 'Rights are by definition claims that are staked within a given order of things and relationships.'[4]

As well as having meaning as a general political term, 'rights' exist within legal frameworks. Some feminists have argued that law is simply man-made and inherently anti-woman. Carol Smart has put forward a more complex theory of social control in which opposing stereotypes of women can be seen to conflict in law.[5] Equally, law is marked by feminists' past struggles, providing the means of recognizing moderate gains and periods in which these are re-appropriated. The extent to which the law concedes women's right to abortion expresses a combination of political forces. The feminist campaign for abortion used arguments based on rights but was also extending their terms of reference. Marguerite Russell,

a barrister, attacked James White's bill in 1975 on the grounds
that doctors accused of carrying out an unjustified abortion would
have to prove themselves innocent, thus reversing the principle
of 'innocent until proven guilty'.[6] The restriction of the right
to abortion thus curtailed civil liberties. However, a year later
in a paper at the Newcastle Women's Liberation Conference, 'A
Woman's Right to Choose' Campaign argued that the existing
interpretation of legal rights could not express the political meaning
feminism gave to the concept 'a woman's right to choose' because
'nearly all rights exist through negative means, i.e. by preventing
something being done to you, rather than positive means'.[7]

Feminists have in practice combined the language of rights
with another aspect of the radical tradition: the ideas of self-
determination and control over one's person. The belief in individual self-realization has been a vital aspect of radical-liberal thought.
In the early nineteenth century radical and utopian socialists who
advocated birth control linked it to the right to sexual pleasure and
enjoyment and opposition to the church's control over knowledge
and life.[8] Nina Woodcock echoed their arguments in her observation, 'If we don't have full control over our bodies we have no hope
of being able to control our own lives.'[9] The idea of control over
one's person has an interesting radical heritage which can be traced
back to the seventeenth century. In the twentieth, it still has tremendous implications for the identification of necessary changes – in
relation to health and the environment as well as fertility control.

Thinking in terms of control over our bodies extends how we
can regard fertility in relation to social transformation. The concept
goes beyond the 'right' to have access to available contraceptive
technology. It has been a powerful means of contesting belief
in a fixed natural sphere for women outside social action. It
also potentially extends the way in which material life and social
relationships are conceived. However, it has certain limits. It
assumes that control rather than harmony with one's body is the
aim in all circumstances. It also focuses on the individual rather
than the wider relationships in society.

The campaigns for abortion have highlighted these theoretical
shortcomings. They have also encountered difficulties with the
Marxist tradition, in which the social circumstances of reproduction
were considered but the individual needs of women disregarded.
Another obstacle has been a tendency among some Marxists to
narrow the definition of 'the material' to mean the economy,

or even heavy industry alone. Other aspects of life were presented as somehow less 'real' and of secondary significance in shaping consciousness. Or they were simply regarded as 'natural'. Socialist feminists criticized this because it did not correspond with their experience of life, but were repeatedly caught between two political vantage points: control over work and control over fertility. The focus on production and reproduction still assigned women the sphere of biological reproduction and men the sphere of production, ignoring the fact that men too contribute to the biological reproduction of the species and women are contributing to production through both domestic labour and paid work. The wider perspective of human life and patterns of relating remained obscured.[10]

In *The Origin of the Family* Engels wrote:

> . . . the determining factor in history is, in the last resort, the production and reproduction of immediate life. But this itself is of a twofold character. On one hand, the production of the means of subsistence, of food, clothing and shelter and the tools requisite therefore; on the other, the production of human beings themselves, the propagation of the species.[11]

In innumerable small groups feminists returned again and again to Engels's phrase. For it clearly asserted the significance of having babies as the means of carrying on human life in the world. What was missing was recognition of the social relationships involved in human propagation. This detached the material activity of fertility, birth control, conception, birth and child-rearing from human culture. Engels's presentation of the 'propagation of the species' stresses deterministic forces. He does not take into account the importance of women's own activity in relation to reproductive freedom. The orthodox Marxist view thus appeared to be completely at variance with the utopian idea of control over one's body which was being put forward in women's liberation. The two positions were popularly designated as 'the Marxist' and 'the feminist' – and many a meeting has divided in acrimony between the two. While the 'feminist' approach, rooted in radical liberal notions of the right to control one's person, stressed the individual's exertion of control by an act of conscious rational will, the 'Marxist' approach focused on the significance of bearing children for economic life. Both perspectives contained their own snags and blind spots which were ignored in the heat of political argument.

Because the demand for control over our bodies emerged from
the women's liberation movement, the concept has been worked out
specifically in the context of the power relationships between men
and women. This has created the unfortunate impression that only
women have bodies, that our bodies only have a political significance
in relation to sexuality and procreation, and that otherwise the way
we regard our bodies and the bodies of others is not affected by
historical and social circumstance. At the 1979 Socialist Feminist
Conference in London, in a paper entitled 'The Politics of Control
of Our Bodies', Parveen Adams and Beverley Brown pointed to
this problem of isolating the female body from social existence as
a whole: 'The very conception of body only makes sense in terms
of the social institution and practices in which we all necessarily
engage.'[12] In the process of making this point, however, they
tend to disembody the body: it dissolves into the social means of
understanding it. Yet our bodies are still going about our business
in the world and being affected by physical and material change
and circumstance.

A way of correcting the narrowness of the tunnel-vision approach
to the body has presented itself in the 1980s through a range
of movements and campaigns showing how control over 'nature'
can endanger human beings. As we take our bodies to work and
bring them home, stress, chemical pollution, radiation have become
part of daily life. All these extend the political meaning women's
liberation gave to the call for 'control over our bodies'.

In another widening of thought, feminist anthropology has drawn
creatively on Marxism to examine the social relationships involved in
procreation, as one aspect of material life.[13] When the 'propagation
of the species' is seen not simply as 'production' but as culture,
its social organization can be seen to give rise to new needs. Ros
Petchesky has suggested that this concept of social self-realization
is a way of giving historical meaning to the demand for control over
one's body.[14]

Within feminist thinking there has been an intense struggle
to find a new balance which gives weight to both individual
and society. Sue Himmelweit has argued in relation to abortion
that the insistence on individual choice is an inadequate political
basis.[15] But is is almost impossible to imagine a state which would
not be alien to the individual on such an intimate question: a state
which merged with society – a society in which every individual
felt at one with the collective process of decision-making. It is

even less conceivable that all people in this projected future society could be as attuned to one another as intimates. At present there is a negotiation between lovers about decisions connected with procreation. For, while inequality and dominance are features of our loving, there is mutuality, receptivity and union too. But how could such a negotiation be with a collectivity of people? Will there not always be a certain tension between the individual's choosing and the wider group's organization of biological reproduction?[16]

It is impossible to do more than speculate about such futures. We are at a much earlier stage in clarifying new guidelines for our human realization of the potential of birth-control technology. It is evident that existing traditions of thought are not adequate to solve the new dilemmas which the extended possibilities of human intervention open up. The Canadian feminist philosopher Susan Sherwin has suggested that a re-balancing in ethical thought is necessary:

> Our inherited ontology places primacy on the concept of the individual and treats social arrangements as artificial constructs. I think feminism is impelling us towards an ontology that recognizes social arrangements as being fundamental as well; but unlike fascism and Marxism (on some interpretations), and many versions of religious dogma, it cautions against a perspective that values groups *above* individuals. The picture we need is not of competition of interests between the individual and society (which the leading political and moral theories seem to be offering), but rather one that views each as integral to the other.[17]

This would enable women's control over fertility to be understood in the widest sense – not simply in relation to abortion or even birth control, but as involving the social circumstances necessary to allow all women to make choices about child-bearing and child-rearing. It would necessarily involve challenging the relationships of power in the state which deny access to resources for the creation of a technology that meets women's needs.

The ramifications of the potential techniques of birth control and the political and philosophical implications of the abortion campaign are, as we have seen, far-reaching. Their exploration has brought many women into radical political activity. In the process the terms in which politics can be conceived have altered. The demand for abortion is just one aspect of the wider contention of the women's liberation movement that the personal is political.

Nonetheless, there remains the political problem of the limited and immediate gain itself being under threat not only from the traditional Catholic organizations but from new, militant anti-abortion groups which have used violent direct action against clinics in North America. It is not much good if you become wise in all the philosophical implications and yet are unable to uphold the specific reform you sought in the first place. As Eileen Fairweather's article 'The Feelings behind the Slogans' put it, 'I didn't want to raise my consciousness if it was only so that I could stay calm on some back-street abortionist's table.'[18] It is still vital to defend the existing provisions for legal abortion. The time when there was only the grim alternative is not after all so long ago. It still haunts the lives of many women. Joyce Lister wrote in *Spare Rib* in 1980:

> I am now 46 years old with three nursing qualifications and also the mother of three children. When I commenced my training, I held very different views on abortion to those I have today.
>
> For the rich it was a case of pop down to London for your abortion in a private nursing home. For the gynaecologists' wives, or nurses who doctors had got pregnant, it was down to the theatre for a scrape for heavy periods – surprise, surprise, a little foetus dropped out.
>
> For the poor it was a case of do-it-yourself, or a visit to the back-street abortionist. My father-in-law had a pub at the time and an SRN did abortions for a fee. One male customer kept getting girls pregnant, introducing them to the abortionist and actually getting commissions.
>
> Saturday night was abortion night on our gynaecological ward. We knew a man went around on Saturdays carrying out illegal abortions; many women arrived just in time to have their lives saved. Personally I never saw anyone die, but dead bodies are not brought into recovery wards.
>
> Some of the doctors' attitudes were disgraceful. If the woman showed embarrassment when being internally examined, comments like 'Pity you didn't close your legs before' were made.
>
> For God's sake let's not put the clock back. Contraception is still far from ideal. I myself had a stroke 18 months ago as a result of taking the Pill. Let women have their abortions in sterile and caring conditions.[19]

While the need to defend what gains have been made continues, the years of campaigning have also brought a determined resolve to break the 'taboo' and acknowledge the 'Mixed Feelings' about abortion examined by Gina Newson in the film of that name in 1982 and, with Angela Neustatter, in a later book.[20]

Abortion as a political issue challenges the scope of existing theories about demands, rights, individuals and society, and social need. It does not find a comfortable expression in a form of politics geared to campaigns. Nor is it easy to draw up a 'line' which can admit ambivalence. In Kathleen McDonnell's words:

> Gradually I found myself coming back to a basic feminist truth: that our 'politics' cannot afford to be divorced from our authentic feelings, no matter how vague or contradictory they may seem. Our real task is to search out and find ways to reconcile the two.[21]

6

Disentangling Desires

Women's liberation as a movement created a political space in which women were able to consider the whys and wherefores of motherhood. A formative tenet of the movement has been that there should be a conscious decision whether or not to have a child. Michelene Wandor reflected on the contrast between this questioning approach and the prevailing attitudes when she married and had two sons in the early 1960s:

> I assumed that all women were like me and simply wanted children. The question was 'how soon?', not 'whether' and certainly never 'why?'.[1]

In the early years of Women's Liberation the emphasis was on challenging the myth that motherhood was woman's inevitable destiny. It has been very important to contest the idea that happiness comes only through motherhood and to attack the myth which denies women a range of possibilities. Feminists have maintained that motherhood as we know it carries both oppressive and fulfilling elements. It is far from being a liberating and enriching experience for all women. Consequently, feminists have insisted that motherhood must be freely chosen and socially transformed.

The complaints of young women with children were significant in movement literature. There is a tremendous sense of release in the accounts of struggles, dependence, exhaustion and rage. Women began to talk about the most taboo aspects of this darker side of mothering – depression, derangement, violence.

In the early 1970s Nemone Lethbridge wrote a play for television called *Baby Blues* about a woman who drowned her baby. It received hostile, incredulous reviews. How could anyone seek to understand such a monstrous act? *Baby Blues* was written out of the author's own contrary response to the birth of the baby she desperately wanted:

I saw visions, heard voices – especially Shakespearean ones, remembered from childhood visits to the Old Vic – 'When first we smell the air we wail and cry that we are come to this great stage of fools.' I cried and cried. In fact I couldn't stop crying for eighteen months.

Baby Blues touched a painfully raw nerve. The letters poured in. 'I put a pillow on my baby's face and climbed a mountain 4,000 feet high' (Cumberland). 'I thought I must be the most wicked person in the world to have thoughts like these' (Aberdeen).[2]

Annette Muir wrote in an early issue of *Shrew*:

We are bombarded on all sides with the image of motherhood as a radiant woman who has achieved her ultimate fulfilment by holding a sweet-smelling, sleeping baby in her arms. The reality is more likely to be a harassed dishevelled mum with a foul-smelling, yelling baby. I think the shock effect of this gap between the myth and the reality is underestimated and not discussed enough. . . We seem committed to a conspiracy of silence.[3]

There were two sources of protest. Young middle-class educated mothers found that the contrast between their assumption of equality and the reality of their domestic confinement was acute. They were not necessarily poor, but they were dependent and isolated. Single mothers, both middle-class and working-class, also experienced economic hardship and state harassment. The release of their feelings of dissatisfaction challenged the propaganda about the joys of motherhood. Women also argued for changes in domestic life and work which would mean caring could be shared by both parents or by other carers. The early women's liberation groups were linked closely to organizations offering advice and help: Claimants' Unions, Gingerbread and Mothers in Action. All these emphasized practical steps which could be taken for mothers' 'survival'.

The question of mothering was an important element in the emergence of the women's movement. Many of the earliest meetings discussed child care. But there remained a gap between those of us who had children and those of us who had not. I was among the have-nots. I can remember in my twenties listening dutifully to tales of the crimes and charms of little Bloggins and feeling secretly restive. Oh, if only we could pass on to more exciting stuff like the domestic labour debate or the relevance of Rosa Luxemburg or something. Theoretically I recognized the politics of everyday life. But, not being a mother, I still found the chit-chat exceedingly dull and depressingly dismal. 'How do they put up with it?' I wondered. 'How do they remain relatively sane?' Their lives were not their own at all. Yet I wanted to have a child – but always in the future. In the present there were so many things to do. I was wary about having a baby because I was terrified of the dependence it entailed. The denunciation of motherhood intensified my fears – though it did not make me personally ever imagine I would never conceive. In 1977, breast-feeding a baby at women's meetings, I gazed at childless feminists in amazement as they intellectually galloped along. 'How can they think so fast?' I wondered, and yearned for the child welfare centre where we were all hypnotized by the micro-world of the babies.

By 1980 Liz Heron was commenting on 'the latterday feminist baby boom':

> In the early days of the movement, feminists with children discovered their oppression and had the support of their sisters in throwing off guilt and finding independence. Those founding mothers were striving to challenge the mystique – and the material realities – that made them prisoners, to live like those of us who weren't hemmed in by maternity.[4]

She noted wryly that many feminists seemed to be 'melting into motherhood'.[5] The move towards having children was also noticeable in many other countries.

During the 1970s complaint about motherhood, denunciation of its mystique, and emphasis on choice had put women who wanted children on the defensive. Were they simply the victims of delusion? Was the choice of motherhood an indulgence? Freewheeling childless feminists could appear to be saying, 'You made your bed, now lie on it.' Writing of the French context, Claire Duchen said this led to 'the ironic equation: enslaved motherhood + voluntary motherhood = voluntary slavery'.[6] However, the biological clock was having its effect: '. . . women have very different attitudes to motherhood when they are 20 and when they are 30'.[7]

Readiness to consider why women want to have children, without attributing the inclination completely to external conditioning marked an acceptance of a complexity which had been absent from the earlier literature. Terry Slater came to understand her longing for a child as an inward existential quest:

I have been trying to work out what has been driving me to have a child, what has made it worthwhile for me. . . Other mothers have given me various reasons: someone to look after you in old age; it's easier to 'fit in' and be part of the world if you have a child; it's part of belonging to natural cycles of life and death; and one friend just told me she wanted someone to love and be loved by. . . When I am low and down on myself I feel that perhaps even now I really needed a baby to fill some empty gap inside me – a kind of deep loneliness which needed that baby, tenderness and skin contact with someone who doesn't go away (you're never alone with a baby). When I am feeling cheerful and OK, I see it in a different way: that having a baby has been a way of exploring and recovering part of myself, of somehow reliving and reshaping my own childhood and through it perhaps getting a bit mature.[8]

After the initial release of lifting the guilt from complaint, the ambiguity of desire began to surface. A movement which had asserted that areas of life defined as personal had political implications reflected on its original impulse and began to suggest, in Claire Duchen's words, 'that not everything in our lives can be explained and analysed'.[9] The assumption that the personal is political led into deeper water than we had imagined. It was innovatory indeed for a political movement to embark on exploration of 'experiences and feelings' in 'an area that defies political analysis'.[10] Claire Duchen pointed out that when women in France formed groups to discuss motherhood, they 'found that they might try to disentangle culturally conditioned desires and "real" desires, to find out what women's "real" attitudes to motherhood were, but they couldn't actually do it'.[11] Not surprisingly the women's liberation movement yielded no clear answers. What has become apparent is that a movement for change which envisages the transformation of personality has to live under a tension: 'The tailoring of desire to the logic of politics is not always possible or acceptable.'[12]

It is not in fact true that in the early days of the women's liberation movement in Britain there was an outright rejection of motherhood. The change really was that it became possible to express the negative aspects of mothering without feeling such a sense of failure. As Nell Myers put it:

The women's movement has been caught up in the necessary exorcism of our rage and frustration; when you are told that your only real value is as a reproducer and you know that isn't so – what can you do, initially, but deny that value as loud as you can in order to create some kind of balance?[13]

This was not the only response of course. I can remember in many early discussions women complaining about the practical problems of child care but expressing happiness in being mothers. Underlying the anger was the impulse to make a life in which there could be a new balance between mothering and a range of other activities for women. We did not see this as an 'either/or' choice. We explicitly rejected the emancipation of the middle-class 'career woman' who was forced to remain childless. Instead, we wanted new relationships and conditions in which we could have children and lead fuller lives.

Denial that our only value is as 'reproducers' has not been the only response from feminists. Another approach has been to argue that motherhood is a source of female power that men seek to control. Linked to this has been an affirmation of the 'motherly' values of nurture. As a total political concept this leads to a dead end. It results in an idealization of motherhood which confines women again to a separate sphere as nurturers.[14] As Liz Heron argues, 'to celebrate child-bearing and child-rearing as "woman power", as one strand of contemporary feminism has done, risks bringing us full circle to another kind of biological determinism'.[15]

This approach undermines women who are sharing child care and combining mothering with paid work, and disregards the material reality of large numbers of working-class and black women's daily struggle with low-paid work and child care.[16] But, in acknowledging how some women can experience mothering at certain moments, it is an important assertion of aspects of experience which have been disregarded as a source of alternative social values. Amidst all the testimonies of desperate and harassed mothers in the early issues of *Shrew*, for instance, there were also descriptions of harmony and creative fulfilment in giving birth:

> I had always felt inadequate, not only in everyday life but in my relationships with my family and with men. I felt I had failed in everything. Here was the greatest test of all, and I was sure I'd fail this too. . .
>   . . . When I looked at that beautiful baby, so perfect, I thought very clearly, 'This is the first time in my life when I've done something *well*.' I knew thousands of women did it every day, but that didn't minimize

the great sense of achievement I felt. I had created something good
within myself for the first time. . .

. . . I felt the outside world could go and tie itself up in knots
and I didn't care. This simple deep relationship between her and me
was real.[17]

The sensual pleasure of mothering has also been described in
women's liberation literature. In *Only the Rivers Run Free*, Eileen
Fairweather, Roisin McDonough and Melanie McFadyean interviewed women in Northern Ireland about the effects of war and
their feelings about their lives. Mary Nelis, a Catholic community
activist and mother of ten children, was unusual in breast-feeding
them all: '. . . it was breast-feeding that first really made me
aware of my body, the pleasure and pride it could give me'.[18]
She went on:

We hear so much about the horrors of the female body, and everything
that can go wrong with it, but next to nothing about its marvels. Well,
to me, the fact that women can feed their young through their own
bodies is almost magical. I loved it. . .

. . . Really, I think that men are just jealous of women. They can't
feed, and they can't have babies either, so they've tried to turn what
we alone can do into something that's as shameful and unpleasurable
as possible. . .

. . . But I carried on, regardless. And you know, breast-feeding gave
me a sense of my own power – would you believe that? I come from as
puritanical a background as anyone else, but when I gave birth and fed
my first baby, I felt the most intense emotion, and sense of happiness
and pride, that I'd ever felt in my life. I didn't care what anyone said:
this was beautiful and this was right.[19]

Feminists have been 'saddled with the image of the Mrs Kramer
mother who abandons husband and children to find freedom and
herself'.[20] There is a persistent popular stereotype of feminists
as curious beings, distinct from 'normal' women and immune
to contrary emotions. In reality feminists have grappled with the
contradictory extremes of female destiny that mothering embraces.
To dismiss the delights it can bring denies intense and passionate
aspects of women's lives. But to elevate these into an alternative
ideal is to deny the negative feelings, to return women to the sphere
of reproduction and subordinate childless women to a maternalistic
hierarchy. It is hardly surprising that the persistent determination

to change the conditions of mothering in the women's liberation movement has come up against the evasiveness of desire. As Liz Heron points out, the tension between mothers and non-mothers is not just a matter of 'freedom' and 'divergence of commitments',[21] but also springs from the complexity of the 'decision to have children or not, turning as it does on the experience of our own childhood, our individual strengths and weaknesses, our relationships, work, housing and, crucially, economic security'.[22] Then there is pride in maternity, traditionally a source of women's self-esteem. This has included a competitive element which still lingers emotionally, along with even deeper feelings about fertility.

The effort of transformation in an area of human experience often regarded as natural and not subject to social modification has involved a tremendous upheaval. It has caused feminists to challenge medical, anthropological and psychological assumptions, as well as questioning the scope of politics. Tessa Weare, for instance, describes how she struggled for an alternative to the medical typification of pregnancy:

> I tried to rebel against the NHS image of motherhood, but the only image I could find was that of the Great Earth Mother, deprived of her magic and evil, now merely the round, loving all-provider. She bakes, knits and sews and sits in passive contentment, breeding. . .
> . . . Although it is a more constructive image than the previous one, going to women as primarily physical, earthy beings is no help to someone like me who wants to have an active, working, intelligent image of themselves when pregnant. I don't feel I can counter my rejection of my physicality by worshipping it. The thought brings out all my fears of being engulfed by my body, becoming only tits, cunt, womb and no me.[23]

Although the Earth Mother is a symbol in our culture of a 'natural' source of female power, there is a real dilemma if feminists accept the existing dichotomy and celebrate woman as 'nature'. Mary Kelly has argued that there is a psychological ambivalence in the existing symbolic meanings of motherhood. It is too simple to elevate motherhood and represent it as 'nature':

> 'Mother art', identification with the woman who tends: i.e. the mother who feeds you. She produces milk and therefore all 'good things', patchwork quilts, candles, bread and assorted magic rituals. She is the phallic mother, the uncastrated 'parthenogenator' of the pre-oedipal

instance. But there is also the castrated and (unconsciously) despised mother of the Oedipus complex. Her labour of love is signified as 'women's work', a kind of iconography of victimization. . . obsessive activities like scrubbing, ironing and above all preparing food.[24]

This would suggest that it is not just a matter of challenging how motherhood is portrayed in the external culture. Women bring to the decision whether or not to have a child a psychological image of motherhood as power and submission bound together. The problem for feminists is whether this is a fixed, unalterable structure or whether it can be changed. If it can be changed, where should we concentrate our efforts? On psychoanalytic exploration, on attempting to represent mothering differently, on changing the relations in which we mother, or on transforming the social conditions of mothering? Not surprisingly, there is no unified strategy. Feminists have busied themselves in all these areas. As the women's movement has become more fragmented it has been harder even to consider how the differing forms of activity and inquiry might interrelate.

It may seem a relatively simple question: Why do women have children? But there are no simple answers. The inquiry is a tremendous tussle, truly a riddle of the sphinx, which has brought feminists up against those old chestnuts of nature and society, the biological and the social. As Laura Mulvey put it in a discussion of her film *Riddles of the Sphinx*, 'Motherhood can be seen as one of the very important areas of misunderstanding.'[25] The women's liberation movement has been no more able to produce absolute explanations than other political and intellectual currents. Nor is there a coherent 'position'. What is apparent, though, is the development of a series of practices which oppose the prevailing meaning of motherhood. Women's attempts to reinterpret and to change have served to redefine the problem. One strategy has been to oppose the power of male-dominated institutions to define maternity.

This opposition has involved challenging the alienation of women's experience of pregnancy and labour by the hierarchies and technology of the modern hospital. Ann Oakley has argued that behind the medical approach to motherhood, with its apparent scientific objectivity, lurk less rational fears. The woman

has to be protected from the consequences of the invasion of her body by the alien foetus, but, also crucially, society has to be protected from the dangers of the indeterminate state represented by the pregnant woman and her unborn child. In this sense, pregnancy is a form of spirit possession requiring elaborate rituals for its taking into a non-disruptive element of the social order. Such rituals may be carried out by spiritual healers whose function is the domestication of wayward spirits, or by medical professionals working with a physicalist model of reproduction and a feminine construction of women within the orbit of medical 'science'. . .

. . . In producing babies, women seem to cause, or at least represent, an untidy and dangerous blurring of the boundaries between bodies and the social space they occupy.[26]

Ann Oakley notes a contradictory duality in how pregnant women are seen. In the medical manuals they are presented as passive machines to be programmed with the conventional advice literature into efficient production. In the popularized psychoanalytic model, on the other hand, pregnancy is the apotheosis of femininity.[27]

It is not just feminists who are confused about motherhood: the received images in a male-defined culture contain their own contradictions! Within the iconography a pregnant woman is both weak and powerful, sick and serene. Susan Hillier contested this representation by juxtaposing fragments from her diary with a sequence of photographs of her own body taken at regular intervals during pregnancy. The customary images appear, but the woman artist comments on her own belly. FFor Rosie Parker, this interaction seeks to overcome the division in the person caused when pregnancy is made to symbolize. nature: '. . . our culture both practically and theoretically divides the body who bears the child from the artist who acts and observes'.[28] Dana Breen's study of pregnancy presents a similar interaction between the growth and development of the mother and maternity:

Pregnancy stimulates in the woman ideas of life and death, mortality and immortality, purposefulness and futility, ideas connected with her own infancy, mothering and fathering, about the ability to nurture, to be relied upon, about dependency, about her own capacity to be intimately and bodily involved with a new-born baby and later a child while at the same time able to retain a sense of individuality.[29]

The biological event of pregnancy is thus socially conceived and represented. It is also experienced psychologically in different ways.[30] Feminists have been aware of the need to alter both the images of pregnancy and the individual perception of child-bearing. Thus the 'natural' can be conceived as symbiotic with human consciousness rather than its polar opposite.[31]

This has far-reaching intellectual implications which go beyond the immediate experience of pregnancy. But they have barely been explored. The argument returns persistently to the prevailing polarities. So one strand of feminism has challenged the 'natural' as socially constructed, while another has attempted to reassert the 'natural' against a male-defined society. Feminist anthropologists, however, have been particularly preoccupied with the boundaries between the two concepts.[32] Carol MacCormack says that it is impossible

> to absolutely verify that the nature–culture opposition exists as an essential feature of universal *unconscious* structure, and there is ethnographic evidence to suggest that in the form in which Europeans now conceive it, the contrast is not a universal feature of the consciously held folk models.[33]

So the very dichotomy between nature and society could in fact be cultural.

While European capitalist society has been preoccupied from the seventeenth century at least with dominating the environment, with social control over nature, this cannot, according to Gillian Gillison, be taken as a universal 'underlying metaphor for men's subordination of women'.[34] Examination of the assumptions of other societies about nature and culture shows that these do not correspond to ours. They do not associate nature with women in the way that a strand of European thinking has done, as a universal social fact taken for granted in much political thinking. For instance, Marilyn Strathern describes how, among the Haga people of the Papua New Guinea highlands, 'humanity is bounded off from the non-human, but does not seek to control it'.[35] Control comes from within, a self-defining attribute of the social world.

Theoretical difficulties also arise because feminism as a political tradition comes from a Western capitalist context in which control over nature is equated with power and freedom. So the social changes which brought so many women to question motherhood are also interrogating some of the assumptions of feminism as a system of thought. The movement of women for their liberation starts from varying predicaments and journeys with a variety of theoretical baggage. En route there is a great deal of chucking and swapping and appropriation of this baggage.

There are wider social factors in the questioning of control as an adequate radical strategy for change. Women have more chance to decide whether to have a baby because both birth control and maternal medical technology are more reliable – if not safe. However, the psychological and social assumptions about motherhood are rooted in the experience of generations of human beings who did not possess the means of choice. Feminists are thus torn between approaching women's desire to conceive as a socially constructed phenomenon which can be rationally explained and subjected to conscious control, as a psychological structure, or as an assertion of women's natural power. There are signs of a more muted quest to dissolve the boundaries and to approach maternity as a continuing interaction between physical growth and mental perception. The implications of such a model for political thought and social change remain unclear.

A generation of women, in Western capitalism, found they had stumbled into uncharted historical territory. The relation between our conscious will and giving birth grew closer, while society's arrangement remained based on the assumption that women as a sex were naturally ordained to be bearers and rearers of children. The movement for women's liberation continues to touch nerves which have become raw from the conflicting changes in our predicament. The effort to find a way through has led women to reach out towards contradictory understandings and test these by trial and error. In 1973 the radical feminist issue of *Shrew* described the dilemmas of the unknown as 'dragons':

> We are in a place now which, if it were marked on a medieval map, would say 'Here are Dragons'. A no-man's-land full of unexploded mines. But it is precisely in this area, this apparent limbo we traverse in our stumbling circuitous passage on our way from passion to action, this no man's land in which we begin to be energized, begin to realize our desires.[36]

The 'passage. . . from passion to action' in seeking change in the circumstances of fertility and child care has led to a radical search for alternative social possibilities, including both changes in relationships and the division of activity and greater access to and control over the resources of society.

7

The Mother Knot

At the first British women's liberation conference held in Oxford in 1970, Rochelle Wortis argued that the liberation of women required changes in how we reared children.[1] An American child psychologist, involved in one of the earliest women's groups formed in Britain, the Tufnell Park Women's Liberation Workshop, which had started meeting in 1968, she saw child care as part of a wider commitment to creating new relationships in society as a whole. Rochelle Wortis set the new movement clearly and calmly on course for a radical transformation of society which combined with personal change when she argued that patterns of child-rearing are socially and culturally determined, not biologically determined. Any change in children's upbringing, any transformation of society in order to liberate women as well as men, must incorporate, from the beginning, more shared responsibility for the care and socialization of children at all levels of the process.[2] She added:

> It is hoped that this weekend will provide the opportunity for discussing ways to attempt to change our own lives, so that we determine for ourselves the practical solution and the political solution for our own emancipation.[3]

It was to prove a long discussion. Rochelle Wortis probably did not realize how many 'weekends' were ahead of us – nor could she have envisaged the ramifications of her programme of action, which are still evident after two decades.

In practice of course it has proved to be easier said than done to connect the analysis of the need to change society with the search for solutions in our personal lives. The two endeavours have lurched along together in a rather rickety tandem. They have held together but it has often been a strain. Nonetheless, the attempts to change child care have revealed a new range of social possibilities and uncovered dimensions of psychological complexity which would not otherwise have been conceivable.

In *Shrew* in 1971 a woman married to 'an ardent revolutionary' who politically supported the women's liberation movement wrote about how the ideas remained external to their lives. They assumed 'they were OK'. Yet she frequently had bouts of depression. It took time to see the obvious.

> I challenged him on the hypocrisy of his political attitudes. Wasn't I oppressed too? He hadn't even come to terms with this fact, let alone the fact that he was my oppressor. I looked after the home and kids so that he could be free to do what he liked.[4]

After several big rows which nearly brought an end to the relationship, she demanded he looked after the children equally and did half the housework.

Other women wanted shared parenting outside the nuclear couple. A writer in *Black Dwarf* in January 1969 said she did not know who the father of her baby was.

> What seemed to me much more important than the single male–female relationship was some sort of community, not necessarily a self-consciously defined one of individuals living in the same house, but some sort of network of people with whom the child can identify. . .[5]

Attempts to alter particular aspects of women's subordination always come up against the interrelatedness of differing elements of oppression. The involvement of fathers and indeed mixed groups of adults who are not biological parents can bring about significant shifts in consciousness. However, changing the form of child care is not in itself sufficient. The social meaning of sexual difference and the notion of male superiority is not *only* carried, maintained and enforced in particular families, but by people in their relationships and activity outside the family. In any case, it seems to me a fatal illusion to expect one's children simply to reproduce one's own views – even if these are without ambiguity. Instead, I think they extract from a range of contraries. We can certainly alter the range, but can no more programme our children than our parents were able to ensure that we turned out as they wished.

When men and women care for children equally this does not mean that the relationships are the same. Clearly personal experience is limited and there is a wide range of male and female behaviour. Nonetheless, there is a common factor in that we all bring our male and female upbringings and culture to parenting. Without exaggerating biology, I feel that the experience of carrying a child and breast-feeding did affect my connection to my son, although he was looked after by both parents. So equality of care does not dissolve difference – even though the cultural context in which differences between men and women are expressed can vary exceedingly.

There is also the fact that in general we relate to people of the same or the opposite sex in different ways. As well as the infinite individual differences, there are broad social differences in which gender plays an important part. Here considerable ambiguity has developed among feminists, which was not so evident in the early impulse to change the way the world was divided in child-rearing. Do we want men and women to relate to boys and girls as if there was no difference in sex? Or are we aiming for more diversity and a wider range of response which allows for greater choice for children of both sexes? It seems to me that the second is more realistic though less fundamental. The first appears to be more radical but it ignores the fact that children do notice whether they are girls or boys from an early age.

The interaction of child-rearing with the 'larger domains' of social organization, the ambiguity over sexual difference and the complex relation of personal feelings and political aims have continued to cluster around the arguments expressed by Rochelle Wortis at that first conference. It is important to admit practical snags in the arguments for changing child-rearing, while affirming the radical potential of the concept.

This potential takes us beyond the personal encounters of men and women, or parents of the same sex, or even a collective of carers – out into the realms of state policy and paid employment. The tremendous difficulties in changing these 'larger domains' have restricted the attempts to change child-rearing which arose from the experience of young middle-class radicals. The alternative to child care for these mothers of the early 1970s could be fulfilling employment or continuing education or creative leisure. But they were options confined to a minority. Since then the economic crisis and subsequent restructuring of capitalism has closed down some of these possibilities, even within the intellectual middle class. Politically, the idea of dividing child care equally has become more widely acceptable, while the material difficulties have intensified. Yet the need is desperate and experienced by more and more women.

It is much harder for working-class people to combine earning a living with child care, partly because both men and women are likely to earn less than many middle-class people, but also because of the organization of manual jobs. Women's wages are still on average way below men's, so role-switching would mean a very low standard of living. For the employed male manual worker there are shift arrangements, time taken in travel to work, the physical exhaustion of the job, all of which militate against the possibility of shared care.[6]

For Rochelle Wortis's vision of shared parenting to become a reality there would need to be a transformation of society in which the organization of production was geared to human need, and equality rather than profit and competition was the fundamental basis of society. These are long-term changes. But we all live in the short term. In the short term we shift what we can. As more women with young children have gone out to work, the issue of sharing labour in the home has assumed a wider relevance. The double workload is frequently exhausting and women can see that the division is unfair. In some cases women getting jobs means men are prepared to help more with the children and housework – but this is far from general. It is hard to fit in even a part-time job and looking after children. In Sue Sharpe's *Double Identity* some of the women interviewed complained, not surprisingly, of tiredness and irritability. The strain of home and work are apparent. Obviously, women doing low-paid monotonous work do not necessarily see this as emancipatory. The combination is a matter of necessity.

It is also the case that the involvement of men in the home is still seen as an invasion by some women.[7] Noting this apparent contradiction, Diane Ehrenshaft suggested that unless shared parenting was accompanied by changes in power outside the family it could feel threatening and undermine some women's sense of self-worth – despite the evident advantages. She maintained that being a mother was more meaningful than most women's work outside the home: 'As a mother she is afforded the opportunity for genuine human interaction in contrast to the alienation and depersonalization of the workplace.'[8]

Would it be the case, though, that simply improving work would dissolve the tension women express in combining employment and motherhood? I think it is rather more tricky, because a certain unease has been expressed even among the minority of women who earn relatively high wages and have flexible jobs. The intimate relating of mother and child is not the same as even creative and rewarding work. There is a strain in moving between two quite different spheres. The reflective assessment of fulfilment through work seems to have appeared most noticeably among the women who postponed motherhood because they were busy out in the world building successful careers. Confident in their ability to achieve and to control their own lives, they found that mothering contradicted the previous structuring of their identities. Linda Blandford tackled this puzzling conundrum in the *Guardian* in 1981:

> It took the woman so long to find out that being human is the prize, not the apology. . .
>
> . . . It is as though some dam were unstopped, releasing a reservoir of feeling, giving, serving, loving and experiencing of joy. In short, at 38, the woman has become a bore.[9]

As for the father's involvement: 'He, who after so many years alone was eager for the equal parenting to which they paid lip-service during pregnancy classes, now has to fight for his share.'[10]

Diane Ehrenshaft assessed the benefits and difficulties of shared parenting. The gains were evident for women and for men. But she noted that some women remained equivocal:

> We women who have shared parenting with men know the tremendous support and comfort and luxury of not being the only one there for our children. We see the opportunities to develop the many facets of ourselves not as easily afforded to our mothers or to other women who have carried the primary load of parenting. We watch our children benefit from the full access to two rather than one primary nurturing figure, affording them intimacy with both women and men, a richer, more complex emotional milieu, role models that challenge gender stereotypes. We see men able to develop more fully the nurturant parts of themselves as fathers, an opportunity often historically denied to men. And we develop close, open and more equal relationships between men and women as we grapple with the daily ups and downs of parenting together. The equality of our lives no doubt has been improved immensely by the equalization of parenting responsibilities between men and women.
>
> Yet we also know another side of the experience that shared parenting is easier said than done.[11]

One explanation has been that shared parenting can mean a loss of power and status for women without any equivalent gain in terms of job opportunity outside. But this would not explain adequately the intensity of the passions Linda Blandford described. Perhaps the successful women who have babies when they are older have become somewhat disenchanted with the 'male' world of competitive careers, so that motherhood is a release from pressure and a certain hollowness in external worldly achievement.

Whatever the reasons, it is important to recognize that trying to change sexual inequality in the family involves confronting a wider context of mutable economic, social and psychological factors. This is even more apparent in the attempts to create wider collective groups to rear children, and in the problems faced by single parents and lesbian mothers. One of the obvious material problems faced by people attempting group child-rearing is that of housing. Just like people with large families, they are excluded from the planners' notion of normal requirements: modern housing is designed for the nuclear family with two children. The group has to be wealthy enough to buy an old house large enough to contain them all. So communal alternatives to the family have been socially restricted. There are of course less self-conscious intermediate sharing arrangements between parents in flats or in next-door houses. But these are networks of practicality, not attempts to prefigure a future. During the Seventies there were many attempts to make an alternative family in an explicit and conscious manner. There were advantages for both parents and children but there were also obstacles which had not been anticipated, largely because the new families existed in a wider society which did not endorse their values. Lynne Segal wrote in an article on alternative families in 1979:

> One thing that's always worried me about collective living situations and collective child care is the rights of non-parents. It is really hard for them to be confident, if they're having a relationship with the child, that their commitment to the child will actually be taken into account. Because in the end it comes down to the fact that all society sees the mother as responsible, so therefore the mother is going to be responsible.[12]

This can also be a problem for lesbian women who are not biological mothers because there is no social recognition of their relationship to a child for whom they have helped to care. There is not even a special kin name yet for this relatively new kind of family.

The children of lesbian women might have two mothers, or mother and a friend. In some cases the children and their peers might regard this as unremarkable; in others, consciousness of difference might result in discomfort or persecution. In the mid-Seventies, for instance, *Spare Rib* carried an account of a lesbian mother of four, Sheena, living on a council estate in Lancashire and married to a man who was a driver. She loved her husband and he accepted her lesbianism. She believed in being frank about sex and nudity with her children and had explained to them about homosexuality and lesbianism – but she did not know how to tell them that she was herself a lesbian.[13]

The parents' choice of differing relationships also presents a dilemma about how far to accept other people's standards in child-rearing or to stick out for your own approach. This tension has appeared in the collective families. Marsha Rowe described a Leeds radical group family in 1978:

> Fran disagreed with Louise's ideas about the children's dress, which conformed to 'traditional working-class respectable' standards of the area where they live. Louise disapproved of odd socks, which Fran thought were invisible under dungarees.[14]

One-parent families are becoming more numerous now but there is still a stigma attached. Single mothers especially are likely to be poor and dependent on the state. Unmarried couples, collective families and single mothers all face a system of law and state policy in which they are deviations from a concept of the normal married couple with the average small family.

There is a particular legal bias against lesbian mothers, and this form of alternative child-rearing has come up against the most prejudice and obstacles. In 1978, for instance, the London *Evening News* tried to whip up hostility to lesbian women becoming pregnant through Artificial Insemination by Donor. Women retaliated effectively by invading the paper and won the right to reply.[15] A direct challenge rather than a defensive apologia exploded the hypocrisy of media scapegoating. But when the law rather than the press is involved, the power of a judge's assumption can leave a lesbian mother in a child custody case more vulnerable and direct action is not always a viable course.[16] Lesbian parenting thus requires a significant shift in the assumption of the law, which continues to define a lesbian as a deviant. In a paper at the Socialist Feminist

Conference in London in March 1979, Bernice Humphreys summed
up the inequality in the power relationships which the law expresses
and reinforces:

> . . . there exists in British courts no hope of justice on equal terms
> with heterosexuals for lesbian mothers. She will only win if there is
> a substantially greater risk if the children live elsewhere, or where the
> possibility of living elsewhere is almost nil. . .[17]

The unevenness of power in the overall relations of the sexes in
capitalist society produces a pincer-like dilemma in which some
women find themselves fighting for men to take more responsibility and care for children, while others are struggling against the
prejudice of male-dominated courts for their right to live with their
children.

It is always easier to argue for political strategies which ignore the
contradictory forces in our lives. The extraction of certain aspects of
need can produce what appears to be a more cogent argument for
action. The initial desire to escape from the 'smothering' of full-time
child care underestimated the pleasurable aspects of mothering and
thus assumed that sharing was an unproblematic solution. The
counter-argument portrayed shared parenting as a male plot to
take away the 'power' of maternity from women by making their
capacity to bear and rear children redundant. This was also an
over-simplification.

The designation of prevailing technology as a male force which
assails women is also a trap. It assumes that women have inherent
qualities as a sex which bring them closer to 'nature' and thus make
them incapable of devising forms of technology inimical to life.
Ironically, this disregards another, similarly one-sided but quite
opposing, line of thinking in feminism which sees technology as
a neutral force and a means of overcoming biological difference
in order to establish equality. The portrayal of women as close to
'nature' ignores that our activities in society affect how we see the
world. High wages and equal opportunities could well be acceptable
to many women in capitalist society employed in developing and
manufacturing harmful technologies. It is material circumstances
and political attitudes rather than sex in itself that determine whether
people question the development and use of technology. The social
situation of women *can* foster critical questioning. But this is uncer-
tain and far from being an automatic response.

Similarly, the assumption that only men are capable of creating technologies designed to dominate, exploit and destroy life and the environment evades the possibility that, given the opportunity, some women will take such jobs. Profit and military factors determine forms of technology rather than the supposed male/female characteristics of individuals.

The argument about how technology could enhance work and everyday living has tended to become confused with the assertion that men are inherently vicious, a view that ironically reasserts biological destiny in a feminist context, and is conservative in its implications. At its origins feminism shared with other radical theories of the Enlightenment the optimistic view that human beings have the potential to change. From the vantage point of the late twentieth century, it is apparent that change is complex and problematic, but nonetheless the possibility of egalitarian social transformation depends on human beings' capacity to desire alternatives, and must involve rejecting the notion of an immutable human nature. The assumption that a group, by the chance of sex, is rigidly fixed into unchangeable evil is a profoundly pessimistic concept which rules out the possibility of any social solution. Also, the conviction that the nature of 'manhood' is pre-ordained by a male supremacist culture or 'patriarchy' misses the dialectical relationships between the thoughts, feelings and actions of individuals in the web of connections in which we find ourselves.

These debates have been, and still are, impassioned.[18] It has been a strength of women's liberation politics that personal feelings have been touched, but this has also been too painful sometimes. The emotions released in conflicts have exploded the boundaries of political disagreement and seared through intimacies.

'Are Fathers Really Necessary?' asked the radical feminist issue of *Shrew* in 1973. The writer of the article concluded that they were more trouble than they were worth and likely to abuse children sexually.[19] By the late 1970s and early 1980s the assumption was being made more commonly and became interwoven with the decision of some feminists to bring up their children together without men. The separatist choice to live with women sprang from a positive preference combined with a generalized suspicion that men were not to be trusted with children. The response from women living with men was that this was yet another way of making women feel guilty, all the harder to deal with because it came from within the feminist camp. This divide has produced some bizarre spectacles at conference crèches, with one group of women demanding that men do the child care while others hiss the men who turn up for the crèche and insist their daughters go to a girls-only group.

The assumption that all existing 'masculine' social characteristics are bad has led to fundamental disagreements about mother–son relationships. Angela Hamblin gave a paper at a women's conference entitled 'Thinking about Men':

> This summer my son will be ten years old . . . Does he yet understand that to succeed as 'a man' in this male supremacist culture he will have to turn his back on me and everything I have tried to teach him since infancy?
>
> How long must I go on waging battle, against the patriarchal culture, for the heart and mind of my son? Will I be able to bear the pain if I lose?[20]

Amanda Sebestyen reported on the vehemence of the response to her speech:

> Experiences flooded the room: sons who'd almost destroyed their mothers, sons who'd accepted their feminism and stood by them; feminists who'd been willing to share a mother's fight and feminists who'd withdrawn from . . . male children.
>
> A childless woman listening was angry – hers was no easy way out, she'd chosen childlessness rather than risk caring for someone who'd grow up into an enemy.
>
> But were enemies born or made? Either way, there were some women in the room who felt that change could only come when women stopped caring about men and boys altogether. And more who felt that feminist mothers of sons were in the very front line.[21]

Changing 'child-rearing practices' is a more ferociously passionate affair than Rochelle Wortis imagined in 1970. This was partly because of political disagreements about the role of men, partly because it encroached upon emotions about kinship and fertility which could not be crudely transposed into political arrangements. There was another snag, too, in the assertion that women's liberation would be impossible without changing child care. Much of the discussion about the role of fathers presumed that there existed a universal family structure and that women's needs could be generalized. But there were situations in which the involvement or rejection of fathers was not a matter of choice. It was rather that responsibility was forced upon women by circumstances of class or race.

The United Black Women's Action Group told *Socialist Woman* in 1978 that a problem they faced was the tendency for black men not to feel responsible for rearing children. The men were inclined to think that

> the woman can have babies for you and then bring them up – and you come in and do your bit when you want to. But the women don't see that as a problem because they've managed to cope, bring up their kids – even though the system here never stops reminding them that they need a mother and a father.[22]

Black women have thus taken a great deal of responsibility but, instead of respecting them, white society regards their single status as a mark of inadequacy. In *The Heart of the Race*, Beverley Bryan, Stella Dadzie and Suzanne Scafe seek to balance respect with rejection of the assumption that this role is to be taken for granted as an ideal of black womanhood:

> The reality today is that many Black women do bring up their children, and the children of other relatives, on their own. It is our mothers and other women who provide the support which the men so often fail to give us, reflecting a long tradition whereby responsibility for our children has been shared. Recognizing this reality does not, however, mean that we would wish to romanticize the role played by Black women who raise their children without the support of a man. We do not raise our families in this way because we are superwomen, or 'sturdy Black bridges', but because we have been compelled to accept this responsibility both historically and as a result of the internalized sexism of many Black men today. There is no power or respect to be gained from performing such a task, particularly in a society which invalidates any family structure which does not conform to the nuclear model, with men as the providers and decision-makers. The fact that Black women are often prepared to raise a family without a male figure around does, however, attest to a different kind of strength, and an independence which the pervading oppressive sexual stereotypes have not undermined.[23]

The early assumptions about changing the sexual division of labour did not explicitly take into account the question of biological difference. There has, however, been disagreement among feminists committed to sharing child care equally with men about whether or not to breast-feed. Some women have asserted the sensuous pleasure of nurturing. Jenny, a Sheffield feminist, maintained, 'I wanted to use all of me and see what happened and what it felt like. I felt I could get closer to the baby and love and enjoy the baby more.'[24] But other women find breast-feeding difficult, either because their milk dries up or because it is not practical to combine with a job. Gwyn, another Sheffield feminist, pointed out that emphasis on breast-feeding could make women feel guilty: 'We've got enough to worry about without making each other feel guilty too.'[25] Information about benefits to babies' health and awareness of the sales propaganda of multinationals seeking to persuade women to use their products for bottle-feeding – especially in the Third World – strengthened the case for breast-feeding, but Zelda Curtis argued that the point was not to pressurize women who cannot or do not want to breast-feed but to make sure women had information and could choose.[26]

If you do choose to breast-feed you have also to choose to be pretty cheeky about your right to feed your baby outside the home. Society is not at all designed for breast-feeding mothers and babies. In the mid-1970s Constance Whippman advocated public libraries, and, for the shy, the feeding rooms of some large department stores.[27] I had not thought very much about breast-feeding. Committed to sharing child care, I discovered I enjoyed physical nurture and that here I was not inclined to put equality before difference. I resolutely breast-fed on beaches, buses, trains – and in the Marx Memorial Library. But it made me aware of how the design of cities completely disregards nurture. Weaning was more traumatic than I had thought. It is still an area of experience that is relatively undiscussed as if it were simply natural. I felt a sense of both loss and relief after breast-feeding for about seventeen months.

Breast-feeding is a biological mark of difference. It is also experienced psychologically and in varying social situations. 'Nature' is not separate from human beings' perceptions and assumptions. There is a continuous interaction. The experience of breast-feeding, and indeed of maternity as a whole, affects us and contributes to the development of conflicting wants. Jane Lazarre, an American feminist who wrote about the apparently irrational tendencies released by motherhood, described this phenomenon as the 'mother knot'. Women expressed a yearning to be with their children and a desire to be free from them in the same sentence.[28] Motherhood expresses in an intense microcosm a wider reality of human consciousness which is frequently contradictory.

The women's liberation movement has been more open than other forms of contemporary radical politics to exploring future utopias.[29] It is not possible in the abstract to delineate what kind of society would give scope for both equality and difference, nor to imagine how these could be less of a wrench between the intimate love for a small child and activity in the world outside the family. But at least we can glimpse that there could be an alternative. Scattered through women's liberation writing there are many hints. From these can be gleaned the potential for social change behind Rochelle Wortis's endeavour in 1970. Transformations of child-rearing on a large scale would require a society in which mutual caring was the norm rather than the exception. Angela Phillips's description of a woman's needs immediately after a baby arrives suggested just such a social possibility:

> There is really only one thing you need now – someone to mother you. Looking after a new baby on top of recovering from birth is extremely physically demanding. In any properly organized society, all new mothers would be waited on hand and foot for at least a fortnight. Our society isn't, so do your best to get lovers, friends or relatives to take the housework out of your hands and provide the support you need. Your baby will only be born once. You have a right to enjoy the occasion.[30]

The celebration of birth is here based on the material needs of the mother, not on a mythologizing of what motherhood ought to be.

The recognition that needs change within the process of mothering would suggest a society in which it is not such an effort to assert tenderness and in which those changing needs can be more flexibly met. Gill Hague wrote to *Spare Rib* in 1978, explaining:

> The experience of having a baby revolutionizes your whole outlook on life – or at least it did mine, and you end up being really rather a different person. I've become more conventional, careful, settled; I experience great maternal feelings of love and protectiveness. I find it easy and not at all loathsome to sacrifice myself where the baby is concerned: and I don't care so much about myself and my career. (Hopefully some of these are only temporary.)[31]

A society in which these temporary changes could be experienced and it was easier to readjust later, when the cycle of child care altered, so that women could find a new balance between the qualities developed by mothering and by other activities, would make for a less stressful synthesis. As it is, in our society even privileged women feel torn in two, as Linda Blandford observed:

> Eventually, of course, she must redeem herself. She is a person not a pledge. She must gather up the wet and soggy tangle of her present being and rework it into some recognizable shape. It will not be as it once was, of course, for the reality of her has been altered. Humbled by the existence of what she helped to create, she may never recapture that past assurance.[32]

Perhaps this process of loss in which a new realization of self is also gained is not susceptible to social transformation. This is something we cannot verify from within the existing forms of the relationships we know. How could one play a responsible part in a different kind of industrial society and be sensitive to the microcosmic life of a baby? Linda Blandford describes the split world of work and mothering graphically. No longer concentrating on control but on openness and responsiveness, the mother with a career has been able to meet her own vulnerability and overcome some fears. Yet, 'it now cripples the will. Her nerve has failed.' She continues:

> The unaccustomed tenderness of her private world leaves her bewildered outside it. How does she hold a child at dawn, quivering with her love and the blessing of their mutual need, and then glitter at some impersonal lunch in quest of work she's not sure she wants – or in her state of present turmoil can even manage?[33]

Women's liberation as a movement has not produced blueprints for a future society, but, rather, intimations of needs which aare disregarded in our own because the experiences that give rise to them are denigrated.

An aspect of mothering which in our present circumstances can be experienced as oppressive might be a means of reassessing the general emphasis placed on the need for control. There is a complementary quality of receptivity that is also necessary to society. Ann Mitchell and Nell Myers describe this everyday experience which marks off someone responsible for caring for young children:

> It means being open *all the time* to an infinite, galactic, cosmic spectrum of. . . what can we call them? 'Demands' is such a quiet, lifeless word for what we want to convey! Never mind, open to

demands which range back and forth: from tying shoelaces to buckling straps, to finding pencil sharpeners to dewaxing ears to plastering cuts to dispelling nightmares to spelling out words. . . to standing over a cot for an hour when someone can't drop off to sleep to hunting in toy boxes for jigsaw puzzles to trying to retain lines of thought in hopeless attempts at conversation with a captive adult, to hunting for socks on a school morning to getting them to change their underwear, to brush their teeth, to brush their hair, to organizing hair-cuts to hunting for gloves in cold weather.[34]

Without endorsing concepts of 'women's values' or a 'female social character', we can acknowledge broad divisions in experience and perception. The liberation of women requires that those aspects of life at present confined to women should, rather than being abandoned, find a less oppressive expression. At present, in a male-dominated capitalist society, having the capacity for responsiveness means you risk losing contact with your own needs, and you will be likely to fare badly under the competitive pressures of employment. Care is not highly valued, resources are restricted. Serving people could be socially pleasurable and rewarding. It would be better if so much care and responsibility for the young were not confined to women and if relationships in society at large were able to be more open to this quality of loving. In a poem by Eve Fitzpatrick, she wrestles with the memory of her father:

> I turn to my son, got so deliberately,
> and wonder if my love can beat the pattern back,
> can teach him to admire equally
> the grace of women, the good gifts of men.
>
> Or must my shame be his shame
> and my needs his helpless pain. . .[35]

'Motherhood' has clearly been a repository of conservative iconography in our culture. Women's liberation has indicated that mothering can be the source of a profoundly radical social inspiration. From the contradictory experience of the 'mother knot' the desire for a more humane society can arise.

PART THREE

Self-help and the State

8

Sharing the Caring

'We believe that it is up to the individual woman to determine the sort of pregnancy and labour she wants,'[1] announced the group of Leeds women who produced the *Leeds Pregnancy Handbook* in the mid-1970s. This was part of the wider assertion of women's reproductive needs, which also involved contraception, abortion, changes in sexual attitudes, changes in relationships in the family and at work.

Demanding 'the service we want' was necessarily going to affect employment – there would need to be demands for maternity and paternity leave and shorter hours, for instance. It involved tackling the inequalities of the womb, infant mortality and low birth-weight, which had been central campaigning issues in the earlier feminist and socialist movements. But there was also a great emphasis upon the *type* of care required, showing a militant impatience with remnants of the Poor Law which had passed on into the welfare state and contesting the assumption that recipients should be passive and grateful. Moreover the campaigners scorned the paternalism – or maternalism – which assumed that professionals in health or education knew best. The women's liberation movement was, albeit critically, the offspring of the 1960s. Its early politics took the expansion of capitalist welfare for granted and contested the forms of provision. Even the welfare cuts did not quell the search for alternatives. The women's movement frequently shared with left libertarianism a wariness of the state official even in a benign guise. Medical and educational professionals tended to be presumed guilty and had to prove their innocence by demonstrating good faith. If this approach erred on the side of over-simplification, it challenged the deference towards public institutions that enabled the welfare services to get away with authoritarian and bureaucratic behaviour.

'How can we expect women to go for ante-natal care in a cattle market atmosphere?'[3] exploded Dewsbury midwife Joyce Lister in *Spare Rib*. In 1979 the *Sheffield Women's Paper* described the ante-natal department at Mulberry Street Central Health Clinic:

'. . .tension and no toys. . . Most prisons have much better facilities
for children on visits.'[4] A woman reported from Jessop Hospital in
the same city:

> At my first visit I had to wait an hour in the waiting room before
> being weighed and having a history taken down, then another wait
> in a cubicle wearing a thin gown, 15 minutes, and then to the inner
> sanctum to wait for the doctor. I waited here for 45 minutes pacing
> the small room, felt like a caged animal – the heat – no clothes and
> nobody in sight – I felt as if all my strength had gone and I was
> reduced to a crumbling mess. Finally the doctor came in and sat
> on the bed – he looked at my notes and said, 'Come back in 4
> weeks.' I couldn't believe it – had I waited 2 hours to be told that?
> I said nothing but burst into tears – I couldn't talk – Doctor turned
> round and walked out. Nurse said, 'What's the matter dear?' Me still
> sobbing – 'Been here 2 hours.' 'Bit upset dear?' says she – cried some
> more – went home and cried most of the evening. Vowed never to go
> to ante-natal again.[5]

Bangor Women's Liberation Group tried to change this impersonal
attitude to maternity care which subordinated the individual to the
hospital's routine. The women went to put their proposals to the
Area Health Authority and discovered considerable resistance:

> Even on simple points – like starting an appointment system to prevent
> mothers waiting hours – they wouldn't budge. They argued that to
> change this would mean calling three or four committees that would
> cost thousands of pounds. They refused to give more information to the
> mothers-to-be on the grounds that this would confuse and worry them.[6]

The 'cost' to the mothers stuck in the ante-natal clinic does not
come within the NHS social audit, of course.

A practical example of what could be done on a wider scale
was demonstrated by a project at a health centre in Homerton,
London. Jo Robinson, a feminist who had been a midwife, talked
to women waiting for ante-natal appointments at the centre during
1980–81. The women's perceptions and responses about how the
local health system treated them enabled her to identify the following problems:

● Mystification of birth: a perfectly normal and healthy event was
  being made into a medical mystery, and sometimes even treated
  as a disease.

- A lot of fuss and wasted time was spent just in collecting a urine specimen and taking the blood pressure.
- One did not have the right to ask questions or make demands.
- The waiting area could be make more attractive and suited to the needs of waiting patients – e.g., play facilities for children, more comfortable chairs, drinks available.
- The waiting time could be more usefully adapted to be also a time of learning and looking at books and films.[7]

Jo Robinson began by humanizing the waiting time at the health centre with tea-making, toys for children, a book-case with books and pamphlets and information about childbirth. People started talking to one another and from this they formed an ante-natal group in which choices in childbirth, information about local hospitals, the effects of pregnancy on life, emotions, and relationships and preparation for labour were discussed.[8] The women wanted to discuss not only the physical aspects of pregnancy but its effects on their feelings and connections with other people. The group came to act as a collective means for working out what they wanted. Their perception of what they needed was not a fixed entity which could be met with a 'facility', beloved term of the bureaucratic model of welfare. Their definition of need was a process of mutual discovery. Jo Robinson explained, 'Women in a group can use each other's personal experiences. It's a way of feeling more confident about getting what you want from the health service.'[9]

In the report on the first year of the 'Health in Homerton' project Jo Robinson said she felt there was much that still needed to be done to change the experience of labour in local hospitals. She also stressed the importance of taking on the problems of health workers, exhausted by working under the strain of the cuts.[10] This typified a growing awareness among feminists trying to change the conditions of the health service that it was a mistake to assume that workers in the field were unsympathetic. Jo Robinson raised the wider issue of how democratic control could resolve conflicts of interest – especially when resources were short: 'Could the whole system of ante-natal care in the health centre be changed in some way that would suit both the workers and the consumers?'[11]

If it is difficult to be pregnant in circumstances of your own choosing, it is even harder during the actual birth – for you are not in a strong position to argue. There is no doubt that much needless unhappiness has been caused by the circumstances in which many women have given birth in hospitals. These have come under sustained criticism from feminists. For example, Nell Myers described in 1977

> the dark loneliness of the labour ward wherein my only friend was the rubber mask that brought me pain-killing gas; the nurses not deliberately unkind but much too busy with too many cases who could not become people because there wasn't enough time.
>
> The need to keep things moving (for what, for whom?) was the metronomic tick to which I had my babies.[12]

Feminists have resisted this mechanization of birth in the interests of the institutional routine of the hospitals, though the need to understand the positive uses of technology has also been asserted. This has involved questioning both the nature and use of medication and equipment and considering how they could aid rather than control the rhythm of the mother in birth.[13] There has been disagreement over drugs and epidural anaesthesia. Some feminists have been against them as artificial interventions but others have demanded them, pointing out that being under pressure to experience pain in the pursuit of nature can be as oppressive as being drugged to relieve pain without realizing the possible consequences.[14] There has also been some uncertainty about whether to campaign for improved hospitals or for the right to home deliveries. This issue was publicized in the Tower Hamlets area because of the disciplinary case brought against the London Hospital consultant Wendy Savage in 1986. Her belief that women should have the choice to deliver at home became an issue in the inquiry. But in fact there had been a less visible struggle in the previous decade. A home birth can be very pleasant and intimate but should some complication occur there can be a danger to the child and the mother.

In fact a resolution to the problem of what to aim for has emerged. Feminists have argued that if the inadequacy of the midwife service and the poor pay, conditions and status of midwives were tackled, both home and hospital births would benefit. At the same time there have been campaigns for a better atmosphere and more maternal choice during hospital deliveries and for accessible maternity services. Throughout the 1970s and 1980s this has included the defence of hospital facilities threatened by health cuts or 'rationalization'.[15]

Despite disagreement about methods, there has been general agreement on the right to choose how to give birth. But this is not as unproblematic as it appeared in the mid-1970s when the *Leeds Pregnancy Handbook* proclaimed it with such conviction. 'A woman's right to choose' assumed a middle-class patient earnestly consulting *Our Bodies Ourselves*. Myra Garrett, a socialist feminist campaigner on health and child care matters for over a decade in London, observed that on issues like maternity 'you can't have a campaign about choice. . . The campaign is about having enough knowledge and information to be able to make a choice.'[16] But even when information is available there are real problems in controlling your own birth. Gilly Westley of the Bangor women's group took her demands to the consultant in her last ante-natal visit:

> . . . No shaving, no drugs unless medically necessary; lights and voices to be low at birth for the baby's sake; the cord not to be cut until it stops pulsating so that the baby has two sources of oxygen; the baby to be laid on my tummy until the cord is cut; then the baby to go to my breast for colostrum and love. . . and for my husband to be there all the time even if complications arose.[17]

He told her these were routine procedures. However, even consultants are not omniscient – the real routine proved to be rather different.

> At the birth it was a different story. The nurses refused to tell me what stage I was at, saying 'She's been going to classes, reading books and got herself all confused.' When my baby came the nurse deliberately cut the cord while it was still pulsating although Dave pleaded with her not to. She said you have been reading that French stuff, meaning Leboyer. The nurse refused to put the baby on my tummy, but put her in a plastic cot. Only when I threatened to yell for a doctor was I given my daughter to nurse, and to put to the breast. And I was stitched.[18]

However, several months later at the same hospital, another midwife was happy to go along with the Leboyer approach.

It is hard to distinguish between professional bossiness and medical necessity during a birth. There could be circumstances in which decisions have to be taken quickly and medical staff simply have to assert professional authority if there is conflict with the parents. Births are not the easiest times to weigh the pros and cons of various methods. A concept of absolute choice, which would accept medical risk, is hard to maintain. There is also a real problem in applying the notion of control, which dwells in the realm of reason, to all aspects of birth. In my own experience it was fine for the first 14 hours or so. After 29 hours of contractions, when the consultant consulted me, my decision to go on without artificial acceleration was based more on some Yorkshire childhood idea of the virtue of 'seeing a job through' than philosophical reason. Nonetheless I am profoundly glad he asked.

My short stay in hospital of 48 hours in 1977 also made me aware that the 'feminist' demands, no shaving, no enemas, the baby brought to you for the night, the right to leave hospital quickly, came from a very specific social context. They involved particular cultural attitudes to one's body, probably a first child, and a network of friends and supporters at home. The East End women in my ward were exasperated that the hospital routine had changed because of support from the doctors for ideas generated by the women's movement. They complained of neglect, felt their babies were not being looked after in a professional way. Though they all appreciated as well the recognition of the consultant, Peter Huntingford, that women who had already had a baby knew some things he did not. They valued the respect of the consultant. The changes he had made in the doctor–patient relationship were valued, even though the altered arrangements for birth were not. As I padded down the corridors, in agony from my stitches, I thought ruefully about the complexity of needs.

Information, choice, control are partial remedies. There exist in our society different cultures of health and different assumptions about the meaning of birth. The medical hierarchy can be uncomprehending about how class, gender and race mediate encounters between medical professionals and users of the NHS. If it is difficult, given the structure of the NHS, for women in general to feel that the health service will respond to their needs in pregnancy and birth, it is even harder for women who have to negotiate two cultures of maternity. In Tower Hamlets in the mid-1980s women set up the Maternity Services Liaison Scheme, which received some initial funding from the GLC Women's Committee. They work with women in the Chinese–Vietnamese community, Somali women, Bengali women, and others who do not speak English as a first language. They have formed close working links with workers in the NHS and with the Health Authority. They stress that they are not simply interpreters but community health workers who act as advocates for the women during maternity. They began as a voluntary group but want to be more securely established and for groups to exist on a wider scale.[19]

While the issue of democratizing birth is not a simple matter, the fundamental principle that a public service like the NHS exists for the public has been reasserted through these struggles. Testimonies from Tower Hamlets women about the maternity services bear witness that, amidst the bureaucratic indifference which can make birth a humiliation, the attempts by a doctor like Wendy Savage to relate her medical judgement to the wishes of the mother created the basis for trust which is so vital in medical care: 'She takes into account your feelings and treats you like a person, not like a lump of meat.'[20]

The memory of a birth stays with you all your life but child-rearing consumes a much greater part of it. The need for child care was one of the first issues raised in the early women's liberation groups. The contradictory situation of the mother with small children, expected to care and yet denied an environment in which this was possible, was one of the factors that brought many women into the movement. Along with the emphasis on changing the division of labour in the family and involving men in child care, there was the more traditional labour-movement emphasis on nurseries as a material necessity. The Camden Women's Action Group expressed this early in 1970, demonstrating for nurseries with a giant 'bovver boot' and a rhyme:

> There are too many women living in shoes,
> With so many kids, no bathrooms or loos,
> Abortion's expensive, there's no free birth pill
> She has unequal pay and jobs with no skill
> Now is the time for all women to fight
> For more nursery schools and an end to their plight.[21]

The first women's group I was involved in started the Islington Nursery Campaign in 1970–71 – all six of us went round knocking on doors and trying to arouse a mass movement! The 'campaign' was a non-starter. But we did learn, green as we were, that there was more to it than nursery schools. Women complained they could not get out at night. From this came the idea of 24-hour nurseries so that children might be left in the evening, or at more flexible times than nine to five.

There was, though, another approach to child care. Instead of demanding facilities from the state, radical self-help projects were being set up by the American New Left, in the German students' movement and in Paris by the students after the May Events. The German student movement was preoccupied with the internal acceptance of authority. They were intensively reading Freud, Reich, A. S. Neill and Vera Schmidt, a psychoanalytical theorist of children's education in the Russian Revolution. At the same time the personal tensions and problems that appeared amidst large-scale and violent confrontations with the police provokked consideration of how feelings linked with politics. Isolated from the working class and often estranged from their own families, who had lived through fascism, they argued the need to release the capacity to imagine alternative modes of life. They sought a culture in which people could grow up who would not accept authoritarian regimes. They believed that people clung to existing society because of unconscious fear. If children were brought up without fear they would be critical and rebellious. Politics was thus not simply demanding changes and improvements, but also meant consciously developing a new culture: '. . . prototypes of future forms of organization can be productive factors in shaping a new society,'[22] wrote 'An Authors' Collective' in a book about the students' crèches which squatted in shop-fronts in Berlin.

The *Kindershop* idea travelled to Britain but proved rather difficult to transplant. In 1969 one of the first women's liberation groups in Britain, which included several American women with a political background in the New Left, began to link the German ideas to women's liberation. Susan Cowley reported in *Shrew*:

An essential part of the German *kindershop* and of our projected group has been the necessity of men and women, parents and non-parents being involved in order to break down the women's role as child-minder and to develop the concept that children are the responsibility of the community. However, some of the men at our first meetings seemed to want to immediately co-opt our crèche into their already existing political framework. Others of us felt that the crèche should not be cramped by traditional political forms but that a new and more radical interpretation of 'political' should be allowed to evolve out of the experiment itself.

At our first meetings with children and adults we found we had nothing to say. All of us at one time or another had talked articulately about a crèche. But there we were with no compelling interest in one another, and while the kids were happy we weren't. The German experience was not totally relevant, here we were in England with no 'movement' to base ourselves on, no storefront to provide a public and permanent place for the crèche and not much idea of what could hold us together besides the kids. We came out of our separate isolations and had no unifying experiences.[23]

Despite this discouraging experience the Tufnell Park group continued to think about the implications of different relationships in caring for children. In 1971 they wrote:

Women's liberation is not only about getting away from things – in this instance the children whose need for care confines us to the home and can inhibit our existence and development as people in our own right. Women's liberation is perhaps more importantly about coming together. One does not want to release women as isolated units from the care of children. One wants to bring women and men together to care for children.[24]

The practical need for child care thus led to an aspiration for community.

In 1970 in *Socialist Woman* Audrey Wise extended the concept of workers' control into the domestic life of mothers and children.

Community control should *not* be a next demand – it is an imperative, which should be put *first*, last and all the time. Without it, in fact, the child-care facilities which might be provided might well be a trap.[25]

Seeing child care as a means of developing new forms of relationship and of democratizing control over everyday life differed from arguing for nursery provision in terms of women's right to work. Audrey Wise was critical of this more traditional labour-movement approach, which she believed subordinated human need to the maximization of productive efficiency:

Technological society treats people as adjuncts to machines. Our hands and brains are just extensions of the hardware. From this point of view large numbers of hands are being wasted caring for small numbers of infants separately. Why not gather the infants together into larger, more economic units (very suitable for machine-extensions in the making). Make sure that families become more and more dependent on the earnings of both parents (as is happening) and there will be all these extra workers to be either a reservoir of additional labour power or a pool of unemployed according to the 'needs' of the 'economy'. We may well get our child-care facilities in this context. But the only criterion will be whether the mothers can be profitably utilized. And we know whose profit will be intended! Not the mothers! Not the babies![26]

Writing in *Red Rag* in 1973, Sue Cowley struggled to combine the early women's liberation vision of prefigurative forms of child care which would overcome the isolation of mothers with the perspective of nursery provision to enable women to choose whether to go out to work or not.[27] But there was a persistent tension between the two approaches. In later years they were to merge pragmatically but remained theoretically unresolved. In the early years this discordance of perspective was one factor which made it difficult to establish a campaign for child care. Val Charlton, who had found herself at the second Women's Liberation Conference in 1970 singlehandedly responsible for a nursery campaign and had suffered under the burden, observed in *Red Rag*:

> Women in women's liberation were confused, suspicious, uncertain. They didn't want nurseries for everyone if the nurseries remained hotbeds of sexist ideology and authoritarian organization.[28]

Another difficulty was the kind of provision which was to be proposed. The demand for 24-hour nurseries had been developed out of the need for flexible hours in child care. But it conjured up a horrific 'Brave New World' of baby farms and impersonal, heartless child-rearing. Angela Rodaway made a pertinent criticism of 24-hour nurseries in the Bristol Women's Liberation journal, *Enough*. Did we really imagine under-fives being delivered at ten and collected at six when women came off shifts? Did we want 24-hour schools? What about breast-feeding? And what, indeed, about the children?

> What if they are unreasonable and want to be put to bed in their own homes? Then they're very obviously insecure – maladjusted. Are they? Well people of all ages tend to live like that. So what happens? They must go anyway, because a parent's job depends on it? And night after night there are scenes with a screaming, sobbing child whom you love.[29]

Angela Rodaway argued that in fact the fulfilment of child-care needs required a series of changes in the organization of life and work rather than an over-simplified 'demand'. Meanwhile, according to Val Charlton, who spoke with feeling, the nursery campaign proved 'a non-starter, though many went grey in the process of not starting'.[30]

A wider concept of child-care needs appeared from several sources. The Sixth Report from the Expenditure Committee (1972–3), which dealt with the employment of women, recommended holiday play schemes in schools and parks, with meals laid on, for children of working mothers.[31] In 1973 the Edinburgh women's liberation group reported: 'We have started a campaign for better nursery and school services – a broad-based campaign including for example a demand for holiday facilities and for more and better-paid nursery nurses.'[32]

In the mid-1970s groups were organized around the Working Women's Charter, which put forward demands for the trade-union movement. One aspect of this campaign was the effort to bring women as workers and in the community into combination.

In 1974 recognition that the nursery was not simply serving a need but was also a place of work stimulated two meetings held by social-ist feminists in London. These brought together users and workers and asked, 'How might trade-union and community-based struggles be linked through the Working Women's Charter?'[33] Along with the extension of democracy which this connection implied, they also discussed what values might inspire a socialist-feminist approach to child care. In practice, though, 'Working Women's Charter' was no more able to develop a concerted campaign than the women's liberation movement.[34] However, the activity generated by the Charter groups contributed to the organization of child-minders. The most under-resourced and isolated workers in child care, they went on to demand from councils collective provision like training, toy libraries and transport. The Charter also influenced trade-union branches to take up demands for workplace nurseries and more community-based provision.[35] In 1976 the TUC set up a working party on under-fives. The benefits of nursery education for working-class children were stressed.

Within women's liberation the relation of child care to employ-ment continued to cause argument. In Scotland Esther Breitman maintained that the demand for child-care facilities was about the right of women to work.[36] This emphasis was evident in a Working Women's Charter poster in 1976: 'Kids are a full time job? No, but they can stop you getting one.'[37] This provoked an angry response from Brenda Freeman: '. . . If child care carries on being so persistently demeaned as it is by the Working Women's Charter and others, then it will always be seen as something *inferior*, which is what this society wants it to be.'[38]

The *Spare Rib* collective argued that Working Women's Charter over-simplified what feminists wanted. They cited an alternative form of child care which had developed out of the women's liberation movement. This was the Dartmouth Park Children's Community Centre opened by Camden Women's Group in 1972 as an example of 'community-run, non-sexist and anti-authoritarian day care'.[39] Exasperated by holding meetings for campaigns which never materialized, and with a practical need for child care, Val Charlton and others had turned to the local council for resources. Dartmouth Park Children's Community Centre was funded by the council but controlled by the parents, who worked in shifts along with one full-time paid worker.[40] This was an early example of an interesting process in which practical need and the desire to retain control combined to create new forms of nursery provision. In Notting Hill a militant struggle of women involved in the Powis Square playgroups led to the creation of a community nursery in which the transformation of relationships was stressed.[41] In Hackney in 1975 two women who needed a playgroup squatted a short-life house in Broadway Market. With the help of a few male supporters they kept the group together for a year. As a result of determined pressure they managed to get a grant from the council through Urban Aid. In 1977 Market Nursery was re-housed in better premises, an old deanery left standing in the midst of new council housing. The workers, along with others from community nurseries, joined the public sector union NUPE. From an informal friendship network a democratic structure developed in which workers and parents made decisions together. The attempt to change the forms of child care was present, as well as an emphasis on the practical needs of working mothers.

Thus the original demand for 24-hour nurseries did evolve over the years in the meandering way in which ideas develop in a social movement. New forms were found in practice which could better express the desire in women's liberation for a different kind of provision. In 1973 Sue Cowley suggested a possible future of communal care:

In many ways, what we in the women's liberation movement are
, pointing towards is a community centre in which education of children

would be one of the many activities going on. Old people, students, workers, women and men not working, as well as teachers, might all be able to come together around activities which concerned them and hopefully all would be involved with the children.[42]

Locally, efforts were made to take some of these ideas into the state nurseries. For example in Islington, London, in 1974, Working Women's Charter's Nursery Action Group tried to bring parents and workers together to get more say in the running of nurseries. They also convinced NALGO of the need to recruit local nursery workers, who were suffering from poor pay and conditions and petty discipline.

As more and more nursery workers joined trade unions throughout the country, Working Women's Charter launched a nationwide campaign for a 35-hour week. However, by 1975 there were ominous references to cuts in the reports of the Nursery Action Group's local branches.[43] By 1975 the Group had been forced to change its orientation from democratizing and improving conditions in local nurseries to opposing cuts. They concluded:

> . . . you cannot fight an isolated campaign: if you do you get fobbed off with answers like 'if we give you your nurseries we'll have to cut the old-age pensioners'. Now we have joined with the OAPs and other people fighting the cuts in the Islington Cuts Campaign. . .
> . . . We have also made steps to contact the other unions in the borough. In particular we are in contact with the building workers on the site where some of the planned nurseries should be built.[44]

This recognition of the need to link up had been manifested in the growth of 'under-fives' campaigns locally. They brought together a powerful and militant lobby on councils for all forms of provision – not only nurseries but toy libraries, changes in the kinds of children's books stocked in public libraries, and improved playground safety.[45] The London Nursery Campaign developed out of these initiatives and held an inter-union workshop on under-fives in March 1977. Similar links were being made elsewhere in the country. In 1980 the Bradford Under-Fives Group asserted, 'Every mother needs a break.' They pointed to the isolation of young children and their mothers, to the demands of housework which meant mothers were always 'on call'. They argued both for the mothers' need for the same job opportunities as other adults and for the importance of men's involvement in child care.[46]

At last, in 1980, a National Child Care Campaign finally got off the ground. The influence of women's movement ideas was important, but the campaign includes fathers, men and women in the trade unions and workers in the social services. It has worked closely with those local authorities which have been more open than central government to the problems women face in combining employment with bringing up their families, and more responsive to the right of all children, including those with special needs, to good-quality care.[47]

During the 1980s questions of race and ethnicity in child care have been discussed more extensively than before. Barbel Pollack from the National Child Care Campaign, along with other black community and under-fives workers, gave evidence to a DHSS committee on 'Service for Under Fives from Ethnic Minority Communities'. Their testimony, said to be 'beyond the remit' of the working party, was published in an appendix to its report in 1985. They demanded:

1 That black children are no longer identified by the authorities as having 'special problems'. It needs to be recognized that the 'problems' of black children are due to individuals and institutions which acknowledge all too rarely that we live in a multiracial and multicultural society.
2 That Social Services departments should more readily respond to child-care initiatives from parents and be prepared to assist with premises and funding; but not to take over the running of schemes – something that commonly happens when fixed-term funding runs out.
3 That government departments, local authorities, schools and nurseries recognize that they have a responsibility to take a more committed approach to combat racism and the mono-cultural approach in and around education and to take concerted positive action towards doing so.[48]

Race is clearly not just an issue in relation to the state but also has to be tackled among groups struggling for change, otherwise slogans of choice and democracy are rhetorical. Thus in 1982 the Childminders' Association announced 'childminding information now available in Urdu and Punjabi'.[49] Local-authority support has meant that translation of material has been possible on a much wider scale. But the problem goes deeper than language alone. In 1976 a worker in a playgroup in Chapeltown, Leeds, pointed out that the formal right to speak was not enough:

> West Indian and Asian people are given the opportunity to speak, but most of them don't say much at all. I think a lot of them think that there's no point, because the staff are mainly White and it's a White country and all that. Mrs Ram [the supervisor] feels that because she's Asian she isn't taken much notice of. It's never brought up on staff or committee meetings. Mrs Ram just brought it up privately with me.[50]

Kum-Kum Bhavnani has also pointed out that nursery campaigns should be conscious of the need to employ black workers and make sure that they do not work only in white 'catchment' areas so that they end up providing only nurseries for white children.[51]

Just before the abolition of the GLC in 1986 a conference was held to celebrate what had been achieved in child care with GLC backing. The workshop on child care in different cultural communities was the best attended. There were reports of a Cypriot nursery in Camden which had been helped by association with a group of older Cypriot women, a nursery serving Latin American children, which had links with the Latin American Association, and a Rastafarian nursery started by a childminder.[52] The Tower Hamlets Mobile Crèche had two Bengali-speakers, enabling women in the Asian community to attend classes. GLC abolition threatened and held back the development of these new initiatives in child care.

Child care in the widest sense has begun to move up the agenda, but tragically this is at a time when all welfare services are being devastated. The recognition that child care is not simply a matter of nurseries but of wide-ranging services is, however, more widely recognized in the 1980s. Instead of the assertion of the *right* to work, the fact that so many women *have* to work is now more likely to be a starting point. The questions then are: what form of care is best, and how could work be organized so parents can combine jobs and families?

The urgency of practical need has led to a more matter-of- fact tone in debates on child care. However, some of the wider political issues raised in the 1970s remain unresolved. The attempt to put ideas into practice revealed, as it always does, some of their contradictions. Already in 1973, for instance, Sue Cowley was questioning the abstract invocation of community. She said that the Community Centre should not be seen as 'an "empty space" waiting to be filled with "the people" '.[53] 'The community' could be bitterly divided by religion or race.[54] Nor could it be assumed that 'the community' necessarily shared the assumptions of the people who started nurseries. The project of prefiguring new forms of relations has come up against this political difficulty over and over again. Community nurseries, for instance, have sometimes found there is a contradiction between serving the expressed needs of parents in the area on the widest basis and challenging attitudes to child care and relationships. A Birmingham group's account, 'Out of the Pumpkin Shell', said that some parents wanted stronger discipline and were not interested in changing sex roles.[55] The same problem can arise in the state sector, of course. A balance has to be found. A child-care worker in Chapeltown, Leeds, observed:

> You can't suddenly say to a girl you're wrong to be in the kitchen, and give a dishcloth to the lads. You couldn't do it fast anyway. Because the parents are at home and they're doing it differently.[56]

Workers, including feminist ones, can also disagree among themselves, for instance on whether to involve men in child care, on how to educate young children in anti-racist and anti-sexist ways, on the role of fantasy in play, or on attitudes to infantile sexuality. There are awkward decisions in child care about who has the right to decide – not only about how to care for and educate children but also about the running of a nursery. In raising the important democratic principle of control, the problem has been how best to achieve this in practice. Community nurseries have developed a variety of forms of worker–user control involving parents or other groups using the centre. Informal networks have been converted to more formal structures because disagreements among friends proved painful and explosive.[57] Many parents are busy and under pressure and after the first wave of enthusiasm participation flags. This can result in a lack of continuity which makes it difficult to pass on what has been learned.[58]

The voluntary child-care groups face all the problems of how to make direct participatory democracy work.[59] This is far from being a new problem of course. It puzzled the Ancient Greeks after all! What *is* unique is the way these relatively recent direct forms have been entering new relationships with the elected democratic structures of local government. In seeking access to state resources the 'self-help' groups have necessarily ceased to be totally autonomous.

Yet without these resources, to which the people involved have of course contributed, they are left to struggle with providing child care on the cheap. Both children and nursery workers suffer from this. The conflict has usually been expressed in terms of the control of provision once money is received from the local council.[60] As Suzy Beresford put it, 'Often when a local authority pays lip-service to participation it means, "You participate, but we'll control the purse strings." '[61]

There is another aspect, however. In theory the local authority, or indeed the state, is representing the interests of all the people who have contributed to its resources. Access to these has to be combined with some measure of responsible monitoring to make sure they are not squandered but put to good use by the groups who receive them. Not only is the autonomy of particular forms of child care involved, but also the way the resources and effort of society as a whole are to be divided. The financial connection, however imperfect still in practice, symbolizes a wider process of sharing which cannot be encompassed by direct democracy. As Sue Himmelweit remarked, 'Recognizing child care as a popular need would involve accepting that the welfare of children is not just an individual question but a responsibility to be borne by any community concerned about its future.'[62] The direct democracy of the nursery *combined* with local-authority involvement indicates the possibility of mutual aid and a wider communal responsibility as an alternative to relying simply on *either* state-run services *or* self-help projects.

Some elements of the radical suspicion of the bureaucratic state ironically fuelled the attack on public services by the Conservative government in the 1980s. Instead of trying to improve on existing provision, Margaret Thatcher invoked self-help in the community. Feminists have pointed out that the Thatcherite rhetoric of voluntarism pushes more and more work back on to women in the home and is anyway hypocritical, as government finance to the voluntary sector has been cut.[63]

Trying to create ways of bearing and rearing children which recognize the needs of both mother and child has landed feminists in the middle of conflicts about the kind of state and the kind of economy this would necessitate. The frail collectivity which the existing form of the state signifies through maternity legislation or Child Benefits partially expresses the principle of social responsibility. But state provision also carries many other assumptions which feminists, among others, have disputed. So the argument has been made not simply for more direct democratic control over provision but for more involvement of women in the planning process – which would mean a different kind of state. In a draft for a report on child care for the GLC's Industry and Employment Committee, Julia Phillips wrote in 1982:

> If the needs of women have been largely ignored in the economic planning process, the needs of children have been left out altogether. It is important that the GLC positively promotes the benefits of collective child care for children as well as parents and that the needs of children are taken into account in local planning.
>
> Both child care and domestic labour are productive activities which remain hidden by being left as the responsibility of the individual and being work for which payment is not made. A radical economic policy must consider how to challenge this position.[64]

In 1982 Ken Livingstone, as leader of the GLC, made an explicit commitment to 'treat child care and other areas of housework as an economic sector'.[65] With limited powers and resources, the GLC was able to put this into practice only at a basic level and create jobs from child care.

The basis for this approach had been laid by Sue Wallis in Wandsworth in 1979 in her report to the Council from the Working Party on Employment Policy in Planning. She argued that 'it is of crucial importance to shift the topic of day care from being a "women's issue" kept out of the economic debate to the central issues of productivity, the economy and employment'.[66] This is absolutely vital but creates a problem. The economic contribution of domestic activity and its consequences for women's employment need to be acknowledged, and changed, but not on the terms of the market within current economic values. It is not such a great idea to have everyone shunted off into paid employment, with paid professionals responsible for the care of all infants over a few months old. This is rather like the unfortunate Lancashire mother of Albert who was eaten by lions at Blackpool Zoo. When the 'magistrate chappie' said he hoped she would have more sons to her name Albert's mother expostulated, 'To feed bloody lions, no thanks!'

We do not bear and rear children for them to be chewed up by the abstract category of productivity. Caring contributes to the wherewithal of life but that is not the reason for caring. It is really the other way round. We produce so that we can care for one another better. Or that is the way round it should be. At present in society there is a contradiction. Most people would agree in a common-sense way with Albert's mother. But the economists and most politicians seem more impressed with the magistrate chappie's more distant approach. For this reason Anna Coote suggested that we should begin with the question, 'How do we want to take care of our children?'[67]

In the mid-1970s Gillian Pinkerton produced a pamphlet entitled *Values in Child Care: Hidden and Explicit.* She listed 'first-step' aims of a socialist feminist approach to child care as follows:

- To challenge competition and individualism. . .
- To develop group awareness and interdependence. . .
- To build up self-confidence and interdependence of each child so that they can take a full part in the group. . .
- To break down hierarchies. . .
- To challenge the domination of the weak by the strong. . .
- To break down stereotyped sex roles. . .
- To develop warm emotional relationships not exclusive to the nuclear family
- To develop an understanding of political questions and struggles.[68]

There is no doubt about it, in the last decade it has got pretty heavy being an 'under-five'. I must confess to the somewhat irreverent fantasy of turning a blind eye for a bit to the 'under-fives' slogging it out with Lego guns as substitutes for their banned military toys and somehow kidnapping the economic policy-makers at a formative age and ensuring they learn these precepts thoroughly – perhaps in the course of cooking the dinners for a nursery on a tight budget or relieving a few hard-pressed childminders.

The precise forms and values of a better society cannot be projected from here into an ideal future. But we can start from present disgruntlement and say what we imagine. In my contribution to the GLC's London Industrial Strategy I argued:

> The long-term aim is to find a new balance between freedom and loving association, a society in which economic and social independence and interdependence between equals is possible.
> This means imagining new forms of collective aid which can meet needs which people in present-day families cannot resolve. It also

means that values and relationships which people cherish in their existing families could be resources for developing wider forms of co-operative associations. In creating new relations of waged work and domestic care, the more humanizing elements of both could be combined and the oppressive aspects of both reduced. Perhaps we might make a future in which the meanings of work, creativity and care were transformed, so that work was not onerous toil, creativity not for the favoured few and care not the responsibility of a single sex.[69]

Christine and Glynis, women from the Yorkshire coal-mining community, described how the collective kitchens set up to relieve the poverty of the striking families not only served an immediate social need but were a catalyst for new relationships and a re-conception of values.

Being faced with small children on a daily basis, the miners have become more determined to fight for jobs for future generations. I've seen older men, not usually bothered with children, actually nurse youngsters while their parents eat their meal in peace. I can't express how much of a morale-booster this kitchen has been to us all, even those not directly involved in the strike.[70]

It is a long way from Berlin to Barnsley. There was no direct theoretical link between the German students' *kindershop* and the Yorkshire miners' kitchen. But in both the practical organization to meet need stimulated a vision of what the human purpose of an economy might be. Surely it should be up to all of us to determine the kind of economy we want?

9

*In and Against
the State*

The women's liberation movement in Britain has not produced a consistent theory or single political line about the state. Instead, ideas have arisen to meet circumstances. These have presented themselves in a rather disorderly manner, remaining in an incomplete form – half assumption, half query.

Women's liberation has not been hermetically sealed from wider radical intellectual influences. In the early 1970s there was a strong anti-statism in much feminist writing which drew on the American New Left and libertarian Marxism. Welfare was seen as a form of control. For example, a pamphlet called *Housing in Crisis: Women's Offensive* argued that the welfare state ensured that women 'produce and reproduce labour power'.[1] The state was 'the institution which ensures that the labour force is adequately housed, fed, nourished in infancy, educated, kept in reasonable health, reproduces itself at the right rate and presents itself daily on the labour market'.[2] Because the state was seen as exercising total control over everyday life, there had to be confrontation in all areas of existence. The anti-statist strand was committed to direct resistance wherever the tentacles of the state struck, defending unsupported mothers in the Claimants' Union, or squatting empty properties or occupying town halls in defence of the homeless.

Militant tenants' struggles and the growth of squatting meant that many middle-class feminists were learning from working-class women, some of whom were single mothers, of the harshness of council housing departments and the impersonal bureaucracy of Social Security. They learned to see social workers from the other side of the class divide. Cambridge Women's Liberation Group became involved in the early 1970s in the case of a woman called Ann Baxter, an unsupported mother. In the course of a protracted struggle her Social Security money was stopped, she was threatened with eviction and two of her children were taken into care. Writing on 'Social Insecurity and Ann Baxter', the Cambridge group maintained:

> . . . through our analysis of the role played by the various social services and the voluntary social workers we can see the basic contradiction between the stated aims of the social services, e.g. to help the unsupported mother, and their real aims, to help clients live respectable lives, i.e. to put as top priority tidiness, punctuality, deference to experts and above all not to blatantly flaunt the rejection of conventional sexual morality. . .[3]

An approach to the state thus developed which argued that welfare was a form of control which had specific manifestations in sexual control over women.

This anti-statism revealed aspects of the welfare state which had been ignored by most socialists. It was not just a question of setting up welfare structures which could offset the unequal distribution of wealth, it was also necessary to challenge the unequal power relationships which remained in the administration of welfare. Behind the policies and practices of the welfare state there were specific historical assumptions which were often about regulation as much as the common need.

The problem was, of course, that this perspective took welfare so much for granted it failed to acknowledge that it had been an enormous struggle to get even these limited provisions in the first place and that, inadequate as they were, they still served real needs. The welfare state was presented simply as undifferentiated control, a veritable Leviathan of social engineering which left the individual powerless. Nor did this approach solve the problem of how women with small children or dependants were expected to live. This 'between the devil and the deep blue sea' attitude to the family and the state led to some extraordinary contortions. One woman on Social Security in the mid-1970s maintained that she knew she was facing

> the State, my enemy, my boss. It was a straightforward battle – no matter how intimately the State knew me through its files, my relation to it was purely self-centred. I didn't have to consider anybody's feelings except my own and my child's. I had no sympathy for the S. S. I know that they had the cash.[4]

In an attempt to shift the log jam some feminists began to argue that we should examine the role of state institutions in propping up the existing family. This was the perspective outlined in 1977 in Elizabeth Wilson's *Women and the Welfare State*, which grew out of an earlier pamphlet published by the socialist feminist paper *Red Rag*. Similarly, in 'The State and the Oppression of Women', which appeared in the collection *Feminism and Materialism* in the following year, Mary McIntosh asserted that the emphasis upon women's direct confrontation with the state was borrowed from 'the libertarian and radical left'.[5] She did not think it illuminated women's specific relation to the state:

> . . .the state intervenes less conspicuously in the lives of women than of men, when it does so it appears to be done more benevolently. The relation of women to state agents is much more often indirect than that of men.[6]

The obvious snags in these assumptions are that the state is not always busy propping up the family and that it is capable of quite conspicuous intervention.

An opposing view of women's relation to the state has been asserted by many feminists in the black communities and by women who support the Irish Republican struggle. They have also challenged the political marginalization of their very direct conflict with the state that follows from accepting that the state's intervention in women's lives is indirect and apparently benevolent. For example, Pratibha Parmar noted the prominence of women in defence of black people in the urban uprisings of the early 1980s:

> As mothers, while fearing for their children being beaten up and arrested, they joined in the street fighting from their homes and as young women they experienced physical violence from the police force either in the front line or in their homes.[7]

The extension of police powers during the 1980s has made increasing numbers of black women in Britain deeply sceptical of a state they see as expressing racist attitudes and intervening all too directly in their lives. It is clear that the imperialistic British state has always been more directly coercive towards its subject peoples than within Britain itself. Women have not been exempted from racist immigration laws and the harassment and repression of black people. They have been subjected to raids, sexual searches to prove virginity, deportation and psychological distress.[8] A black feminist from Brixton observed: 'At present white women get stopped by the police to be asked if they're all right. Black women get treated with hostility and suspicion.'[9]

Nor can we assume a uniformity in women's relations to the 'benevolent' aspects of the state. Amina Mama asserts that, far from there being less intervention, black women come into *more* contact with state welfare agencies. Even within the working class, black people have unequal access to state resources – she instances the allocation of inferior housing to them. Amina Mama is also conscious of the role of the state in carrying attitudes and ideas. She argues that the racist assumptions behind welfare provision mean that the seemingly benevolent aspects of welfare are geared towards the social regulation of black people. Pressure can be brought on black women not to have children. Racist values are evident in the criteria that result in a disproportionate number of black children being taken into care, in the classification of many black people as being in need of psychiatric care, and in the tendency to treat mental illness with physical methods, drugs and electro-convulsive therapy, rather than using a psychoanalytic approach or counselling.[10]

Mary McIntosh's statement that 'the state frequently defines a space, the family, in which its agents will not interfere but in which control is left to the man' is thus true only for certain groups in specific situations.[11] Eileen Fairweather, for example, quotes a Derry housewife and community activist in an article in *Spare Rib* in 1979, 'Don't You Know There's a War Going On?'. She describes the state moving quite literally into this family 'space':

> Although the British government keeps telling us it's a 'law and order' problem or a Catholic and Protestant problem, or civil unrest or just the 'troubles', to me it was a war situation from the very beginning. Because you know, when I looked out of my window what I saw was a soldier with a gun pointing in the window, and when I went out to the back garden to hang up the washing there was a tank sitting in my next-door neighbour's garden and the turret moved around after me . . . and the soldier came into my house and put the gun up against my neck and said 'Up against the wall'. I just couldn't think of that in terms of a law and order problem, or a civil unrest problem, to me that was war . . . So of course the British presence affects us as women. How can't it? They're here.[12]

Rose McAllister went to Armagh jail in the 1970s, aged 40, just after giving birth to a son, Christopher, because five incendiary devices were found in her house. She told the authors of *Only the Rivers Run Free*: 'They try to treat you as an imbecile in jail by making all the decisions for you. And if you let them, they take away your dignity.'[13] The supposedly 'benevolent' approach of the state to women, once breached, reveals the other side of the coin. Contempt:

> It's twice as bad for a woman because they have this idea that good mothers, good wives and good girlfriends shouldn't be in jail and the reasons why you're there is because you aren't good. By going to jail you're destroying their ideals of what a woman should be like.[14]

Because it is hard to know how to resolve the conflict in Ireland, many people in Britain have been inclined to switch off and ignore the ways in which the British state has disregarded rights and human dignity. These is no agreement among feminists in either Britain or Ireland about who is right or wrong, though the greatest weight of support would be with the Catholics and the Republican cause. But it is inescapably true that the abuse of state power in Ireland has had consequences in Britain in times of crisis. Many women in the mining communities in 1984–5 experienced the unbeenevolent state in their back gardens and in their homes; they also were treated as women who were not 'good' when they picketed in defence of miners' jobs and their communities. Since then this extension and intensification of state control has continued.

The state thus relates differently to women according to their race, class and political situation. Also, if a woman's actions take her outside the state's bounds of benevolence, its protective aspects can quickly turn to a peculiarly sexual scorn and brutality. These factors significantly alter the degree of leeway the state is prepared to allow women.

The specific problem Mary McIntosh was addressing continues, however, to create debate among feminists. She was concerned to show that women are treated in contradictory ways by different aspects of the state:

> Women are now full citizens in most purely legal respects: they have the right to vote, to own and dispose of property, to make contracts, to go to law, to hold passports. In many ways, however, the state relates

to married women through their husbands, especially in income tax and the social security system. . .'[15]

In this view the state is not seen as a homogeneous entity detached from the circumstances of society. Its contradictions express historical pressure and existing social relations.

In rebellion against women's partial citizenship, the Women's Liberation Campaign for Legal and Financial Independence argued in 1975 that feminists had to contest 'the web of state regulations' which 'hinder the development of women's social, psychological and economic independence by enforcing their dependence on men or making their lives intolerable if they rebel individually'.[16] But in opposing the unequal treatment of women in state policy and legislation, modern feminists have come up against exactly the same dilemma as that which divided the earlier feminist movement. The demand for independence made sense in some contexts, but it did not provide a solution to the material dependence of women with small children and low wages. Yet, if social measures were to be based on the differing positions of women and men in society so that economic inequality was accepted and institutionalized in state policy, how could women achieve equality? The feminist determination to, in Denise Riley's words, 'shake the family members apart, and speak about the clashes of needs between ages and sexes'[17] has reduced women's invisibility within the aggregate of 'the family'. But, once 'disaggregated', the individual units are left dangling and the social and economic forces which make mutual interdependence impossible mean that women, especially mothers, remain subordinate.

Some feminists have responded to this problem by emphasizing the issue of low pay, others by focusing on domestic dependence. Zoë Fairbairns argued, for example, that abolition of the cohabitation rule for single women on Social Security should mean that married women could claim benefits. She observed:

> . . . 'the Housewife' has always been a bit of a trial to social policy makers, particularly when they have had to work out the basis on which benefits are to be paid. After all, as things stand, the housewife is an adult who must for bureaucratic reasons be treated as a child; she works full time but is not economically active, ought really to be part of a two-parent family, but must not actually be permitted to starve if she falls short of this ideal; and does vital work, but must remain an exception to the idea that the way to keep key workers at their posts is through money.[18]

The Women's Liberation Campaign for Legal and Financial Independence also struggled over the practical issues which dependence raises. For instance:

> . . . the question of maintenance and responsibility for child care, within and outside marriage. Should the father pay for the child's upkeep or should this be the responsibility of the State? Should feminists pressurize for payment of a home responsibility allowance, or would a better solution be found in the widespread provision of free crèches?[19]

In fact they pressed for a whole series of legal changes combined with social and economic policies in an attempt to avoid over-emphasizing some elements of women's liberation at the expense of others.[20] They aimed for a new and better balance between independence and mutual support. The campaign was originally conceived as a challenge to the state, not 'a simple fight for equal rights within the existing social structure'.[21] But a rhetorical and abstract challenge was clearly an evasion and the women involved turned their attention to detailed propositions. The possibility of legislative changes in the mid-1970s made this seem a worthwhile labour. It also proved to be somewhat time-consuming:

> Because so much relevant legislation was being brought up, we found ourselves spending more time than originally envisaged on parliamentary matters. We submitted evidence to the select committees on the Social Security Pensions Bill and the Employment Protection Bill; also the committee looking at Occupational Pensions and the Special Committee of the Supplementary Benefits Commission enquiry into the cohabitation ruling and finally the Royal Commission on the Distribution of Income and Wealth.[22]

Along with doubts about changes and strategic focus necessary to tackle women's dependence, disagreements have emerged about what we want to the state to do. From around the late 1970s a wide range of debates developed about the state's role as a protector. There are disagreements among feminists about the age of consent, state censorship of pornography, state control of prostitution, and police protection against rape and male violence against women.[23] These unresolved political arguments about sexuality and violence indicate a disjuncture between an abstract analysis of a capitalist, white, male-dominated state as all-controlling and the pragmatic recognition of the need to use this same state. Further confusion arises because of a common tendency in both theoretical and practical writing on the state to slip between confronting the 'male-dominated' state, or 'patriarchy', and the 'capitalist' or 'imperialist' state.[24] The state is presented wearing different hats. Or it becomes stripy, partly good and partly bad. It is also a case of now you see it, now you don't. The dominant interests slither mysteriously about. For instance, feminists seeking to restrict male power in the family, as in cases of domestic violence, may turn to the state as if it were unsusceptible to the prevailing relations of power.

The difficulty in understanding how relations of dominance interact within the state contributed to debate about what exactly was meant by the term 'patriarchy', which was pressed into service to designate women's oppression as a sex, as distinct from other forms of subordination. Its universal usage, however, raised more problems than it solved. The word suggests that there are two separate systems divided along male/female lines, so that 'patriarchy' oppresses women and 'capitalism' oppresses male workers. This makes it difficult to see how relationships have changed historically, since the term implies a fixed structure rather than the kaleidoscopic forms shaping the actual encounters of women and men. It does not carry any notion of how women might act to transform their situation as a sex. Nor does it even convey a sense of how women have resolutely manoeuvred for a better position within the general context of subordination.[25]

Recognition that in abstract the debate about the capitalist or patriarchal state leads to an impasse has resulted in attempts to look at the way the state has related to women in particular historical contexts. These 'specific, concrete studies' have in turn begun to contribute to a more complex understanding of women's relations to aspects of the state. For example, Penny Summerfield's study of the Second World War showed the contradictory assumptions behind policies as the state tried to persuade women to take up war work while continuing to emphasize the importance of their activity in the home.[26] Carol Smart's examination of the conflicting attitudes to women's sexuality expressed in the changes in the law on prostitution in the 1950s suggested that it is misleading to isolate the operation of the law in relation to sexuality or the family from other aspects of state regulation and urban control.[27] Smart asked how far there was a coherent body of law which 'overtly or covertly serves the interests of the dominant male group or, more abstractly, the interests of patriarchy'.[28] Some aspects of law codify women's dependence and subordination in relation to men. However, the existing law expresses contradictory claims:

> It is worth considering, for example, that during the twentieth century the law has reversed its position on the question of custody of children on divorce or separation, so that mothers now are far more likely to win the custody of children than fathers. This may be little more than a legal recognition of the social organization of child care, but it removes from most men the power they once had over their wives via their children.[29]

Recent feminist studies of the history of social policy have unpacked the idea of the state as the expression of dominant interests, examining internal government politics, dissension between ministries, reaction to pressure from groups in society, and the different spheres of central and local government.[30] It has become apparent that social policy as much as law has been a site of political struggle. Various different responses may follow from the admission of complexity. One is strategic paralysis. Denise Riley has observed that a view of 'the state as a dense network of generating powers . . . may produce in the end a new functionalism, mysterious because of the dispersion of its causeless effects, its non-authorship, the more remote and terrifying because its tracks are everywhere'.[31] Another possible response is a pragmatic disbelief that the state operates in anybody's interests at all. Linda Challis in her 'Survey of Day Care Policy', argues that the state, far from acting in a concerted conspiracy to deprive women of child care, is just a muddle. It is in fact the very uncertainties, disagreements and ambivalence of 'people including policy makers' that make a policy consensus hard to achieve.[32]

These studies of social policy shared the problem that the Women's Liberation Campaign for Legal and Financial Independence discovered from their lobbying of committees: they tended to turn inwards towards the mechanism of state power and were inclined to minimize the effects of women's organizations at the grass roots.[33] They focused on the complexities of policy-makers' motivations rather than offering an analysis of the *consequences* of particular policies. Looking at the ways in which law or policy affects women in practice makes it easier to determine whose interests are being served. The fact that in history pressure from women has changed laws and policies, and that, while it is recognized that all women do not have the same interests, some legislative changes are more beneficial to them than others, came to be implicitly accepted in practice by the women's movement.

The initial impetus of women's liberation had not been directed at changing laws. However, as campaigns emerged from women's needs, the importance of legislation became inescapable. The abortion campaign combined, though sometimes under tension, lobbying Parliament with the grass-roots work of leafleting and talking to people in markets, parks, shopping centres. In the mid-1970s the Labour government introduced several laws which aimed at greater equality at work and the recognition of women's situation in the family. The Equal Pay Act, passed in 1970, came into force, the Sex Discrimination Act was passed and the Equal Opportunities Commission set up. A new state pension scheme came in with the 1975 Social Security (Pensions) Act, making provision for people who were not in waged work full time because of home responsibilities and giving more women the chance of a pension. The Employment Protection Act gave women a statutory right to paid maternity leave, protection from unfair dismissal during pregnancy and the right to their jobs back up to 29 weeks after the baby was born.

Thus, while women's liberation has tended to be extremely suspicious of the state in theory, in practice it has drafted and lobbied and given evidence. Clearly, laws have a significant effect on our lives – if they did not, there would be no political conflict in their making or struggle over their retention. But their impact is limited. Over time it became apparent from observation of the operation of these Acts for women's equality that a law is a declaration of intent and a staking out of territory, rather than an achievement in itself. It is a continuing problem to ensure that the Acts are enforced, and that laws passed with the aim of freeing women do not instead serve the interests of men or of specific groups of privileged women – for a law can be put to many purposes depending on who applies it. Carol Smart points to the limits of law in the face of existing relations of power in society and the state:

> . . . treating as equal persons who are manifestly socially and economically unequal can actually operate to further discriminatory practices whilst perpetuating an ideology of total fairness and impartiality.[34]

Bea Campbell and Anna Coote, however, take a more optimistic view of the legislation of the mid-1970s and of the radical implications of 'equality'. They argue that, despite the laws' practical limits, they legitimized the idea of equality and shifted the ideological terrain:

> . . . the effect of having the principle of equality formally endorsed is hard to measure, but it must have helped to develop new expectations and a new sense of confidence among women and it must have begun (however sluggishly) to change public opinion about what was 'natural' and immutable about differences between women and men. The focus of the argument shifted: open disputes about whether or not women were men's inferiors, worthy of equal treatment, gave way to disagreements over what exactly constituted the equal rights that women want.[35]

The state, then, is not simply propping up and enforcing the interests of the privileged, it can be made to work on behalf of the subordinated. Consequently, feminists have broadly accepted in practice that struggle in the arena of the state can result in more favourable laws, and can work towards the redistribution of wealth. It can also offer opportunities to assert countervailing values and principles by challenging what appears to be legitimate. An example of this is feminist questioning of the dominant role of the family in social policy, drawn attention to by Hilary Wainwright in *Beyond the Fragments*.[36] Resistance to the coercive and inequitable features of the state can evidently shift resources and change common-sense assumptions about how the state should act, though many reforms fall short of the intentions that motivated those campaigning for them.[37]

Despite the anti-state strands in women's liberation, the state has also been seen by some feminists as carrying a concept of collectivity which is opposed to capitalist market relations. For instance, in the early 1970s *Red Rag* argued:

> The family allowance campaign could have been seen as a means of acknowledging and extending demands for State recognition of responsibility toward successive generations of children.
>
> Thus it could also be a focal point for raising consciousness of the relationship between the State and the family, and for eroding the notion that each family must be sufficient to and responsible for itself.[38]

The idea that the state *as it is* embodies an alternative principle of social organization and can be a means of correcting the inequalities of the market appears in Jean Coussins's and Anna Coote's *The*

Family in the Firing Line: A Discussion Document on Family Policy.
They argue that through taxation of the childless the government
gives 'the lead in trying to counteract the all too common view that
if people choose to have children, it's their responsibility'.[39] There
is, however, a crucial difference between asserting that the state is
an important terrain of battle for a democratic idea of collectivity
and saying that the existing state is a free association for mutual
support. If the state is regarded as already embodying an alternative,
the problem is evaded of how a state representing various interests
in relationships of inequality has evolved into a state that transcends
the interests of the dominant groups in society and becomes a neutral
instrument for change. So, not only is it unclear how the interests
which control the state interact in the coercive aspects of its relation
with society, there is also a vagueness as to how countervailing values
can be present within the same state. Yet, because the existing state
is the only overall mechanism for the distribution of social welfare
resources, there are practical short-term pressures not to labour its
loaded character.

The cuts of the late 1970s and the policy of the Thatcher government in the 1980s, forced an intense reappraisal among feminists.[40]
Among many socialist feminists the anti-statism of the early 1970s
has tended to move towards an admission that the resources of the
state are needed and the point is to contest how these are controlled
and distributed.[41] There has also been a growing recognition that
the state is not just an abstract 'it' or even an opposing 'them'.
Audrey Wise made this point at 'The Debate of the Decade'
in 1980:

> I don't believe that the state is some sort of abstraction, I believe that
> the state itself depends on acquiescence at least, if not support, from
> ordinary people. And so the big question to which we've yet to find the
> answer is how to persuade ordinary people not to acquiesce while they
> are prevented from achieving the transfer of wealth and power towards
> themselves.[42]

There has been a great deal of discussion among feminists about
how the users of welfare, many of whom are women, can ensure
that the state meets their needs and how women as workers in
the state can themselves act to change how it operates. Socialist
feminists were in the 'London to Edinburgh Weekend Return
Group' which produced *In and Against the State* in 1979. Starting

from the concept of the state as composed of people in specific social relations, they examined both the question of acquiescence and the circumstances in which people resist. The state was thus not presented as embodying alternative principles in an abstract or static manner, but rather as in continuous movement as people take action within and against its boundaries.

An extraordinary range of demands have emerged from women's actions as users and as workers. There has been a sustained challenge to the presumption that the recipients of resources should be passive and grateful. Instead, the emphasis on information, self-help and greater control has promoted the idea of the user as a person who has an active right to make claims on public resources. 'This handbook isn't just information, it's a weapon,'[43] declared the *Unsupported Mothers' Handbook*, produced in the early 1970s by the Claimants' Union. The evangelical dissemination of information has been very much a part of the struggle for women's liberation.

Women have also argued for a more open state in which information is not used as a source of power over people. Maureen Murphy, a single mother, told the authors of *In and Against the State*:

> I had social workers or probation officers at one time when the kids were in trouble. I never hit it off with them. Everything you tell them, you know is supposed to be confidential. But they write it down. I know a girl working down the office and she said, 'I've seen your records.' Well that put me off completely . . . So when I was offered a social worker after that I turned it down. I felt I wouldn't have that aggravation again, always being put down and everyone reading your notes.[44]

Access to information and democratic control became an issue for Newham parents in 1981. Viv Dufill, a member of the Parents' Action Committee, described how they tried to oppose the closure of a local school by putting their case to the council: 'There was uproar at one meeting. They closed the meeting rather than talk to us. They want to take decisions that affect our lives behind our backs.'[45]

Another form of resistance has involved challenging the repressive stereotypes that can be imposed on women. This is easier to do rhetorically than in real life, but opening up the personal feelings of pain and humiliation can relieve the isolation of an individual claimant who resists. In 1980 Anna Briggs described how she represented two friends in Social Security tribunals. One was a former social worker, Wendy, who had been handicapped by an accident and was an Open University student. The other was Kay, a single mother. Wendy's claim was accepted; she fell into the 'deserving poor' category. Kay's was rejected. She recognized that in making a claim she had to maintain an objective relation to the tribunal. She was engaged in a transaction, trying to make a bargain. Nonetheless she felt judged: '. . .it's hard to be objective when you have your life put under hostile scrutiny, then feel yourself being mentally categorized as some kind of brainless, lust-oriented animal.'[46]

One aspect of resistance to controlling and confining stereotypes has been the effort to validate forms of knowledge that go unrecognized in society. For example, the authors of *In and Against the State* pointed out that many women who have to deal with the state, like Maureen Murphy, acquire a great deal of 'know-how' about its actual workings.[47] In 1981 Nicola Murray, Cynthia Cockburn and Jeannette Mitchell said in *Spare Rib*:

> What we need to do is to perceive and unify all the thousand acts of everyday resistance; the refusal to hand over the passport, the refusal to leave the waiting room, the refusal to be forced by the DHSS into dependence on a man.[48]

They see these 'refusals' as part of a wider resistance to the existing relations of the state.

Another way of shifting the state has involved the active assertion of needs through self-help. The Rape Crisis Centres and battered women's refuges have served, like the community nurseries and women's health projects, to reveal unmet needs. They have also created a collective force to press the state for resources, while seeking to develop new relations around women's needs.[49] A group in Birmingham, the Programme for Reform of the Law on Soliciting (PROS), aimed to abolish prison sentences for loitering and soliciting. This was not simply a liberal pressure group for law reform, since it included the prostitutes themselves, arguing for change based on their own understanding of their situation.[50] In this case self-help combined with the campaigning skills of radical state workers.

A crucial element in women's liberation writing has challenged the way people are defined and categorized by the state and understanding is denied to those without power, many of whom

are of course women. It is evident, however, that this process
is not peculiar to the relationship of men with women, since
it also exists in relations between women, especially when they
are divided by inequalities of power such as those of class,
race or age. For instance, in 'Care or Custody?', an article on
long-stay geriatric patients, Helen Ewers described the nurses'
categorizing of one group of old women as 'awkward Alices'.
These were controlled by such strategies as avoidance, being
put in corners of the ward, being left until last by overworked
and underpaid nurses: 'Awkward Alice has been stripped of
her competence to make judgements about the appropriateness
of the care provided for her in her enforced dependency.'[51]

The women's movement has sought not only equality but loving
sisterhood. In certain situations this has resulted in a rhetoric that
conceals actual divisions. Yet, like the desire for equality, this
aspiration contains a profound critique of the prevailing inhumanity
in our encounters as human beings. It challenges customary ways of
seeing one another. 'Poem by Kate' appeared in *Shrew* in 1976:

> What do you see nurses
> what do you see?
> Are you thinking
> when you are looking at me
> a crabbit old woman
> not very wise,
> Uncertain of habit
> with far away eyes,
> Who dribbles her food
> and makes no reply,
> When you say in a loud voice
> 'I do wish you'd try'.
> Who seems not to notice
> the things that you do,
> And forever is losing
> a stocking or shoe,
> Who unresisting or not
> lets you do as you will
> With bathing or feeding
> the long day to kill
> Is that what you're thinking
> Is that what you see?
> Then open your eyes nurse
> You are not looking at me. . .[52]

The strong emphasis that the politics of women's liberation gave to looking at one's own life meant that feminists who worked in the 'caring professions' began to think about how their work in the state affected other women's lives. One approach was 'refusal': 'Women's liberation requires an analysis of *all* the roles offered us within a sexist culture, leading to a refusal to take on these roles.'[53] This position is expressed in the verse:

> The caring roles divide us
> Make us agents of the state
> If we abdicate that power
> We can redirect our fate.[54]

But having refused totally, where did you go? This absolutism resulted in the contortions of guilt contested by Elizabeth Wilson in *Women and the Welfare State*. Feminist welfare workers came to recognize that although they possessed power over other women, through knowledge and control of resources, they also shared their needs for welfare provision. Vanessa Stilwell, writing on 'Women in White Collar Unions' in the radical social workers' paper *Case Con* in 1974, observed:

> Resources such as day nurseries, play space, crèches, special schools, hospitals, housing etc. are particularly important to us, not just as social workers who are faced with the need for them every working day, but also as women.[55]

So there was not only the yearning for sisterhood, the utopian project; women were linked by the shared material needs of everyday life. Reporting the Edinburgh Women's Liberation Conference of 900 women in 1974, Lesley Gilbert stated in *Spare Rib*:

> A common theme that ran through all the workshops I attended was the relationship between clients and workers, in social welfare and health services, between patients and doctors and nurses, between the victims of psychiatrists and mental institutions and women social workers. Was it possible to work politically on feminist issues as a state employee – say a social worker – and if so, how would this link up with claimants' unions' activities? Could women's groups be established in hospitals incorporating ancillary workers, nurses, health visitors as well as medical students? How could we combine creating our own alternatives, like self-examination groups, with campaigns around

NHS provisions? Most people seemed to think that we should try to work both to create alternatives and to attack the system from within, as workers, and without, as clients.[56]

Pragmatically, steps have been taken to minimize the divisions rather than deny that they exist. Health workers producing information have sought to democratize knowledge: 'We feel that too much knowledge is in the hands of too few';[57] social workers have exposed 'anti-feminist casework ideology';[58] members of the London Nursery Campaign have contested social and psychological attitudes in nursery nurses' training;[59] women in NALGO have argued that the union should not only respond to their needs as workers but also take up social issues and campaigns for nurseries and increased Child Benefit.[60]

In trying to overcome divisions between women, feminists have taken part in everyday resistances which sought to connect workers and users of state services. This was a significant element in the political strategy, broadly accepted by many feminists from the mid-1970s, that found expression in hospital occupations like that of the Elizabeth Garrett Anderson, a women's hospital threatened with closure in 1976.[61] The approach was also taken into the anti-cuts campaigns developing in this period.

During the Seventies feminists had played a crucial role in developing the strategic practice summed up by the authors of *In and Against the State*: 'Our struggle is about everyday opposition to the normal condition of things.'[62] However, to move the idea of changing relations between state and society beyond everyday encounters necessarily involves a challenge to executive power. From the early 1980s a profound uncertainty is apparent among feminists about how to translate the experiences of the 1970s into a new context. There has been a widespread search for an alternative that acknowledges women's need of the state but refuses to accept its existing structure as inevitable.

Faced with the limits of small-scale grass-roots struggles, many feminists in the 1980s have become involved in local government. Women's committees have tried to combine the direct democratic forms of local groups with the representative democracy of elected local government. For example, in the South London borough of Southwark, the Women's Committee wrote to about 600 playgroups, mothers' and toddlers' groups, old people's clubs and tenants' associations, as well as women's groups, asking them to come and talk to them and to attend committee meetings. They also went round local groups to find out what they wanted.[63] Sue Goss, writing in *Local Socialism* (edited by Martin Boddy and Colin Fudge in 1984), drew out some of the implications of the attempt to change women's relation to the local state. She said the aim should be that:

● The demands and priorities of women are brought to the forefront of local decision-making.
● Women's committees act as a resource to, and support, women organizing in their areas while respecting their autonomy.
● The new forms of representation and organization developed challenge and change the political organization of local government as a whole.
● Material changes are made in women's lives by responding to the new assessments of employment or service provision.[64]

Not surprisingly, this recent move towards the democratization of the state through local government has run into many difficulties. Hopes have been raised without the resources to fulfil them, since the government has put ever stricter limits on spending and women do not always have the power to make their needs into budget priorities. Notions of 'the enabling state' and 'planning from below' have moreover tended to assume that all women share the same politics and speak with single voice. Divergent interests have become evident in practice. Lesbian women, black women, Irish women, women with disabilities – all have challenged the treatment of women as a homogeneous administrative category. The democratization of relations within local government has proved even harder. It is not clear how large-scale administrative structures can respond to the external pressures of needs and still operate efficiently. Nonetheless, the political experience of women's liberation has made many feminists see that an administrative structure is not a neutral power that can simply apply a different set of policies. If there is extreme inequality in a hierarchical bureaucracy, and no understanding of co-operative ways of working, how can the people within it effectively carry out policies committed to extending democracy and equality in the use of resources? This is not an issue which affects only women, of course, but women's lack of power over the way policies are agreed and acted upon has made it a concern of many feminists in local government.

In 1980 Michèle Barrett maintained in *Women's Oppression Today* that the local and anti-hierarchical emphasis in women's liberation politics had 'tended to deflect attention from attempts to influence the state at the level of national policies'.[65] However, this ignored a real political obstacle which is not the preoccupation of the women's movement alone. An unresolved problem in modern socialist thinking is how to link local democracy with a different kind of central state. The attempts in the 1980s to connect direct participatory democracy with elected representative government have only begun to indicate how this could take shape locally. How such ideas might be applied to change relations between state and society nationally – or indeed internationally – remains unclear.

This was one of the reasons why many socialist feminists who joined the Labour Party in the early 1980s were profoundly disoriented. They had many assumptions about how the state should meet women's needs in more direct democratic relationships. This would in fact mean an extensive transformation of the state both centrally and locally. But the Labour Party had traditionally had an unproblematic attitude to the state, and it tended to incorporate only those aspects of women's liberation politics that could be codified into demands and did not require drastic change in the political process itself.

In the last few years the British state has become more overtly coercive in the regulation of dissent and suppression of rebellion. Central government has also exerted greater control over local government. All this has been done against a background of rhetoric about freedom *from* the state, accompanied by the relaxation of restraints on the market and on employers. These changing circumstances have brought many more women into conflict with aspects of the state, and on a larger scale, than in the 1970s. These struggles are no longer local but national – even international in the case of the peace movement, which involves not only direct protest action but the contesting of military strategies and power in every possible forum. Women as well as men experienced the raw force of the state in the extraordinary policing of the miners' strike, which left long-lasting scars, but women's involvement in the strike also raised the issue of who was to control the future development of communities. Throughout the 1980s, too, women public service workers, many of whom are from ethnic minorities, have fought for their jobs, against privatization, and against cuts in social services. There have been many defeats, but they have asserted with considerable confidence that their work is of value to society. They have shown how resistance can develop within the state itself.

In Belfast, ancillary workers concerned to defend the Health Service decided with the backing of their union, NUPE, to study women's health needs in a historical perspective by interviewing neighbours and members of their own families. As well as collecting a devastating account of working-class women's health they gained a consciousness of their rights. One of the women involved, Anna McGonigle, could have been responding to Audrey Wise's recognition of the way acquiescence holds people in thrall when she affirmed:

> We are never going to be invisible again. We have settled for too little in the past. We working women are part of history. History is us.[67]

When such an affirmation starts to appear within a society, its roots go deeper than a theory. Why acquiesce to a state which denies resources and power to live out your days decently and enjoyably and have hope for the future? Why not try another kind of state indeed?

PART FOUR

The Working Life

10

Impediments to Equality

When I was a little girl I wished I was a boy
I tagged along behind the gang and wore my corduroys
Everybody said I only did it to annoy
But I was gonna be an engineer.

I listened to my mother and I joined a typing pool
I listened to my lover and I sent him through his school
If I listen to the boss, I'm just a bloody fool
And an underpaid engineer!

I've been a sucker ever since I was a baby
As a daughter as a wife as a mother as a dear
But I'll fight them as a woman not a lady
I'll fight them as an engineer![1]

Peggy Seeger's song captures a new mood of confidence in the late 1960s among many women workers who were exasperated by lack of support from men in their trade unions for their demands for equal pay and their efforts to break out of confinement to low-paid jobs. In 1968 at the TUC Miss J. O'Connell accused male trade unionists of 'industrial apartheid'[2] because of their lack of action on equal pay. She told them, 'We want more than a promise of a dream.'[3] The following year Mrs M. Turner told Congress that women had developed 'inferiority complexes'[4] from being relegated to subordinate work:

> James Baldwin once remarked in connection with racial discrimination that the white supremacists had only really succeeded when the oppressed people began to believe they were inherently inferior; in other words they began to accept the discriminators' view of themselves.[5]

The Ford sewing machinists' campaign for equal grading in 1968 was part of this militant rejection of inferior status. The National Union of Vehicle Builders (NUVB), the union representing the Ford women, started the National Joint Action Campaign for Women's Equal Rights (NJACWER). It included men as well as women from the trade-union movement and aimed to consolidate and extend Barbara Castle's Equal Pay Act, which went through Parliament in 1968 and was due to come into force in 1975.

The action of the Ford women and the discussions about equal pay gave impetus to the emergence of the women's movement in Britain.[6] Several of the first women's liberation groups began as equal-pay groups. Two parallel developments can be seen: a growing impatience among women active in trade unions with continuing inequality, which was expressed in terms of 'equal rights'; and the discontent of young educated middle-class women influenced by student politics and the New Left, who were demanding 'liberation'. Links existed between the two groups – there were socialist women active in both NJACWER and the new women's liberation groups. In Britain the emphasis on class and the need for connection with the labour movement was an important feature of the emerging women's movement. From the start there was a commitment to campaign for equal pay and better conditions at work, and these appeared prominently in the demands of the movement.

For most of the young middle-class members of women's libera-tion, however, many of whom were students, young mothers or had only just started work, equal pay and equal rights at work were rather remote concerns. These were demands made with a dutiful nod in the direction of other women's problems and labour-movement politics in contrast to their passionate 'personal' concerns about images in advertising, child care, the response of left-wing men to women's liberation. This probably accounts for the somewhat distant and pedestrian tone of the early writings on work. The exceptions were women like Audrey Wise, who had a lot of experience as a trade-union organizer among women but also responded to women's liberation's emphasis on changing relationships rather than just acquiring 'rights'. Thus, although the Equal Pay Act was a victory, a culmination of a phase of struggle among manual working-class women, it had barely appeared before its limits were being noted. In 1969, for example, Barbara Wilson, from Surrey NJACWER was arguing that equal pay for equal value was needed, along with higher wages, training, access to skilled jobs and better child-care provision.[7] There was division in NJACWER about how to proceed. Sue Pascoe reported in 1969 on a meeting of the Cities of London and Westminster Trades Council: 'The general mood of the majority who participated in the discussion at the conference was that the first aim for women is equal pay, and that equal rights should be left until later.'[8]

The debates on equal pay were complicated by opposition from the Left of the labour movement to the Wilson government's attempt to impose an incomes policy and later to the Industrial Relations Bill - it was argued that women had little chance of equality when the government was acting to restrict workers' industrial rights. In 1969, for instance, in the magazine *Socialist Woman*, Kath Fincham and Sabina Roberts linked equal pay with opposition to an incomes policy and with democratic control by Conference of Labour Party policy.[9] Speaking at a meeting called by the London Women's Liberation Workshop in January 1971, Audrey Wise said that 'women were further behind in the industrial field'[10] and thus had a great deal to lose from the Industrial Relations Bill's restriction on the power of trade unions. She believed that the Bill could make the trade unions 'appendages of the State machine'.[11]

As early as 1969 a divergence of perspective is apparent in women's liberation on the reasons for women's inequality at work and on the role of legislation. These political differences were to re-surface repeatedly over the years. *Socialist Woman*, which was linked to a Trotskyist grouping, the International Marxist Group, emphasized the capitalists' interest in a divided workforce,[12] while in the London Women's Liberation newsletter, *Bird* (later *Shrew*), Janet Hadley said that inequality arose because 'men are still in position to dictate to us the economic terms under which we live'.[13] She also reflected on the inadequacy of equal pay without equal job opportunities and expressed a characteristic view of the time that the government's promise of equal pay in 1975 was simply a 'palliative' for the growing unrest among women.[14]

In the early 1970s equal pay continued to be extensively discussed. The limits of the Act and the dangers of removing protective legislation under cover of the slogan of 'equality' were pointed out; the ways employers would evade the Act through grading and job description were noted. Sarah Boston produced evidence that some trade unions were collaborating with employers to evade the Act. She cited for instance an agreement in Leicester under which male shop assistants were 'designated "Trainee Managers" and paid three pounds more than a female shop assistant who [received] £12.50'.[15]

Criticism of the specific limits of the equal-pay legislation merged
with a political critique of legislation as a means of change. Anna
Coote's scepticism was based on the investigations she and Tess Gill
had made of the limits to women's rights.[16] In 1974 she looked at
the anti-discrimination proposals in the Labour government's White
Paper on Equality for Women and concluded:

> New laws and regulations don't bring social change. The most they
> can do is to create a climate more favourable to change and make
> life more tolerable for some in the meantime. If the Equal Pay Act
> achieves nothing else it will have taught us a valuable lesson: women
> will get nowhere unless they organize and fight for themselves.[17]

In women's trade-union activity there has historically been an
oscillation between trying to get legal changes and stressing the
need for women's organization and action at work. The militancy
of women workers has been beset by many difficulties including
lack of support from men in the trade-union movement. Yet the
limits of state protection are evident, for without mass action, laws
have remained ineffective.

In addition, in the mid-1970s there existed on the Left a strong
syndicalist current which was very wary of laws and the state.
This influenced discussion on the equal-pay and anti-discrimination
legislation. 'Laws Don't Bring Women Equality,' said *Women's Voice*
in January 1973,[18] and the libertarian Marxist *Islington Gutter Press*,
reporting a conference on the new anti-discrimination legislation
held by the North London Working Women's Charter groups
in November 1976, used the headline 'New Legislation: Is It
Worth the Paper It's Written On?'[19] The women writing in *Big
Flame Women's Struggle Notes*, also libertarians, were critical of
the ballyhoo surrounding the new Acts, which they argued were
simply the result of women 'fighting'.[20] The aim of the equal-pay
law in their view was to make industry more efficient. Despite
this theoretical scepticism, however, all over the country women's
liberation groups gave practical support to women on the equal-pay
strikes which broke out in the first half of the 1970s.[21]

The realization that equal-pay legislation had no effect on women
in many low-paid jobs was brought home to women's groups who got
involved in trying to unionize night cleaners, first in London and then
elsewhere. The Equal Pay Act did not benefit the cleaners because
broadly speaking it applied only to women doing the same or similar

work as men working for the same company. The cleaners worked for contractors, their pay was low, they had no job security or legal rights because they were employed by the night. There was hardly any union recognition and no way in which the skill in their work was acknowledged. Many had young children and many were black, Irish or from poor European countries and afraid of deportation. The predicament of exhausted, bewildered and fearful women who could be moved around buildings at the will of the employers, and who joined the union secretly, pointed up the gap between the official world of the trade-union movement and many women's working lives.[22]

The links between home and work made in the cleaners' campaign were being more widely noted by the mid-1970s. For instance, students in the women's liberation group at Essex University drew attention to the low rates of pay in the canteen and printed the demand of Mavis (from the Coffee Bar) for a change in the sexual division of labour:

> The home is such a shambles,
> Off to work in such a rush.
> Not a touch by duster or by brush
> Windows grubby, beds unmade,
> Unless he helps that's how it stays.[23]

The Big Flame women argued that equal rights were an abstraction: '. . . "equality" at work means nothing while there is no equality in the home'.[24] Manchester Women's Liberation Group made a similar point in a conference paper in the mid-1970s. The sexual division of labour had to be considered as a whole: it related not only to paid employment but to domestic life as well.[25] Commenting on the Labour government's Green Paper on Equal Opportunities, they rejected the emphasis on prejudiced attitudes: 'Discrimination against women is in fact deeply rooted in the structure of our society, deriving from a particular organization of the family.'[26] They also thought the document gave too much priority to women in management, the professions and the universities, which they saw as 'class bias'.[27] The prevailing tone of women's liberation writing in the mid-1970s was critical of the 'anti-discrimination' and 'equal opportunities' approach that characterized liberal feminists' studies of women's work. But the awareness of all the interconnecting facets of women's subordination made it difficult to focus on and tackle any particular aspect.

The formation of the Working Women's Charter organization in 1974 signalled a resolve to be practical and effective, though uneasiness persisted that the Charter's approach missed out many aspects of women's oppression and operated as a kind of male Left group in disguise. The Charter's demands were more extensive than the TUC's but, most important, it created a structure through which feminists could continue to work in the trade unions and trades councils.[28] Hackney Trades Council, for example, held a conference on women in November 1974 which was attended by women's liberation groups, Working Women's Charter groups and trade unionists.[29] There was an increase in activity by feminists in the trade unions to which many of them belonged. It is noticeable that the union branches affiliated to the Working Women's Charter were mainly from local government, teaching and clerical unions with a few from manual workers' unions like the AUEW (engineers' union).

The Charter organization had a persistent problem about where to focus. There were so many aspects to women's problems at work that, while everyone agreed equal pay was not enough, it was difficult to agree on which course was most strategic or which issues were most crucial. Moreover the women's movement was insisting on the interconnections between paid work and women's social and personal lives. In 1974 the National Council for Civil Liberties held a conference on women and work in which there were papers not only on pay but on education, training, and child care.[30] The NCCL was able to span the labour movement and older campaigns for women's rights while involving feminists from the new movement. In addition the abortion campaign meant that feminists were beginning to raise wider social issues in the trade-union movement.[31]

There was optimism, despite the range and scale of the problems – certainly until 1976. Even in face of the welfare cuts Michèle Ryan, the organizer of that year's Working Women's Charter Conference, stressed the need for militant resistance.[32] But economic change was to constrain the earlier hopes and mean increasingly defensive resistance to the cuts and then to the privatization of public services that affected many low-paid women workers. Unemployment and the widening gap between the earnings of low-paid and better-paid workers made women's low pay an even more crucial issue in the 1980s. The restructuring of the economy has resulted in changing patterns of employment. Casualization has meant an erosion of job security and 'flexibility' of hours the substitution of part-time jobs with less pay rather than a re-organization of working time to fit women's needs.

The government's policy of deregulation has removed many of the legal protections which covered women's work, for example through the wages councils which used to set minimum rates in low-paid industries.

On the Equal Pay front it was gloomy news too from the late 1970s. Mandy Snell's monitoring of the equality legislation came up with depressing conclusions:

> At workplace level, the legislation has had little impact. Although most women received some increase in pay as a result of the Equal Pay Act, many are still underpaid in relation to the men they work with and in relation to their level of skill and effort. Furthermore, the Sex Discrimination Act has not eliminated discrimination in employment nor has it led to any significant degree of desegregation of jobs. Most women are still concentrated in low-grade low-paid women's jobs with little prospect of better-paid jobs or promotion.[33]

She observed:

> The women's movement has always been ambivalent about the value of legislation in bringing about real change. On the one hand women have campaigned vigorously for legislation to improve women's domestic, economic and political positions. On the other hand, women inevitably find that laws, once passed, are unsatisfactory and that the inequalities they were intended to remove still remain.[34]

A generation accustomed to an expanding capitalist economy, ready to cry co-option and see reforms as palliatives, found itself at an impasse. Militant resistance was often faced with defeat. The prophecies about the laws unfortunately came true - at a time when women were finding it harder than ever to win demands on the shop-floor. The mid to late 1980s have seen several noteworthy gains made by small groups and individuals through tribunals and legal proceedings, but these have not been sufficient to check the overall intensification of inequality.

Why was it so difficult to improve women's situation at work? Feminists have tried to understand the causes of women's subordination in order to find strategic solutions. An explanation common in the early 1970s was that it was in the interests of employers to have a divided workforce:

To prevent united action by the working class the bosses always divide them into categories to set them against each other. It is exactly the same 'divide and rule' tactic they use around the world in the colonies and neo-colonies, and at home where they set white against blue collar, etc. As long as there are those who profit from the work of others there will be 'divide and rule.'[35]

This does not explain, though, why women in particular should be subordinated. And does capital have such clear-cut interests and strategy? Ruth Milkman's studies of the US auto and electrical manufacturing industries in the 1940s[36] led her to question the assumption of 'divide and rule' as a total explanation:

It is certainly plausible to argue that capital has a class interest in a divided labour force. However, on the level of the firm, sex segregation conflicts with capital's interests in profit maximization – at least in firms employing male workers. Treating male and female labour as non-interchangeable (the operating principle of segregation) limits the possibility of substituting cheap female labour for the more costly labour of men. As long as female labour is cheaper, this also limits profits.[37]

Another early assumption was that women were part of a great host of people who would be drawn into the labour force when required and cast out when trade was slack. Janet Hadley adapted this argument in 1969 to stress male power to dispense with women workers.[38] In fact, however, in certain sectors of the contemporary economy women appear not to be simply 'disposable', even in a recession.

A persistent problem for feminists seeking to understand women's subordination in employment has been working out how the power of men over women combines with the power of employers over workers. An early attempt was Audrey Wise's article 'Equal Pay is Not Enough' in 1969:

When you sell your labour-power you are selling part of your life, and if you sell it for a low price in this society you are announcing that you are a low-value person. Equal pay's therefore a very necessary step towards equality, and will have repercussions on the value placed on women in general.[39]

But the keeping down of women is not just a capitalist phenomenon and it is not just capitalists who do it. Other societies based on property have done it and men of all classes take part in it. Audrey Wise believed that women's oppression at work was linked to their position in the family.

> The fact that women are the mothers makes them powerful and vulnerable, and men seek to curb this power and utilize this vulnerability. Children make mothers guardians of the future with a direct and visible immortality, while a man can be dependent on the word of a woman even for his knowledge of fatherhood. This is power indeed. But mothers are vulnerable because their children are also hostages, and by depriving mothers of the guardianship of their children men have made full use of superior physical strength to ensure their dominance.[40]

She argued that capitalism had undermined some aspects of the father's direct control – making some men regard women with antagonism. Competition against women in the workforce thus had not simply an economic but also a sexual basis.[41]

The problem with asserting that men seek to keep women unequal because women bear children is that it leaves it somewhat unclear how inequality is to be disengaged from biological difference. Audrey Wise's argument that motherhood is *at once* a source of power and of vulnerability has been only intermittently explored in modern feminist discussions in Britain. In the early 1970s the stress was on the vulnerability of motherhood; then in the late 1970s it came to be seen as a focus of power.[42] Audrey Wise's approach indicates how the effort to understand the interaction between subordination in the personal aspects of social existence and subordination at work and in the labour movement was already being made by trade-union women in the late 1960s.[43] This was to be one of the main routes by which women's liberation would try to engage with inequality in employment.

It was frequently pointed out that family responsibilities affected women's conditions of employment and their consciousness of themselves as workers. 'Why are women treated as inferior to men?' asked Kathleen Ennis in *Women's Voice* in 1972. 'Obviously it has a lot to do with the fact that our main job in life is to be wives and mothers.'[44] Domestic responsibility explains why some women take part-time low-paid jobs, but it does not account for the fact that women as a group, including the single and childless, remain in a worse position than their male equivalents. To say that discriminatory attitudes determine the kinds of jobs women do is also a partial explanation, for in an emergency like wartime, or when it is profitable, these prejudices suddenly prove to be unexpectedly flexible. You end up with a circular question. Do social attitudes decide women's employment, or is it women's economic subordination that creates the attitudes?

In the early 1970s, in her pamphlet *Women and Workers' Control*, Audrey Wise connected women's low economic status as workers with their consciousness of themselves in society:

> Low wages for women . . . means more than lack of money, important though this is. It also means lack of self-respect and self-confidence . . . It has kept them docile in their relations with employers – and thus low pay preserves low pay.
>
> The whole organization and culture of our society is geared to making and keeping women submissive and subservient. The trade-union movement both helps to do this and is also deeply damaged by it.[45]

She argued that the under-valuing of women's paid employment meant that the care and nurture of the young - also 'women's work' – were under-valued in society. As early as 1969 she called for the equal sharing of domestic work.[46] But the argument was usually posed the other way round – that it was women's responsibility for unpaid domestic duties that led to the under-valuing of their work outside the home. In 1975 the Manchester Women's Liberation Group said, 'The myth that women are best suited to domestic duties determines the type of job they are expected to do outside the home, as shown by the great numbers of women in the service industries.'[47] The comparison with domestic work has been made in descriptions of many 'women's' jobs. A discontented secretary complained in a letter to *Spare Rib* in 1975:

> The work does not only consist of typing etc. but making cups of tea, sewing buttons on jackets, booking holidays for the man's family, covering up for the boss's faults in general, and lastly but certainly foremost, looking your best at all times. In fact, in many cases the secretary is just a substitute 'wife', the only difference being the salary at the end of the month.[48]

Women's domestic and sexual position in society clearly affects how paid work is divided and rewarded. But again it cannot provide a complete explanation for women's position in employment. For one thing, it is evident that such analogies are historically changeable. During the Second World War industrial jobs previously thought to embody masculinity were suddenly discovered to resemble women's domestic work.[49]

Feminists rejected the argument that women's inferior position in the workforce was due to lack of militancy and pointed to the difficulties women experience in joining and participating in trade unions, partly because of the unions' bureaucratic structure and partly because they are dominated by men. They may not formally exclude women, but in their organization, atmosphere and culture they can be alien institutions for women workers. In the first half of the 1970s unions were seen as contributing to women's subordination, but not as its cause. The exception was Selma James's pamphlet *Women, the Unions and Work*, in which she maintained that trade unions were a block to women's autonomous organization and a cause of women's apathy at work. This was received with considerable disagreement in 1972.[50] By the late 1970s, however, the prevailing tone had changed. In 1978 Beatrix Campbell and Valerie Charlton argued in 'Work to Rule' that trade unions were part of capitalism's incorporation of the 'patriarchal system'. They noted

> the intervention of the craft-defensive male trade union movement in excluding women from the labour process. A singular feature of this process seems to have been men's assertion of their wage as the family wage.[51]

Both these statements rested on one nineteenth-century example. But the arguments took off to a life of their own. They were part of a shift among feminists away from theory based on social relationships within capitalism and towards an emphasis on male workers' responsibility for women's subordination at work. In 'Capitalism, Patriarchy, and Job Segregation', Heidi Hartman stated that male workers have an interest in perpetuating job segregation by sex. Low wages for women keep them dependent on and subordinate to men at work and home. Men's power in the unions had given them the means of asserting their gender.[52]

There are specific examples of this craft control, as Cynthia Cockburn describes in her book about the printing industry, *Brothers*. But there are several problems with generalizing from these to find an explanation for women's inequality. Exclusionary craft tradition is not the only strand within trade unionism, which has included large democratic movements of unskilled and semi-skilled workers and has supported social and political campaigns – including that for women's suffrage. Even within the craft tradition there have been varying politics. As Ruth Milkman observed in the mid-1980s, an approach that *only* notes craft exclusion is one-sided. She said that Heidi Hartman

> is unquestionably correct in identifying the predominant historical pattern as one of male workers' (and unions') chauvinism vis-à-vis women workers. But there have also been instances where male workers actively fought to eliminate sexual inequality from the labour market.[53]

Ironically, in the 1970s some of these instances were recorded in British women's liberation periodicals that reported women's strikes.[54] Irene Bruegel pointed out another snag in seeing craft practices simply as anti-women. In a talk on 'Sexual Divisions and Labour Market Processes' at the Sex and Class Group of the Conference of Socialist Economists in January 1980 she commented, 'While there is evidence of the wholesale exclusion of women from certain trades, exclusionary tactics were also used by men against men.'[55] She observed that distinctions have also been made between single women, women with dependants and married women; exclusion had not just been directed against women as women.[56] Charlene Gannagé argued in her study of the Toronto clothing industry that it is too simple to talk in general terms of male trade unionists creating job segregation. We need to ask instead,'. . .what men in what institutions, and in whose interest, structure the labour force along gender lines?'[57] Part of the problem is that the trade unions are seen by some feminists as a monolithic structure pursuing a single set of aims, whereas in fact of course they consist of many different groups – for instance, men and women, black people and white, rank-and-file members and officials – with varying interests and points of view, acting in contrary ways in various historical circumstances.

In the earlier days of the women's liberation movement, feminist explanations of women's subordination at work were being formed in an atmosphere of enthusiasm for change. By the late 1970s it was less possible to be hopeful. Neither legislation nor the organization of women at work was really tackling the inequality of most women workers and the concentration of women, including many black women, in low-paid jobs. The debate about the cause of this continuing inequality took on a greater emotional intensity in response to the urgency of finding some means of breaking through the apparent impasse. The increasing emphasis on the 'male' trade unions' role in keeping women in a lower position can be seen as a reaction to the sense of powerlessness engendered by the situation. It was also part of a growing ideological tendency within feminism to see men as directly responsible for women's oppression.

There is a problem in the construction of the query: why are women subordinated at work? The form in which it is cast tends to imply a single, universal and ahistorical determinant. There has been a tendency for those in pursuit of a 'source' for subordination to push its origins back in time. Indeed one perplexed group of community development workers studying women's work in North Tyneside found themselves holding forth on the historic struggles of Boadicea and blamed it all on the Romans.[58] It is hard enough to examine how hierarchy appears in the labour force when we have comtemporary data. Once we are forced to rely on a valiant queen of the Ancient Britons as an index of women's experience of employment we are on shaky ground!

Suppositions about the causes of women's subordination do not contain any definite answers, they provide questions to test out in particular contexts. Feminism can thus contribute a deeper understanding of how a combination of factors decides the structure of a particular workforce. As Ruth Milkman put it, 'The development of an industry's pattern of employment by sex reflects the historically specific economic, political and social constraints which are operative at the time when that industry's labour market initially takes shape.[59] Veronica Beechey has observed that this can mean noting disunity among women as a group: '. . .we know far too little about the differences between women of different classes, races and ethnic groups, and have not yet developed a theoretical framework which can adequately account for these differences'.[60]

Along with awareness of difference among women has come a realization that the questions feminists have asked carry limitations.[61] When the women's movement emerged, the need to examine what was specific about women workers was vital because male ascendancy had meant the prevalence of studies which assumed that the male worker represented workers in general. Against this feminists asserted that the working class has two sexes. Judy Wajcman has suggested, however, that attitudes found among women workers need to be compared with men's attitudes to work in equivalent occupations.[62] For instance, many unskilled men stress the family's importance to them as a source of value and fulfilment. Male public service workers like ambulance men can believe in the caring aspect of their jobs. Veronica Beechey has shown that by interpreting women's consciousness of work in terms of the family, and men's consciousness in terms of labour relations, we fall into a dualism between private and public spheres: 'We need instead to allow for the possibility that both women's and men's consciousness of themselves as workers is affected by both their workplace and their familial experiences.'[63] In the early 1970s Audrey Wise's 'Trying to Stay Human' did in fact attempt to delineate the differences in women's consciousness at work while holding on to what men and women had in common. She suggested that women were more likely to complain about conditions and relations which men accepted. But she added that there was a shared problem of acquiescence: 'It's difficult to get all workers, men and women, to realize that they don't really need the boss and it doesn't seem to me that we make this difficult job any easier by behaving as though we lived in a strictly sex-segregated world.'[64] She was drawing on the practical experience of trying to organize low-paid workers of both sexes, whereas most of the feminist theories about women's subordination have come from the experience of *distinguishing* women's oppression from men's.

Feminist writing on women and work has not been exclusively preoccupied with the search for the sources of oppression *vis à vis* men. There have been efforts to analyse how capitalist society is changing and what impact this has on women's employment. Issues like control over work, technology, cuts in state services, privatization, unemployment, casualization and the growth of low-paid work have preoccupied feminists, for women's situation is affected by general changes in the organization of work and the nature of the economy.

Women have been the focus of crucial changes in capitalist society. Anne Showstack-Sassoon noted in 1982 that a major structural change had occurred in the pattern of work: 'The norm today is for women to have a dual role: in the home and in paid labour.'[65] The increase in women's paid employment had been in the service, state or clerical sectors and in part-time work. She went on to observe:

And yet, although women are in the labour force on this massive scale, society as a whole has not really accepted this fact of life; the domestic sphere, the world of work, the welfare state are all organized *as if* women were continuing a traditional role. Women remain the backbone of domestic labour; the world of work is organized around a 'male model' which assumes one human being at work for 40 hours a week (plus commuting and possible overtime) plus a partner available full-time for domestic tasks; the institutions and practices of the welfare state are organized around the same traditional model of work and domestic life.[66]

Women's labour also plays a key role in the international movement of capital which is restructuring production globally. Swasti Mitter described how multinationals have embarked on the automation of some forms of labour-intensive repetitive work for which cheap female labour was needed. An accompanying development has been the decentralization of production and the growth of a new form of domestic industry. So the concentration of capital in new technology can be combined with an adaptation of the much older 'putting-out' system:

> The alternative strategy is to channel the work from factories to homeworkers. The death of the factory rather than of the work is the order of the day – a dramatic rise in homeworking is perhaps the most important way that the structure of employment is changing today – and it is no longer confined to the Third World countries.[67]

These attempts to grasp how shifts in the economy affect the circumstances of women's work can indicate the potential for action. But feminists have come up against stumbling blocks in moving from an analysis of what is happening to an assessment of what is to be done. As Sally Alexander remarked in her introduction to Marianne Herzog's account of piecework in Germany, 'It is easier to describe women's work than to speculate how change might come about. . .'[68] It has also been difficult, given all the interconnecting elements in women's oppression and exploitation at work, to find a strategic focus. Jean Gardiner asked in 1975, 'At which point are we most likely to begin to break the vicious circle women are in as both domestic and wage workers?'[69] Over a decade later the question actually appears harder to answer.

Lurking behind the practical and strategic problems is the lack of a theory which can take on the whole range of human activity. Marxism emphasizes the significance of production. Some modern feminists have protested the limits of this view by prioritizing domestic life over employment or gender over class. Others have adapted to the older formulation by simply adding reproduction on to production. The practical struggles of the women's movement have repeatedly come up against the need for a more complete conception of social existence. Cynthia Cockburn has stressed the need to bring 'into a single focus our experience of class and gender'.[70] She argues that there has been a 'tendency to try and mesh together two static structures, two hierarchical systems'.[71] She suggests that this has been unhelpful and we should pay more attention to the 'process of mutual definition in which men and women are locked' and to the 'processes of mutual creation'.[72]

An impediment to re-thinking the connection between material and social existence has been the reduction of 'the material' to 'the economic' or even just 'waged work'. A conceptual split between culture and this narrowed vision of material life has divested the family and household of their material aspects. Feminists have implicitly contested this equation of the economic with waged work, but the demarcation has a persistent theoretical hold. In fact, as Cynthia Cockburn indicates, 'the economic' is too narrow; work is rather a material activity within which human beings form assumptions and conceptions about themselves and others in relation to society.[73] A related issue is that of how to approach women's consciousness as workers. It is not just a matter of acquiring ideas but of internalizing assumptions in a personal way. Sally Alexander has argued that 'the sexual division of labour is a historical relationship which structures both economic relations and unconscious mental processes.'[74]

Charting one's own, never mind other people's, 'unconscious mental processes' is an elusive venture. Yet feminists have stumbled towards a recognition that consciousness at work is intimately bound up with a wider and more personal conception of ourselves. This is an insight of considerable political significance. However, it has not been sufficiently theorized as a means of understanding the relation of consciousness and ideology to material existence. There has been a recurring tension between a political ideal of what women's consciousness 'should' be and the analysis of how consciousness is expressed. In addition, there is a serious and widespread confusion not only among feminists but in the whole radical movement about what we want from work and what kind of economy we can make which would not be hierarchical, unequal, unjust and exploitative of people's creative capacities.

A new vision of material life and culture is not just a subject for scholarly thought. If large numbers of women in working-class manual and service jobs were to be actively involved not only in protesting the conditions of their labour but in developing the rich and varied policies and alternatives which could best express their needs, we would indeed begin to alter social existence and shake up the 'common sense' that confines human beings to labouring for a pittance. Then, for sure, we would see 'more than the promise of a dream'.

11
What's in a Job?

In the popular media 'Women's Lib' still tends to mean successful career women. In fact, several fundamentally different approaches to the subject of work appeared in the women's movement in Britain from the early 1970s. These divisions, which had also occurred among earlier feminists, were partly caused by the real strategic problems of demanding access to a man's world while insisting that it should be changed. When women's liberation re-emerged as a movement in the 1960s an optimistic liberal feminist assumption that work, or more specifically a career, was in itself emancipatory, prevailed. A gradual progress in capitalist society, towards freedom and equality of opportunity was assumed.[1] The new movement opposed these ideals as having no relationship to the lives of working-class women, especially women with children.[2] In the early women's liberation discussions on work there was an acute self-consciousness about class. Leonora Lloyd described this in her pamphlet *Women Workers in Britain*, published by Socialist Woman Publications in the early 1970s:

> First, many women felt that they should get their own problems, which they saw as distinct, sorted out first. Second, they felt that being middle class, without any experience of working-class life and conditions of work, they had no credentials for getting involved – they would be accused of being patronizing. Third, they felt that any involvement in any industrial campaign raised more questions than it answered; such as whether we should enrol women in bureaucratic, male-dominated unions, which would only disillusion them, etc. Fourth was the purely practical question of how women not involved in industry could get in touch and help women who were.[3]

In practice the paralysis did not last long. The tradition of labour-movement politics in Britain had a powerful effect. women's liberation groups got involved with women's struggles at work in many ways, campaigning for better pay and conditions, supporting strikes, and publicizing action and conditions in women's liberation publications. Plays, films, festivals, research groups were developed as back-up for women trade unionists. Feminists organized in their own, mainly white-collar, unions and influenced trade-union politics. Some also took manual working-class jobs. However, amidst all this activity and the great mountain of writing on work that has emerged since those early years, there has been considerable argument about how feminists should see work in women's lives. Behind these disagreements are quite different visions of the kind of society we should be aiming towards. Is this envisaged as one in which everyone is fully involved in paid employment with good pay, or one in which the hours of paid labour are greatly reduced? Do women have to become more completely integrated into the paid labour force in order to be economically independent and 'militant' workers? Or are there some advantages in women's contact with children and elderly people in the community which might be the basis for a better structure to society?

These questions were not entirely new, of course. Older ideas about the means of achieving women's emancipation interacted with the new feminism of the women's liberation movement. As early as the 1870s Marxists had rejected feminist assertions about the primacy of 'sex oppression' and maintained that the abolition of capitalism would emancipate women. One strand of Marxism, following Engels, tended to be optimistic about the potential of women's involvement in the labour force. Marxists still stressed that work enabled women to organize and challenge capitalism – despite considerable evidence that this was not an automatic process because of the kinds of jobs women did and women's position in the family. Consequently the Marxist tradition also recognized that equality with men at work involved changing women's position in the family.

Ideas of how this should be done, however, still returned to themes developed in the socialist movement in the late nineteenth and early twentieth centuries. It was assumed that paid professionals should take over child care and domestic work. The extension of the state's responsibility for welfare was seen as unproblematical under socialism and as a necessary reform in capitalism – an assumption that we have seen was not accepted by the women's liberation movement on the whole. Also, the proposal to collectivize housework had been partially overtaken by the development of domestic labour-saving appliances as commodities in capitalism. The desire for both parents to be involved *more* with children was hardly raised before the modern women's movement. The reorganization of work and life which this would require was persistently dismissed as utopian by women who remained closer to the Marxist approach to the 'woman question'.

In this tradition Leonora Lloyd argued in the pamphlet *Women Workers in Britain* that the aim should be to 'enable women to take a full part in the working force'.[4] Child-care facilities provided by the state were seen as the answer. She presented women's domestic role as a negative factor which prevented organization and restricted the desire for change. At the Skegness Women's Liberation Conference in 1971 Anna Paczuska spoke for the International Socialists (now the Socialist Workers' Party) in linking liberation with work:

> For us in women's liberation, the right of women to work is an important demand. We do not necessarily think that working women are liberated, but we understand that the right to work brings many women immense social gain as well as being vital economically.[5]

When campaigning through trade unions for the demands of the Working Women's Charter began in 1974 the focus was also on women gaining access to work on the same terms as men, along with better nurseries and social benefits. This implicitly downgraded the women's liberation concerns about changing the division of labour and struggling for a new balance between care in the family and paid employment. The Charter was supported by many feminists, but often with an undercurrent of distrust and uneasiness because of its disregard for the need to change the organization of work and the relationships between men and women in society.

The emphasis on the 'right to work' was thus a common feature of the campaigns in the mid-1970s which brought many young women from both colleges and the white-collar unions into women's liberation politics. These campaigns also tried to extend the narrow class basis of the consciousness-raising groups by involving working-class women either in Charter groups or in *Women's Voice*, a paper published by the International Socialists. This approach to work coexisted and collided both with the more tentative tone of the early women's liberation groups – which questioned whether work was the answer to women's subordination – and with the emphatic ideological rejection of work as inherently oppressive in capitalism which appeared in the various libertarian Marxist currents in women's liberation.

In September 1976 the International Socialists organized a 'Right to Work March' to the TUC in Brighton. Women on the march wore badges with the slogan 'A Woman's Right to Work'. Anny Brackx, who reported the demonstration for *Spare Rib*, declared, 'When I first saw people with "A Woman's Right to Work" pinned on their jackets I thought – bad joke – it's about time women felt they had the right to sit back.'[6] She was concerned that many women would feel such a demand denied the labour involved in housework. Nor did she believe we could assume that women's 'specific oppression of being servants of men and children will end with the collapse of capitalism'.[7] Anny Brackx described how she got into an argument with one of the marchers, 'Celia'. Their debate has a wider resonance in the collision within the women's liberation movement of quite different political objectives. Anny Brackx thought that 'working on a conveyor belt sounded more like a punishment than a right to fight for, especially if it meant cramming in the housework later'. Celia summoned Marx – the unemployed cannot withdraw their labour – they have no power – women are isolated at home - only when they get together with other workers outside can they organize against capitalism and change their situation.[8]

The rejection of both work and the family had been a feature of the revolutionary politics of the late 1960s. It was seen as part of the 'Great Refusal' which, rather than asking for improvements within the capitalist system, demanded the transformation of the whole society in single gigantic sweep. At the first Women's Liberation Conference in Oxford, early in 1970, the anonymous authors of one paper said:

> We're not looking for a change in the distribution of existing roles between men and women (pram pushing for men, careers for women); what's needed is an attack on the totality of life styles – to destroy all roles . . . Working wives are curiously expected to be also full-time mothers. Thus women become double slaves, domestic slaves and producer slaves.[9]

And, more succinctly, 'Fuck Work.'[10]

During the Oxford Conference a woman sprayed on a wall, 'Women in Labour Keep Capital in Power', much to the irritation of the University authorities. It must have been a resilient spray-paint for the slogan remained over the years as a defiant expression of that strand in late 1960s libertarian Marxism that rejected compromise in the belief that all gains were co-opted by capital. In the changed atmosphere of the 1970s the politics of the 'Great Refusal' puzzled a new generation. A friend brought up in Oxford told me that as a schoolboy he used to pass the slogan in bemusement, assuming it was some kind of right-wing assertion of capitalists attacking Labour Party women.

The rejection of work also appeared among women active in the Claimants' Union in the early 1970s. A paper on 'Work, Women and Unemployment' for a Claimants' Union Conference in the early 1970s insisted that 'women are never out of work',[11] and argued that men and women should share domestic work and child care equally. They saw women's liberation as part of a challenge to the work ethic that assumed paid labour in capitalism was a source of power and dignity. Behind the critique of work was the belief that it was not sufficient to resist on capital's terms. The starting point should be working-class people's needs. An argument was developed for a minimum living wage for women and men regardless of whether they had jobs.

Exponents of this idea included the Wages for Housework grouping. In 1972 Selma James's *Women, the Unions and Work* had demanded the right to work less and a guaranteed income for women and for men,[12] which she equated with wages for housework: 'All housekeepers are entitled to wages (men too).'[13]

New Left groups abroad, particularly in Italy and France, were also debating these issues. For instance, in the early 1970s criticism of the assumption that a full-time job was the answer appeared in a duplicated pamphlet entitled *Les Femmes et le salariat* ('Women and Waged Labour'), by a woman from the French women's liberation movement.[14] Marina Lewycka, reflecting on these approaches to work in the early 1980s in the *Beyond the Fragments Bulletin*, put them in a wider context:

> . . . Leftists of the 'workers' autonomy' school already realized that working-class struggle for higher wages was the main motor of capitalist expansion. But, they said, the workers' strategy was to try and overtake capitalism at its own game – to go for money unrelated to increased production, and through sabotage and insubordination to attack production itself. (Wages for Housework was the feminist expression of

this tendency.) In this way the 'falling rate of profit' spiral described by Marx would be intensified and brought to crisis pitch.[15]

There was considerable fluidity in the debate on women and work until the late 1970s. Argument moved back and forth between the polarities. In the middle ground, many feminists accepted the significance of work for women while seeking to change its conditions. They also attempted to struggle with the tension between women's economic need to go out to work and the domestic circumstances that made this difficult. 'If you have a job and a child and any sense of yourself, you are a walking triangle,'[16] says a nurse in the film *About Time* by the Women's Film Group and the Wages for Housework Campaign in the mid-1970s. Women caring for children and going out to work have argued for shorter hours and the reorganization of work to acknowledge women's domestic labour because the two demands on their time and energy simply do not 'fit'. This dilemma has cut across class divisions. Frances Cairncross described in 1981 how the only page she could edit on the *Guardian* was, ironically, the Women's Page, as it alone had a lunchtime deadline and she had two small children.[17]

Consideration of women's domestic responsibilities has given rise to some awkward questions about work for wages. For example, Sandra Peers described how some women at a Newcastle TUC School in the early 1970s were anxious that equal pay might involve taking on night work. Others wanted to do night work because it was easier to arrange child care. She struggled to find less grim alternatives:

> To this I argued that women with pre-school children should not *have* to work (everybody agreed) and demanded adequate state maintenance without means test for women with small children (very few agreed here – they said it was the husband's responsibility etc.) So, backtracking, I suggested greatly increased family allowances for pre-school children and everybody liked that. They also agreed on the need for good, free or cheap day nurseries. They feared night work would open up more shift work which would mean seeing their children less. . . Several women had accepted the argument that they must work shifts because otherwise the return on capital would be too low. They feared that their factories would close if they refused to do shifts.[18]

The contradictory pressures of work and care have led women to see time as a resource that is denied them and to seek a different division of labour and time. Mal Varley (mother of two) wrote to *Women's Voice* saying she had bought the paper at the 1977 Matlock

Working Women's Festival and thought that with its emphasis on equal pay it did not tackle the problem of how to raise a family and do a job:

> Please can we fight for radical solutions to this problem? I suggest job-sharing is the real answer; people being employed for 3 full days a week, so that husband and wife could share both earning the income and raising the family. Each would have four days at home with the kids, and women would also have the satisfaction of continuing with the social contact at work. Why should women have to choose between a job and a family – men don't.[19]

Audrey Wise argued that the interconnected nature of women's subordination could be used to challenge the narrow and exploitative meaning of work in capitalism. She described a meeting of the Gloucester Trades Council where she had argued that equal pay should be accompanied not only by the retention but by the *extension* of protection – for example, there should be opposition to night shifts for men as well as women. A male trade unionist said that the economy could not afford it: 'Up got a woman – beautiful creature – and said, "If the economy wants me to work night shifts THEN I WANT A DIFFERENT ECONOMY."'[20]

In the Scottish paper *MsPrint*, Eveline Hunter described how the campaign for protective legislation had involved a long history of struggle between workers and employers over shift-working:

> There is little point in arguing for an abstract equality if it is to be the right to be equally exploited at work . . . real equality cannot be sought by downgrading conditions for either sex.[21]

She added that the ban on night work should be extended to men and women covered by the Factory Acts unless it was socially necessary, when workers should have time off to compensate. The CBI claimed that bars on women's night work were 'archaic' but this was a loaded concept of equality – they were keen on equal pay.[22]

The women's liberation movement has repeatedly opposed the inhuman denial of personal life in the existing organization of both men's and women's work. Women have pointed out that shift work makes relationships impossible because couples rarely meet. The circumstances of a partner's work – physical danger, heightened stress, overtime, long hours of travel, shift work, or rotas which change – affect how life can be lived outside work.[23] The existence of a movement which could express the social dissatisfactions of women has created the political basis for a more wide-ranging critique of economic life.

The women's movement has also engaged with what the Notting Hill Women's Liberation Group called 'the needs of the body'. They were describing conditions in the early 1970s at Chesebrough Ponds, a multi-national company in which the workforce was divided by gender, race and ethnicity. The women wanted time to wash; they complained of the lack of any safety provisions and thought they should have better treatment when they were sick.[24] Concern about health has a long feminist tradition in campaigns for protective legislation. But in the modern women's movement it took a few years before the interest in health and control over our bodies expanded into the area of work.[25] This recognition that how worker's bodies are treated and regarded is of importance, and that appearance, behaviour and personal relationships have significant connections with power at work, has extended the concept of worker's control.

American and Australian publications influenced a group of women in the British Society for Social Responsibility in Science to form the Women and Work Hazards Group, which began meeting in 1978. Sheila Brown commented in *Red Rag*:

> Within the Women's Liberation Movement the subject of health has centred very much around the issue of controlling our own bodies and in particular our reproductive functions. However, our health in general terms probably has a great deal more to do with where we live or, more especially, where we work.[26]

The Group discovered, for example, women suffering from exposure to lead in some industries and dust in textile mills. Others were in danger from packing chemicals. The Group showed how hairdressers were affected by toxic sprays, how office workers could become ill from untested chemicals in photocopiers, and how fast repetitive tasks in both factories and offices caused inflammation of the tendons in hands and forearms. They pointed out not only factors which could be harmful to pregnant women and their unborn babies but also the risks to men using pesticides or working with vinyl chloride (used for making PVC) of fathering still-born or handicapped children. They also served as a practical resource

in specific struggles,[27] for instance giving back-up information
to cleaners who were refusing to move asbestos in a London
polytechnic.[28] The Group also argued that the pressure of combining
a job and work at home affected women's health:

> The women's liberation movement has always made health a priority
> issue . . . But we've made little of the necessary link between women's
> health and work. Stress, for example, which may cause tension,
> digestive disorders, depression and heart disease, occurs at high rates
> in women who are under pressure from two jobs: one paid and one
> unpaid.[29]

In *The Heart of the Race* Beverley Bryan, Stella Dadzie and
Suzanne Scafe noted the impact on black women's health of the kinds
of work available to them, the demands of the family, and racism:
'The effects of long hours, shift work and the frequent need to hold
down more than one job in order to support ourselves and our families are made worse by the particular risks associated with the kinds
of jobs we do.'[30] Bad eyesight, exposure to dangerous substances,
moving heavy equipment, working through sickness and pregnancy,
the stress caused by family responsibilities and by racism – all these
factors have cumulative effect: 'Many of the ailments which are
increasingly prevalent among older Black women such as strokes,
arthritis and rheumatism can be traced directly to the stressful, haz-
ardous working conditions we have faced throughout our lives.'[31]
    The fact that some women have been moving into manual jobs
usually seen as 'male' in our society has led to discussion about
how people learn to use their bodies.[32] Men's physical strength has
been used as an argument for women's exclusion, but, while there
clearly are differences, these also exist among men – not all of whom
are strong. It is also often overlooked that some jobs traditionally
associated with women, such as nursing, can involve much heavy
lifting. Confidence in one's physical capacity has been asserted by
feminists as part of a challenge to the idea that certain kinds of work
should remain male preserves. A woman working on a building site
in Islington in the mid-1970s observed that it is often a matter of
knowing the way to lift and move things and not being intimidated
by machines.[33] One day two schoolgirls aged nine and eleven came
by and, seeing her working there, wanted to try working the pulley.
She allowed them to try and showed them how:

The fact that they could do it, and all these men were watching, for me it just totally destroyed the whole thing about women can't do these things. The girls were really thrilled and the men actually looked quite disturbed. It was destroying the image of themselves as the big toughies.[34]

Rebellion against the physical assertion of male power has proved to involve health and safety matters. For instance, women in jobs like building have challenged the tendency of some men to take unnecessary risks with their bodies in order to prove their 'masculinity'.[35]

Women have also contested the power men have gained through control over technology. Feminists have taken part in a wider project to demystify technology and enable people to question how it is conceived, constructed and used.[36] Women's upbringing tends to discourage them from feeling able to acquire scientific and technical skills and learn to handle machinery. Attempts to counteract this have therefore emphasized not only learning but the development of confidence and physical aptitude. Cynthia Cockburn points out that this is not just a matter of education and training but of how boys and girls learn their gender identity throughout childhood.[37]

Another exclusionary tactic has been men's stressing of sexual difference. Jackey Morgan left farming in the North of England and Scotland after eight years. Describing her experiences in the feminist magazine *Cat-Call*, she wrote:

A woman in a man's world gets her eyes prised open – ears too. I was often teased for blushing at the conversations at tea breaks – my blushes mistaken for embarrassment or prudery. How red, how hot I grew for wives, girlfriends, women. Any remark of mine on their behalf only increased the hilarity.[38]

In *Patterns of Discrimination* Sarah Benton probed men's objections to women doing certain jobs in the film industry. Behind the assertions about women's incapacity she found economic fears of unemployment and the reduction of wage-rates, but also a less tangible social discomfort at the breaking up of an all-male work group.[39] Unease at the inclusion of difference is a factor in men's resistance to women entering 'male' jobs. As well as dwelling on men's control, feminist writing on work has thus also described relationships at work in which bonding is important. Vebeka, for instance, commented on Norwegian building workers:

> The men used to climb on the cranes for fun and do other crazy things like that all the time to show off to each other. That's the way they were – they used to play around like children and have a good time with each other at work. They really adored each other.[40]

There is a real difficulty in disentangling forms of control that men exert over women from other ways in which power can be used at work. This is apparent in feminist accounts of hierarchy. Both Anna Pollert in *Girls, Wives and Factory Lives* and Ruth Cavendish in *On the Line*, for example, note the correlation between management and masculinity in many manual jobs. But is women's resentment against management to be interpreted as class consciousness or as opposition to male control?[41] Black women have also pointed to the power of white people in employment hierarchies. In addition, racial and ethnic divisions in a workforce can strengthen management control.[42]

One expression of male power that has been brought into the open because complaint has become possible in the climate of the women's movement is sexual harassment. This has occurred not only where women are taking up 'male' jobs but also in occupations like teaching and clerical work where there are large numbers of women. Sexual harassment takes many forms, from innuendo through unwanted sexual advances to outright assault, but in all cases it involves men's use of power over women in a subordinate position in the workforce or as students.[43]

There has also been discussion of other ways in which social expectations about women's sexuality constrain women's working lives. Just as the 'motherly role' pervades certain forms of women's work, appearance and demeanour are important in a wide range of jobs. Clare Cherrington said of secretarial work, for example, 'While the factory worker just sells her labour, the secretary sells labour plus behaviour.'[44] Joyce Betries described in *Spare Rib* how as a waitress in America she worked a counter window and the tips were good. The other waitresses worked at the back. She did not think much about it until they began calling her 'Miss America'. Gradually she realized that the boss had hired her because she was young and put her on the window tables to attract attention.[45] Sarah Benton also noted in *Patterns of Discrimination* that in some of the TV companies a PA had a 'dolly bird' image.[46] Assumptions about how women should present themselves are not only imposed by employers but also by the public. For instance, Joyce Betries recalled how some customers expected her to smile: 'Some actually tell me to smile. Sometimes when they catch me in the wrong way, I ask them, "Is that an order?" But I've gotten into trouble with the boss for that.'[47]

Women's fears of each others' sexuality can also reinforce stereotyped ideas about what kind of work women can do. *Spare Rib* reported the case of fisherwoman, Sue Hesp, who lost her job on a Stornaway boat because the men's wives opposed her working with their husbands.[48] In an article on 'Nursing and Racism' in *Spare Rib* in 1978, Amrit Wilson gave an account of a student nurse being rebuked by a matron in which concepts of sexual respectability merged with racism:

> A nurse from Barbados recalled how when a student she had been living in the Nurses' Home and had worn clothes which she had brought with her from Barbados. 'Matron said to me, where are you going dressed as a tart?'[49]

Amrit Wilson also described black nurses who were unmarried with children encountering prejudice, and a nurse from Guyana who was getting married to an English doctor being made to feel she was going above her 'station' as a black woman.[50] Appearance and behaviour at work have been an area of complaint and rebellion. Control has operated through the assumption that there is an accepted form of femininity. This necessarily excludes women who do not 'fit'. For example, hotel workers have complained that black women are excluded from the visible jobs, at the reception desk for instance.[51] Another form of discrimination in catering was described by Marisa Casares-Roach when she was a trade-union organizer in the hotel industry: '. . . if some of the girls have to wear trousers because of their religion and management say no, we have to fight for the girls' religious rights'.[52] Even in jobs which have been accepted as women's work, women from ethnic minorities can be made to feel they are there on sufferance. An Irish bus conductor told how a woman passenger had informed her, 'The English are a very tolerant people really, after all we allow you here.'[53]

The use of power to define what is 'normal' has also been resisted by lesbian women. To be a lesbian is not visible in the way being a woman or a black person is. But codes of dress and appearance tend to define 'normality'. Also, an enforced secrecy affects one's consciousness. Lesbians working in caring professions are particularly at risk because here the social ideology of the heterosexual woman as a naturally maternal carer is most dominant. Veronica Pickles was sacked from her job as a student midwife, for example.[54]

Another area of anxiety and prejudice has been made manifest to lesbians who become 'visible'. City stockbrokers H. J. Symons Holdings sacked Louise Boychuk because they maintained that her badge, 'Lesbians Ignite', was 'displaying a wording at our place of business which is distasteful to others and which could be injurious to our best interests if observed by our clients whose goodwill results in the earning of large amounts of overseas currencies beneficial to our country'.[55] It transpired at the industrial tribunal where Louise Boychuk claimed unfair dismissal that she hardly ever saw any of these overseas currency dealers and that there were no complaints about the quality of her work. She explained that she wore her badge so people would not assume she was heterosexual and to show 'a real person behind the fearful word lesbian'.[56] But the chairman invoked Genesis, recounting how Sodom and Gomorrah had earned the Lord's displeasure, until her lawyer pointed out that this went beyond the prerogative of an industrial tribunal.[57]

'Coming out' as a lesbian at work has been an important assertion of gay pride and a challenge to heterosexual assumptions about sexuality and identity. But it can be a frightening and isolating step, especially for women who are likely to face other forms of prejudice and hostility, for example racism. Black lesbians and gay men can also face a conflict of loyalty and 'feel extremely wary of coming out at work because of fear of rejection by other Black workers'.[58] But to remain invisible can exact 'a terrible toll' in constantly living a lie.[59]

Conventions of appearance can exclude women with disabilities from certain forms of work, and also older women. When my sister-in-law was left a widow in her thirties she was told she was too old to work as a receptionist. The authors of *The Heart of the Race* describe the difficulties of black women made redundant from factory work in their forties and fifties who have little chance of finding alternative employment.[60] Florence Keyworth has pointed out how older women can be made invisible in work relationships. Older women lack social esteem partly because they are often poor and powerless, but also because women's status is largely conferred on them by men: 'So when attractiveness to men is at an end, they become non-persons.'[61] Florence Keyworth described an incident which made her realize she was old:

> I was on a reporting job which involved a long wait outside a government ministry in order to interview a delegation following its meeting with a minister. Three young male reporters were also waiting. I had taken a book to read as we sat on the ministry steps. But the three young men amused themselves by observing each young woman who passed, commenting on her physical characteristics and estimating her likely performance in bed. All this was accompanied by much giggling and falling about. At first I thought they resented my presence and were doing this in an attempt to shock me. But as time passed, I realized the truth was something more disconcerting. They had not noticed me. I was invisible.[62]

The women's liberation movement's emphasis on self-definition and control over our bodies has thus opened up the possibility of examining hierarchy and power at work in terms of material circumstances and social relationships in the widest sense.[63] The significance feminists have given to personal experience has created a political medium for protest against inhuman relationships at work – 'We are like battery hens all cramped together,' a northern factory worker told her daughter in an early issue of *Shrew*.[64] Commitment to the politics of personal experience has enabled women to protest when the existing framework of politics provides no language to convey injury. For example, in *The Heart of the Race* a black nurse described how racism can be expressed in everyday encounters:

> I know I was accused of giving preferential treatment to a Black patient once, because there was a Black woman in the ward and her hair needed doing and when I asked her about it she said there was no one to come in and do it for her. I agreed to do it, but the only time I had was during my break, so I did it then. And I was told off. So I told the sister that it was my break and I'd do what I liked with it, it was my business how I chose to spend my own time. But you need a lot of strength and confidence to do that. If you're in a position where you're on a visa or work permit, this is more difficult.'[65]

A politics which gives significance to the personal does not, however, protect people from pain when they are defined as deviant.

Hilary Stafford wrote to *Spare Rib* from Kirkby-in-Ashfield, telling of the everyday hurt of having to conceal her sexual orientation:

> I have worked in the gay movement for a few years now but still experience a personal crisis every time I apply for a job. A crisis between honesty and integrity and for once wanting to live on a decent wage instead of social security.[66]

Commitment to politicizing areas of life commonly seen as personal has also stimulated observation of the ways in which women are described and represented by men at work.[67] There is an obvious contradiction between ideas of dignity, control and freedom as workers and the objectified images of women displayed in many workplaces. Feminists have engaged with imagery and sexual fantasy used to subordinate women. Jackey Morgan, for instance, described the horrors of the slaughterhouse as one of her worst experiences as a farmworker:

> I shall never forget a visit I once made to a particularly obscene abattoir – I had to go into the men's hut which was situated in the middle of a bloody courtyard full of putrefying corpses in various stages of mutilation – inside this hut four or five men were drinking tea from flasks and all over the inside walls above their filthy heads were pinned up gory photographs of naked women, their pink and bloated flesh indistinguishable and interchangeable with the corpses outside – the parallels were horrifying.[68]

These pictures are, however, open to differing interpretations. The interplay of sexual fantasy with the circumstances of work is elusive. It could be that the men regarded their pin-ups like the animal flesh they had to butcher. On the other hand the naked women who surrounded them at tea-break could represent a thwarted longing for all that was denied and forbidden at work. Pornographic fantasy can be seen both as an extension of control and subjugation and, to quote Muriel Dimen in *Surviving Sexual Contradictions*, as an 'act of make-believe conjuring up what we desire'.[69] Ros Carne described how in a Yorkshire factory the women's cohesion as a group was expressed in a defiant sexuality:

> Comradeship on the track was really startling. On my first station, before they transferred me to the Jelly Pots, there was time for a smoke and a chat . . . sex was the favourite topic. Medium and even

hard-core porn passed up and down the line . . . given a moment women threw their arms around each other or pinched a nearby bum. These women were amazing. They worked their guts out from 7.30 – 4.30 every day, often all evening and weekend too if they had families, but they managed to remain human. They'd complain about the work of course, it was boring, often exhausting and totally alienating, but knowing they'd probably never get out, they'd found ways to deal with it. They accepted me, thinking I was probably a student, though at first they were rather apprehensive. 'I bet you think we're terribly wicked,' giggled a rather attractive young blonde woman as she leafed her way through *Men Only*. Wicked? I found it all amazing, not to mention the surreptitious Guinness she'd been swigging under the track when the supervisor turned her back.[70]

Sent off to the Jelly Pots, Ros Carne found less hedonism and much tighter supervision even within the same factory.[71] Her account indicates that images can be given very different meanings. Thus, even though pornography expresses male-defined sexual fantasy, it can be a means of conjuring women's desire because it symbolizes what is forbidden in our lived reality.

Marianne Herzog, in *From Hand to Mouth*, described rather different fantasies of some German women factory workers:

To put up with piecework the women take refuge in dreams in which they can express all their longings. Frau Winterfeld dreams of an ice-cream parlour of which she is the proprietor. She imagines pastries and ice-cream sundaes and invents names for them. Once, when she had a friend working next to her, she told her about her ice-cream parlour and they agreed to share it and to go on dreaming about it together. Frau Lange dreams of the relationships she had before marriage and how different everything might have been had she married someone different from her husband. . .

. . .Piecework dreams go back mostly to the past. When they are needed, one fetches them; when the bell goes for a break, they disappear. Immediately after the break there are no dreams, then they are needed again and collected, and while you are dreaming and welding you suddenly come across a familiar spot on the third or the seventh or the tenth tube and you think, 'Ah, here I am again,' and then you go back to your dreams until a spot like that comes up once more or a conversation starts in your row or there is a break.[72]

But how do we interpret fantasy, play and dreams? Are they strategies of resistance, or of survival and accommodation? Judy

Wajcman is critical of depictions of shop-floor culture as rebellion:

> Are signs of life amongst the work force in themselves subversive?
> Shop-floor culture is as much about adjusting to and making bearable
> the intolerable conditions of most manual labour. If it cannot be said
> to change and improve those conditions then why call it resistance?[73]

Perhaps we might interpret fantasy as both an aid to bearing an
oppressive reality and a potential source of alternative aspirations
– not in the literal sense of imagining a different way to work,
but as a way of cherishing a sense of self that is not geared to
production.

12

Better Times

If you ask people to imagine the kind of work they would like, those who have been led to expect little from society are liable to have quite modest expectations of happiness. It is hard to envisage what you have never known. In a collection of testimonies, *Our Lives: Working Women*, members of the Eden Grove Women's Writing Group in North London describe their visions of work in a book they produced and wrote themselves in a literacy class. Val, who had attended the class for four years and had participated in writing two earlier books published by the group on childbirth and technology, said:

> If I had to get a job I'd go back to the brewery. I liked putting bottles in the machines . . . I'd really like to work in a nursery because I like to be with children. I'd look after them properly – I'm a very patient person. I've never done it because you need qualifications.[1]

Pauline, a young woman with a child, wrote:

> I like looking after children for a couple of days a week and on the other days I would like to work as a telecommunications officer putting in people's telephones. I know a lot about installing phones because I used to watch my boyfriend putting them in and I know it pays good money.[2]

These longings are for work that is better, but they do not express how work might be changed. However, more ambitious conceptions of what work could be like have also emerged from action, in strikes and work-ins, co-ops and self-help projects. Combined with the discussions in women's groups, these experiences have begun to indicate how work might alter. Through them we can see how women's notions have shifted in specific circumstances. Instead of thinking of something a bit better within the existing system of employment, they have caught glimpses of the ways in which the organization of production might change – how relationships need not be hierarchical, how a differing balance between work time and domestic time might exist, how relations between workers and users might be ones of mutual caring. These observations from practice question both the structure and purposes of production and labour.

In March, 1972, 45 women at a shoe manufacturer's in Fakenham, Norfolk were made redundant when the firm was sold to an American company. They decided to take over the factory and 'work in'. Edna Roach, one of the workers, told *Socialist Woman*: 'By working in it makes it a bit different to a sit in; we're actually doing a job of work, so we don't lose our skills.'[3] They decided to diversify their products, and they also sought to communicate and share their skills:

> The women who hadn't made garments before learned as they went along, helping each other out, seeing the product from start to finish. The factory runs as a co-operative, all decisions are made collectively. When a problem comes up they all meet in the centre of the factory floor to talk it out. The atmosphere in their converted church is miles away from the time-clocked, piecework days of Sextons' with husbands and friends popping in to chat, non-stop music and each worker pacing her own work.[4]

Ten years later, when women clothing workers who were made redundant from Lee Jeans in Romford, Essex, decided to form a co-op, they too envisaged how the older women could teach the younger workers a wider range of skills on the machines.[5] In 1981, Janet Payne described how the same desire to break down the division between skilled and unskilled was asserted in an all-women building co-op set up to convert a building in Lambeth which houses a women's training centre.[6] In another instance, in 1973, women and men at the Lip clock factory in France occupied to save their jobs. There again the need to gain access to skills, to share skills and to understand the work process as a whole were asserted. The women at Lip described how relationships changed and time was experienced differently. Reine J. said that when the occupation was over and she knew she would be reinstated she 'had mixed feelings',[7] including fear and regret:

> It meant for me the end of the freedom which had helped us to develop: a fraternal freedom, a freedom of expression, a form of culture which

we acquired talking to all those who visited Lip. Now conformity and punctuality would return – getting up early, running to work, rushing home in the evening to start a new day with your husband and children. In other words I would once again become dependent on a society which doesn't give me the time to think.[8]

But there was also 'pride in having won a hard battle',[9] there was the memory of how work might be different, and there were bonds of love: '. . .the great friendship which arose during the struggle is still alive'.[10] Another woman said, 'We loved the factory'[11] – an almost inconceivable sentiment in existing industrial relationships.

In less dramatic circumstances, the attempt to structure work-time differently has appeared in negotiations for job-sharing, flexible hours and a shorter working week.[12] Early in 1980 engineering workers, men and women, at Ronson Lighters in Surrey, the Isle of Wight and the North-east won a 35-hour week. Helen Hewland interviewed two of the women involved in the negotiations. Pat Scott told her she hoped it would mean men did more at home. But considerations about the women's time seemed more pressing. They were pleased they got an extra hour off on Fridays, which allowed them to get home before the rush to the shops. There was talk of a four-day week, which they thought would be good, but they were anxious not to lose time in the dinner-hour – again because of shopping: 'So the shop stewards are talking to the management about extending a shop in the factory canteen and making its prices competitive with local shops.'[13]

Another recurring aspiration has been for the democratization of work to combine with the improvement of relationships with the users of a service. In 1985 Liz Heron interviewed Margery Bane, an ancillary worker at Hayes College Hospital, in connection with the GLC's backing for health emergency campaigns. Margery Bane made a distinction between production and service work:

> . . .a hospital occupation is completely different from a factory occu-pation; we tried to keep patients' relatives involved all the time. The occupation committee was totally open, anyone would come along to meetings . . . pickets had their own committees too. . .towards the end of the occupation pickets were coming forward and saying they wanted more and more responsibility . . . It was lovely manning it ourselves. I think it was run much better . . . We were like one big happy family. It was a joy to come to work. It was your hospital.[14]

In November 1977 about 80,000 people marched to Parliament
to protest against the Labour government's public spending cuts.
There was a rally at the Elizabeth Garrett Anderson women's
hospital, which was being occupied to avert closure. Among the
crowd was a tremendous gathering of women workers, many of
them quite unaccustomed to militancy. They came from children's
hospitals and old people's homes, nurseries, the home-help services.
They included cleaners, nurses, social workers, play-group workers,
from Hereford and Yorkshire, Wales and Scotland, and they came
out of desperation because their pay was low or they could not do
their jobs properly because of closure and cuts in facilities.[15] At
the EGA the women patients hung out of the windows to wave
the demonstrators on their way. Claire Fazan and Ann Oosthuizen
who were watching, wrote in *Spare Rib*,

> Out-patients went with the march. Ms Marlow, a pensioner from
> Camden, said, 'What I think about this hospital is that you are
> treated like a human being, which is more than at most places, and
> I'm not going to any other hospital. If I could walk I'd go on the
> march.[16]

Links with users have also been made in private services run
on co-operative lines. Co-ops can be a means of democratizing
work. They can also change the nature of the service provided.
Roz Wollen, Ros Wall and Annette Williams run a garage in
Sheffield. At 'Gwenda's Garage' they try to distribute work so
that they learn from one another, and they explain what is wrong
clearly to customers, admitting their own mistakes. Roz Wollen
said, 'We like to feel that women can come in here and not
feel intimidated.'[17] Jan Clarke reported in *Spare Rib*: 'They can
also chat to disabled drivers and advise on the pros and cons of
special disabled vehicles, how to adapt ordinary cars for different
disabilities and the different schemes you can go through for
motobility.'[18]

The attempt to demystify technology has been an important
aspect of women's efforts to extend control over work. From it
has emerged strong criticism of the use of technology in ways that
reduce people's control and ability to do a good job. Jean Sargeant,
a SOGAT member who refused to go and work at Rupert Murdoch's
Wapping plant in 1986, contested his claim that all the Wapping
strikers were

overpaid printers addicted to old-fashioned technology. I show people my last pay slip with its figure of £123 for take-home pay and I tell them that as for new technology I would be glad to have some. My manual typewriter at the *Sunday Times* may not be as old as I am, but like me it's certainly known better days – or should I say better *Times*. But then in Rupert Murdoch's hands new technology is for putting people out of work.[19]

It has become evident in various contexts that the nature and use of technology are crucial issues in women's liberation. There has been opposition to forms of technology that degrade and devalue people – for example in giving birth. The same process also reduces the worker's human involvement and skill. The Association of Radical Midwives made this point in a paper at the 1979 Socialist Feminist Conference in London:

> Our main fear is that midwives are losing confidence in their own abilities as independent practitioners . . . An increased use of techno-logical apparatus, e.g. fetal monitoring equipment, has led to (a) a lack of confidence on the midwife's part as she feels her basic skills are no longer relevant, (b) decreased learning by students of these basic skills as they are no longer being taught.[20]

The Radical Midwives saw the intervention of technology not only as de-skilling their work and undermining its value but as breaking up the vital relationship of the midwife with the woman in labour: 'The word "midwife" is Anglo-Saxon for "with woman" – which is where we should be, yet our education and our experience is leading us away from this.'[21] The midwives' complaint indicates the low value set by society on creative nurture. The arrangements that determine how we live and associate seem to be based on contempt for the most profound human needs and experiences.

The same ineptitude is apparent in the value given to the cultivation of simple delights. In our society little attention is paid to the weaving of sensuous pleasures into everyday life – especially that of the poor. Trisha Ziff described a form of caring which is low-paid – hairdressing in a working-class salon in London. But this work could have dimensions of disregarded meaning:

> My job revolves around women, and how they think they appear, or wanting to change how they look. I think it's a very important job. I enjoy making women beautiful for themselves. Women enjoy

looking at each other, even heterosexual women, that is what I think is important. I like to think that's what my job is about. I do it to make women feel good. I don't do it to make women be how men would like to see them.

I think women go to the hairdresser's to feel better. It's a sort of therapy, a time to relax and sit down for a change, have a chat, and not worry about the housework or the kids or husbands. For pensioners it's also a time to be with other people.[22]

Control, work relations and the purpose of work have also been questioned in accounts of more privileged and powerful jobs. Mary McCann became critical of the purposes of her scientific work as a woman physicist at Harwell Atomic Energy Research Establishment. At first she was confident and young, shrugging off 'discrimination' and breaking through into the challenge of her work on a huge accelerator, stimulated by her colleague – 'a fiery, sparky young man. Everything I say sets him off. I am very attracted to him.'[23] They worked hard together, competitively and under pressure – but she observed certain differences in their behaviour:

I have more than a touch of the female desire to serve. It is all a little like an imitation old-fashioned marriage – I still have a fearful, magical image of men which prevents me meeting them on equal terms.[24]

Dwelling amidst polarities of which she was barely conscious, Mary McCann became strained and was ill. Away from work she realized she had been 'denying' many aspects of life, despite the satisfaction of the intellectual challenge and stimulation of her work. She tried to reassert the importance of 'closeness to other people'.[25] She also wanted to face 'the question of how to use my head and my aggression in a balanced way'.[26] She came to the conclusion that in her scientific training there had been

arrogance, narrowness. A closed circle. Political unawareness. I read about and faced up to the atom bomb. I think perhaps pure science can go too far.[27]

The attention given in the women's movement to personal experience and specific circumstances has brought about a sustained effort to explore and re-define the received wisdom expressed in old radical slogans about socially useful production, the right to work and workers' control. Women's liberation has put back on to the agenda the meaning of labour and the quality of human working relationships. The Cambridge women's liberation magazine *Bloody Women* declared in the early 1970s, for instance:

> The point to stress is that women being free to go out to work is not sufficient for their emancipation . . . Equal rights are not enough as long as work is separated from pleasure, sexuality from humanity, and production is geared to profit not to need.[28]

The emphasis on 'control' in women's liberation politics has interacted with the insistence on changing the relations involved in production and the reproduction of life. An office worker, Janet Sass, wrote to *Spare Rib* in 1973:

> While the women's movement has helped many of us gain control over our personal lives, it hasn't helped us gain control over the 40 or 20 hours a week we spend in jobs outside the home – and 1/3 of us work in offices. What good will it do women to escape a restricting home life only to find themselves in restricting jobs?[29]

Audrey Wise brought into women's liberation the political concerns of the Institute for Workers' Control, which during the 1960s was discussing the implications of democratizing work. In her pamphlet *Women and Workers' Control* she asserted:

> Women are in fact deeply alienated from the uses to which technology is put. They say, 'Who wants to go to the moon – what about houses or a cure for cancer?' They have tremendous radical potential which is almost untapped and which would become of great importance if and when we really start to challenge not only the ownership, but also the purpose of production.[30]

The radical potential of the desire for alternatives in women's liberation was suggested by the Marxist philosopher Herbert Marcuse in an interview on British television just before he died. He made the distinction between positing an essentially female utopianism and recognizing that aspects of women's historical circumstances could point towards a critique which also conceives how society might be fundamentally reconstituted. He stressed that this utopian capacity for creative imagining was a great asset, to be used by all who wished for a better society.

It is this ability to desire beyond what we know that can provide an impetus for re-shaping society as a whole rather than merely pushing for more for a particular section. Embarrassed negligence towards aspiration has been a weakness of socialism in modern times, so sources for alternatives are particularly needful. The women's liberation movement has contributed to the mapping of discontent and desire in many dimensions simultaneously. The mapping is partial and sometimes contradictory, but it is of great social value in the effort to make radical changes in how we live. One of the strongest cards held by people with a vested interest in keeping things as they are is the ability to make people feel foolish and ashamed because they want alternatives. Part of their power consists in marking the boundaries of admissable goals. These boundaries can be moved when people take collective action in rebellion against a particular constraint.

In this process what we remember, and how we remember, is not a matter of chance. The significance is often measured according to whether they are uttered by powerful and important people – who are of course mainly men. Implicit in the rebellion of women has been a re-coding of significance, yet this is constantly in conflict with the prevailing assumptions about how concepts are developed. 'Learning through doing' is an old adage popular in the working-class movement and re-discovered by women's liberation. The ideas and language of doing are important because they increase the impetus for change, and their chronicling should be more seriously regarded.

Another source of power is through personal narratives – channels of communication which pass on historical memories of resistance. Black women in Britain communicate not only their immediate grievances but a history of defiance. In *The Heart of the Race* Beverley Bryan, Stella Dadzie and Suzanne Scafe insist that 'today's generation of young Black women are refusing to admit defeat', for part of their inheritance as workers is 'their mothers' struggles . . . that obstinate refusal to bow down to the requirements of the economic system has left behind a rich tradition of militancy and dogged determination'.[31]

The power of desire and the fortitude of memory are not enough, however. In setting a course for utopia, complications emerge. It is perhaps tempting to ignore these, but the attempt to seek short-cuts leads only to dead ends.

It has become increasingly obvious that women cannot be assumed to have a single interest. Class interest and politics will divide women just as they divide men. Similarly, divisions of race are apparent, and so are the differing circumstances of the young, the old, heterosexuals and lesbians, women who are able-bodied and those with disabilities, those with children and those without children. Even when political aims are shared, differing circumstances can result in the inability to notice the needs of others. This has been the cause of considerable tension in women's liberation. It has also restricted the development of the movement. For example, Anne Day, a works representative in a Stoke-on-Trent pottery who has three children, heard about a women's liberation group at Keele University in the mid-1970s. Angela Phillips describes what happened:

> Out of curiosity she went along with one other woman but was very disappointed. It was just a bunch of students sitting in a pub. They wanted young wives to join but they weren't really interested in our problems. I'd expected an active group willing to give up a few things, even a few hours at weekends looking after kids so that women who are stuck at home all day can get a chance to go out. They wanted to know all about trade unions but they didn't want to work in a pottery in the holidays, they just wanted me to tell them what happened.[32]

Disappointment and estrangement led Anne Day to try to form her own group. Many women who have got as far as going to a women's group have felt excluded by a consensus of interest different from their own and by the unconscious acceptance of privilege. So the movement for change also expresses, to a certain degree, the relations of power within society, even between women as a group, and this limits the possibilities of creating radical alternatives. Finding organizational forms that can counter hidden power imbalances remains a crucial problem for contemporary social movements.

A rather different awkwardness has arisen from the feminist emphasis on transforming the relationships of work in defiance of the trade unions' male-defined emphasis on economic militancy.[33] Jill Tweedie wrote an article entitled 'Money Will Not Buy What Women Want' in the *Guardian* in 1981:

> For countless generations women have gained their strength and their pleasure from liking other people and wanting to be liked in return . . . I believe that women are the last half of humanity to value what money cannot buy and are currently making financial sacrifices in

order to conserve those values albeit unconsciously. Yet exploitation is good for no one. . .[34]

The values that set women at odds with the male world of work can also be invoked to construct a conservative utopia of self-sacrifice and thrift which has been one of the motifs of Thatcherism. In 'Women in Control' Judy Wacjman shows in fascinating detail how this tendency intertwined with the creativity and democratic release of the Fakenham co-op. The Fakenham effort to democratize the relations of production floundered in the face of market forces.[35] This problem, inherent in co-operative enterprise in a capitalist economy, is especially acute for women's co-ops, which are often set up in low-paid, labour-intensive areas of employment.

Another difficulty in questing for utopia, or the change beyond the change, is that re-designing work can eliminate people's jobs. For example, feminist criticism of women clerical workers' role in serving men led to proposals by Anna Coote and Laura King for a reconstructed office which were debated in the union TASS.[36] Their ideas included self-servicing for many tasks, the recognition of typing as a real skill, and a degree of co-operative democracy. However, this would have meant the effective demotion of women who had reached a better-paid, more interesting job after a long climb through low-grade clerical work. They would have been understandably disgruntled. Women's movement zeal to challenge the meaning, purpose and value of employment may result in disregard for the views of those most closely affected. This approach also ignores the question of how it is to be decided what is good and bad work. It can appear that middle-class feminists are planning change at the expense of less privileged women.

One such zone of contention has been the employment of the body. One strand of feminism has regarded stripping and prostitution as jobs that are oppressive to women. Accordingly in 1976 the National Union of Students decided to ban acts from student entertainment 'which objectify the male or female form'.[37] Joy Mallert said in *Spare Rib* that she thought that 'working as a stripper can only entice men into rape'.[38] But Janet Feindel asserted that she was a 'stripper and a feminist. . .I also enjoy my work and resent other sisters trying to deprive me of a job. Or perhaps I should get a job at the censor board?'[39] Susan Read called for equal opportunities: 'What *is* sexist about stripping is the lack of male strippers, and the outrage over the few male strip shows that have taken place.'[40] Clare Cherrington developed a complex feminist critique of the law in an account of the arrest of a male stripper for aiding and abetting keeping a disorderly house in Nuneaton in 1976. In 'What Went On at the Frog and Nightgown?' she described how the court tried to establish whether he had simulated masturbation with his right hand (he was left-handed) and heard how you could tell a G-string by the amount of buttocks exposed. Nuneaton women had debagged his driver and mobbed him. Clare Cherrington saw bias in the tolerance of female strippers and the tendency to define women's pleasures as 'disorderly'.[41] It was not clear whether she wanted more or less acceptance of women strippers.

There have been similar problems in relation to prostitution. Some feminists have wanted to stop kerb-crawling that goes on in areas where prostitutes work. Ruth Wallsgrove commented that feminists had been suspicious of prostitutes 'because they make a business out of what we hope will *some* day be done for pleasure between equals who care for each other'.[42] She argued that women become prostitutes because of lack of choice in employment,[43] a view endorsed by Tricia Dearden in an article in the radical magazine the *Leveller*.[44] This interpretation does not, however, illuminate why all women with restricted options in employment do not take up prostitution. A more complex version of the 'lack of choice' interpretation was presented by Helen Buckingham, a member of the English Collective of Prostitutes, who had worked as a call-girl in the more up-market part of the trade. In a paper presented to a socialist feminist conference she wrote:

> Until women are taken into consideration in the evolution of social and political structures and in their own right rather than as appendages of men, the financial rewards to be gained by selling sexual services far outweigh any advantages that alternative life-styles present.[45]

Some prostitutes have argued that their work should be seen as 'just a job like any other'[46] and conditions improved rather than the job eliminated through feminist zeal. There has been some support from feminists for this position. Tricia Dearden criticized the tendency for the women's movement to become 'an exclusive kind of club, with a moralistic emphasis on what women should be doing to get out of their situation'.[47]

How the moral economy without exploitation which has been an important objective of feminism engages with the meantime is a tremendous problem. Qualitative transformation can be at variance with the defence of existing jobs. In Britain most feminists would probably tend to be opposed to military work. But in the United States some have campaigned for equal opportunities in the army.[48] Hilary Wainright found conflicting versions of women's role in the attitudes of women making weapons in Britain. While one woman described approvingly people's willingness to work overtime during the Falklands war for 'our boys', another was unhappy she made weapons which would harm life: 'In my opinion women are more worried about working here. I think this is because women's instinct towards their children makes them think that way.'[49]

There have been certain difficulties over job-sharing and shorter working hours, particularly important feminist demands because of women's domestic responsibilities.[50] Just as the TUC officially came round to calling for shorter working hours, the economic situation changed. There have been a few scattered gains of shorter hours, and a brief debate erupted in the early 1980s about whether a shorter working day or a shorter working week best served women's interests.

But instead of spending less time at work while earning a good wage, many women in the late 1980s have found themselves forced to do low-paid part-time jobs. Thus feminist demands of the 1970s for job-sharing and part-time work have now assumed a different meaning. Equal opportunities and 'flexibility' can be invoked to cut full-time work to part-time and split shifts into unsocial hours. In the present context it is flexibility for the employers rather than the employed. Veronica Beechey has suggested we should recognize that workers' needs change and that what is required is a job structure in which people can move from part-time to full-time work and have long periods off like sabbaticals.[51]

There is a tension over time even in the visions of change. Co-ops stress commitment arising from a new and fulfilling meaning to work – but they also often involve heavy responsibilities and long hours. Similarly, the effort to make public services truly caring would be demanding and exacting even with good resources. So there is an unstated confusion about how to regard work. One strand in feminism favours shorter hours while another is asserting the potential liberation in new forms of work which involve women more. Yet the commitment to Gwenda's Garage means spending less time with children.[52] The practical inconsistencies of the women's movement indicate a theoretical indecisiveness in modern radicalism about work in a future society.

Feminism has also taken part in the wider social critique of technology and its uses. Two arguments have intertwined: one is that in capitalism technology is designed and used in the interest of making profit, not for human benefit; the other asserts that technology is an expression of male dominance which exerts control over nature. Some feminists have dismissed technology, control and reason as 'male'. This denies their advantages to society and assumes that they have universal rather than historically specific meanings. It is moreover too simple to assert alternative women's values of nurture, nourishing, cultivation, for there have been cultures that stressed nurture in which women were nonetheless subordinate. Also, women have collaborated in regimes in which 'instrumental reason' assumed a grotesque shape like fascism. The chief danger, however, in characterizing forms of thought as 'male' is that women are presented as belonging to a separate 'female' sphere and there is no potential for change. It also sets up an illusory ideal which is incapable of dealing with uncomfortable realities, as when women display supposedly 'male' attitudes to technology, fail to protest against inhuman 'economic goals or accept a detached and hierarchical system of command.

Some of feminism's unease with technology indicates the need for redefinition of reason and of human beings' relation to nature. For example, Jessica Benjamin has identified a non-coercive form of control over nature 'in a sense of growing mastery and knowledge' which does 'not imply that nature is given the status of object or other'.[53]

There is a problem in deciding what we would want to discard and what we would wish to hang on to in re-making a male-dominated culture. This can have various meanings for women in different situations. I was once corrected in a meeting by two elderly working-class women for assuming that 'professionalism' was exclusive and elitist. To them it had another meaning – responsible pride in a product or service. It is perfectly true that it would be a dismal world if we attacked all the values of skill which have also been part of the heritage of resistance to exploitation, to replace them only with shoddy muddle and incompetence. Cynthia Cockburn suggests:

Somehow we have to keep the best of the old skill ethic while discarding the worst. Pride in the ability to produce must stay, but in the form of a pride of being collectively responsible for the making of a socially useful product.[54]

I wonder? For in a world where relationships were free and equal, individual crafting would not threaten. It would involve an exchange of gifts in which skill was appreciated and not envied.

In a period of intense restructuring, when the assessment of worth and the establishment of social identity through work are being assailed, strategic opposition actually requires a utopian element. The possibility of giving shape to a more human-oriented economic system depends on there being space to imagine new values and explore how human beings might create, communicate and maintain their lives without exploitation. If these projections are to retain dynamic complexity there has to be a continuing interaction between the vision and specific, invariably conflicting realities.

Similar debates have arisen from feminist attempts to make alternative forms of culture – in art, music, publishing, theatre, dance and film, for instance. A continuing problem of the 'alternatives' has been how to change the forms and relationships of culture while still engaging with the economic constraints and ideological power of the dominant culture. Although only a small number of women work in these alternative areas, their situation illustrates in microcosm the real tensions between work and creativity. There has been a persistent tendency for feminists to find themselves caught in an alternative ghetto. For example, fringe theatre has given women a chance to direct plays – still largely a male prerogative. But this makes for experience gained on a financial shoe-string which in the long run hampers creative development. Yet competition in the mainstream cuts women off from the sources of support which the alternative networks can provide. Also, women are constantly expected to be emblems for their sex. Women film-makers, for instance, are assumed to work from a 'women's angle'. This can inhibit when it is imposed as a form of containment. There is a real problem for women artists: how do they challenge the way 'women's' skills like embroidery are devalued, while also advancing into the forms of art which have been dominated by men?[55] These recurrent debates among feminist cultural workers raise important issues about how work is valued and how to develop alternative forms that are not marginal to the prevailing power structure.

Discussion of the social value of work was raised by Lucas Aerospace workers who, during their struggle against redundancy in the mid-1970s, developed alternative plans for socially useful prototypes. The Lucas workers defined social usefulness in terms of products. Ursula Huws entered the debate as a feminist to question this emphasis on meeting needs simply through new commodities. She argued that the self-servicing economy proposed by the Lucas approach recognizes technological skill but disregards nurture, and suggested a different perspective:

> When devising strategies for the future which seek simultaneously to create jobs and to meet social need, the starting point should not be the assumption that a product will necessarily be the answer. If it is, then in all probability forces already at work in capitalism will find it. On the contrary we should start from an analysis of the unmet needs, which means listening to the view put forward by the needy themselves through their own organizations. Do child-bearing women really want more foetal monitoring, or would they simply rather have, more, and differently trained, midwives? Do the severely disabled want more gadgets or would they prefer more money, more home helps or differently designed homes?[56]

Ursula Huws's questions bring new dimensions to the social definition of need which do not tie it solely to production. Democratizing an economy is not simply a mental process. It may be possible to start with a rough common sense of need. But we are all bound by the limits of our life experience. By learning from people's past actions and by listening to the proposals of groups and movements, a deeper understanding can be reached through trial and usage. Needs change while policies fossilize. A dynamic economic transformation requires a continuing search to discover what is needed, given the infinite and changing variety of necessity. Women have a practical stake in the creation of such an economy, for the present system not only treats women badly, it dismisses their social experience as trivial and by the way. How a new economy is made will determine its shape.

There has been a sustained critique by feminists of theories of development in the Third World. They have engaged with the fundamental economic inequalities which engineer poverty and have insisted that the labour and needs of women are taken into account. For example, Irene Dankelman and Joan Davidson write:

> . . .the training and support programmes (including credit) which might enable small farmers to manage their land well are most often directed at men. In many countries women are denied title to land, cannot enter into contracts and cannot raise loans. Technologies, too, are transferred mainly to men: it is they rather than women who are

reached by agricultural extension programmes and who are taught how to install and maintain water pumps or biogas pumps. Grinding mills and stoves are used by women but designed and built by men.[57]

This perspective on aid has brought into plain view many of the economic realizations that feminists in Britain have only glimpsed in imagination or been able to put into practice only briefly at the micro level through left local authorities.[58]

As the international economy becomes increasingly interconnected, the consequences of restructuring bear particularly harshly on the poor in every country. Women, who are a significant group of the poor, are, in many different places, coming to realize the necessity of understanding fully the forces behind the immediate difficulties in their lives. In the summer of 1984 some women from the Yorkshire mining communities attended a meeting at the GLC. Stumped by a man who spoke on alternative economic strategy, Betty Cook, from Woolley, considered hard and replied:

> Now, flower, I'd like to get this straight. We're miners' wives. That doesn't mean that we're simple, only that we're not used to many of the phrases you used. I, for one, admit to not knowing a lot of the words and most of the concepts. But this I promise you: I've had three months up to now on the picket lines and my political education is being acquired at a gallop. Stick around and I'll come back in a year's time and answer all your questions.[59]

It seems to me that no one knows, when all forms of inequality grow more marked, how we might move towards an economy directed by popular needs. But the urgency of creating the means for such a transition is desperately evident and here women's experience, with all its diversity, has a vital political part to play. In Cynthia Cockburn's words, ' . . we are led to face the fundamental issues of human society from the moment we embark on the project of enabling women to saw a straight cut or tighten a nut'.[60]

13

A Woman's Place is in Her Union

'A woman's place is in her union' has become an international slogan. It was on the badge that had lost its pin proudly presented to me by a young Canadian trade unionist from the West Coast. 'Make sure you get a pin for it,' she said, in the summer of 1985. I smiled to myself wryly, thinking of so many meetings, so much argument and anger. What histories these slogans have!

There is no single 'feminist' approach to trade unions. Attitudes and assumptions are both opposed and overlapping, for there have not simply been feminist critiques of the labour movement, but a historical relationship between feminists in the women's liberation movement and women and men in the trade unions. This relationship has been sometimes one of argument, sometimes one of approval. In some cases the feminists *are* trade unionists; in other cases feminists have supported trade-union struggles. Trade unionists, both men and women, have also acted with feminists – for instance on abortion, nurseries, against welfare cuts.

In 1982, reviewing the collection of essays *Women, Work and the Labour Market*, Judy Wajcman observed a certain inconsistency. While Judith Hunt declared 'A woman's place is in her union', other writers berated the male-dominated trade unions.[1] Joanna de Groot also noted a contradiction among feminists who 'encourage women to take hold of union structures at the same time as criticizing them. Surely we ought to be able to make up our minds.'[2]

This dual vision has been a persistent feature not only of the present women's liberation movement but of feminist movements in the past. Women need unions, yet power in the unions, as with most institutions, is held by men.

The very emergence of the women's movement was part of a wider radicalization of the young educated middle class who were to have considerable impact in 'white-collar' trade unionism, which grew

massively over this period. The relationship of this group to manual
workers is historically complex and feminists have been caught up
in its unresolved ambivalence. Investigating this involved inquiring
who 'we' were, and reflecting on whether the structure and ideas of
the women's movement expressed a specific class position. Arsenal
Women's Liberation Group tried to raise this at the second Socialist
Women's Conference held in London in September 1973:

> The class composition of the movement, from our observation, is pre-
> dominantly middle class – at the very least most of us have had an
> education beyond the age of 15. Obviously although many women
> are middle class by background/education/occupation, they may (a)
> have rejected this for political reasons, (b) be in desperate financial
> dependence on men or the state. We are not even sure that we are
> very representative of the middle class as a whole – is this true and
> if so in what ways? There are historical reasons for this phenomenon
> which have not been sufficiently examined.[3]

The conference paper went on to suggest that these social factors contributed to the movement's political emphasis on 'choice', challenge
to notions of 'womanhood', and assertion of economic independence
from men.[4]

The women's liberation groups of the 1970s included students,
clerical workers and women doing many educational or welfare jobs.
There were women with young children who did not have jobs and
were on social security or living with men whose jobs could be either
middle class or manual working class, but who were often part of a
socially defiant radical subculture. Women in manual and service jobs
active in trade unions joined in with specific activities and campaigns,
while working-class housewives more often participated in groups
involved with playgroups and schools. In the early 1970s feminists
tended to be in their twenties or early thirties. Older women were
the exception. Sandy Kondos and Lucy Draper looked back on this
period at the Socialist Feminist Conference in 1979:

> When we first became involved in the women's movement, it was at a
> time when a lot of the women involved were either students, on the dole,
> or working in alternative situations of one kind or another – which gave
> us the time and space to work out a lot of the issues involved in feminist
> politics.[5]

By the end of the 1970s, however, they had become aware that
things were changing. These women were now more likely to be

in full-time jobs with people who did not share their politics. This meant, that 'the purity of our politics'[6] was being threatened, but also that feminists had a less marginal position within society. Feminists of the 'first wave' were becoming more prepared to engage with mainstream politics.

Women's liberation as a movement gained much of its momentum from that section of the post-war generation which scrambled out of the working class and lower middle class through higher education. This was a sociological event and an intense psychological process. The accounts in *Truth, Dare or Promise*, in which feminists describe girlhood in the Fifties, express the enthusiastic resolve to 'get out' and yet, in retrospect, recognize what was left behind. Liz Heron introduces the collection with a comment on class:

> The experience of class mobility (from working class to middle class, through education or through the development of a particular kind of confidence connected with the workplace and arising out of material improvements in working class life) was given expression during the Fifties and Sixties in both fictional and sociological form. But the protagonists were almost exclusively male (the working class hero), their conflicts and dilemmas assumed as masculine by their very nature. The experience was neither examined from a woman's point of view nor looked at in terms of what it meant to women.
>
> This is partly because class is usually not seen as having the same meaning for women as for men. Class for women is both simple and more complicated. It is marriage, traditionally, that eases a woman into another class; it is her rite of passage; another place of belonging no matter that her husband's class is different from that of her father.[7]

Liz Heron suggests that women who are uprooted from their class and challenge female destiny retain an 'unease and sense of not belonging'.[8] Many of the post-war generation of women who were part of the expansion in higher education were to enter the middle class through their occupations, rather than through marriage. It was no longer simply a matter of ' "My face is my fortune, sir", she said'. Valerie Walkerdine describes going to grammar school in Derby in the late Fifties as an upper-working-class girl:

> They held out a dream. Come, they told me. It is yours. You are chosen. They didn't tell me, however, that for years I would no longer feel any sense of belonging, nor any sense of safety, that I didn't belong in the

new place, any more than I now belonged in the old. So, around every
corner of apparent choice lurked doubt and uncertainty. Leaving one's
class was to be both admired and scorned.[9]

For many women the changes in capitalist society and the expansion
in education meant entering a different world from that of their
mothers. In Valerie Walkerdine's words:

> My mother in this history has no history. She lurks silently in the
> kitchen. . .I cannot find her in my dream because the kitchen is where I
> am most afraid to look. . .What if winning in one place is simultaneously
> always a loss?[10]

The composition of the women's liberation movement can thus be
seen as a reflection of changes in class relations in post-war capitalism
by which more women became socially mobile through education
and employment rather than marriage. This shift in female destiny
opened up opportunities, but it was also an unresolved source of
barely articulated pain, for it estranged young women from their
families.

Meanwhile, some of the more privileged tried to shed their class.
Three women doing working-class jobs, Barbara in a sterilization
unit of a hospital, Carole, a cleaner, and Sue, a post office accounts
clerk, who were in a small Marxist group, 'The Red Collective', in the
mid-1970s, wrote in a paper for a women's liberation conference:

> It seems to us that one of the political problems facing the movement
> is that up until now its only real base has been among young middle-
> class ex-students, while we *all*, wherever we place ourselves on the
> Marxist/Feminist spectrum, recognize that we have no political future
> unless we can relate women's liberation to the mass of women.[11]

The relationship of women's liberation and the labour movement
has been further complicated by the formation of the very concept of
class in terms of men – and indeed of class solidarity, which is often
expressed by women as well as men in terms of 'brotherhood' and
'fraternity'. Militancy has been equated with 'standing up and being
a man' and 'having balls', bureaucratic inclinations with 'old women
– of both sexes'. The emergence of women's liberation challenged a
male-defined culture within trade unions.[12]

In retrospect it does not seem so surprising that women's liberation should have such a tense relationship with the male-dominated labour movement. Nor that there should be such embarrassment about privilege in relation to working-class women. The uprooting meant that beneath the political debates there was an intensely emotional desire to situate the self. Feminists, whose class displacement remained unsung, grappled with the working-class heroes of the 1970s, their very taunts betraying the intensity of the encounter. In 1980 Bea Campbell was still waving the red rag to the bull with 'our brave lads on the shop floor', 'they say you always hurt the one you love', and – delivering the *coup de grâce* – 'Trade unionism will be left loitering without intent in the pre-history of modern capitalism, a muscle-bound Tarzan, a man of few words wielding blunt instruments.'[13] In a passionate affray there is a tendency to go for the bits below the belt.

Ambivalence towards trade unions has been due not only to their male-dominated character and the social complexities of class relations in Britain but also to a political rejection of many of the older labour-movement assumptions. Women's liberation as a movement was profoundly influenced by the American New Left's ideas: the extension of the political sphere into personal life, emphasis on direct experience, and faith in participatory democracy. It has, however, been extremely difficult in practice to keep hold of the positive and creative impact of these ideas and at the same time to recognize their limits.

It was to become apparent that there were a number of snags in the political perspective that prioritized subjective experience. While it enabled unrecognized social grievances to be expressed, it did not explain the necessity of extending self-organization. The emphasis on the personal not only raised problems about how to go beyond the existing class base of the movement, there were also difficulties in relation to race. Black feminists pointed out that the emphasis upon the personal was subject to manipulation and was not in fact being extended to all aspects of experience. Race was central to their lives and yet was obliterated in versions of women's liberation that focused exclusively on the experience of gender. Ironically, the emphasis on personal politics could evade aspects of experience.

This tendency to muffle differences was fiercely attacked by Afro-Caribbean and Asian women in Britain from the late 1970s. They rejected an invoked unity of sisterhood based on hegemonic privilege. Similar criticisms came from many other groups of women – for example, lesbians, women with disabilities, and older women.

The political legacy of the 1960s inherited by the women's movement provided no theoretical basis for overcoming the resulting fragmentation. While the assertion of one's own experience is a useful countervailing force against the scholastic deployment of a detached and authoritarian version of theory, it cannot transcend the particular. In practice, looking beyond one's own specific circumstances was often impelled solely by a sense of guilt. There was no means of articulating a politics which could promote the stategic benefits of alliance and unity.

Another and curious feature of the New Left inheritance was that while it emphasized subjectivity, it had in fact no means of examining its own assumptions, either psychologically or theoretically. Any self-consciousness tended to become stuck within a repetition of the particular rather than analysing how one form of subordination interconnected with others. A related problem was that the stress on personal consciousness did not necessarily equip one to tackle institutional forms of power in society and the state.

Thus, although this subjectivism had the advantage of being able to ground theory, its disadvantages have become evident. What is needed is a means of balancing the benefits of direct experience with theory and strategy. Throughout the practical struggles of women's liberation, this theme persistently emerges. Amina Mama has stressed the importance of theorizing from 'the experience and realities of the specific Black women concerned',[14] synthesizing the 'contingency of action on experience'.[15] In 'United We Fall' in 1980 Bea Campbell also wrote positively of a connection to feelings and experience:

> The women's liberation movement has evolved a practice from the theory of 'the personal is the political'. More than any other political force it is feminism which is today the bearer of practising direct democracy.[16]

She points out, however, that it is far from clear how this emphasis in women's liberation relates to the 'national political culture'[17] in the sense of existing parliamentary parties and trade unions at national level. Feminist experience can illuminate the immediate relations of women and men in trade unions in particular workplaces, and can be extended to take in the complexities of class and race. But the more distant institutional structures also affect women's lives. Here feminist practice is less developed and has lacked creative confidence in making theories of politics in this wider sense. Somehow there has to be 'another level of political intervention'[18] – both everyday experience and the positions in which power is concentrated have to be tackled.

The lack of agreement among socialists about the relation of the grass roots to executive power in the trade unions has made it all the more difficult to make good this shortfall in feminist theory. Various political ideas about trade unions were carried into the women's movement, but these tended to be stronger on criticizing existing structures than on bridging the gap between direct and representative democracy. The discussion of male domination in the unions became intertwined with the agendas, hidden or otherwise, of varying political tendencies. For example, in 1972 in *Women, the Unions and Work*, Selma James generalized from ideas developed on the autonomist wing of the Italian Left to argue that trade unions co-opted and fragmented 'autonomous class action'[19] and were responsible for divisions within the working class which resulted in unequal pay. She also maintained that the trade unions modified the intensity of conflict between workers and capitalists by confining struggle to wages and ignoring the social gains needed outside the workplace.[20] Disregarding the specific context that had produced the original ideas, she recommended that women simply withdraw from trade unionism. Big Flame women, on the other hand, brought a more engaged libertarian critique of the bureaucratic nature of trade unionism to feminism. International Socialism (later the Socialist Workers' Party) emphasized rank-and-file organization, wage militancy and workers' control. Some Trotskyist groups and the Communist Party – which had members in official positions – were less critical of trade-union bureaucracy but quite prepared to criticize right-wing leadership.

Bea Campbell's influential writing on trade unionism has been partly shaped by political arguments in the Communist Party, and is directed particularly against a labour-movement old guard who have clung on for dear life to a fossilized notion of trade-union struggle. In her writing on women and work from the late 1970s a peculiar passion is reserved for a polemic against a particular economistic image of class militancy which is continually equated with male domination. This feature is shared by much feminist writing on trade unions from this period. There is an elision here. Certainly there have

been historical connections and certainly demands for higher wages
cannot solve all social ills. But by the mid-1980s what had begun as
a critique was in danger of becoming a frozen stance. A beleaguered
and battered labour movement was being depicted as if it was still as
strong as it had been in the previous decade.

Angela Weir and Mary McIntosh have argued that this approach
throws the baby out with the bath-water,[21] since it seems to present
male workers as the main enemy and ignore the power of the employers. They maintained that women's relation to trade unionism could
not be encapsulated in a polemic that focused on gender relations
alone. A much deeper historical process was at work.

> The battles are tough ones and the opposition often appears hydra-
> headed. A fine resolution at national conference is often ridiculed or
> ignored at branch level; hard work in recruiting new women members
> can be sabotaged by full-time officials who refuse to take part-time work-
> ers seriously; local militants can be thwarted by right-wing leadership.
> The style of work of trade unionism is notoriously male in its assumptions
> and often alienating to women. It is not perhaps surprising that women
> sometimes see the unions as an obstacle to their aspirations rather than
> a strong arm to help achieve them. Yet at the end of the day, unions
> are membership organizations, and women are a growing part of that
> membership. They can change and they are already changing as those
> women make themselves felt.[22]

There have now been two decades of interaction between feminists
and trade unionists in Britain. This has shaped the history of
the women's liberation movement as much as the inheritance
of political assumptions from the American New Left and from
European Marxist traditions. Despite the assertion of personal
experience by many feminists, and despite the tendency to see
trade unions as homogeneous structures of patriarchal bureaucratic
authoritarianism, in practice there has been persistent engagement,
particularly of socialist feminists, with the struggles of women
workers and with trade-union battles that include men. This
impulse has been especially powerful in Britain, where the break
with the Old Left was less sharp than in the United States,
and where the Communist Party has exerted less control than
in Europe. It was originally fuelled by the extraordinary upsurge
of militant working-class action in the early 1970s. While this
might have been male-dominated and economistic, it nonetheless

exerted an enormous social and cultural influence beyond the labour movement. It was the background to a series of interactions between the radical subcultures of the middle class and the older forces of labour. Feminists were affected by this process and it served to transmit political and organizational traditions and form personal links which influenced the developing women's movement.

This involvement of feminists with organized labour has enabled the women's movement to transcend its original social base, and has had a slow but undeniable effect on the trade-union movement as well. From the struggles for equal pay or the unionization of night cleaners in the 1970s to the bitter battles of the 1980s against privatization or in support of the miners or seafarers, feminists have joined picket lines, helped produce strike papers, raised money, monitored civil liberties and organized innumerable meetings and conferences. Among myriad local encounters, two predominant themes can be traced: the insistence that class conflict be gendered – or that the working class has two sexes; and an empirical recognition that an exclusive emphasis on gender cannot provide a full account of society, lacking as it does the vital dimensions of class and race.

There are two important processes which await their historians: one is the experiential encounter of feminism with the labour movement; the other, even more deeply buried, is the remarkable transformation in consciousness that has been taking place among working-class women. The latter has been expressed to a limited extent within the trade-union movement, but also surfaced in their writing during and after the miners' strike. While in one sense these have been two distinct historical processes, there have been significant convergences. In the very early days feminists oriented themselves towards the poorest working-class women, but from the mid-1970s they were becoming increasingly active on their own account, mostly in 'white-collar' trade unions. The groups formed to promote the demands of the Working Women's Charter were an organizational expression of this development, which has persisted during the 1980s with the result that feminists are now present at every level of trade unionism. As Bea Campbell and Anna Coote observed in *Sweet Freedom* in 1982:

At the TUC annual conference of women workers, the feminist presence has grown visibly stronger year by year. There have been growing numbers of younger delegates with prior experience in women's groups, and at the same time older delegates and women in traditional blue-collar jobs have been voicing their demands in increasingly feminist terms.[23]

Meanwhile, of course, the character of the women's movement has altered. A hint of the complexity of its relationship with the trade-union movement was expressed in an article by Jill Brown, Pamela Trevithick and Carol Metters, 'The Forward Face of Feminism', in *Marxism Today* in 1981. Reflecting on the women's movement in Bristol, they questioned the concept of the movement as 'a monolithic body with a clearly defined boundary'.[24] This led into

> a trap. . . which says there is a gap between feminists inside the WLM and other women working outside, for example, in trades unions. It might be more accurate, from our experience, to describe the WLM as having a semi-permeable membrane through which ideas, practices and women move in both directions. The monolithic description does not take into account any dialectical relationship between movements and organizations.[25]

This is certainly a more accurate way of assessing social movements. It does, however, make the historian's job much harder, and it represents a veritable nightmare for the politician or journalist under pressure to come up with tidy formulas.

Although there is as yet no definitive history of this interaction of feminism and trade unionism, a rich patchwork chronicle can be pieced together in the meantime from reports scattered through socialist and feminist journals like *Socialist Woman*, *Women's Voice*, *Spare Rib* and *Outwrite* (the latter especially strong on racial and international issues), and in some cases gathered into books about particular aspects of the movement. These accounts provide glimpses of the complex understandings that have accumulated from the excursions backwards and forwards through the membrane.

Detailed examination of disputes soon vindicates the view of Mary McIntosh and Angela Weir that complex processes are at work and that a single-minded focus on gender is historically incomplete. Feminists have been aware of the implications for women's equality of attacks on the welfare provisions which had been gains won by the working class as a whole. The battle to defend public services has encouraged yet more links and alliances.

As the main 'carers', both paid and unpaid, women are acutely aware of the vital importance of the health, education and welfare

services. As cuts began to bite in the 1970s, they were in the forefront of opposition. *Spare Rib* reported on one mass protest against
low pay and welfare cuts in 1977. The women demonstrating were
concerned not only about low pay and the threat to their jobs but
also because, as nurses from Nuneaton told *Spare Rib*, 'Our own
kids are doing sponsored walks and sponsored spelling lessons to
raise money to pay for books. They're sending the children home
from school earlier so they can shorten the dinner time and cut
back on dinner ladies.'[26] Social workers in Kensington, London
were worried because holidays for the old and disabled had been
totally withdrawn in that area. And nursery workers were distressed
that toys were not being mended and they could not afford paper
for the children to paint on. So they were organizing jumble sales.
'Why should *we* raise the money?'[27] these public-service workers
asked.

Unfortunately neither the Labour leadership nor the TUC could
offer convincing solutions. Soon the Thatcher government would
launch its offensive against the trade unions and the welfare state, and
a beleaguered working class would find the banners it was expected
to rally behind looking increasingly threadbare. Nevertheless, there
has been continuing resistance, even if desperate and fragmented.
Women are not of course the only sufferers from the new order, but
disproportionate numbers belong to the overlapping groups that have
been hardest hit – the low paid, public-sector workers and people
dependent on welfare benefits. Within households containing men
it is also still largely women who care for dependent family members
with even less public help than before, and who try to feed and clothe
everyone on inadequate money.

Women have thus had every reason to fight back. They have
marched in thousands against the cuts in public services. They
have picketed and occupied to contest the closure of hospitals. They
have resisted privatization, not only through protest, but by showing
that the result would be deteriorating services. Barking Hospital
cleaners went on strike for over a year against the contractors,
Crothall's, who wanted them to do more work for less money,
with insufficient time, as the women pointed out, to do the job
as they knew it should be done. Women teachers and nurses have
been prominent in the long and bitter campaign for the value of their
work to be recognized. Women clerical workers have spearheaded
the movement against the unhealthy and oppressive use of new
technology. Women have argued within the trade-union movement

for shorter hours to be a priority, and have gone on battling against low pay, taking on employers like the bed manufacturers Silent Night, who were paying even less than the minimum set by the wages council (whose 'restrictive' role would soon be abolished by the government). Women have fought to get and keep union recognition and agreements, and have opposed anti-trade-union laws and government bans like that at GCHQ. Wherever major disputes in defence of jobs and conditions have occurred – the miners' strike, News International, P & O – there have been the women, masses of them, as workers, relatives, supporters. Thus, while they have often acted from a specific social position as women, their concerns have not simply been about inequality with men in the trade unions but have extended into a wide range of social and economic issues.

Even when gender equality has been the major issue, the historical evidence reveals that there have been various and contradictory responses from men in the trade unions, for example during campaigns for equal pay, as recorded by feminists in the early 1970s. In 1973 Bea Campbell wrote about women clerical workers recently recruited into TASS at the Nuswift fire extinguisher factory in Elland, Yorkshire, who were campaigning for equal pay and getting the support of male workers.[28] Marsha Rowe reported a series of strikes against GEC.[29] South Wales miners donated a little yellow fibreglass hut for the women picketing at the GEC plant Eccles in Lancashire, and the women installed cooking facilities, chairs and a table. One day management was so incensed by this 'homely' picket that they hoisted the hut up and lifted it over the factory fence, leaving the perplexed women still sitting there.[30] Engineering workers supported women at Bronx Engineering in the West Midlands in October 1975. There was male support too for women office workers striking for equal pay at Louis Newmarks, an Ipswich engineering factory, in 1976. Norma Eltringham, an assistant buyer, told Ann Scott, 'You don't know what it felt like on Monday when we stood out here on our own and the men came out. I could have hugged every one of them.'[31]

There were, however, also cases of opposition from men. In July 1973 Coventry women in the Amalgamated Union of Engineering Workers at GEC Spon Street decided to go on strike against low pay. Their union convenor, Albert Beardmore, told drivers to please themselves about crossing the picket lines. 'I'm not going to have my men laid off by a bunch of silly girls,' he said. He then tried to get the union card of his deputy convenor, Elsie Noles, taken away from her because she supported the women. This was overruled by mass meeting. He then organized a kangaroo court of other stewards who voted to expel Elsie Noles, but she was hastily reinstated by the AUEW committee.[32]

The AUEW women at the Trico car-component factory in Brentford, London, who struck for equal pay in defiance of an industrial tribunal ruling did not have the full support of the men at the plant. Nevertheless, mounting a round-the-clock picket with help from feminists and trade unionists, they won their claim in full. At the end of 1976 the women marched back together in triumph, and two days later one applied for (and got) the previously all-male job of forklift truck driver.

A crucial element in the history of women's trade unionism in the recent past has been played by Asian women living in Britain who have, against all the odds, organized themselves as an impressive force within the labour movement. In *Finding a Voice* Amrit Wilson shows how they have had to tackle racism as well as gender inequality in the course of class struggle. For example, in the early 1970s Asian women workers walked out of the Imperial Typewriters factory in Leicester because the firm had raised the speed of work beyond endurance with no breaks. This also meant they could not get their bonus. In the course of the dispute it was discovered that the union had actually negotiated and agreed production levels which management had disregarded, and the women were entitled to backdated pay. The bonus dispute also opened up wider issues of democracy and trade-union representation.[33] One of the women told *Race Today*:

We are mostly Asians in our section, but our shop steward is a white woman. She doesn't care and the union doesn't care. I pay 11 pence a week to be a member of the union but I really think it is a waste of hard earned-money. Don't get me wrong, I am not against unions, but our union is no different than management.[34]

The union negotiator George Bromley went on Radio Leicester and said of the 'Asian ladies':

. . .they have got to learn to fit in with our ways, you know. We haven't got to fit in with theirs. And the way they have been acting, that means they will close factories and people won't employ them – that's all.[35]

Larger themes can be discerned in these specific battles for equal pay, against low pay and against racism; they all contribute to a practical reassertion of the political concept of equality.

Democratic equality has internal implications. Jenny Beale's book *Getting It Together*[36] examines the effects feminists have had on trade unions in Britain. She argues that issues of democracy and hierarchy have been of key importance. Very few women hold high office in unions and on the whole women's interests do not get priority. Questioning differentials, or the right of men to earn more than women, has been a manifestation of feminist concern to achieve fundamental change in the nature of trade unionism. Women's difficulties within unions thus have more general political implications.

Democracy has not only been raised in terms of women's representation in the echelons of the trade unions, it has also been an issue in the personal encounters between feminists and men in labour-movement struggles. An article by Bea Campbell and Val Charlton in *Spare Rib* about the 1977 Grunwick strike records graphically a positive and critical interaction between people from differing situations and political traditions:

> Gail Lewis, a Black feminist who joined the picket line virtually every day with other feminists, commented that she felt impressed by the trade unionists' 'sense of solidarity and caring in their discipline. They were really caring, trying to see that our people didn't get hurt.' And Maria Duggan, another feminist who suffered a fractured leg when she was stamped on by police, said she felt 'very solid with the support of the men, particularly the miners'.
>
> But they also confronted sexism on the picket-line. 'In one struggle with the police you would hear men testing manhood by saying things like "What sort of man are you, hitting a woman?" to the police,' said Gail Lewis. 'So I said "Hey what's this, we are here as part of the struggle and if you are suggesting that women are more feeble then we'll have that out with you here and now." When another woman overheard male pickets complaining that "We'd have got that bus if it wasn't for those silly women in the way", she countered, "Wait a minute, it's those silly girls who have been holding that gate all this time." '[37]

An important feminist assertion has been that democracy is not simply about formal participation: people can also be excluded by the use of images and language that diminish them. This insight is relevant not only to women but to workers with disabilities, gay and lesbian workers, black workers and those from other ethnic minorities. Even white male workers can be divided by demarcations of 'craft' and 'skill' that foster a culture based on the skilled worker's sense of superiority over those classed as unskilled.

It is a curious fact that those elements of the women's liberation movement that have related to trade unionism have re-discovered tenets that the labour movement had half forgotten as it became stronger, more established and able to make economic gains. Equality, well-being and democracy were the radical watchwords of the early working-class movement. Another, of course, was internationalism.

Feminist writing has served as a vehicle for generalizing the experience of women in many countries. For instance, in *Feminist Review* Catherine Hoskyns describes how in Italy women entered the major car factories in large numbers in the late 1970s as a result of equality legislation necessitated by the EEC's Equal Treatment Directive. Once there in large numbers, the women raised complaints not previously voiced by the unions about the conditions and organization of work.[38]

Increasingly, however, internationalism is coming to involve making links not only with Europe or the United States but with women in 'Third World' countries. In *Common Fate, Common Bond* Swasti Mitter documents the ways in which the need to respond to the international movement and organization of capital is bringing together women in the 'North' and the 'South'. She instances a feminist conference of women workers in the electronics, clothing and textiles industries which was organized in 1983 at County Hall in London by War on Want and the Archway Development Education Centre and resulted in the setting-up of the network Women Working Worldwide.[39] This conference was one of many meetings that have tried to counter the monopolization of information by international capital and break down the rivalries and suspicions their strategies create among women in the 'North' and the 'South'. While the international grass-roots links are fragile as yet, they are significant as indications of a wider vision of trade unionism which recognizes the importance of social needs and political questions that have often been marginalized in the modern labour movement.

The women's liberation movement has not only provided the means for feminists to develop understandings that have influenced trade unionism, it has created a cultural context in which women in the trade unions can gain a voice that can be heard beyond the labour movement. One aspect of hierarchy and privilege in Britain is the exclusion of the views and experience of most working-class women from political and social discussions. Women's movement periodicals and books have contributed to a struggle to break down this cultural barrier. For instance, back in 1969 Kath Fincham, who had considerable political and workplace experience, wrote in *Socialist Woman* criticizing those men in the Transport and General Workers' Union who refused to accept women as bus drivers:

> How can we expect to see greater democratic control for working people generally if there is no democracy within their own ranks? How can we expect to move forward in industry against the employers' undemocratic practices if you are not willing to support us in our struggle?[40]

In *Spare Rib* in 1974 she described the antagonism from male bus workers and inspectors against women driving or becoming inspectors. The executive of the TGWU were by this time committed to equality and pushed it through but the men themselves felt hostile:

> It was all the usual things about a woman's place being in the home and the women ruining the job. . ., there is a feeling around with all the men that women are content with a smaller wage. It's a vicious circle, because women are having to be content with it.[41]

The feminist movement also enabled women who were new to trade unionism to express their views, which were hardly heard even in the organized labour movement. A night cleaner, Jean Wright, wrote in the *Cleaners' Voice*, an organizing bulletin in the early 1970s:

> Women night cleaners work very hard and have much to do, but there is too much work to give a good standard. If there are complaints, it is not the women's fault. When contractors take on buildings where there should be 25 women and put in only 12, they can't expect the standard of work necessary.
> That is why we must have a union to get work cut down and to put the right number of women in the buildings. Why should we kill ourselves for them so they can get more profit? Don't be afraid, Londoners, we are strong enough to fight them for rights we should have had years ago.[42]

The voice of one cleaner from a deserted city building in the night resounds down the years in what now sounds like prophetic warning.

The trade unions were to find themselves faced with an enormous problem as this kind of casualized employment proliferated during the 1980s. Tragically, organized labour has paid for its disregard of workers at the bottom of the pile – when the employers' offensive came there was a serious weakness in the extent of trade-union organization.

Among these disregarded workers were many black and ethnic-minority women. For them, unionization has had more extensive personal and cultural meanings because it has been an intense struggle. They have described both an individual sense of power and a determination to change the way unions relate to ethnic minorities. For example, during the Imperial Typewriters dispute Amrit Wilson observed that the local union bureaucracy in Leicester was controlled by the right, which further diminished the Asian workers' chance of support from the union.[43] They went back to work without winning their demands, but when the foreman taunted Shardhar Behn with defeat, 'I told him I had lost a lot of money but had gained a lot of things. I told him he couldn't push me around any more like a football from one job to another.'[44]

In an interview with Bea Campbell and Val Charlton, Jayaben Desai assessed the effect of the Grunwick dispute, in which she played a leading part:

> The dispute is bringing up so many good things. Before the mass picketing began in June the issue was not so clear in our community, it was misty before. But now the Asian community sees what we are fighting for. And before the trade unions in this country were feeling that our community was not interested – that was always a gap in our community. But this will bring the distance nearer. We can all see the result – people coming here from all over the country are seeing us as part of the workers now.[45]

Her optimism was often tempered with exasperation, and as Pratibha Parmar documents, some of the white male trade unionists still could not recognize the Asian women at Grunwick as fellow trade unionists. One miner declared, 'We are right behind the lads here, they have our full support.'[46]

Strength to oppose this kind of unthinking arrogance, which has both right-wing and left-wing manifestations, has often come as a result of cultural and community struggles against racism. Sometimes political memories of the country of origin contribute to a radicalization expressed in trade unionism in Britain. Filipino domestic workers in Britain, for example, linked community and workplace organization and also recognized the importance of the freedom to unionize because they had experienced overt coercion from the state in the Philippines. Their resistance to deportation from Britain brought them greater confidence at work. They said in 1982:

> At first it did not seem natural to many to resist, because in the Philippines we had been used to martial law and general repression. We did not have the idea that it was possible to resist. . .

> It is really something when a Filipino from an oppressed society is able to stand and say 'this is enough'.

> Unions are strong in Britain and are an important source of help to us. Until our campaign grew most Filipinos did not realize unions could help an individual. . .

> The campaign is a long educational process. It seems slow, but then suddenly one event can do so much to create new awareness of the possibility and the means of struggle. . .

> There are many common threads in building resistance to oppression here and in the Philippines. If you could pull out just one, it would be 'education'. Perhaps the most important element in the campaign is that Filipino women have been learning that they can take part in public affairs.[47]

It was not that the women's liberation movement created workplace rebellion; rather it provided practical support and acted as a vehicle to disseminate accounts of women's actions at work. As the years went by it became a reference point for a dissenting mentality. Even the disclaimer 'I'm not a women's libber but. . .' acknowledges that an alternative to the prevailing culture exists.

Already in the early 1970s, ideas were travelling along diverse routes, not simply through the feminist movement but as part of the general context of working-class activity. For example, Pat Sturdy, an engineering shop steward in Burnley, Lancashire, tried to organize a separate women's industrial union in 1971. Her approach to the process of unionization was to go around and listen to complaints and grievances from women. She said a year later that she had not intended it to be separate from men workers on issues like pay, hours and holidays but to take up 'problems that bother women – nurseries, welfare committees to help unmarried mothers'.[48] In fact the separate union joined the AUEW but Pat Sturdy was undeterred. She was forty at the time and thus had a general sense of the previous two decades. She perceived a new spirit:

> You know over the last twelve months there's been a new awareness in the big trade unions of the importance of their women members. Could be the Equal Pay Act that's done it. And the women workers themselves, we're seeing the sixteen and seventeen-year-olds keen to join us.[49]

In 1972 a shop steward, June Marriner, involved in a dispute in Goodman's loudspeaker factory in Havant, Hampshire, which had not previously been unionized, said the women workers read about and discussed women's liberation and were encouraged by the action of other working-class women who resisted redundancy at Fakenham.[50]

For Jayaben Desai the idea of organizing came not from feminism or specifically from women's issues but simply from seeing other strikes on television. She saw the unions as a power to resist exploitation, but also intimated another dimension of their potential as a moral force, a kind of collective reserve of will for a better human existence:

> All this time I have been watching the strikes and I realized that the workers are the people who give their blood for the management and that they should have good conditions, good pay and should be well fed. The trade unions are the best thing here – they are not so powerful in other countries. They are a nice power and we should keep it on.[51]

There is a volatility in the movement of consciousness. Jean McCrindle was to become treasurer of Women Against Pit Closures in 1984 and was closely involved in the emergence of a women's support group in Barnsley. But just before the strike she had done interviews about pit closures with miners' wives in the area: 'At that time nearly all the women I interviewed were aggressively antagonistic to Scargill himself and his media image, but also quite hostile to a strike.'[52] Within a few months there was to be a dramatic transformation. But after the strike Jean McCrindle was still turning over in her mind some of the ideas she had taken part in voicing a decade earlier in the Arsenal Women's Liberation Group paper on class:

> I grew up in a tradition in which to say you were political. . .meant that you had to have a connection with working-class movements. To say you were political and just write articles and be a feminist academic or something was never my conception of what being political was.
>
> And I just took that through with me, as have other socialist feminists, right through the women's movement, and still have it. You needed to be building bridges between ideas and some working-class movements. . .[53]

This political conception forms a counterpoint to the feminist emphasis on expressing the subjectivity of one's own oppression. It has exercised an immensely important influence on British feminism.[54] The effort to extend the initial social composition of the women's movement has had a political dimension which to some extent offsets the dubious inspiration of personal guilt about class privilege. During the 1980s, however, it has become increasingly apparent also that the historical experience of the previous decade has not equipped feminists to comprehend the scale and singlemindedness of the offensive now being faced by women workers. The politics of the women's movement during the 1970s inclined towards enabling women to act at the grass roots with greater effect. This was important, but not adequate to deal with the onslaught that workers have met from employers and the state.

The 1980s have seen feminists in many countries engaging with the problem of power. In Britain the Thatcherite era has presented an acute dilemma to those socialist feminists who seek to build the political bridges described by Jean McCrindle. Aware of both their marginality within the power structures of the unions and the overall threat to the labour movement, they have oscillated between challenging male domination and defending the working class as a whole. Thus, contemporary feminism has had to struggle with a classic political conundrum of sectional interest versus wider alliance.

In the early 1980s, writing in the *Beyond the Fragments Bulletin*, Joanna de Groot argued that the problem of male power in the unions was not just a matter of the positions occupied. Men had a wider hegemonic power to determine priorities and keep issues which bear closely on women's circumstances down in the second division.[55] This was not to deny the impact women were nonetheless having on the labour movement. To some feminists, however, the changes appeared slow and derisorily small. Bea Campbell's dismissive phrase of 1984, 'the men's movement',[56] was a pithy expression of feminist complaint about male domination, but it has had an unfortunate effect in implicitly negating women's actual achievements. It presents an ahistorical and unchanging structure of male power rather than a dynamic picture of struggle and change.[57]

It has been extremely difficult simultaneously to challenge male power and assert the need for women and men workers to unite strategically on common ground – for example, against low pay and job loss, and in campaigns for shorter hours or trade-union rights. Despite the lack of conscious strategy, however, both joint action by workers and solidarity from social movements have persisted. There has been a profound recognition of interconnecting commitments not only by feminists but by groups of gay men and lesbian women who have also been assailed by the policies of the Conservative government.

A further obstacle has presented itself, however. There has been a greater ease and certainty about solidarity with strikers, male as well as female, whatever the feminist critiques of male power, than about modes of intervention in the formulation of union policy. Here the problem with power has not been simply that men have it. Feminists have had enormous difficulties in developing a political strategy for posing an overall alternative to conservatism, given that this would necessitate moving beyond grass-roots resistance. It would be unrealistic to claim that a female alternative was waiting in the wings, prevented only by 'patriarchy' from taking the stage amidst popular applause. Yet the political and trade-union activity of women in the last two decades has left a rich deposit of experience which could be a source of valuable insights. A recurring concern has been how women can find ways of influencing decisions and policies without abandoning the ideas and supportive forms of organization they have developed.

The difficulty is not simply political or organizational. There is a cultural presumption about a public political role which gives it masculine accoutrements – despite the extraordinary phenomenon of Margaret Thatcher. In different ways this bears on women as well as men. The effects have probably been accentuated by the strong distrust of power as inherently corrupt that marked the women's liberation inheritance of American radical politics.

Barbara Gunnell achieved election to the vice-presidency of the National Union of Journalists as a job-share candidate with Scarlett MccGwire in 1987, after feminist campaigning had opened all union positions to this form of tenure, and in 1988 they went on to become joint presidents. But in the early 1980s she had noted an ambivalence among women trade unionists about taking power on existing terms:

> Women are good at encouraging women to take office at the bottom of the union and at helping new office-holders. But some of us seem distinctly uneasy, nervous about seeing women at the top. . .It could also be that men get the disapproval and hostility all the time but don't mind, while women can't be thick-skinned. After all they aren't used to being in the firing line.[58]

Perhaps it could also be that women are undermined by pressures from several directions. Joan Bohanna, a convenor at Glaxo Operations, described how when she became a shop steward she found male members paid lip-service to what she said in the committee but informally agreed with management that women were 'too emotional to make a serious evaluation of a situation'. Women who hang on and fight, however, face attack on quite different grounds:

> You get many titles, not least being that you are unfeminine and hard. This seems to be a standard maxim of men when faced with the problems of how to deal with a woman who decides to invade what they consider to be their domain. . .Your own sex tend to become frightened of you and, as I have been told many times, you make them uncomfortable because you make them think about things they would prefer to leave hidden.[59]

Joanna de Groot is a university teacher who has been active in her own union and involved with trade-union education, which has brought her into contact with many women trade unionists. Her impression is that they feel power needs to be 'redistributed so that women get the share to which they are entitled', and that they also want 'a redefinition of power and political activity which will be more relevant to them'.[60] This could perhaps make it easier for more women to take responsibility and power, and to feel less isolated in doing so.

Hilary Wainwright has also argued in 'A New Trade Unionism in the Making?':

> Our relations, as feminists, with male-dominated trade-union organizations shouldn't just be determined by their policies and actions as far as women are concerned. . .we should also be on the look-out for deeper developments which can affect whether a trade-union organization is moving in a direction potentially favourable to women.[61]

She suggests that questioning the conditions of work, the purposes of production or the nature of state involvement in industry all exemplify this kind of development. Workers' attempts to draw up positive alternatives to the traditional forms of state intervention in order to secure greater control over resources could be compared with the women's movement's emphasis on control in community projects like nurseries.

Although this was one of the ideas that drew many socialist feminists to the conference and network which developed from the book *Beyond the Fragments*, the search for political convergence as a basis for strategic alliance with labour has not been the prevailing focus for feminist discussion of the unions. Perhaps it could only have assumed this position if a strong and united women's movement had survived into the 1980s and organized labour had not been forced on to the defensive.

It has, however, become evident to many feminists that improving women's circumstances at work means not only engaging with the unions but tackling power in the state, where employment conditions are increasingly being determined. During the 1970s state regulation took the form of industrial legislation and government attempts to implement incomes policies. One debate on the connection between the unions and the state erupted in the late 1970s into a brief controversy about the need for a feminist incomes policy. In 1978 Bea Campbell and Val Charlton wrote 'Work to Rule' in *Red Rag* in a mood of despair over the débâcle of Labour's economic policies which had embittered so many of the party's supporters. They argued that the consensus of militant trade unionism to fight for higher wages was a dead end in itself (as gains would be lost by inflation) and would not solve the problem of women's inequality in relation to men's wages.[62] Later, in 'United We Fall', Bea Campbell developed her argument: 'Two years ago, in our first lurch into the wages debate, we went against the grain of the Left's dismissal of the social contract by suggesting the need for a feminist incomes policy.'[63]

Behind their proposition was the insistence of the feminism of the 1970s that women's interests should not be disregarded in the distribution of wealth, and that more is needed by people than can be expressed simply through wage bargaining. They can be seen to be reacting both to the defeat of women's hopes of the early and mid 1970s for equality in earnings with men and to an assertive phase of trade unionism which characterized the 1960s and still had force in the 1970s, in which workers in relatively powerful positions (mainly men) were able to bargain confidently for higher wages.

The onslaught on workers' power in the 1980s has confirmed feminists' rejection of a narrow notion of economic struggle confined to the workplace. On the other hand, turning to the state in its present form as a means of achieving a more equitable distribution of wealth clearly presents problems in terms both of class and of men's and women's incomes. Angela Weir and Mary McIntosh pointed these out in 'Towards a Wages Strategy for Women':

> There is no automatic mechanism by which wage rises for miners or printers must come out of the pockets of clerical workers or cleaners; nor would successful struggles by shop workers or nurses necessarily weaken the power of the steelmen or the dockers. There is no real evidence that holding down men's wages would improve women's pay. The real weakness of women on the wages front is a weakness in relation to their employees.[64]

Under Thatcher, any notion of benign state intervention on behalf of sections of workers has become inconceivable, but the issue of how workers could gain access to the resources of the state in order to enhance their economic power remains of great significance. A related problem is how to combine economic militancy with strategic demands for legal change and state intervention. These questions are of particular relevance to women workers, since in the past, precisely because of their weak bargaining position, they frequently turned to the state for protection in the form of both laws and social benefits. Clearly the character of the laws is important. But, however beneficial they might be, as the militant movement that forced them through subsided they could become ineffective, or even in some cases be used against women by employers or male workers. It is thus not just a matter of gaining the political power to use the state – to get legal restrictions on working hours, for instance, or welfare provisions – but of building enduring forces that can fight ferociously for such measures to operate in the interests of working-class people. If this idea were to be theoretically assimilated by the Labour Party and become the basis for a new combination of political and economic power, it would mark a decisive break with that party's traditional acceptance of the existing framework of the state as neutral.

What is at issue is the relation between organized economic power and the state. As these have become more closely entwined in the interest of capital, the questions of how the state might act differently and what kind of state it would become in that event have been discussed by some socialists. The issues raised concern not only the legal framework but also direct economic intervention. There have been several employment struggles involving women that have led them to conclude that changes in the operation and structure of the state are needed. For example, when young women workers at Lee Jeans occupied their factory against the threat of closure in the early 1980s, Lindsey German pointed out the economic irony behind their dispute. The UF Corporation, who made Lee Jeans, chose to set up in Greenock because it was a depressed area in which sugar refining and shipbuilding had declined:

> The government has been willing to give new industries large grants to bring any work at all to the area. What is now becoming clear is that these companies have taken the money and run as soon as it is no longer available. Now that grants and tax in Ireland are more favourable they have decided to transfer all production to their factories there.[65]

Big sums of public money were being given to employers – by Labour as well as the Conservatives – during the 1970s, on the assumption that this would result in the creation and maintenance of jobs where they were needed. The money had come partly from working-class people's taxes, and it was given away to corporations whose priorities were unlikely to include loyalty to the depressed regions. From the late 1970s rank-and-file trade unionists began to ask why the state was handing over public money to the employers so trustingly. They demanded forms of state intervention in the economy which would give workers greater control over state subsidies, investment, and the products and markets of private firms. In the course of their fight against job loss the Lucas workers produced an alternative plan for socially useful production. This sparked off debates among trade unionists which also drew in socialist feminists like Jane Barker, Hilary Wainwright and Ursula Huws.

The ideas that emerged from this discussion found their way into left local government, where they influenced economic strategy, but have been left hanging in the air because of the Conservative government's success, through cuts, rate-capping, and the abolition of large local authorities like the GLC, in thwarting the practical development of such initiatives, both locally and nationally. Also, the Labour leadership has been exceedingly unwilling to follow through the implications of these ideas for democratizing economic policy.[66] Nevertheless, this line of thought suggested more general questions about the kind of state that could work in partnership with popular forms of workers' and users' democracy, and how these groups might retain a defensive autonomy while extending their power to decide political objectives.

Clearly the resolution of such questions is not just a matter for the women's movement in Britain, but is a broader, indeed international, preoccupation. Nor has the exhaustive attention given by feminists to the welfare state been applied to the ways in which the extension of women's economic strength might involve changing power relations in the state. This problem has, however, arisen in several different areas of debate in the course of the movement's recent history.

The complexity behind the slogan 'A woman's place is in her union' is partly due to the multi-faceted manifestations of inequality within trade unions. But it also springs from wider changes in the social composition of organized labour and from economic restructuring in which women have been vitally concerned. The labour movement itself has been going through a decisive transformation. Not only has it been assailed by accusations of sexism and demands for change from feminists, but also changing employment patterns have meant that many traditionally male jobs have disappeared. The situation has been further complicated by the peculiar grafting of New Left ideas on to older labour-movement assumptions – neither of which proved adequate for an overall assessment of the social changes the unions were to face in the 1980s. We have also lacked a theoretical means of understanding the combination of received knowledge, experience and consciousness that have influenced both women's liberation and trade unionism.

Despite these tangled threads, women workers' determination and breadth of activity have contributed to an intense and creative historic change in the trade-union movement, even in the face of a ruling-class offensive. Amid the demoralization of the last decade it has been difficult to hang on to the positive ideas produced as extended meanings of trade unionism have been hammered out through innumerable disputes. Nor has it always been possible to transcend the sectional and defensive terms in which feminism has sometimes phrased its critique of women's subordination. However, there has been a vigorous and insistent strand in feminism to oppose that approach.

The capacity of a democratic trade unionism to survive, expand and overcome the new economic and social divisions created among workers by economic restructuring is inseparable from the issues of inequality raised by women in the unions and in the women's movement. This is far from being a parochial matter. In *Common Fate, Common Bond* Swasti Mitter quotes the early radical credo that has been emblazoned on the banners of trade unionism:

> The world is my country,
> Mankind are my brethren,
> To do good one to another is my religion.

She observes, 'The time has now come to make explicit room for womankind. . .'[67]

Part Five

Identity and Community

14

Breaking Images

In August 1968 a group of young women protested against the Miss America beauty contest by crowning a sheep and depositing objects of female torture in a rubbish bin. Girdles, curlers, issues of *Ladies' Home Journal* and bras were discarded. This rebellion against a manufactured ideal of feminine beauty generated its own legend. Henceforth 'women's libbers' were to be 'bra-burners'. It was an early warning of the power of symbols, always important in politics, but in feminist politics touching particularly acute and sensitive nerves.

The contested borders between public and private, evident in the changes in everyday life at home and at work, were beginning to find a political language in the late 1960s.

An important influence was the movement of black consciousness which had compelled French left-wing thinkers like Sartre to discuss identity as part of the political process. In the United States black Civil Rights activists drew on spiritual concepts to express connection between self-perception, culture and social transformation. The movement used symbolic direct action to contest white 'space' by sitting in at lunch counters. It also struggled to go beyond formal democratic rights to reveal and challenge hidden forms of power based on internalized racism.

As Bernice Reagon says it was Civil Rights which was 'the centering, borning essence'[1] of the subsequent movements.

Feminists applied the Civil Rights movement's political innovations in differing international contexts. Many groups of women inherited the focus on identity, the attempt to recreate the self in relation to a social movement. They challenged both physical and cultural territory and admitted implicit restraints on freedom as well as evident claims to 'rights'.

In France situationist writers in the Sixties had developed a critique of the emphasis upon exploitation in Marxism, which they argued ignored other areas of human oppression. They pointed to the control exercised by the display of a consumer society and the media's power to reproduce symbols which evoked and shaped desire. They coined a new political term, 'the spectacle'. The fulfilment of subjectivity thwarted by the whole context of everyday life in modern capitalism required the recreation of social relations in the most profound manner. The subjective in struggle was seen as the means of realizing human wholeness.[2] This was to be a powerful theme in the student uprising of May 1968 which influenced many European 'First Wave' feminists.

In the States the student movement produced the phrase 'the personal is political', which challenged the existing scope of political issues and presented an alternative kind of political process. One strand in American radical politics took this a step further and asserted emotion against old theories and reason, which was characterized as the tool of the oppressor.[3]

Kathie Amatniek (Sarachild) produced an early definition of women's liberation consciousness-raising in the USA: 'In our groups, let's share our feelings and pool them. Let's let ourselves go and see where our feelings will lead us.'[4] Leaving nothing to chance, however, she adds hastily, 'Our feelings will lead us to ideas and then to action.'[5]

It was to prove true – up to a point. Many young women inspired by the new movement found the release and exploration of accounts of personal life empowering and a means of recognizing the social oppression of women. The separation of personal and public spheres was seen as a way of restricting women's articulation of grievances.

In Germany the student movement, painfully aware of fascism as a reality in their parents' lives, rediscovered traditions of radical psychoanalysis. They believed it was vital to create prefigurative forms as the basis for a new anti-authoritarian culture. The men were strong on theory. The women demanded practical measures, crèches for instance.

At a conference in Frankfurt in 1968, Helke Sander took up this demand and commented:

> The separation between private and public life always forces the woman into lonely endurance of the problems of her role. . .women can only find their identity if the problems previously hidden in the private sphere are articulated and made into the focus for women's political solidarity and struggle.[6]

Ideas circulated internationally and this awareness of the political nature of private life awakened in young radicals interest not only in psychoanalysis but in strands of Marxist thought which had pursued the links between subjectivity and social transformation. There was, however, a real difficulty in the convergence of these strands of radical thinking. In one breath subjectivity was put to the fore, in the next, individual human will and personal emotion were demoted.

In Herbert Marcuse's words advanced capitalism was ' "a psychological economy"; it produces and administers the needs demanded by the system, even the instinctive needs'.[7] In the process of extending the scope of politics into confrontation in every aspect of life, capital's tendrils were seen everywhere. It was a daunting and pessimistic picture of Leviathan's power, summed up in the term 'conditioning'.

The women's movement, in seeking to reveal and understand the wider implications of oppression, thus inherited contrary theoretical assumptions. One was unstintingly convinced that individuals could will themselves to freedom. Another presumed that every crevice of our consciousness was determined by capital. This rather tense juxtaposition was to be a source of friction and confusion.

However, as we sat in an early women's liberation group in North London in 1969 we were not giving the situationists and Marcuse a thorough theoretical overhaul. Elements of their ideas were current in a whirl of slogans, assertions and stances. But we were preoccupied with the jutting vaginas which loomed large in the swimwear ads as you went down the Holborn tube. Emotionally affected by the more overtly sexual portrayal of women in the media – camera angles from below – we were trying to work out why the ads affronted us and what to do about them.

Deciding that they reduced women to mere bodies and denied our humanity, we decided to answer them back, as we had done for the Vietnam war by putting contesting stickers on adverts of war films. We made oblong white stickers with 'This exploits women' written clearly in black and white, and we produced another set for good measure advertising the forthcoming equal pay march. We cautiously embarked on 'the new politics' with older left formulations and causes in tow. This was characteristic of the movement in Britain, which has cherished the custom of 'something old, something new'.

Sue O'Sullivan captures the mood of the early consciousness-raising groups vividly in her article, 'Passionate Beginnings: Ideological Politics 1968–72'. She records that the sticker campaign aimed to subvert what we saw as 'anti-women or woman-as-object advertisements'.[8] Our tiny band had the evangelical enthusiasm of those who have seen the world in a new light. All around us in adverts, the cinema, and television were images of a distorted man-made femininity. We had an overpowering desire to communicate the clarity of our recent understanding to other women.

In November 1969, women in Britain, influenced by the Americans, demonstrated against the Miss World contest. In 1970, during the next demonstration, a bomb exploded under a BBC outside-broadcast van and five women were arrested amidst a blaze of publicity.

The demonstrators produced their own pamphlet, *Why Miss World?*. Again the disruption of 'the spectacle' was linked to resistance against material oppression. *Why Miss World?* traced the economics of the competition and Mecca's business interest. It tried to connect the women in the contest with the social subordination of women. Beauty was a source of inequality and division among women. Compliance with men's gaze made it impossible for women to find their own identity. 'We have been in the Miss World contest all our lives. . .dividing other women up into safe friends and attractive rivals. . .we've all been through it,'[9] wrote the battle-weary twenty-year-olds.

The passionate desire for union among women was a necessary first step towards the fused identity of a new social movement. The symbolic disruption of a spectacle which ordered divisive conceptions of our female identity was part of a wider challenge to the power of men to define and judge how we were to be valued.

However, it was not to be that straightforward. Even at this early stage there was a cluster of indications that this form of political action had snags. They were to call into question some of the premises of the theory of subjectivity versus the spectacle, which the modern media were seen as orchestrating. They also suggested problems of method. Guerrilla theatre and direct action invaded and caught the attention of the media to redirect the message. But implications could boomerang. Sue O'Sullivan writes of our sticker campaign: 'For one week we saturated the escalators, station and train ads. And we did get publicity but not one paper mentioned the sticker which had all the details of the Equal Pay rally and most articles made a joke out of the attacks.'[10]

In opposing a representation of women which we saw as offensive we wanted to express our conception of an alternative, liberatory sexuality. Instead we were caught up in the dominant culture's fascination with women as sexual beings. 'Women's Lib' was titillating. Equal pay was not. In attempting to transcend the split between the personal and the economic we had become fenced in neatly by the media in the domain of sexuality which made us newsworthy. It was not only that we had insufficient control over the media's recording of our action to turn around the meaning of the spectacle. We were to learn that once you take political arguments to eros, interpretation can get hazy.

For Sue O'Sullivan's baby-sitter, a Catholic schoolgirl at the time, the 'This exploits women' sticker did not signal a call to women to cast off their chains as the objects of desire. She assumed they were planted by '. . .puritanical crazed nuns racing through the subways in outrage at the display of nudity in the posters'.[11]

A feminist challenge to images we perceived as oppressive and degrading could simply look like an attempt to suppress women's sexuality. This was to become a familiar theme. The meaning of a symbolic protest depended on the social assumptions that influenced one's perception. There was no single meaning in a defiant gesture against the ideology of an image, because gestures can carry a multiplicity of meanings. Indeed, if communication were not a complex process the job of advertising would be without risk. The problem with entering the media and attempting to turn around the presentation of women was that you could be incorporated within a quite different set of terms and come over as demonstrating what you actually opposed. Also, we were so convinced that the media were the enemy that we supped neurotically with the devil, refusing to explain ourselves. As Sue O'Sullivan remarked with hindsight, 'There is something self-defeating in the politics of the movement which is prepared to burst onto the screen of seven million viewers one minute, but withdraw the next into a jealously guarded privacy.'[12]

Many of the women involved in the Miss World demo subsequently turned quite determinedly away from big-splash political actions. They worked in Claimants' Unions with unemployed women and single mothers. They organized in trade unions, community struggles and the newly formed gay liberation groups.

Instead of communication through symbolic propaganda by deed
they adopted the longer-term forms of agitation over which they
could exercise control – local community newspapers lovingly pieced
together with scissors and paste.

But the memory of the challenge to beauty contests remained.
Protests were repeated in other towns throughout the 1970s. In the
late Seventies women in the libertarian group Big Flame were still
pressing the arguments of the early demonstrators:

> It has always been clear to us as feminists that women are first and
> foremost seen and valued in terms of their role as sex objects for
> men. That's why one of the first big protests of the recent women's
> movement was against beauty contests, the disruption of the Miss
> World Contest in 1970.
>
> We were angry at being made to feel that our most important qualities
> as women were simply our physical attractiveness to men. We know
> this divided us, humiliated and degraded us, forcing us always to see
> ourselves through men's eyes, living to please them, competing with
> each other.[13]

However, the participants in the beauty contests maintained they
did not see competition in these terms. Their bodies and appearance
were matters of pride. One response from feminists when faced with
opposing conceptions was to assume simply that everyone else was
duped. But this approach to consciousness veered towards elitism
and had the disadvantage of putting feminists immediately at odds
with other women.

Rosalind Coward approached the problem from another tack. In
the early 1980s she suggested that we bring meanings to words and
images from our own social experience. She was concerned with the
problem of pornography, which from the late 1970s was coming
to dominate feminist discussions of how women are portrayed.
She thought the concentration on pornography was obscuring
an attempt to understand the wider implications of 'codes of
submission' and fragmentation' through which aspects of being
a woman were portrayed in the media.

She also pointed to the notoriously indistinct border between the
erotic and the pornographic, arguing that an image could not be
contested in isolation: '. . .their meanings arise from how various
elements are combined, how the picture is framed, what lighting
is given, what is connoted by dress and expression, the way these
elements are articulated together.'[14]

But the theoretical attempt to decode complexity of meaning had remarkably little impression on the political assault against pornography which was developing among some strands of the British women's movement. Pornography was assuming a new political significance as the symbol of male violation of women.

In the early 1970s the London Women's Liberation Workshop had refused to be drawn into the anti-pornography lobby, insisting that the point was to change social relations between men and women, not to direct one's fire at symptoms of a distorted sexuality. There was the lurking assumption that a pure sexuality dwelt somewhere – presumably locked within women – which could be released on the world. Quite what this was or how it had retained its innocence we could only intimate. As the years went by the quest for an alternative sexuality which was to be at once unrepressed and harmoniously democratic became increasingly convoluted in both lesbian and heterosexual relationships.

One of the problems was that desire was not aroused on democratic decree. The effort to control eros could smother lust in heterosexual relations, which turned into brotherly–sisterly love, dissolving passion. Disputes among lesbian feminists were also fraught. I remember a fierce argument breaking out after a women's liberation conference cabaret in the mid-1970s. One woman insisted that the humorous portrayal of male/female roles confirmed oppressive stereotypes which feminists opposed, while the other saw the comedy of manners as an expression of cultural power. This split had extensive ramifications.

The feeling that there was something amiss with the faith that relationships could be changed at will made some feminists incline towards psychoanalysis, both as a means of theorizing and as a therapeutic practice. However, as Michèle Barrett pointed out in *Women's Oppression Today*, the political implications of this shift grew more remote.[15] Psychoanalytic practice had its own exigencies and they made political conclusions even more difficult.

These problems are still unresolved in feminist thinking, though they have led to extensive and innovative theoretical enquiries, for example into the impact of images on our consciousness, the relation between conscious will and unconscious inclination, between culture and material life, between action and fantasy.

The move towards psychoanalysis was not simply intellectual, it was part of a wider uneasiness among many feminists with earlier assumptions which had equated the personal with the political.

Ten years or so of intense political activity had left a need for deeper, more private sources of psychic and spiritual renewal. The directions of this new inwardness were varied: apart from psychoanalytic practice, there was interest in therapies, Eastern religions, alternative medicine. Some feminists turned towards poetry, fiction and autobiography.

These responses were not about contesting ideological points but implicitly they were expressing a rejection of an approach which had attempted to politicize personal life by folding subjectivity into a conceptual framework devised to understand the external manifestations of social forces rather than inner processes. It was not that all these women abandoned feminist politics but that the axis of their politics shifted.

Instead of the *fusion* of the personal and political there was a more confused exploration of a range of responses which could be in a contrary and ambivalent relation to political concepts. Space to consider and perceive the play between conscious and unconscious influences was sought because the earlier optimism about a neat and easy 'fit' had begun to develop a suffocating, authoritarian character.[16] It has, however, been hard to hold together the recognition of the significance of a complex process of interaction while defending the space for speculation. Moreover, intellectual doubt and emotional and spiritual exploration are ineffective in head-on political conflict. As one strand of feminists became more confused, another grew much more decided. In 1979 the Leeds Revolutionary Feminist Group was arguing that heterosexuality was a form of male control.[17]

Moving away from a feminism which sought to examine the whole spectrum of social relations, identifying interlocking and sometimes conflicting forms of subordination, the focus was now on sexual violence. This had the advantage of clarity and gained considerable influence as a new feminist consensus.

The stress on violence was based partly on the grim realities revealed in the Rape Crisis centres and battered women's testimonies in the Women's Aid Centres. It was also stimulated by a growing fear among women as the city streets became more dangerous. A series of murders in the north of England by Peter Sutcliffe contributed. Women in northern towns were terrified to walk home at night before his arrest. All this inclined many feminists to accept Jalna Hanmer's argument: 'We focus on rape and violence against women in the home without being fully aware that violence in all its forms makes up a crucial dimension in the social control of women.'[18]

There followed a series of elisions in which specific acts of rape or physical attack were present as manifestations – of a violence which characterized all aspects of heterosexual relations and was the determining constraint which decided woman's subordination. As Rosalind Coward pointed out in 1982, this led to 'a reductive sort of politics' in which every aspect of women's social subordination 'was seen through the lens of the one issue of male sexuality'.[19] It was, moreover, a rather specific social definition of male sexuality as a ravaging potency constantly seeking passive female prey. This denies that women have active desire towards men and, despite social constraints, are as inclined to pursue as to be pursued, even within the codes of submission.

Because some men raped and many fantasized rape, all men were described as potential rapists by some feminists. But there is not a simple connection between fantasy and reality. Also, both men and women have the potential for cruelty and murder, yet we know we also have other potentials.

Moreover, some feminists began to equate pornography with the act of rape. The scope of coercive violence was extended: 'Pornography is the theory, rape is the practice.' 'Pornography is violence against women.'[20] These made pithy slogans but they led to the conclusion that a physical violation was the *same* as an offending image or fantasy. This had extensive and alarming implications. It was linked to the assertion that heterosexuality was a form of control and thus inherently violent. The physical act of penetration was said to be necessarily oppressive. Anger against specific actions in which particular men violated women was magnified into an interpretation of social relations in which all men became simply 'the enemy'.

A danger in the prioritization of male violence as the explanation of women's subordination is that it leads towards a profoundly conservative pessimism, in which human beings appear to be determined more or less from birth. Also it leaves us without strategic recourse. There is simply the reiteration of anger satisfied only by the elimination of men or the contradictory demand for more law and order from the 'male-dominated' state.

Because there is violence at one end of the spectrum, this does not mean there is *only* violence and that all forms of male–female culture and relationships only express violence. Without such distinctions it is impossible to consider what kinds of circumstances increase or diminish violence in society. It is also impossible to conceive of alliances with men who also suffer forms of subordination.

The logical strategy to spring from the emphasis on violence and its extended interpretation into sex and fantasy was separatism. Some feminists have seen the liberation of women as impossible in a society with men. Others have argued for a strategic withdrawal from any political links. Yet others have preferred to live without personal contact with men.

But women have many problems which require dealings with men. In the 1980s, as the economic recession deepened, these became less easy to avoid in practice. Feminists of various views turned to main-stream politics, many joining the Labour Party. This brought about a re-alignment in which some of these assumptions were modified but were also taken up by many women in the Labour Party who were new to feminist ideas.

So a political perspective which was bound up with a separatist politics was grafted on to labourism with some curious results. In the context of the Labour Party this has resulted not in a challenge to interpretations of socialism as a whole in the manner of socialist feminism, nor in a more sophisticated working of the relation of autonomous organizing to a party, but in a split between Labour 'politics' and 'women's issues'.

The parliamentary traditions of the Labour Party also substituted for the direct-action tactics feminists had used against sex shops and pornography and in the symbolic taking of the male 'space' of the streets in the Reclaim the Night marches. This has introduced the question of using the law to bring harsher penalties against sexual violence and harassment. Using the law is, however, problematic in all these areas. It is not clear how laws are going to be enforced; moreover they can rebound. Evidence of the improving effect of harsher penalties is also controversial.[21] The attempt to legislate against pornography presents particular difficulties because not actions but images and impressions are at issue. As Lynne Segal points out, the attempt to censor pornography is liable to be applied in the courts to work by feminists, lesbians and gay men.[22]

The involvement of some Labour Party women in the anti-porn strand of feminism has meant that the attempt to suppress pornography has assumed a public profile. Disagreements which had long simmered among feminists have thus been brought out into the open.

In a 1987 *New Statesman* article, 'Adventures in the Soho Skin Trade', Melissa Benn looked critically at the assumptions behind anti-porn feminism, which holds that 'pornography is both cause and symptom of women's poor economic, employment and domestic situation. It also argues it is a precipitating cause of actual violence against women.'[23]

As this is being asserted as 'the feminist' position, her reminder that this approach has been disputed at length among feminists is timely. She also outlines some snags in the anti-porn analysis. Pornography plays with more than one theme. One species arouses by presenting women in positions of powerlessness, immobile, wounded, humiliated and submissive to the point of physical annihilation. However, another fantasy is of male helplessness, passivity, even torture and death. In others the male becomes infantile before the woman as sexual initiator and organizer. These can be briskly nurturing nurses, bossy school teachers, *femmes fatales* or the female dominatrix who snuffs out the male entirely.

If pornographic fantasy is so clearly linked to reality then, as Melissa Benn asks, '. . .why if so much porn is about women doing violence to men, don't women go out and sexually attack men?'[24]

Pornography as the iconized representation of a political perspective about masculinity as violence blocks further interrogation. Anti-porn feminism thus leads to an unnecessary dead end in thinking about sexuality. Many interesting questions are over-shadowed by its moral fervour. Do pornographic images pattern lust, or do the social and psychological interactions of physical desire generate emotions pornography codifies and transmits? What on earth makes people find one another sexy?

When violence and masculinity are equated, whole zones of sexuality are eclipsed. Sensations and emotions are artificially polarized by gender. For women *and* for men sex can evoke not only 'acceptable' emotions of openness, union and courage, but those that are less sunny – antagonism, dread, fear, submission.

The slogan 'the personal is political' began as an assertion of new perceptions, by being treated as a received fact it rigidified into a new source of hypocrisy. For we found ourselves clutching a lodestone which fused ideals, prescriptions, wants and desires and gave conflicting directions.

Joan Nestle, who was involved in early lesbian feminist groups in New York, observed with prescience that new boundaries were being constructed even in the process of dismantling others:

I learned that class played a role but wasn't to be talked about and certain sexual practices were taboo. . .Now I was living another double

life in feminism. . .I knew that something was missing in the world I
saw around me; understandings were missing. Just as feminism had
given me things, I was also losing something.[25]

One of the losses was a capacity for openness and receptivity
which could explore contradiction and ambivalence. Mandy Rose,
an independent feminist film-maker, argues that the emphasis on
an ideal sexuality in anti-porn feminism leads to 'the creation of yet
more silences and suppressions about sex'.[26]

Buried within the argument about pornography there is an unresolved problem about how aspirations for alternative cultural forms
of expression can have a dialectical relationship with actual cultural
practices. If we simply brandish ideals of what we decide ought to be,
we neglect expression of existing wants. For example, one aspect of
the silence imposed by anti-porn feminism is that it makes it difficult
to look at how pornography can arouse women apart from returning
us to the deterministic concept of 'conditioning'. Its challenge to
male-defined sexual culture is in terms of a feminist convention of
a woman-centred 'good' sexuality, in which the tangled range of
women's sexual desires are nicely sorted. Out goes a lot of scruffy
unlabelled jumble and we are delivered a salutary, nurturing,
non-violent, co-operative loving.

However, the imposition of such a fixed female identity can
enclose as much as the male-defined images which forced the
original challenges to the beauty contest. The 'virtuous' woman
is part of a male culture too. Morality, like allure, has always been
a double-edged womanly weapon. In exasperation a group of New
York feminists in the early 1980s exploded against the connection
between feminism and purity, forming a woman's group called 'No
more nice girls'.

Mandy Rose breaks out of the purity enclosure energetically:

> Women should be allowed the freedom to seek out, to consume and
> buy images that we find sexually exciting. Although porn is in many
> ways flawed and particularly for women, the fact is that porn is the only
> sphere that exists for a non-moralistic exploration of women's sexual
> fantasy and desire.[27]

But this presents as an alternative to anti-porn feminism a free
market in fantasy, suggesting that we could simply lift existing
images off the shelves of an abundant sex hyperstore to satisfy.

This cultural relativism rescues freedom but obscures a real problem which anti-porn feminism catches emotionally. The images are not just flawed. There is a profound incongruence for women's sexual desires in a culture of desire which is fundamentally male-defined. This was the starting point for the sense of not belonging in existing culture which led many women towards feminism.

A variant on the old Marxist adage about human beings acting on their life and times, though not in circumstances of their own choosing, is applied by Muriel Dimen to sex in *Surviving Sexual Contradictions*. (A real 1980s title, that.) She argues for the explicit recognition of contradictory perceptions of sexuality. She observes that pornographic images can both contain women and be a means of subverting containment. They can arouse both because we are trapped in a male definition of desire and because our desire is barred from expression. Pornography, like other images, can carry more than one meaning. Muriel Dimen suggests that in enjoying pornography women

> are playing with a normally forbidden part of themselves. They are toying with a consciously public representation of their private, lustful wishes. They are entering, and allowing to flower in them, the power of desire, which though it is tabooed because located in men nevertheless belongs to them as well.[28]

Pornography can thus be a symbolic means of bringing ambivalent sexual feelings into the open and through play portraying collisions in sexual assumptions and ways of relating. This avoids the traps of projecting an idealized sexual convention as a feminist morality. It also retains an element of critique.

It is true, though, that some people take better than others to being sent off to live contradictions. The dialectics of desire confuse the agendas. There are yet others who belong to the persuasion of the East London typists in a further education college whom I faced in one of my first liberal studies classes in the early 1960s. Their first comment on sex was curt: 'There are them that talk and them that do.'

Rather than ponderously arguing the point, some feminist writers, artists and film-makers have explored and affirmed aspects of sexuality which if they were not categorized as art (which we all know is for the toffs and thus erotic) might have got listed under the rubric of pornography. Consider for instance Angela Carter's 'The Company of Wolves'. In this reworking of Little Red Riding Hood, Grandma is consumed by the wolf-man. The last thing she sees are hairy legs and his genitals. 'Ah! huge,' she exclaims and expires. Undaunted, Little Red Riding Hood strips and moves in on the wolf-man.[29]

Now you see it, now you don't. In 'Upsetting an Applecart' a most searching essay is made by Sue O'Sullivan and Sue Ardill into the labyrinthine implications of aspects of life that politics rarely reaches. Reflecting on nearly two decades of intense struggle among feminists to change sexually, they say, 'We approach our sexuality to capture it. But is it ever steady enough to capture? To haul into the political arena?'[30]

The women's movement has made a sustained effort of enquiry. How do we in fact create an opposing culture? Can there be transformation in sensibility which produces new images and fantasies, new wants and new desires? Or is it that we shuffle existing images into contexts in which they take us in new directions?

There has been a tremendous feminist cultural offensive to create new images of women in the visual arts and to challenge how women are portrayed in books, newspapers, films, theatre, comedy and television. This engagement with the prevailing terms of culture has taken many forms, not only stickers and demonstrations. Its manifestations have ranged from learned debates in universities to the attempt to live and act differently, from women's communes to styles in dress. In the process, though, snags and complexities have emerged which we could not have conceptualized in our early consciousness-raising groups. These dilemmas have not been confined to Britain – internationally there has been a protracted argument among feminists over how to change the way women are presented in culture. For when we moved from protest to the attempt to exert power over visual, oral and written forms of representation, real differences in assumptions, aims and means came to the surface. Were we to try to eradicate the cultural experience of gender by prohibition? This is always a labour of Sisyphus, for the banning of fantasy in one sphere makes its allure all the more excitingly covert. Nor is it clear who is qualified to draw boundaries about what is permissible and who is to have the power to decide. There are some knotty problems ahead for feminists who propose to change culture by decree.

The attempt to live an alternative has also presented many problems. Cultural imagery is not just out there, it is present in how we ourselves appear. One strand of feminism has opposed restrictive styles in which women are presented as doll-like possessions of men. At times this has meant disregarding or opposing mainstream fashion. In some cases a completely new style of dressing has been invented, like the androgynous smocks and bloomers of early-nineteenth-century utopian socialists. So in the self-presentation of dress and style the same cultural arguments about imagery and fantasy can be detected.

However, the denial of delight in the body and appearance can limit as much as being defined only by one's looks and dress. It is yet another statement. It does not end the hold of fashion but creates a new sub-cultural style. In the 1970s feminists adopted a variety of styles in rebellion against the fashionable image of women. In *Adorned in Dreams* Elizabeth Wilson examines the implicit values in these rebellions. One was the nineteenth-century value of utility, another was the New Left critique of consumerism which emerged with a contempt for conspicuous display in the fashion of 'retro-chic'. Yet another was the authenticity and naturalness which has always been an element in romanticism.[31]

But the meaning of styles change too. The outlaw libertarianism of the 1970s turned into what Elizabeth Wilson calls 'polytechnic dressing' as a generation grew older.[32] It became somewhat dull. The association of virtue with dowdiness is rarely attractive to the young. A new outlaw wrote to *Spare Rib* in 1983,

> Recently I have been the target of a lot of criticism from women. . .because they do not like the way that I dress and wear my hair (i.e. Mohican, Bondage etc.). They tell me that I am ignoring its racist and sexist overtones, that it is not 'feminist', and that I am allowing myself to be exploited by the fashion market. . .
>
> Do you criticize your sisters because they don't wear dungarees and kickers? Is a woman any less emancipated because she 'chooses' to wear make-up and stilettos?
>
> Is not the whole point of feminism to help a woman to realize her right to control her own life and make decisions for herself?
>
> If so, why are we as feminists oppressing women with a new set of rules. . ? would anyone with any individuality call that liberation?[33]

This approach illuminates how over time a defiant style can become a self-satisfied orthodoxy. But it uncritically endorses the view that freedom is simply a matter of atomistic characters floating about in a free market – ironically one of the prevailing orthodoxies of the monetarist conservatism of the 1980s.

So in rebelling against cultural forms we use a combination of existing political and social values. The opposing images that we fashion change in meaning depending on context and period. This may sound obvious but it has been hard to hear it in the heat of battle. When feminists first began to write about appearance, this involved a real tussle between what felt important personally and what was seen as trivial in the male definition of existing politics. But somehow a new split occurred and it became difficult to admit that desirability and appearance could matter to us, regardless of our sexual orientation, more or less acutely at different times in our lives.

In all radical movements there is a certain tension between the explicit drive to focus all forms of self-expression upon the conscious desire to transform and the implicit recognition that a new culture is impossible without the rising power of thwarted imagination. But because women have been oppressed as playthings this has peculiar difficulties for feminism. The artistic movements which have elevated the imagination have tended to do this on male terms and women have remained transfixed as the objects of desire. But to deny imagination, fantasy and play is to curtail impulses which have been a powerful force in the modern women's liberation movement. Writing on fashion, Elizabeth Wilson argues the subversive value in the pointless, the contingent, the decorative, the futile, in play. She argues that fashion is one 'vehicle for fantasy'.[34] Instead of a fixed utopia of the perfected, or an aesthetic based on functionalism, she says:

> there will. . .never be a human world without fantasy, which expresses the unconscious unfillable. All art draws on unconscious fantasy: the performance that is fashion is one road from the inner to the outer world.[35]

Dress can be 'performance art' in which we 'express and explore our more daring aspirations'.[36]

The contemporary feminist movement has been preoccupied not only with images, fantasy, style but also with the power of definitions in opposing a male-dominated culture. Again, this was a theme inherited from the movements of the Sixties and had been discussed extensively in the black movement. Like gay liberation, feminism drew on these political ideas and gave them varied and far-ranging applications.

An important strand in feminism is a respect for memory and a desire to reinterpret history. Beverley Bryan, Stella Dadzie and Suzanne Scafe in *The Heart of the Race* listen in order to redefine:

> Black women in Britain today are faced with few positive self-images and little knowledge of our true potential. If we are to gain anything from our history and from our lives in this country which can be of practical use to us today, we must take stock of our experiences, assess our responses – and learn from them. This will be done by listening to the voices of the mothers, sisters, grandmothers and aunts who established our presence here. And by listening to our own voices.[37]

They add, 'It is not easy to record history as it is still being made, particularly when so much of our story lies buried, so there is much which has yet to be said.'[38]

While there are specific circumstances for the search of particular groups for cultural image and identity, this has been a persistent and intense aspect of the radical social movements of the last few decades. Tension on the borderlines between the personal and the political has been accompanied by the struggle to redefine power around one's social identity. This has involved placing oneself, hence the search for a past, and the process of declaring or naming oneself that is crystallized in the gay liberation phrase 'coming out'.

Bridget Hutter and Gillian Williams suggest in *Controlling Women* that one of the implications of the movement for women's liberation has been a challenge to the categories of what is acceptable:

> When women start appearing in classifications which fall outside this – system, or reject the categories themselves, this may be seen as a serious threat to fundamental equality, this threat may be lessened and women may be made to remain, both symbolically and actually, within 'their place', retaining a primary commitment and loyalty to 'womanly tasks'.[39]

Categorization of women in terms of sexuality has been a means of control by division. Feminists have thus made attempts to contest this separation.

During the trial for murder of Peter Sutcliffe in 1981, the distinction was often made by commentators in the press between those of his victims who were prostitutes and those who were 'totally respectable women'. Both prostitutes and feminists pointed out this amounted to a judgement 'that the lives of prostitutes were worth less'.[40] Prostitutes are often seen in the media or by the police as less entitled to protection than other women. Attacks on them, even murder, are unlikely to cause outcry.[41] Similarly, they have, in practice, few civil rights, so police action towards them can be governed more by personal whim, than by formal legal controls.

Prostitutes as a group are likely to experience serious physical assault. They have tried to counter this threat through organizing to campaign for the decriminalization of prostitution. One step has been to break through their containment in a private and secret zone of sexuality, to find a public voice. This is part of a wider political challenge to a process in which certain groups are encircled by social definitions which remove them from the formal concept of equality before the law. They become not part of 'the public', but part of disorder and deviance. Just as a lesbian is presented as a contradiction to mothers, a prostitute is distinguished from women. A Birmingham woman, Susan, said she joined the Prostitution Reform Organisation (PROS) 'because it's wrong if prostitutes can't stand up and say what they want to say: they should be able to say, "I'm a prostitute", and not be looked down on.'[42]

Another group of women who have resisted stereotyping are those with disabilities. Merry Cross describes how feminists with disabilities, who first began meeting around 1980, also had cause to challenge the power of how they were defined by society. They resisted their representation in the dominant culture by 'never acting as if the stereotypes about us or the limitations placed on us are rational'.[43] Echoing the 1960s concept of consciousness raising, she wrote in 1984:

> I think now that we provide a model for putting into practice the concept that the personal is political and that the women's movement would do well to check back with us, as it were. Even when we meet to look at a particular issue with the interests of developing a policy on that issue, we deal with our feelings first. The more we flush them out, the more confident we are about the rationality of our decision.[44]

Merry Cross says that instead of 'heated intellectual discussions . . .humanity, honesty and the quality of attentive listening'[45] are valued at their meetings. Such an approach could be a safeguard against the manifold forms of sectarianism and exclusivity that can arise in the course of naming one's difference.

The needs of both women and men with disabilities relate to a challenge to the power of stereotyping and the creation of mutual care and confidence as a group and in relation to others. But all this is hot air which stays out in the cold without access to resources and the reorganization of many everyday aspects of social existence, along with feelings and relationships. For instance, their network experienced considerable practical difficulties in demonstrating at a conference where able-bodied experts met 'to tell each other what people with disabilities needed'. They had great 'communication and transport problems' in getting there and then 'toilet and warmth problems once you've arrived'.[46]

In the case of both prostitutes and women with disabilities, the struggle against how society defines and categorizes them is inseparable from a challenge to power relations and the need for material changes.

The assumption that the oppressed are best able to determine their own needs has also been of considerable radical significance for many other groups of women who have asserted their feelings and needs. Once this was done, though, many differences of perception began to emerge among women. Everyone asserted their ranking in an inverted hierarchy of subordination. Lack of power could become a power ploy.

Sue Ardill and Sue O'Sullivan have pointed out that our recognition of the power of naming our sectional oppression is not without internal organizational snags.[47] The emphasis on identity in women's liberation politics can become a claim to a superior moral authority. This is an interesting extension of the old problem on the left of 'workerism'. How is a balance to be found between contesting privilege within our own ranks and indulging in a political gambit to suppress argument simply by notching yourself up on a hierarchy of oppression? This dilemma is important, for it has been a persistent, often destructive, problem in the women's movement. However, it has a wider political significance too in strategic thinking about how groups can claim a conscious identity in ways which open up possibilities for extending the scope of political action rather than imploding in subjective recrimination.

There has been a recurring danger of the politics of identity narrowing the possibilities for democracy by fostering an authoritarianism which makes all opposition outcast and demotes reason as 'male'. A more sophisticated understanding of the differing implications of 'naming' is vitally needed. It cannot be assumed that the act of claiming identity is itself politically radical. It depends on who is claiming what. It is necessary to enquire more closely into the context, the specific power relations, the consequences of the asserted identity in terms of power and resources.

It seems also that problems of democracy arise when people take elements of a group's experience and raise these as a battle standard, rather than seeing the expression of identity in the terms described by Merry Cross – as a process which retains a cultural fluidity. Identity defined only through an enclosed and guarded difference can swiftly lead to acrimony. A more resilient politics is capable of combining what is distinct and what can be recognized in the predicament of others.

In attempting to break the images of femininity and to claim new ways of being women, the feminist movement has encountered twists and turnings we could never have imagined when we started the early groups. Problems are evident now that we could not conceptualize then. We began with snatches of theories which found a subjective resonance. They took us off into perilous territory where there were many dragons, some even of our own making. We can witness honestly to a creative if fraught twenty years of innovation in politics. This makes it possible to note the snags in some of the early assumptions about subjectivity and the transformation of daily life. Theory opens up a vista. It can take the long view. But when you cover the route on the ground you know all the bumps and blockages which do not appear on the maps.

The historical existence of feminism as a movement has meant that ideas have become lived politics and partially assailed prevailing common sense of what can be done. Not surprisingly the women's movement has also left many questions hanging and given rise to real differences of strategy and perspective.

There is a need to defend the scope for disagreement and critical rethinking of concepts which contain contrary political implications, rather than snuffing out dissidence with the accusation of betrayal. 'Naming' can be a means of individual self-realization strengthened by mutuality or a collectivity fortified and walled in by fear.

It would be a terrible wastefulness to foreclose on the creativity which the contradictory movement of circumstances in the late 1960s released, simply because many of the new ideas about politics came up against some dead ends and quagmires. The quest to transform all aspects of social relationships, the search for mutuality, equality, freedom and ecstasy is not diminished because it enters a bleak

landscape. We can take courage and continue. We have a choice
– in Alison Fell's words,

> To pace the moor, and mark it
> like a cat bruises the grass
>   for its bed,
>   or be claimed instead –
> scars of burnt heather, dead
>   weariness, the sheep paths
>   misleading, and the bogs pitted
>   with white water. . .[48]

15

Making Links

In Meg Luxton's *More than a Labour of Love,* a study of three generations of women in a Canadian mining community called Flin-Flon, one of the women says:

> What I'd really like to do is to change pretty well everything about the way people get fed, clothed and live. It takes lots of time, lots of work and not just one person to make such big changes. It seems if you don't do something no one will, but if one person starts and keeps things going others will.[1]

This puts in a nutshell how a vision of radical social transformation can arise from a reconsideration of domestic tasks which have been allotted to women in society. In certain contexts women move into social action to demand, as Temma Kaplan puts it in her description of working-class women's resistance in Barcelona between 1910 and 1918, 'the rights that their obligations entail'.[2] This insistence on rights has sometimes meant a demand for resources and organization in the community, sometimes that women are drawn into the defence of their children and men in social uprisings or strikes. In an account of women's contribution to the 1983–4 Arizona Copper Strike in the United States, Judy Aulette and Trudy Mills show not only how domestic activities can extend outside the 'traditional' sphere of the home but also that everyday domestic life can become fiercely political. They quote an auxiliary member:

> For one thing, women are more aggressive when they see something harming their kids – and when the strike-breaker or scab, he's taking her husband's job away, taking the food away from your kids, taking the shoes off their feet, I think women are the first to respond to that. . . They're seeing the destruction of the family, and they are going to come out with tooth and claw.[3]

The women's interests are embedded within their relationships with the men and children. The antagonism they feel is not motivated simply by support for the men; it also involves resistance to an attack upon themselves. Although this is an American example, the same is true of Britain and other countries as well.

It is possible to see in contemporary feminism an interaction between several sources of rebellion, including both a challenge to existing ways of being female and resistance to conditions which prevent women from fulfilling traditional responsibilities. The popular forms of collective action can extend the range of feminism, preventing it from being ghettoized. Liz Heron argued in an article in the *New Statesman* in 1983 against what she described as the 'politics of retreat', a narrowing of feminism to a 'hostile refusal to engage with existing social and sexual relations in ways that can lead to change'.[4]

There is in fact a great body of experience of such engagements in our immediate past. Along with women's activity at work, these forms of resistance continually push outwards towards other aspects of oppression and extend the social meaning of women's liberation. Feminism can be of help to these fragmented rebellions by asserting a recognition of the links made in action which can give them greater strength and cohesion.

A material resource which has figured a great deal in accounts of what women have regarded since the late 1960s as rights 'that their obligations entail' has been housing. While these struggles about where we live have not been couched quite in the terms of Virginia Woolf's *A Room of One's Own*, the attempt to get better housing has appeared in several political forums in the contemporary feminist movement. Obviously housing struggles are not restricted to women. But it is true that, as a Birmingham International Socialist paper for an early Women's Liberation Conference argued, 'blocked drains, broken lifts, damp, condensation',[5] are particularly important in women's lives because they are the people most likely to be at home dealing with these problems. Valerie Clarke and Kathy Sims argued in *Women's Voice* in 1972 that the tenants' movements were particularly relevant to working-class women because often they paid the rent out of their house-keeping.[6] Housing problems also entered women's liberation politics in Britain in the early 1970s because it became evident that the economic dependence of single women, especially if they had children or were old forced them to the bottom of the housing market. Another group likely to become homeless were Asian women deserted by their husbands, as Rosie Boycott and Christine Aziz noted in *Spare Rib* in 1973.[7]

In the 1970s squatting became an alternative for families who were living in one room or in council hostels. *Islington Gutter Press* ran an article in 1975 on 'Squatters and the Housing Crisis' in which they asked people why they had squatted empty property. One woman, said:

> I squatted because I couldn't get anywhere to live when my marriage broke up, we'd been in a furnished flat. Before we'd found that flat we'd been round all the agencies, even to Shelter. They told us to squat at the time.[8]

Alison Fell wrote in *Spare Rib* in the mid-1970s:

> An increasing number of women take matters into their own hands and meet their own needs by squatting, by direct action forcing the urgency of their situation on unwilling local authorities – there have been single women's squats, gay women's squats, unsupported mothers' squats.[9]

In a general political sense squatting was seen as a direct assertion of control over life. It was also seen on the libertarian left in the early 1970s as offering an alternative to the family, an opportunity for children to be cared for by a wider group.[10] Another aspect of squatting was that many women learned 'male' manual skills, – electrical wiring, plumbing, plastering, carpentry.[11] And it was a means of creating networks that cut across the divisions of race and class and put the ideas of mutual aid and free association into practice, with street parties and campaigns for better amenities.

It soon became apparent, however, that all this self-activity could simply mean squatters were confined in short-life houses which they improved only to lose them through demolition. They also placed themselves outside the responsibility of council re-housing. So new forms of cooperative housing association developed and there was a turn to putting more pressure on councils. When Sophie Watson and Helen Austerberry wrote in 1980 about their experience working for some years with homelesss women, a marked shift of emphasis was apparent. They described in *Spare Rib* the detailed implications of state housing policy and legislation for women. As well as issues like security of tenure and the sale of council housing, which they argued would force women even further into having to rely on second-class housing',[12] because it would remove from the public stock the better council-owned houses, they considered the psychological effect of homelessness. Not having a home, they could observe, was not simply a material deprivation, it was a psychic injury. It contributed to women's feelings of failure.

Formed by the feminism of the 1970s in which female stereotypes were contested, Sophie Watson and Helen Austerberry struggled with an apparently conflicting notion of rights to social resources based on women's upbringing to be home-makers. 'It is important to challenge the idea that women's place is in the home,'[13] they wrote. Yet clearly their work with homeless women revealed the desperate need for accommodation in which women could make a good home for themselves and their families. As feminists they were troubled about the terms in which demands could be made on the state without 'reinforcing our position of total responsibility for our children. . .as if we accepted that it was somehow written in our biology'.[14] Nor did they want to play on the vulnerability of single women or gain the housing on conditions set by the state that curtailed choice of how the women might want to live – for instance with another man or woman. Sophie Watson and Helen Austerberry were also aware that housing is not a woman's need alone; children and men need homes too.

There has been a tension in Women's Liberation politics around the interconnection of women's everyday needs with human need as a whole. In the early 1970s some Communist Party women who inclined toward the new feminism contested making a connection between women and demands for better housing. Florence Keyworth, for example, argued against what she saw as the older labour-movement assumption

> that women can best be brought into mass action. . .through the tenants' movement, the peace movement, parent–teacher associations and so on.
> Of course the tenants' struggle, the campaigns for better education and other social services are all vital, but they are the province of men and women equally.
> To see them as the particular interest of women arises from the bourgeois notion that woman is always a relative creature – someone's daughter, wife or mother – never herself.[15]

However, younger left women in the Trotskyist groups and in the libertarian Marxist group Big Flame had not experienced a tradition of women's needs being defined and explained by a party in the domestic sphere. They were conscious of the limits of a feminism which dealt only with equal rights or the personal liberation of young middle-class women, and they saw housing struggles in terms both of challenging social inequality and of raising confidence.[16]

From the mid-1970s there is a record in women's liberation writing of working-class women challenging the quality and design of housing, pointing to domestic and environmental health hazards, showing the consequences in terms of health and stress, tackling technical issues about energy and water pollution. Present in their concern is both an understanding of the social problems they experience directly and a preoccupation with the lives of their children and their dreams for their future. For example, women in Manchester on a council housing estate pointed out:

> They never should have put families with kids in these flats, as it's one avenue on its own surrounded by main roads. The children are given two choices of where to play, one is a factory and one an empty croft, so of course any kid will choose the factory. This means a lot of kids in the avenue have been prosecuted for 'breaking and entering'. The only other play areas involve crossing three main roads. It's bad for women with young babies on the verandas which are invaded by flies and earwigs, otherwise they don't get any fresh air. Last week an 18-month-old baby fell from the top floor and now has massive internal injuries. There is no safety gate at the top of the stairs either, that means the only way to keep the kids safe is to keep them prisoners.
>
> The flats are built with old drains that are too small to take the waste. Every day they are blocked and rats and sewage waste spill into the verandas and streets, causing a real health hazard. Ancoats has one of the highest T.B. rates in England. No wonder.[17]

Black women in North London who met through a tenants' association formed a group to defend their children, who were being harassed by the police. Martha Osamor described in an interview in *Socialist Woman* in 1978 how concern for their children was an important motivation in their politics: 'You have dreams for them and when you sit back and watch that dream smashed, you've got to do something about it.'[18]

Women's housing struggles have also addressed women's fear of violence, which has become even worse in the economic conditions of the 1980s.[19] Along with proposals for better lighting and design, links have been made between the material inadequacy of the buildings, their damp, lack of safety, overcrowding and psychological stress. 'All the women here are on nerve tablets,' a woman from

Haigh Heights in Liverpool told *Spare Rib* in 1975. 'In other places people borrow butter or sugar from their neighbours. Here we ask for a pill.'[20] Val, secretary of a Leeds tenants' group, wrote, 'Leeds tenants don't need tranquillizers to relieve our depression – we need healthy damp-free houses.'[21]

The process of resistance and its effect on consciousness has also been described. For instance, Maria O'Reilly, an organizer of a flat-dwellers' action group at Netherley, Liverpool, told *Spare Rib* early in 1977 how residents began to mobilize after a child was fatally hurt in 1973. Resentment over council inaction exploded, and Maria and other women came up against opposition and yet gained a power among themselves.

> I have faced male chauvinism I failed to see existed before. . .we came to understand politics, usually thought of as a man's world, and expected more of ourselves – knew more about what we could and couldn't do for ourselves. People now call us women's libbers. I never realized but we must have become just that, though we're not aware of it. Of course some of the men around regard us suspiciously and think that we hold ritual bra-burning sessions to which we might invite their wives.[22]

When women from Pontypridd, South Wales, became involved in a campaign for suitable heating on their estate, at first they asked themselves what they could do as women for the tenants' struggle. Then they began think what the tenants' struggle had done for them:

> When we started the Action Group I was really nervous meeting people. And he used to tell me I was like a mouse and ask me why I didn't stand up for myself. Now he tells me I'm dictatorial and bossy, so you can't win.[23]

Realization about one's situation as a woman can grow in the process of a collective struggle which is not only about the needs of women. There have been diverse meanings in the slogan of women's liberation 'The personal is political'.

In 1986 Marie Mulholland, coordinator of the Divis Joint Development Committee in Belfast, told Loretta Loach in *Spare Rib* that the people who lived in the Divis flats were the ones who knew what the problems were. They wanted the flats pulled down and to be re-housed together. The flats, which were only built in 1968, are damp, infested with rats and dangerous for children. There is asbestos flaking from them. The tenants are predominantly Catholic and an army helicopter on the Divis tower kept them under surveillance. Marie Mulholland said, 'The people in Divis know that living there is damaging their health but the authorities keep asking for proof.'[24] The tenants, with help from professionals, began analysing the water and sewage, and they made an exhibition of the estate which was shown at the Town and Country Planning Association early in 1986. When they returned to Northern Ireland, however, some of the tenants were arrested in a dawn army and police raid. The demolition of the Divis has been opposed on Belfast Council by Ian Paisley's Democratic Unionist Party, though other parties, including the Constitutional and Nationalists, support the tenants' argument. In the context of Northern Ireland, tenants' complaints have become an issue not only of community but of power politics. Marie Mulholland argued that the Divis tenants' struggle was about an assertion of collective power: 'The campaign to end Divis is more than just destroying an eyesore – it's about asserting the dignity of a people.'[25]

In Northern Ireland the political divide between Catholics and Protestants makes for special difficulties in working-class community action. But even in Britain itself there are big problems for groups like tenants in gaining a wider political voice. This is not only a women's issue, of course, but it is often the case that women are prepared to protest locally yet do not have the means to put their demands into practice.

Connie Hunt has had a long experience of resistance in tenants' struggles in North Woolwich. When she learned in the early 1980s of the London Docklands Development Corporation plans to build a quick-take-off airport, the Stolport, in the area, she was concerned about noise and unconvinced that the project would provide many good jobs in an area which, with the collapse of the docks, had been economically and socially devastated. Through a local action group she got in touch with Hilary Wainwright in the GLC's Industry and Employment Branch. Local residents, some of whom had worked on the docks, met together and with backing from the GLC found out what local people needed by going around to a wide range of groups. Schools, mothers' and toddlers' groups, local industry and trade unions were approached. They also assessed the skills which were being wasted with the decay of the docks and began to put a new value on the experience of women in the area. They drew up a People's Plan – an alternative proposal for economic regeneration which took community need and resources as its starting point rather than the interests of finance capital. The GLC was abolished early in 1986 and the London Docklands Development Corporation disregarded the People's Plan. Nonetheless it strengthened local people's understanding of how alternatives could be developed. It also shifted attitudes towards elected local authorities. After all, representative institutions control resources which come from working-class people and they should be made to serve the people who have elected them.[26]

Working-class women are among the last groups to presume that state resources are theirs by right. In fact they have a stronger claim than many people because they are often carrying a double work-load of low-paid employment and domestic work – on top of which many working-class women manage to do voluntary work of various kinds.

But it is not just a matter of injustice; power is involved too. From the mid-1970s in women's liberation writing the connection between housing and powerful financial interests was recognized. As Alison Fell put it in *Spare Rib* in 1975,

> Whenever women envisage the possibility of the security of a decent place to live and a choice of ways to live – such a modest-sounding demand – and maybe even decide this is their right, the whole ugly picture of housing profits, land speculation and powerful vested interests reveals itself.[27]

She believed the assertion of those rights meant challenging 'the power of the city bankers whose interest charges on building loans cripple local authority housing programmes'.[28] It would mean clamping down 'ruthlessly on land and property speculation', and possibly the 'requisition' of empty properties.[29]

The following year, Pat Olley, then a member of a tenants' association in Newham, London, told women in Big Flame that the land should be nationalized: 'The land belongs to us, they didn't make it so why should they own it?'[30] Tenants should be involved in planning – 'After all it's us that's got to live here'[31] – and protest was no longer enough: 'The working class has to begin to think about how the system works and what the alternatives are.'[32]

The notion of developing alternatives in relation to housing emerged in the women's liberation movement in the early 1970s. In 1971 Sue Crockford and Nan Fromer asked in *Shrew*, 'Who knows most about what it's like to live in the houses we've got?

Women and children. Who better to define alternatives?' New housing, they found, simply took the nuclear family for granted rather than being designed for larger groups. They suggested that part of the problem was that most people did not assume they could affect their environment. Emma Charles took up this theme in an article in *Spare Rib* in 1973. She wanted design to be democratized in several ways. Council tenants should not be banned from choices and changes in how they lived, links could be made between building workers and tenants, and there could be closer integration between building and architecture. The architect could be a technical adviser rather than a person who imposed living styles on people. Instead of structures determining living arrangements, needs could be reflected in the built environment. It might even be possible to develop forms of building which were more flexible and would meet the changing needs of groups of people.

Emma Charles also looked at architecture as a male-dominated profession. Mythically it was associated with a masculine deity. God was the Great Creator on high, building order out of chaos – real planning from on top.[34] A few years later Denise Arnold, an architect in the Matriarchy Study Group, argued that if our society were organized around reproduction as well as production we would have quite different architecture and design:

> Our settlement patterns. . .give preeminence to the realm of the men's huts, whether the office, the factory, clubs or pubs, at the expense of the world of women's huts, and all power, production, decision-making, and 'rites of life', birth, learning and initiation, healing, caring, sickness and dying have now been excluded from the domestic realm.[35]

This dichotomy is too simple, for women work in the 'men's huts' – offices, factories, as well as schools and hospitals. Nor does it seem to me sensible to say you want to return all these activities to the household. Nonetheless, polarities of inner and outer space have consistently preoccupied women's liberation writing.[36] They can reveal how social assumptions and power relations are built into our environment.

In 1975 *Women's Report* linked bad housing with the low value put on domestic work in our society:

> This means that the domestic environment is not usually designed to conserve effort – sub-standard housing requires extra time and energy

for a woman to maintain, but this is not generally accepted as an argument for better housing.[37]

The writers point out that the disregard for domestic need means that delay in repairs is more likely than in unionized places of work like offices. Yet a lift breakdown on an estate affects old people, the disabled and women with small children particularly severely:

> The development of the built economy has always been closely linked with the needs of the economy, and since the prime function of our society is production, domestic and social needs have tended to take second place.[38]

Irene Bruegel and Adah Kay argued in *Architectural Design* in 1975 that the physical structure of many urban areas and the effects of economic planning reinforce the subordinate position of women.[39] Questioning the priority of production and profit does not take us back to the 'women's huts', but on the contrary leads outwards to a challenge to the real power behind the 'men's huts', finance capital, power politics, and the military-industrial complex.

Feminists have oscillated between demanding an environment geared to women with children and arguing that men's work and life should accommodate children. Emma Charles believed that women architects could foster demands from community groups on planning for women and children's needs. In 1973 she made three suggestions for basic guidelines:

(a) That any new factory or office building employing substantial numbers of women must provide space for a supervised crèche. At the moment the world of work is geared entirely to the needs of men and childless women.

(b) That every supermarket and department store must provide space for a closely supervised pram park, where women, the most courted consumers of the high street, can leave their babies.

(c) That every new housing estate must provide a women's centre where a launderette, family planning services, a legal adviser and meeting place would be grouped under one roof.[40]

Thirteen years later when Islington Council Women's Committee surveyed local women in the London borough about planning for child care, similar needs were reiterated and further ideas put forward. There was also stress on the inconveniences and dangers women face in getting about.[41] Planning for children, though, has to be regarded as not only the responsibility of Women's Committees. For the inter-connection of children with the 'men's huts' has also been at issue. Why always assume, for example, that women change babies? A woman in the Lesbian Custody Group said on Radio London, 'I will know that our society takes fatherhood seriously when in motorway service areas the gents' has a baby's changing room as well as the ladies'.'[42] Such a transformation of gents' lavatories in the direction of civilization would be startling!

Existing material and social circumstances have made women conspicuous in protesting against the way inequality is structured not only into the built environment but into the organization of mobility. In 1975 *Women's Report* observed:

> Car ownership may seem high, but in practice it is generally the man who has the car, and the woman must use her feet or public transport. The woman pushing a pram loaded with both baby and shopping will encounter endless obstacles. With these experiences it is not surprising that women's organizations have pressed for much of the legislation to help the disabled in wheelchairs, including improved access to buildings.[43]

In 1986 the Islington borough plan noted that only 39 per cent of women in London had a driving licence.[44] Friends of the Earth Transport Campaign showed that two thirds of women do not drive.[45] Women are thus predominantly walking and using public transport. Walking means that the dangers of crossing roads, pollution, fumes and noise caused by traffic are part of everyday life.

In 1974 Constance Whippman wrote about the struggle she had had to transport herself and her eight-month-old baby to the *Spare Rib* office in West London: 'London Transport could scarcely have designed a bus less accommodating for mothers and wheeled vehicles than the currently promoted model which has two-aisle entry for automatic ticket dispensing machines.'[51] She observed that 'mothers, prams and bus transport' did not have to be incompatible – Swiss buses were designed with provision for parents with wheeled vehicles.[52] On the tube, escalators are difficult with pushchairs and impossible for the disabled. Trains are easier for babies but even those have their snags:

I've spent a fair amount of time cursing British Rail for making the doors
to the regular carriage compartments just a quarter of an inch too small
for me to pass my carry-cot through but have since discovered that my
neighbour's model just makes it, so I've decided to curse the Marmet
company instead. Either way couldn't there be a little coordination?[53]

Fittings have been standardized, so it would be possible to relate
the design of private commodities to public activities. Constance
Whippman pointed out that breast-feeding and nappy-changing
could be extremely difficult when you are moving about a city.
Museums sometimes banned pushchairs. There were consequently
parts of the city from which parents were virtually excluded, and
some of the elements that created this 'zoning' effect also affected
the elderly and disabled.

The connection between transport design and planning was made
in the early 1980s during the London struggle in support of the
GLC's fare-reduction policy, which was reversed by the Law Lords'
decision and then modified. Wider problems came out during later
conflict with the Conservatives over transport policy. For instance,
it was shown how the inconveniences and dangers of passengers
are linked to the illness and stress faced by bus workers – which
becomes especially acute with One Person Operation buses.[54]

The fear and threat of violence which is increasing in large cities
like London is also a bar to women's mobility. And new industries
have created new forms of loneliness. Members of Aberdeen Wom-
en's Liberation described in 1980 in *Spare Rib* how 'oil wives' were
stranded on special estates built outside the city – only management
could afford to buy in Aberdeen. There were few shops and schools
on these estates and public transport was poor. The women felt
depressed and lonely in a strange place with the men away for
two weeks at a time: '. . .alcoholism and psychological problems
are common. . .Televisions are switched on early to make time
pass more quickly and the postman becomes a VIP.'[46] Women's
isolation contributes to a great deal of psychological depression,
as Anna Briggs pointed out in 1977 in 'Who Drives the Family
Car?'[47] She went on to found a self-help group for women who
were tied to the house because they were caring for elderly or sick
people.[48] The problems of 'carers' began to receive more attention
in the 1980s and the right to a small allowance has been won.[49] But
the mobility needs of people who are barred from access to public
transport services remains a pressing problem.

Bad planning of the environment and transport consumes women's time and effort. For example, a woman in a rural area with a man on a low wage told me they could not afford a washing machine. There was not an adequate bus service so she could not reach the nearest launderette. Consequently she did all the washing by hand. Even in a big city, time taken delivering children and travelling to work, even part time, on public transport which does not run along convenient routes can take up several hours a day.[50] High-powered people in the business world and politics would put a money value on those hours. 'Time is money', as the saying goes. There is a completely unequal estimation of the value of time taken from people's lives.

The tragedy is that after a decade or so of making the arguments they are beginning to make a wider impact just at the point when public services of all kinds are being dismantled and the profit motive applied to the most basic human needs for association, security, sociability, pleasure and recreation. Without sentimentalizing 'public services' or 'communities', there is compelling evidence of the need to conserve social gains, public assets, informal bonds of friendliness while trying to make a better life. For their destruction brings not progress or freedom but disintegration, fear, violence and despair. Although women's liberation is a movement for radical change it has also contained a recognition of what can be lost in the arrogant desecration of human bonding. Community formed even amidst hardship over years, is of value beyond measure, yet it has been squandered at a terrible cost.

As for the development of a new Britain, Milton Keynes has the promise of prosperity. It is in this region that the booming electronics industry has arisen. Yet when a group of women got together to make a video in 1979 it seemed all was not well. They sang of the 'Things Mother never told us about life in Milton Keynes'. They had not got a hospital. It was 'five long miles to the nearest pub'.

> The city centre's still not built
> And I can't afford new jeans,
> But the fresh air's good, and we've Dial-A-Bus. . .
> So come to Milton Keynes.[55]

What alternative can we make to the bleak future which can be glimpsed in this rhyme and in those oil-rig estates near Aberdeen?

Part of the weakness among critics of the society geared to profit and to the market has been uncertainty about how life might be better.

Implicit within much feminist writing has been a dissatisfaction with communal forms which had been patterned by Communist and social democratic traditions. These tended to emphasize the state taking over domestic activities rather than the promotion of community control from below. When some of these ways of 'socializing' domestic labour were incorporated into welfare capitalism it became evident that they were not peculiarly socialist solutions. In fact, they could be means of making capitalism more efficient rather than increasing people's control over their everyday lives. In 1975 Marina Lewycka argued that certain forms of 'socialization' were consistent with the logic of capitalism, whether provided through the state or private services. She wanted to examine whether this process might be turned to the advantage of women and become a means of exerting power.[56] From the Italian women's movement, Mariarosa Dalla Costa's *The Power of Women and the Subversion of the Community* attempted to tackle domestic activity within a tradition of direct action which had been the practical experience in the early 1970s in Milan and Rome, where tenants and workers had squatted and occupied properties together.

Unfortunately, the application of the tactics of direct action and refusal to work to the resistance of the housewife is difficult in isolation and unrealistic in relation to caring for children and dependants. Mariarosa Dalla Costa's approach, however, contained a significant insight in recognizing that capitalism's power to organize people's time was a necessary terrain of struggle. She looked at how time at work, domestic time and 'free time' were balanced and argued that they had to be considered together. There was no point in reducing time spent in domestic tasks simply to replace it with work time. Or, more specifically, it was no good making a communal canteen in the neighbourhood without fighting for shorter hours. The combination of confrontations was a more general theme on the Italian Left at the period in which she was writing, for it had become evident that wage increases were being 'passed on' to employees in higher prices and rents. *The Power of Women and the Subversion of the Community* is weakest on the manner in which women can develop new forms of communal power. Its contribution was the recognition of the inequalities in daily life.[57]

In practice the women's movement oscillated between engaging in small-scale communal self-help activity and falling back on socialist models which had been made somewhat archaic and inappropriate by the technological inventiveness of capitalism. Fast-food restaurants glitter more brightly with fantasies of the good life than 'communal canteens' or the municipal restaurants of the Second World War. The problem of defining differing needs and reflecting on the relationship between those needs which could be met with commodities and those which required communal activities was emerging out of the practice of contemporary women's liberation, but was not examined theoretically in Britain.

Washing provides a good example. As many people now have washing machines and find them convenient, and in the 1970s many at least had access to a launderette, there was not much point in insisting that washing must be 'socialized', in the manner of the community wash-houses which had been initiated in the nineteenth century and then campaigned for by groups like the Women's Co-operative Guild early this century. Nor is it the case that public washing was always an enjoyable activity. On the other hand, the communal laundries that councils neglected or closed in the 1960s were still serving certain groups – as protesters, mainly older women, proclaimed outside Kensington Town Hall, according to *Spare Rib*'s report in 1974.

The Notting Hill Laundry Group, backed by the local women's liberation organization, had formed to fight the council's decision to demolish the public laundry, which was part of the swimming baths built in 1888. The council said it was no longer needed because the cold-water flats in the area had been pulled down. The protesters said it still served as 'a communal meeting place' for local women and was particularly important to pensioners.[58] Communal facilities could be useful for people who lived in small flats, could not afford washing machines and wanted to get out to chat.

The laundry campaign had some success because it created links between several community groups in Notting Hill, and with the help of sympathetic architects they showed how alternative use could be made of the space under the new Westway motorway for child-care and other community projects. After struggles and negotiations lasting about seven years the Laundry Group was among those able to move in under the Westway, and building started in 1974.[59] A decade later the laundry got a grant for improved machinery from the GLC, and one of the Technology Networks set up by the GLC developed a device to save energy which was pioneered there.[60]

The exertion of the 'power of women' in the 'subversion of the community' proved to be a rather lengthy and exhausting process. To save and preserve one small laundry consumed hours and hours of endeavour. Nonetheless, one example like Westway can suggest certain broader principles. The market has proved itself deft in meeting some kinds of wants but inept and soulless where other aspects of human need are concerned – for example care and conviviality. Westway introduced an alternative communal form which meant a practical task could be done in contact with others. It extended choice, which does not deny the usefulness of individual products, but questions their value in particular contexts.

Other examples have been food co-ops. The food co-op on Lincoln Estate, Bow, in London, for instance, was motivated both by practical interest in lower prices and ecological concern about the quality of food. It involved the idea of making housework communal and bringing women together. It was part of a range of other community activities which developed on the estate after the collapse of the mass rent strike of the late Sixties.[61]

But the scattered attempts to alter the social conditions and relationships affecting domestic life in order to transform the daily existence of women have been only spasmodically recorded and little theorized. They seem to be most prevalent in periods when extraordinary events – long strikes, sit-ins, police action in community rebellions, civil war – disrupt pre-existing patterns of life.

During the upheavals of the early 1970s prices rose in Britain. A group of socialist women in Nottingham decided that the difficulties women faced shopping around for cheaper foods, the time expended and the tensions price rises provoked in the family were problems of a 'social nature':

> It is our task to show women that we can *join together* in protest against these attacks on living standards. Women, as the main consumers, have the strength to oppose price rises, and to combine with workers who are fighting for wage increases, to unify the struggle against the effects of inflation.[62]

They knew there had been a long tradition of women's collective action in the area of consumption in the eighteenth and nineteenth centuries. They also noted that the National Housewives' Association was organizing against price rises but blamed the 'obstinacy' of the miners for causing the crisis.[63] Towards the end of 1973 the Nottingham group began to demonstrate. The campaign was launched at a Trades Council rally in solidarity with the miners and imprisoned Shrewsbury building workers. A boycott of Fine Fare over the 'marking up' of goods already on the shelf embarrassed the management into making a public statement that they would stop this. In the course of their protest the women came across various other actions around prices. They reported that in Glasgow workers at Allied Supplies had taken industrial action against the hoarding of lentils, which had almost tripled the price. Also, during the miners' strike of 1974, they learned that 'housewives in Calverton, an isolated mining community in Nottinghamshire. . .during the '72 strike succeeded in reducing some prices, while freezing others at least for the duration of the strike'.[64]

The organization of women *against* strikers received publicity when Carol Miller led a rebellion of wives against left-wing car workers' leader, Alan Thornett, at British Leyland's Cowley plant in Oxford in 1974. A larger mobilization of Cowley wives, with support from Women's Liberation and trade unionists, occurred in retaliation. The situation was complicated by the attitude of some of the male workers, which was simply that women should not meddle in men's affairs.[65]

There has not been a history in Britain of sustained organization on, for example, the American Women's Auxiliary model, but there have been many instances of women taking action around consumption and reorganizing domestic activity during workers' resistance. In the mid-1970s wives of Triumph workers at Meriden formed action groups to back the sit-in for jobs and to give women access to information which would help them claim Social Security.[66] In 1977, when workers at Wildt Mellor Bromley in Leicester sat in, wives organized a baby-sitting rota so they could visit their husbands during the occupation.[67]

Communal forms of organization seem to have occurred particularly often in mining communities. In Calverton, Nottinghamshire, in 1972, women not only reduced the prices in local shops, they started buying food collectively – for example fish from Grimsby – and getting food parcels out to every family. In another instance, 'Women in Donisthorpe, South Derbyshire, got the fish and chip shops to reduce their prices during the strike while the clubs reduced beer by 2p a pint.'[68] Also during the 1972 miners' strike, women from the Kent coalfields travelled round the pickets at the power stations in London. They went to the Saltley picket and began their own meetings – sometimes with opposition from the union. They too went to shops to get prices reduced and took action on Social Security. Many tactics were used to ensure that Social Security was paid in full. In Rugely women took their children out of school and down to the DHSS, leaving them there until money was paid for accommodation costs. They occupied the Stafford County Council offices until eventually they got coal, food and some money. At Keresley in Coventry, women decided to feed the people on the picket lines.[69] According to a bulletin published in 1973, *Housing in Crisis: Women's Offensive*, 'They liberated a bread van and then organized bulk-buying with the money collected from various factories.'[70]

In the 1984–5 miners' strike, the denial of Social Security payments and the desperate need for food galvanized collective organization on a scale far beyond the previous years. On 12 May 1984 the Women's Action Groups called a rally. They expected a relatively modest gathering in Barnsley, Yorkshire. Instead, Jean McCrindle recalls:

> Ten thousand women suddenly arrived, from everywhere. Some came dressed in Welsh costume and they were singing. And there were these home-made banners that they'd brought. People came from pit villages that we hadn't even heard of. They just arrived. And Barnsley of all places! Barnsley, it's such a male town. Somehow to have this extraordinary working-class women's rally in the midst of this town was amazing, actually amazing.
>
> Well they all turned out. Then the majorettes, these girl drummers turned up. We had this consultation and decided that they were to lead the march. They were overwhelmed because on all previous miners' rallies it had been the brass bands and the miners who came first and the little majorettes came on last.
>
> And we marched round Barnsley, I think to the utter astonishment of probably every citizen who watched us.[71]

The year-long collective effort to provide food and money was on a much larger scale than in the previous strikes. It involved women in contact with groups not only in Britain but all over the world. Around a million pounds was collected, the donors ranging from Bruce Springsteen to pensioners.

In August 50,000 women marched through London on a boiling hot day to a south London green where men from the print unions served them tea as they listened to speeches. Women in the mining communities had organized before, but never on such a scale or with such power. By 1984 some of the women worked in the collieries themselves, in the canteens or as cleaners. Some had experience of unions in other jobs. They started to go on the picket lines as the men were being turned back by road-blocks of police. The women were thus on the front line of the 1984–5 miners' strike.[72] A new and alarming feature of this strike was the scale of policing. It became impossible to see the police as a neutral force. To people in the mining communities and a wide range of observers concerned about civil liberties, the police were simply the instrument of government policy to break the power of working-class people in the mining industry. When people arrested went to court they were frequently judged by magistrates from rich landed families, yet a South Yorkshire magistrate married to a striking miner told me she was not allowed to take cases because of suspected bias.

Outrage against a law and state which appeared in overt collusion against them was one factor in taking the political meaning of the strike beyond saving employment. Another was the women's commitment to their domestic responsibilities, made impossible by the threat of pit closures with no long-term negotiations for economic renewal. Jean McCrindle observed: '. . .it clearly wasn't any longer about wages or even just jobs. It was about who's got the right to decide really how you live.'[73] Ann Suddick, a clerical worker, described in 1986 in 'Making the Links' how her women's support group in Durham began to make connections. Blyth Power Station closed. The National Coal Board then shut down Bute Colliery which had provided the coal to fuel it:

> I realized in five years' time, if things continued in this direction, there would be no coal mining in the North East; that meant there would be no alternative to the Druridge Bay nuclear power station. We won't be able to say 'No thanks' to nuclear power because there won't be any alternative.
> By then we had already met up with women from Greenham. We went down there. And talking to people about plutonium and nuclear weapons made me realize why the nuclear programme was so important. It dawned on me we were fighting something bigger than pit closures.[74]

They linked up with a series of local anti-nuclear and anti-apartheid groups and began to piece together an analysis of the powerful forces shaping a world for their profit. British Nuclear Fuels bought uranium mined from the labour of black Namibians; Pacific Islanders had been hounded, irradiated and dispossessed for nuclear tests; the people of Chernobyl were suffering from an accident which could have happened anywhere; millions were starving while the super-powers spent on weapons rather than on food and agricultural development.[75] Ann Suddick and others got together and wrote all this down. They called it 'our philosophy', adding: 'We will be polishing it up and distributing it for discussion.'[76] They called for the creation of 'informal networks of communication and action to multiply the effect that any one group can achieve, to widen the web'.[77]

The problem is that, without coordination, isolated examples of resistance of this kind can be exhausted and forgotten. Part of making links is making sure a memory of interconnections created in the past is retained. Even for the 1970s we have only an intermittent record of women acting in various kinds of defence movements, in which their own political purposes intertwined with those of people in their families. For instance, in 1976 Pat Turnbull, whose husband worked with asbestos, formed 'Women Against the Dust'.[78] Another area of organizing has been among wives and relations of prisoners: Maggie Tuttle formed a union for prisoners' wives in Britain in 1973.[79]

In Northern Ireland, sectarian conflicts and opposition from many Irish people to the presence of British troops have added a political dimension to prison organizing. In 1976 in Derry, a Relatives' Action Committee started, and others were developed in Belfast and elsewhere. They mainly consisted of women who campaigned for better conditions in prison. The groups also acted as a support network for Catholic women drawn into resistance to the army. Until the death of Katie Thompson, who was shot dead for rattling a dust-bin lid – the rough music of women in the community – it was safer for women to protest than men. However, the civil-war situation meant that women who became involved had desperate child-care problems which the network helped. The prisoners' relatives also mobilized in response to an outbreak of dysentery among children at Turf Lodge, an estate in West Belfast.[80] Through the action committees, the women moved from defence and practical support to more general political thinking 'about the sort of changes needed to produce a New Ireland and specifically about women's role in this Ireland'.[81]

These actions of defence and support do not fit neatly into the concept 'feminist'. Rachel Wilson asked of the 'Wildt Wives':

How do feminists work with women who don't question the fact that their lives revolve around men and see their activity as mainly in relation to men? In this case supporting their husbands, though through doing so they gain solidarity as women?[82]

Amrit Wilson said of 'Women Against the Dust' that they were 'not explicitly feminist. But neither are they acting under male direction. They are women fighting back along with men in the best way they can.'[83]

Some of the women in the mining communities rejected feminism initially because they saw it as a narrow movement which was just anti-men. Some of them changed their minds during the strike because understanding and friendship developed. But a certain uneasiness towards forms of feminism that deny class has remained. The experiences of being working class and being women are intertwined; they cannot be separated.

In an *Outwrite* interview in 1986 Pragna Patel, Smita Bhide and Rita Dia of Southall Black Women's Centre compared the women's politicization in mining communities with their own struggles against racism: 'Miners' wives, like black women, were fighting initially to save jobs, save the community and in the process started asking questions about male domination.'[84] Many black women too have felt uneasy with expressions of feminism which deny race and class. They have criticized the abstract codification of feminism as a set of universal values and emphasized instead the significance of a politics based on everyday oppression in all its complexity.

So, in certain contexts, women's collective action in defence of the rights required by traditional duties takes on a radical political meaning. The limitation of the definition of women's liberation to a feminism which detaches women from the lived web of social contradictions is evident. The response to this entangled reality cannot simply be ascribed a feminist meaning; gender can confine. Also, collective action can be conservative in implication, as with the New Right. Being a woman and resisting does not in itself guarantee radicalism.

It is also patronizing to assume that all women are bound to agree. Women can have fierce loyalties in opposing economic and political circumstances. And feminists like any political tendency, can be at loggerheads over strategy. Christina Loughran describes in 'Armagh and Feminist Strategy' how the Northern Ireland Women's Movement has been torn apart by division over whether to engage with the central question in existing political life –

that of the legitimacy of the state – or to organize around the 'appalling social and economic conditions' which affect both Catholic and Protestant working-class women:[85] 'Feminists are caught in division. They organize on opposite sides of the sectarian divide with mutually exclusive strategies.'[86] She argues that this has a wider strategic significance, for it raises the issue of priorities. Should women concentrate on autonomous struggle or be working in a broader movement?

I do not myself believe that there is an absolute solution which can be applied regardless of history.[87] To a certain extent, people work out their politics by thought and consideration, but political allegiances develop implicitly within certain cultures of resistance. These are shaped by historical traditions. By the memory of humiliation, subordination and rebellion that can pass through families and communities. Political development is also a continuing process of response to specific relationships which structure encounters with other people.

Pratibha Parmar has argued against confining a concept of resistance to a rigid model of gender. She describes how the will to resist has developed among Afro-Caribbean and Asian people through struggles:

> . . .deportation trials, industrial disputes, on the picket lines, in mourning for the deaths of Black people caused by racists and fascists, and through such organizations as the Black Parents' Movement, the Black Students' Movement, Asian Youth Movements and local defence committees.[88]

Out of these movements self-help projects developed which have contributed towards asserting Afro-Caribbean and Asian culture and have acted as a means of revealing inequality and racism. Through them also black people have begun to claim back some of the resources which both imperialism and racism in Britain have engrossed and denied to them.

But the poverty, bitterness and despair which form the experience of much of black youth have been allowed to fester amidst contempt and neglect from white society. Since the early 1980s violent conflicts have erupted in the cities, in poor areas, and especially in the desolate and dangerous housing estates which increasingly resemble fortresses of fear. These uprisings come from desperation and a vista of a future without hope. There is nothing left to lose.

The political gains of riot are dubious. Innocent people get hurt in these urban rebellions and injustice is done to working-class people of all races, especially the old and women. Rich people do not suffer because they do not live in poor urban areas. On the other hand, if a government remains impervious and there is no effective means of political change, what other response can there be but a reversion to an older form of pressure, the action of the urban crowd? Struggling against a simple response of fear and anger, many black people have persisted in making links: supporting the striking miners, for example; arguing against the stocking of South African goods in the shops in which they work.

Afro-Caribbean and Asian feminists have had to challenge the attitudes of white feminists towards black communities, yet continue to struggle as women. For example, Southall Black Sisters said in *Outwrite* that they were concerned about class and race and yet equally resolved to raise issues that specifically oppress women, like domestic violence. They wanted to defend their culture, but not without denying conflict and tensions – for instance, they sought the means of caring for young women who leave home to avoid arranged marriages.[89]

Women of colour experience conflicts of culture, class and politics not only with white women and with men of their own communities, but among themselves. Yet at the same time theirs have been among the strongest voices arguing that there is a need to combine, and not only with women. A black American feminist, Bell Hooks, has argued.

> Women do not need to eradicate difference to feel solidarity. We do not need to share common oppression to fight equally to end oppression. We do not need anti-male sentiments to bond us together, so great is the wealth of experience, culture and ideas we have to share with one another.[90]

This is difficult to live out in practice. But what are the alternatives? As Ann Suddick put it: 'We damage ourselves by feelings of guilt and competition among struggles which we *know* to be part of the same huge iceberg of exploitation, male violence and capitalism.'[91] Somehow we need to find a means of preventing the reproduction of inequality within movements for radical change without damaging one another so much that we become ineffective and bitter. Women's liberation as a movement has expressed love and care; it has also given vent to rage and guilt. Perhaps our political experience of both the positive and negative tensions could be a resource for others in the difficult and challenging times ahead. Learning from women's active resistance to subordination could thus enable us to draw on a deepening cunning which would be of wider value.

One impulse for feminist rebellion was expressed by Rob Hunter Henderson and Liz Cooper as 'Don't Break Down, Break Out', in 1976.[92] Ten years later when the women from the Durham mining community called a conference which involved anti-apartheid and peace groups, they called it 'Make the Links – Break the Chain'. It is vital that the movement for women's liberation holds on to both these understandings. Greenham Common Peace Camp has become a powerful symbol of women breaking out of conventional existence to surround the military base with the most direct and simple forms of human links. Greenham has also communicated to women as a symbol of making links all over Britain and in many other countries. As one woman said of her visit to Greenham: 'It's like coming alive.'[93]

Lynne Segal observes that Greenham has been an attempt to live the 'strengths (and weaknesses) at the heart' of the modern women's liberation movement. It has also been important in 'drawing women into political protest and action against militarism and the arms race'.[94] Women in Greenham support groups have taken part in many struggles, for instance opposing the spending of money on defence instead of the NHS, and helping to occupy South London Women's Hospital. They joined women from mining communities on picket lines and acted against nuclear dumping in the Pacific and other seas with the National Union of Seamen, CND and Greenpeace.

Sue Finch from the Hackney Greenham group recognized that there are feminists who reject the assumption that peace is specifically a women's or feminist issue. She says: 'The simple fact remains that unless we choose to make peace a feminist issue. . .we may all be dead.'[95] There is no single basis on which feminists have theorized women's involvement as women in the peace movement. (Ironically, we have replayed the contradictory arguments which featured in the earlier movement during and just after the First World War.) The feminism and Non-Violence Study Group have emphasized 'The continuum of violence emanating from patriarchal power'.[96] Mary Coghill and Sheila Redmond, in 'Feminism and

Spirituality', say: 'men are to be held accountable for the wars, disease and famine that are rampant in this world', and 'men's future is death'.[97] Other women in the peace movement have emphasized women's role as nurturers, organizing as 'Families and Babies Against the Bomb'.

There is a difficult area on the border between drawing on a social experience of a subordinated group and accepting the role permitted by more powerful groups in society. Sarah Green, a woman in the Greenham peace movement, said:

> I think that most women are really in touch with what life is about. You can't even contemplate having a child without considering the value of that life and the struggle people have bringing up children, putting in all those hours and and hours of caring.[98]

But this is not the only social experience of women, nor is it a feeling completely strange to fathers. It is historically and socially inaccurate to place all the responsibility for evil with one sex and all the capacity for caring on the other.

Another connection to peace has been women's spiritual insight, denied within male-dominated forms of religion. Although I am not a religious person, it seems to me we can do with all the spiritual insight we can muster against the danger of destruction and mendacity. But religion is not an ideal, set apart from human foibles. Spiritual folk, regardless of sex, are capable of disputes and sectarianism in manifold guises. Even among the religions of the oppressed there can appear forms of stiff-necked spiritual arrogance. While spiritual wisdom can be found in many religions, it is not exclusive to women.

Organizational reasons have also been put forward for women's autonomous action on peace. For instance, Sue Finch expresses a preference for the imaginative and creative forms of activity which women have developed. She stresses an important recognition of women's liberation which is expressed in a Greenham song:

> It's not just the web
> It's the way that we spin it
> It's not just the world
> It's the women within it
> It's not just the struggle
> It's the way that we win it
> That's what makes us strong.[99]

The realization that 'our way of doing things is consistent with the future that we'd like to build',[100] has been a strong political influence in feminism. It was one of the themes Lynne Segal, Hilary Wainwright and I raised in *Beyond the Fragments*. But to be quite truthful, hasn't our experience as feminists been that it is easier said than done, and that the harmonious connection of means and ends does not have a simple organizational form? We can be caught in the very web we weave.

A more pragmatic approach has been that knitting webs, surviving through winters in benders of branches and plastic sheeting, moving the essentials of life on prams and trolleys to escape the 'crunchers' – refuse-disposal trucks which crunch everything a woman cannot carry – and the encirclement of camps by women's hands can be effective against police, soldiers, courts and governments unaccustomed to such behaviour. The action of women at Greenham has inspired women and men all over the world to see that people do not have to acquiesce to state policies which make the servants of the state act with destructive inhumanity. Stephanie Leland describes a moment when the forces of peace were joined by some of the forces of the state – as human beings. On 12 December 1982, after long discussions with the policemen and policewomen on duty at the Greenham camp: 'We stood in a circle holding hands and sang "Give Peace a Chance" to each other and the stars overhead. The police joined with us in our circle.'[101]

The invocation of motherhood is always double-edged; it concedes a power to women while denying the constraints caused by the confinement of responsibility to domestic concerns. On the other hand, it is not surprising that women and men should feel a yearning to safeguard the world for their young. This has been one of the calls of patriotism and has often led to war. If it serves peace, this is surely a better purpose. Many feminists feel uneasy with the mobilization of 'Babies Against the Bomb'.[102] On the other hand, it is undeniable that toddlers stomping down the road reach a few parts other protests would not. There are passions and lives and a future at stake, after all. Also, women have not dwelt only on the time-honoured emotions of mothering. They have sought cultural extensions for familiar experiences. Mary Brewer, a member of Halifax Women's Action Group and Labour Party Women's Section, describes being at Greenham on 12 December 1982. She uses giving birth as a metaphor to express a political vision of intense and loving communication:

I'll never forget that feeling, you know; it'll live with me for ever, will
that. . . the lovely feeling of pinning the things on; and the feeling,
as we walked round, and we clasped hands, the feeling will stay with
me for ever. . . The feeling was absolutely – it was like – it was even
better than holding your baby for the first time, after giving birth –
and that is – that is the loveliest – one of the loveliest feelings you
can ever have. When your babe's put in your arms and you give it a
cuddle. . . because that is a self thing – selfish thing, really, between
you and your husband, isn't it? The baby. Whereas at Greenham – it
was, it was for women; it was for peace; it was for the world; it was
for Britain; it was – it was for us; it was for more.[103]

Women have also taken off into issues of military strategy,
defence, state security, energy policy and arms conversion.[104] They
have argued for ecology and alternative forms of technology. Women
in the peace movement have thus in practice struggled against a
division of society into spheres labelled 'masculine' and 'feminine'.[105] Just after Chernobyl, when the Durham women called
their conference, Ann Suddick recalled their petition:

It demanded a halt to the building of nuclear power stations; the phasing
out of existing stations by 1995; and immediate action to implement a
sane and safe energy policy based on coal, conservation and renewable
energy sources. In the course of one week we got 75,000 signatures.
That is one signature every eight seconds. [106]

Part of the 'polishing up' of feminist 'philosophy'[107] is the
recognition that, while the collective actions of women can be
contradictory, while they can take the forms of movements to
conserve rather than to transform, the understandings that develop
within their myriad manifestations constitute a vital part in the
creation of social concepts. This may seem to be stating the obvious,
but the prevailing assessment of knowledge tends to assume it is
held by academics and intellectuals and sits in books. Women are
as susceptible to prevailing power as men. Much that is of value is
conceived in a bookish way, but a great deal is ignored. Being paid
to think does not ensure an all-encompassing wisdom – even among
feminist professors. Indeed, it can put limits on the opportunity
to gain 'sapiential authority'. Within women's action for liberation
there is a wealth of experience which is frequently disregarded and
undervalued, even by feminists. This chronicle of mine is partial,
but I hope that it will help the process of learning from doing. My

view of what can be learned from women's actions for change is expressed by Liz Heron in her article 'Sisterhood Re-examined' in 1983:

> . . .if the struggle for women's liberation is to mean something vital and positive to the majority of women, it has to engage in a supportive way with the realities of their lives and everyday experiences. It has to offer the prospect of change for the better, and acknowledge that it can be achieved through co-operation with men, even though women still need to struggle for independence. The utopian vision that linked the transformation of social and political institutions with the transformation of personal relationships needs to be regained.[108]

It would be easier to understand social movements from below if it were just a matter of fitting together the pieces. You can do a certain amount like this, but because a movement is a process, it moves: so to write of movements is to be a spinner and a weaver. Yet at times even this metaphor cannot express the moving which occurs within movements. Sitting listening to Greek feminists talking in Athens in the early 1980s, I was puzzled by their frequent references to the cinema. When I enquired, my friends laughed and explained that the word for cinema in English is derived from the Greek word for movement. Observation of a social movement can sometimes seem like an electronic spinning and weaving in which textures dissolve and patterns merge so that words and a pen cannot keep up with them. It is not therefore surprising that even a rather general label like 'feminism' cannot convey the complexities of women's collective action for liberation. It is somewhat owlish to ask ponderously, But is it feminist? The question sometimes has to be, Is feminism enough?

Conclusion
The Future is Behind Us

Ideas generated by a social movement do not present themselves in an orderly manner. They are thrown up by circumstances, shaken by destinies and left hanging in mid-air. Expressive of political tensions within the fabric of society, they are raw with interests.

It may be because I incline to politics and history rather than appreciating philosophy for its own sake that I perceive concepts in movement as wider and deeper than the voice of the study alone. The making of ideas through social action and political process challenges not only theory but existing axioms. It reaches the very axis of assumption even though the knowledge that emerges remains unpolished and awkward.

It is immensely difficult to craft the new thoughts of a movement. At first they cascade and resist being caught, the next moment they make channels and become obvious. Mapped out, they serve up to a point. When the point sticks, the routes they have made can be reassessed.[1]

It is a curious experience to try to sort out ideas which you milled around with in your own past. For example, I remember when it was not obvious that housework was work – hence the initial excitement created by this assertion. But the memory became overlaid with the wearisome bemusement of meeting after meeting arguing about wages for housework or totting up surplus value. Debate simply spiralled away from mopping and cooking until it clouded the brain rather than illuminating the experience. In the process of writing about the discussions and descriptions of housework a pattern began to emerge. By concentrating so much energy on trying to equate housework with existing forms of employment we had neglected the other aspect – how it could be a source for radical questioning of the existing nature of work. As I wrote, connections and indeed inconsistencies appeared which I had only partially grasped at the time.

Some themes were actually more pervasive than I had remembered. I was aware of course of the phrase 'the personal is political', but I had not been prepared for some aspects of the slogan to pop up in more or less every chapter. In retrospect its significance is not as some universal political truth, but as an indication of the contradictory forces which brought contemporary feminism into being.

Modern feminism has shifted the conceptual boundaries which confined domesticity within the category of personal life. It was consequently possible to reveal an oppressive social reality and conflicting interests. This enabled needs to emerge which had been ignored or dismissed within a male-defined concept of political, economic and social priorities. Another politicization of the personal has been the struggle for choice and control over reproduction. The social structuring of identity has also generated considerable debate around culture and representation, while the attempt to explore within a political movement subjective feelings in the family and at work has altered the very conceptualizing of politics.

Because political reworkings developed from women's situation in society and were expressed by an autonomous feminist movement, their more general implications have tended to be obscured. For instance, the persistent extension of the meaning of 'material life' beyond the confines of the economic has arisen in various aspects of women's liberation thinking and activity. In feminist writing the 'material' has included the body and the environment – not, I think, because of a prior theoretical recognition, but rather because of the particular sitings of our subordination. This development has coincided with the growing awareness of the threat to the environment and the human body posed by existing forms of industry and technology.

A recurring problem for feminism – and the modern movement is no exception – has been how to give value to those aspects of life called 'personal' which, within the cultural inheritance of Western capitalism at least, have been designated as women's sphere, and to do this without retreating into idealized secret gardens of feminine difference. The other side of the coin is summed up by Liz Heron, in *Changes of Heart*. Commenting on Naomi Mitchison's epic fantasy, *The Corn King and the Spring Queen*, she elaborates on the dilemma of the Spring Queen:

The Spring Queen herself is trapped by the cosmos that is the source of her enchantment and can only free herself by finding or inventing other cosmologies, other possibilities within which human beings can act. To do this she has to leave behind the familiar structures and setting of her domestic power.[2]

The powerful longing to break out of existing relations in the family and seek a new female destiny that has been expressed by so many women in the last two decades can be comprehended in terms of contradictory shifts in capitalist society. Our migration as a sex has been part of a wider process which has assumed some negative and disintegratory features. There can only be a temporary evasion of the question, When the Spring Queen leaves, what then?

Even while travelling through a blighted landscape, many women radicalized by feminism have maintained, along with a radical pursuit of freedom a quest for new forms of community. This is not exactly easy, for so many gallant attempts to transform the circumstances of everyday life have been left stranded as cranky sub-cultures. Still, this is not to deny the continuing significance of the quest – which is certainly not to be accomplished simply by women. Being lumbered with the exclusive burden of finding salvation from the negative features of capitalism is a dubious honour.

Equally difficult has been the feminist endeavour to change personal relationships within existing institutions in a culture dominated by men – for example in trade unions, parties or the state – without bypassing the existing framework of power. This has been most evident whenever meeting the needs women express politically would require a redistribution of resources or the redefinition of priorities.

Feminists have become increasingly aware of the traps inherent in redefining politics in terms of personal relations without following through the implications by challenging the existing political framework. Yet even with this realization, there has been a drawing back. There is a bewilderment, a sense of loss, which sends some feminists down a false trail, in search of a distinctive women's language. The incongruities that have jolted our consciousness are evident in the terms feminists use to express women's predicament. Is it to be the subjective description or a sociological overview? The movement towards conscious theory or existing positions of power is also a leaving, a relinquishing. The question is there *sotto voce* among feminists, Is it all worth it after all?

This questioning of the initial impetus of the movement of the late Sixties and early Seventies has resulted in strenuous efforts to recoup femininity. Motherhood, after all, is perceived to be a source of power, and shared parenting not what every woman wants. Home is a terrain of creativity, not just the prison house, and so on. Feminists are deeply at variance over what to dump and what to hang on to, and the disagreement cuts right across existing political groupings.

The idealization of female characteristics is a dead end. In order for feminism to remain a living politics it has to extend its scope continually. There are many levels of personal subversion of image, behaviour and style through which feminism acquires inflections which expand the range of its political capacity to manoeuvre. Women's liberation has expressed attachment towards what it means to be a woman, as well as renunciation. It has also carried a yearning for possibilities beyond our present imaginings. The tension is there within feminist politics because it exists in the culture of inequality.

A continuing political divide which appears in many contexts is over the difficulty of explaining in clear and simple terms the reasons for women's subordination. Take those codes of submission often visible in the portrayal of women in our culture. Are these simply the result of a male conspiracy to gull us into compliance? I think at one level this was what we assumed when the women's movement began. I realize this is still what some feminists believe. One snag appeared, however, even in those early demonstrations against beauty contests: were we saying that women were all being so easily taken in, or was there something in it for women after all? The emphasis on the active agency of men avoids a remote theory of systems and structures of oppression, but it takes us towards the politics of plots and plotters. It does not provide the means of understanding why certain women in specific circumstances start to question in particular ways. There are similar problems in depicting the operation of power in the state. Is it just a male state? If not, what else is it? How do the bits hinge together historically?

Caught up in the hinges are problems of agency and consciousness. In the early feminist groups there was a relatively straightforward assumption that if women talked long and intimately enough their real desires could be detached from those with which they had been lumbered by men or capitalism. We talked and talked for years and in this time we also lived, acted and changed. The talking did enable women to express feelings in a process of social exchange that could validate grievance beyond complaint.

Needs were brought to politics which had been disregarded and unrecognized within male definitions of politics. But the 'real' desires were more elusive than we had thought.

The problems within this form of political organization became apparent when feminist women disagreed, for instance over sexuality, pregnancy or child care, or had different attitudes to marriage, men or work. Consciousness-raising could illuminate and reveal, but it could also stifle and steer. In some cases new groups could form from the old, but at other times the breaks were explosive, with unstated resentments which could not be quieted by political debate. Two stark emotions loomed persistently: betrayal and coercion. The small group sought a consensus which had ramifications within the politics of the women's movement. Repeatedly, as consensus disintegrated and the community of sisterhood could not hold, the inclination was towards ostracism. It has been painfully difficult, under the banner of 'the personal is political', to admit that it is well-nigh impossible to untangle our desires, and that there is not going to be a uniformity of wants among women.

It is not easy to let go of a new-found union or to acknowledge dissimilarity and discord. But nearly two decades on it is incontrovertible that there are many feminist visions of the future we seek. There remain divisions of right and left, and there are differences between women based on class and race, for example. Other variations of circumstance – whether women are caring for children or other dependants, the nature of women's work, age, or disability – can all affect how women define their needs.

No movement can live on old certainties, yet radical ideas often take root on rocky ground and once they sprout there is a feeling that we must keep watering them, regardless of whether they are misplaced. The radical inside me says, 'Out with them, root and branch.' Then the conservative says, 'There, there; let them be.' It is always difficult to know what to chuck out and what to put by. Uncertainty in politics is always disturbing. Perhaps this is an inevitable restriction of engagement and one of the intellectual attractions of quietism. You falter when you become unsure and amidst conflict this can be a disadvantage. Yet popular movements require the means to doubt. Within a movement can be detected both a culture of politics and a culture of intellectual enquiry. The two are not always in accord.

An uncertainty which rather alarmed me in the writing was that I began to see the slogans of choice and control – which have had extremely radical implications – as limited and somewhat one-dimensional. They could take us only so far, after which they returned us to a point along the route. It was as if feminists were trying to take off to a new conception which combined reason and sensuous apprehension and yet were missing certain crucial connections. This was most noticeable in the debates around fertility. Might there be some theoretical convergence between the individualistic values of choice and control and the collective needs of a community? Could there ever really be a society in which relationships were truly free and equal, and trust so total that our personal concerns might balance harmoniously with those of others, not simply in couples or even within a family but on a large scale? It seems to me pretty well inconceivable. Yet there is just an intimation that perhaps it might be possible. More immediately, thinking about how we bring new life to the world needs to take into account the individual desire for procreation and the implications for society.

Throughout my account of ideas in the women's movement a difficulty is apparent in combining the personal perceptions of relationships and the attempt to understand these in social terms. There are sudden transitions from intimacy to social theories which can either surprise or simply be stylistically indigestible. The chronicler has prevailed over the aesthete here. For even the jerkiness in switching from one mode of perception to another expresses the significant effort of women's liberation to combine differing facets of knowing within a single movement.

Uncertainties and awkward combinations are hardly recipes for success in conventional party politics. Perhaps it is a strength of movements that they can disperse, splinter, form and re-form to re-create themselves. They are perhaps better suited to finding sources of renewal. However, unlike parties they have no institutional forms of conserving memory. They avoid the narrow tracking of time gone by through which the official history vindicates the party, but at the cost of vanishing altogether. They are liable to leave a much reduced intellectual legacy, and from rich experiences has come little received thought about how best to proceed. In saying we want a movement to remember the doings and sayings of its past we are not assuming a single interpretation. It is simply that by mining our memories we might save someone time in the future.

Women's liberation has raised questions that range beyond feminist organizations. The strains in the translation of needs into demands and policy, or the difficulty of campaigning when it is not so much a matter of achieving goals as of changing relationships, are not gender-bound. Nor are the radical challenge to existing forms of political planning and the search for the collective development of ideas which have been present in contemporary feminism. Not only women have sought forms of organization which reach further into social existence than the rituals of public meetings, canvassing and leafleting. Nonetheless, in the last decade or so women have been particularly inventive in extending the social and cultural space of politics.

But the growth of a women's liberation culture in the widest sense has not, as we have seen, solved the problem of how this social force can change the existing framework of political power. In Britain this conundrum has landed on the women's sections of the Labour Party and the women's committees of local authorities. They have found themselves puzzling away between diffuse concepts of politics which have arisen in a social movement and the neater if more tired formulas, geared to goals, polls and campaigns, which are the rules of thumb of Labour Party politics. This has tended to present itself as an internal debate about democracy and the constitution. Certainly, a politics that was organically linked to the expression of social need would require new structures and procedures to enable it to take effect. These necessitate thought and deliberation, but also partly arise through changing the scope of political activity. For it is not just a matter of conceiving the organizational framework anew, but of determining what kinds of radical changes would lead to a better life. It is a new combination of utopia and strategy that is wanting. If the women's movement has been hotter on utopias than strategies, the reverse has been true of modern socialism. It would seem to me an element of exchange might be helpful. The utopias of women's liberation have tended not to be like the fantasies of science fiction or the moral homilies of political theorizing. Rather, they have been the crystallized longings that have arisen from action because the existing social patterns of women's lives have proved so uninhabitable. These utopias are life-lines rather than diversions or pedagogic exercises. Their pursuit has thus been repeatedly renewed even beyond the boundaries of the existing political conceptualization of women's liberation. Organization, even the semi-permeable membrane of modern feminism, cannot keep up with the movement of people, any more than planning or policy can adequately express the spontaneity of uprisings and the complexity of desire. Feminists are therefore part of a continuing search for forms of organizing which are at once open to wider social needs and capable of strategic effect. As the experiences which provoked and formed a feminist consciousness have, to paraphrase the American writer Sara Evans, recreated themselves beyond their original constituency within the diverse circumstances of women, the sources of discontent have developed new ramifications. They have not only been about women's situation as women, but about the denial of access to material resources and about the transformation of the everyday life of whole communities of the disinherited.

While the future is behind us and prophecy most perilous, the past really is before us, so the charting of experience can bring a sense of direction. The process of a movement in transforming itself can link past and future without attempting to impose the past upon the future. A left dissident in the early days of the Russian Revolution, Ante Ciliga, observed that the thought of the past can prevent us 'from battering down open doors, but too often it caused entirely new phenomena to be overlooked'.[3] He went on to quote Goethe: 'All thought is hoary, but the tree of life is eternally green.'[4]

The hope of renewal has been called into question in our times. To gaze at our elusive past can seem an insufficient contribution in such circumstances. Yet there is a great power in memory to release as well as to constrain. Because the tree of life is in danger, all the more reason not to lose our heads and that hope for a better world in which feminism is a creative element. The future, being behind us, is always likely to surprise.

References

Introduction

1 Sara Evans, *Personal Politics: The Roots of Women's Liberation in the Civil Rights Movement and the New Left*, Knopf, New York, 1979, pp. 226–7.

2 For an account of contemporary feminist debates, see Lynne Segal, *Is the Future Female? Troubled Thoughts on Contemporary Feminism*, Virago, London, 1987; and Anne Phillips, *Divided Loyalties: Dilemmas of Sex and Class*, Virago, London, 1987.

3 For a discussion on similar lines of how to approach the thought of a social movement as participant and analyst, see Wini Breines, *The Great Refusal: Community and Organisation in the New Left, 1962–1968*, 1982, pp. xi–xiv.

Chapter 1

1 Jan Williams, Hazel Twort and Ann Bachelli (of Peckham Rye Women's Liberation Group), 'Reflections on Politics and the Family', *Shrew*, February/March 1970; reprinted as 'Women and the Family' in Ellen Malos (ed.), *The Politics of Housework*, Allison & Busby, London, 1980, p. 113.

2 ibid.

3 Michelene Wandor, 'Family Ever After', *Spare Rib*, November 1972.

4 See, for example, 'Should Marriage be Abolished?', *Shrew*, Autumn 1974; Lee Comer, *Wedlocked Women*, Feminist Books, Leeds, 1974, p. 121; Sue Todd, 'Remember Me', *Red Rag*, 12, n.d.; Lee Comer, 'The Act of Forgetting', *Women's Liberation Review*, 1, October 1972.

5 Williams *et al.*, 'Women and The Family', in Malos, *Politics of Housework*.

6 Suzanne Gail, 'The Housewife', in Ronald Fraser (ed.), *Work*, Penguin, Harmondsworth, 1968, p. 149.

7 Williams *et al.*, 'Women and the Family', in Malos, *Politics of House work*, p. 114.

8 Gail, 'The Housewife', in Fraser, *Work*, p. 149.

9 Mary Michaels, 'Evening', *Spare Rib*, March 1973.

10 Emmy Smith, 'Doors are Opening in My Mind', *Spare Rib*, 33, March 1975.

11 Gail, 'The Housewife', in Fraser, *Work*, p. 149.

12 Jeremy Hunter Henderson, 'Thoughts of an Onion', quoted in Roberta Hunter Henderson and Liz Cooper, 'Don't Break Down, Break Out', *Shrew*, Autumn 1976.

13 Smith, 'Doors are Opening in My Mind'.

14 Wandor, 'Family Ever After'.

15 Comer, 'The Act of Forgetting'.

16 See, for example, Jane Baker, 'How I Changed My Sex', *Shrew*, Autumn 1974.

17 Anon., 'Guilt-Edged Insecurity: How Did We Get Here?', *Shrew*, Summer 1974.

18 ibid.

19 Janice, 'A Day in the Life of. . .', *Spare Rib*, 65, December 1977.

20 Anon., 'Something about being Honest', *Shrew*, September 1970.

21 Annette from Dundee Women's Aid Centre, quoted in Ingrid Muir, 'Refuge from Dundee', *Spare Rib*, September 1976.

22 ibid.

23　Anon., 'You're either Someone's Daughter or Someone's Wife', paper at London Women's Liberation Conference, 1977.

24　ibid.

25　Ruth Hall, Introduction to *Women Against Rape* (pamphlet), December 1976; reprinted in Feminist Anthology Collective (eds.), *No Turning Back: Writings from the Women's Liberation Movement, 1975–80*, Women's Press, London, 1981.

26　Bea Campbell, 'A Feminist Sexual Politics: Now You See It, Now You Don't', *Feminist Review*, 5, 1980.

27　ibid.

28　Nell Myers, Annie Mitchell, Adah Kay and Valerie Charlton, 'Four Sisters', *Red Rag*, 11, n.d.

29　ibid.

30　Sue Todd, 'Remember Me', *Red Rag*, 12, n.d.

31　Myers *et al.*, 'Four Sisters'.

32　Astra, 'mother and daughter', in Astra, *Back You Come, Mother Dear*, Virago, London, 1986, p. 36.

33　Anon., 'Dear Mother', *Shrew* (issue entitled 'Let It Bleed'), Winter 1971.

34　Smith, 'Doors are Opening in My Mind'.

35　Betty McArdle, 'Ballad of a Single Woman', *Spare Rib*, 95, June 1980.

36　ibid.

37　Cathy Kerr, review of Nancy Friday, *My Mother, My Self* (Delacorte, New York, 1977; Sheldon, London, 1979), and Marilyn French, *The Women's Room* (Summit Books, New York, 1977; Deutsch, London, 1978), *MsPrint* (Scottish feminist publication), 4, 1979.

38　Kathy Gott, 'Accepting Their Ideals', *Women's Voice*, 13, January 1978.

39　ibid.

40　Sarah Brown, 'Soaking Dirt at Barnsley Public Baths', *Spare Rib*, 73, October 1977.

41　See Sheila Yeger, 'My Mum Doesn't Know How to Draw Elephants', *Spare Rib*, March 1978.

42　Sheena Adams, 'Just an Ordinary Woman', *Working Class Women's Liberation Newsletter*, 7, n.d.

43　ibid.

44　ibid.

45　ibid.

46　ibid.

47　See Jean McCrindle and Sheila Rowbotham (eds.), *Dutiful Daughters*, Allen Lane, London, 1977; Penguin, 1979, p. 4.

48　Kay, 'On Being a Have-not', *Socialist Worker*, 31 August 1974.

49　Ann Whitehead, 'Sexual Antagonism in Herefordshire', in Diana Leonard Barker and Sheila Allen (eds.), *Dependence and Exploitation in Work and Marriage*, Longman, London, 1976, p. 148.

50　Rozsika Parker, 'Being Jewish: Anti-Semitism and Jewish Women', *Spare Rib*, 79, February 1974.

51　Julia Wright, 'Coming Out to My Mother', *Spare Rib*, 51, October 1976.

52　ibid. See also Ros Carne, 'Homosexuality: Sexual Problem or Political Problem?', *Spare Rib*, 36, June 1975.

53　J.R., letter to *Spare Rib*, 14, August 1973.

54　Alison Fell, 'For Ivan Aged 9', in Alison Fell *et al.*, *Licking the Bed Clean: Five Feminist Poets* (published by the authors), London, 1978, p. 17.

55 Ursula Owen, Introduction, in Ursula Owen (ed.), *Fathers: Reflections by Daughters*, Virago, London, 1983, pp. 10–11.

56 Sara Maitland, 'Two for the Price of One', in Owen, *Fathers*, p. 34.

57 ibid.

58 Elaine Feinstein, 'A Legendary Hero', in Owen, *Fathers*, p. 167.

59 Gail Lewis, 'From Deepest Kilburn', in Liz Heron (ed.), *Truth, Dare or Promise: Girls Growing Up in the Fifties*, Virago, London, 1985, p. 231.

60 ibid., p. 232.

61 Fay Weldon, *Remember Me* (Hodder & Stoughton, London, 1976), quoted in review by Sue Todd, *Red Rag*, 112, n.d.

62 See Lynne Segal, ' "Smash the Family?" Recalling the 1960s', in Lynne Segal (ed.), *What is to be Done about the Family?*, Penguin, Harmondsworth, 1983, pp. 25–64.

63 Sharon Barba, 'A Cycle of Women', in Laura Chester and Sharon Barba (eds.), *Rising Tides: Twentieth Century American Women Poets*, Washington Square Press, New York, 1973, p. 356.

64 See Ann Oakley, *Subject Woman*, Martin Robertson, Oxford, 1981, pp. 106–9.

65 See Sue Llewelyn, 'Woman Centred Therapy', in Feminist Anthology Collective, *No Turning Back*, pp. 150–57; and Luise Eichenbaum and Susie Orbach, *What do Women Want?*, Fontana, London, 1984.

66 Sheila Ernst and Lucy Goodison, *In Our Own Hands*, Women's Press, London, 1981, pp. 3–4.

67 Sally Alexander and Barbara Taylor, 'In Defence of "Patriarchy" ', *New Statesman*, 1 February 1980; reprinted in Raphael Samuel (ed.), *People's History and Socialist Theory*, Routledge & Kegan Paul, London, 1981, p. 372.

68 See Michèle Barrett, *Women's Oppression Today: Problems in Marxist Feminist Analysis*, Verso, London, 1980, p. 198; and Kate Young and Olivia Harris, 'The Subordination of Women in Cross-cultural Perspective', in Women's Publishing Collective (ed.), *Papers on Patriarchy*, Women's Publishing Collective, Brighton, 1976, pp. 38–52.

69 I owe this point to Paul Atkinson.

70 Juliet Mitchell, review of Jonathan Miller (ed.), *Freud: The Man, His World, His Influence* (Weidenfeld & Nicolson, London, 1972), *Spare Rib*, 6, December 1972.

71 ibid.

72 ibid.

73 Anna Coote and Beatrix Campbell, *Sweet Freedom: The Struggle for Women's Liberation*, Picador, London, 1982, pp. 100–101. See also Wandor, 'Family Ever After'.

74 Rayna Rapp, Ellen Ross and Renate Bridenthal, 'Examining Family History', *Feminist Studies*, 5:1, Spring 1979.

Chapter 2

1 See Mica Nava, 'From Utopia to Scientific Feminism? Early Feminist Critiques of the Family', in Lynne Segal (ed.), *What is to be Done about the Family?*, Penguin, Harmondsworth, 1983; and Sue Sharpe, 'The Role of the Nuclear Family in the Oppression of Women', in Michelene Wandor (ed.), *The Body Politic: Writings from the Women's Liberation Movement in Britain*, Stage 1, London, 1972.

2 Rosalind Delmar, 'Sexism, Capitalism and the Family', in Sandra Allen, Lee Sanders and Jan Wallis (eds.), *Conditions of Illusion: Papers from the Women's Movement*, Feminist Books, Leeds, 1974, p. 231. For a re-working of ideas on choice and

consumption, see 'Domestic Work and Child Care', in *The London Industrial Strategy*, Greater London Council, London, 1985, pp. 195–217.

3 See Ellen Malos (ed.), *The Politics of Housework*, Allison & Busby, London, 1980.

4 See Sheila Rowbotham, 'Search and Subject: Threading Circumstances' and 'When Adam Delved and Eve Span. . .', *New Society*, 4 January 1979; reprinted in *Dreams and Dilemmas*, Virago, London, 1983, pp. 199–207; Rayna Rapp Reiter, *Toward an Anthropology of Woman*, Monthly Review Press, New York, 1975; Carol MacCormack and Marilyn Strathern (eds.), *Nature, Culture and Gender*, Cambridge University Press, 1980; Heleieth Saffioti, *Women in Class Society*, Monthly Review Press, New York, 1978; Stephanie Coontz and Peta Henderson, *Women's Work, Men's Property: The Origins of Gender and Class*, Verso, London, 1986; and Jane Humphries, 'Class Struggle and the Persistence of the Working Class Family', *Cambridge Journal of Economics*, 1:3, 1977.

5 Examples of this perspective are Kathleen Ennis, 'Notes on the Family', paper at International Socialism Day School, 1972; and North East Region Women's Liberation, paper at Acton Women's Liberation Conference, n.d. For an overview of the debate, see Malos, *Politics of Housework*, pp. 7–43.

6 See Dorothy Thompson, 'Women and Nineteenth Century Radical Politics: A Lost Dimension', in Ann Oakley and Juliet Mitchell (eds.), *The Rights and Wrongs of Women*, Penguin, Harmondsworth, 1976; and Barbara Taylor, *Eve and the New Jerusalem*, Virago, London, 1983. For an American comparison see Martha May, 'Bread before Roses: American Workingmen, Labor Unions and the Family Wage', in Ruth Milkman (ed.), *Women, Work and Protest: A Century of US Women's Labor History*, Routledge & Kegan Paul, London, 1985.

7 See Kum-Kum Bhavnani, 'Racist Acts', *Spare Rib*, 117, April 1982; Parita Trivedi, 'To Deny Our Fullness: Asian Women in the Making of History', *Feminist Review*, 17, Autumn 1984; and Valerie Amos and Pratibha Parmar, 'Challenging Imperial Feminism', *Feminist Review*, 17, Autumn 1984.

8 North London Women Against Racism and Fascism Group, report in *Spare Rib*, 77, December 1978.

9 See Sheila Rowbotham, *Woman's Consciousness, Man's World*, Penguin, Harmondsworth, 1973; Michèle Barrett, *Women's Oppression Today: Problems in Marxist Feminist Analysis*, Verso, London, 1980, pp. 227–47; Amina Mama, 'Black Women, the Economic Crisis and the British State', *Feminist Review*, 17, Autumn 1984; and Lynne Segal, 'No Turning Back: Thatcherism, the Family and the Future', in Segal, *What is to be Done about the Family?*.

10 Irene Bruegel, 'What Keeps the Family?', *International Socialism*, 2:1, 1978.

11 See Malos, *Politics of Housework*; Sue Himmelweit, 'Production Rules OK? Waged Work and the Family', in Segal, *What is to be Done about the Family?*; Christine Dupont [later Delphy], 'L'Ennemi principal', *Partisans*, Paris, 54–5 (issue entitled 'Libération des femmes, année zéro'), July–October 1970: translated into English as Christine Delphy, *The Main Enemy: A Materialist Analysis of Women's Oppression* (Explorations in Feminism, No. 3), Women's Research and Resource Centre, London, 1977; and Barrett, *Women's Oppression Today*, pp. 211–13.

12 'Dot', 'Social Security', *Women's Voice*, 9, November–December 1973.

13 Alison Langan, 'Social Class Five', *Socialist Worker*, 26 October 1974.

14 'Women and Unemployment', paper at Claimants' Union Conference on Unemployment, n.d. (early 1970s).

15 Juliet Mitchell, *Woman's Estate*, Penguin, Harmondsworth, 1971, p. 157.

16   See Fran Bennett, 'The State, Welfare and Women's Dependence', in Segal, *What is to be Done about the Family?*

17   See Hilary Land, 'The Introduction of Family Allowances: An Act of Historic Justice?', in Clare Ungerson (ed.), *Women and Social Policy: A Reader*, Macmillan, 1985; Jane Lewis, 'Beyond Suffrage: English Feminism during the 1920s', *Maryland Historian*, vi, Spring 1975; Sheila Rowbotham, *A New World for Women: Stella Browne – Socialist Feminist*, Pluto, London, 1977; and Eleanor Rathbone (with introductory essay by Suzie Fleming), *The Disinherited Family*, Falling Wall Press, Bristol, 1986. On the Marxists, see Sheila Rowbotham, *Women, Resistance and Revolution*, Penguin, Harmondsworth, 1971. For a comparison with Austrian social democracy, see Reinhard Sieder, 'Housing Policy, Social Welfare and Family Life in "Red Vienna" ', *Oral History*, 13:2, Autumn 1985.

18   See Denise Riley, 'Force of Circumstances', *Red Rag*, 9, June 1975; reprinted in Feminist Anthology Collective (eds.), *No Turning Back: Writings from the Women's Liberation Movement, 1975–80*, Women's Press, London, 1981.

19   Bhavnani, 'Racist Acts'.

20   Nell Myers, Annie Mitchell, Adah Kay and Valerie Charlton, 'Four Sisters', *Red Rag*, 11, n.d. For an interesting comparison with some feminist critiques of 'science', see Hester Eisenstein, *Contemporary Feminist Thought*, Unwin, London, 1984, pp. 98–101.

21   Myers *et al.*, 'Four Sisters'.

22   Anna Coote and Beatrix Campbell, *Sweet Freedom: The Struggle for Women's Liberation*, Picador, London, 1982, pp. 99–100.

23   Anon., 'Fuck the Family', *Lesbians Come Together*, n.d. (early 1970s).

24   Anon., 'Bringing Kids Up in a Commune', *Spare Rib*, 35, May 1975.

25   ibid.

26   Coote and Campbell, *Sweet Freedom*, p. 100.

27   ' "Once they've got a baby by you they've got a hold of you. . ." ', *Shrew*, 3:8, September 1971.

28   Mina Jones, 'Think Darts', *Spare Rib*, 29, February 1979.

29   ibid.

30   Frankie Rickford, 'There's a Female in Here', *Spare Rib*, 95, June 1980.

31   Sharda Patel, 'Refuge', *Feminist Review*, 17, Autumn 1984.

32   ibid. On the GLC, see Maureen Mackintosh and Hilary Wainwright (eds.), *A Taste of Power: The Politics of Local Economics*, Verso, London, 1987.

33   Beatrix Campbell and Valerie Charlton, 'Work to Rule', *Red Rag*, 1978; reprinted in Feminist Anthology Collective, *No Turning Back*.

34   Angela Weir and Elizabeth Wilson, 'Why be a Wife?', *Link* (Communist Party women's journal), 20, Spring 1978.

35   Katherine Gieve, 'Dependence and a New Political Consciousness', *Spare Rib*, 25, n.d.

36   ibid. See also Eisenstein, *Contemporary Feminist Thought*, pp. 64–86; and Lynne Segal, *Is the Future Female? Troubled Thoughts on Contemporary Feminism*, Virago, London, 1987.

37   Rose Ades, 'Women's Liberation is Not Redundant', *Spare Rib*, 44, March 1976.

38   Ulrike Prokop, quoted in Nancy Vedder-Shults, 'Hearts Starve as Well as Bodies', *New German Critique* (University of Wisconsin [Madison]), 13, Winter 1978.

39   Anna Coote, 'The Sexual Division of Labour and Relations in the Family', in

Report on Conference on Alternative Strategies for the Labour Movement, CSE, London, 1981. A version of this paper also appears in Anna Coote, 'A New Starting Point', in James Curran (ed.), *The Future of the Left*, Polity Press and *New Socialist*, London, 1984.

40 ibid.

41 See Sheila Rowbotham, 'Hopes, Dreams and Dirty Nappies', *Marxism Today*, 28:12, December 1984.

42 Anon., 'The Family, Heaven or Hell: So What Would You Put in Its Place?', *Women's Voice*, 34, October 1976.

43 ibid.

44 Eve Lyn, 'Bits and Pieces from a Shattered Mind', *Working Class Women's Liberation Newsletter*, 1, May 1978.

45 Myers *et al.*, 'Four Sisters'.

46 ibid.

Chapter 3

1 See Kathy Henderson, Frankie Armstrong and Sandra Kerr (eds.), *My Song is My Own*, Pluto, London, 1979, pp. 126–7.

2 Pamela Greenwood, 'Job Satisfaction', *Spare Rib*, 38, October 1976.

3 Margaret Benston, The Political Economy of Women's Liberation', in Ellen Malos (ed.), *The Politics of Housework*, Allison & Busby, London, 1980, pp. 119–29.

4 Peggy Morton, 'Women's Work is Never Done', in ibid., pp. 130–57.

5 Lee Comer, *Wedlocked Women*, Feminist Books, Leeds, 1974, p. 83.

6 See, for example, Sheila Rowbotham, *Woman's Consciousness, Man's World*, Penguin, Harmondsworth, 1973, pp. 67–80. The section on housework in that book was based on an unpublished paper for a seminar at the Institute of Race Relations, Spring 1971. It also drew on Jean Gardiner, 'The Economic Roots of Women's Liberation', paper at the International Socialism Conference on Women, June 1971. A different approach was taken in Political Economy of Women Group, *On the Political Economy of Women*, CSE pamphlet, Stage 1, London, 1975. Mica Nava discusses some of these early ideas on housework in 'From Utopian to Scientific Feminism? Early Feminist Critiques of the Family', in Lynne Segal (ed.), *What is to be Done about the Family?*, Penguin, Harmondsworth, 1983. Ellen Malos, in her Introduction to *The Politics of Housework* (Allison & Busby, London, 1980), provides a summary of the debates. Another summary is Eva Kaluzynska's 'Wiping the Floor with Theory', *Feminist Review*, 6, 1980. Susan Himmelweit, 'Production Rules OK? Waged Work and the Family', in Segal, *What is to be Done about the Family?*, takes the discussion down new and interesting paths.

7 Pat Mainardi, 'The Politics of Housework', in Malos, *Politics of Housework*, p. 99.

8 Michelene Wandor, 'Family Ever After', *Spare Rib*, 5, November 1972.

9 Rosalind Davis, 'Community Politics and Industrial Politics', *Socialist Woman*, Feb.–March 1973.

10 Priscilla Allen, Preface to *Wages for Housework* (duplicated pamphlet), Power of Women Collective, 1973.

11 Sandra Kerr, 'The Maintenance Engineer', in Henderson *et al.*, *My Song is My Own*, pp. 136–7.

12 On the family allowance campaign, see Sheila Rowbotham, 'Women. . .How Far Have We Come?', in *Dreams and Dilemmas*, Virago, London, 1983, pp. 89–90. For a Wages for Housework account of the campaign, see Suzie Fleming's introductory essay in Eleanor Rathbone, *The Disinherited Family*, Falling Wall Press, Bristol, 1986, pp. 93–5.

13 On the care of dependants, see Greater London Council Women's Committee, *Chance or Choice: Community Care and Women as Carers*, GLC, London, 1984.

14 Editorial, *Journal of the Power of Women Collective*, 1:1, March–April 1974.

15 Caroline Freeman, 'When is a Wage Not a Wage', *Red Rag*, 5, Autumn 1973.

16 Angela Phillips, letter, *Leveller*, 2, December 1976.

17 Jill Tweedie, 'Slave Wages', *Guardian*, 3 May 1976.

18 See Himmelweit, 'Production Rules OK?, in Segal, *What is to be Done about the Family?*, p. 108.

19 Pamela Greenwood, letter, *Spare Rib*, 28, October 1974. See also Jan Williams, Hazel Twort and Ann Bachelli (of Peckham Rye Women's Liberation Group), 'Reflections on Politics and the Family', *Shrew*, February–March 1970, reprinted as 'Women and the Family' in Malos, *Politics of Housework*; Anon., 'Housewives' Choice', *Women Now*, March–April 1971; 'M.R.', 'Contact', *Shrew*, October 1971; Michelene Wandor, 'Family Ever After', *Spare Rib*, 5, November 1972; Sheila Rowbotham, 'Women's Liberation and the New Politics', in *Dreams and Dilemmas*, pp. 20–34; and Rowbotham, *Woman's Consciousness, Man's World*, pp. 67–80.

20 Ann Oakley, *The Sociology of Housework*, Martin Robertson, London, 1974, p. 45.

21 Betty Friedan, *The Feminine Mystique*, Norton, New York, and Gollancz, London, 1963; Penguin, Harmondsworth, 1968, p. 256.

22 See, for example, Anon., 'Housewives' Choice'; Rowbotham, *Woman's Consciousness, Man's World*, p. 76; Wandor, 'Family Ever After'; and Barbara Marsh, in Jean McCrindle and Sheila Rowbotham (eds.), *Dutiful Daughters*, Allen Lane, London, 1977; Penguin, Harmondsworth, 1979, p. 262.

23 Maggie Fuller, in McCrindle and Rowbotham, *Dutiful Daughters*, p. 127.

24 Linda Peffer, in ibid., p. 381.

25 'M.R.', 'Contact'.

26 Wandor, 'Family Ever After'.

27 Ann Whitehead, 'I'm Hungry, Mum: The Politics of Domestic Budgeting', in Kate Young, Carol Walkowitz and Rosalyn McCullagh (eds.), *Of Marriage and the Market: Women's Subordination in International Perspective*, CSE Books, London, 1981, p. 108.

28 I argue this point at greater length in 'Domestic Work and Childcare', in *The London Industrial Strategy*, Greater London Council, London, 1985.

29 See Chapter 10 below for an account of the connections made between domestic responsibilities and employment.

30 Christine Dupont [later Delphy], 'L'Ennemi principal', *Partisans*, Paris, 54–5 (issue entitled Libération des femmes, année zéro'), July–October 1970; translated into English as Christine Delphy, *The Main Enemy: A Materialist Analysis of Women's Oppression* (Explorations in Feminism, No. 3), Women's Research and Resource Centre, London, 1977.

31 Critical notes made by Françoise Ducroq and the issue of *Partisans* cited in n. 30 formed the background to *Woman's Consciousness, Man's World*. I combined these with arguments from Marx's *Grundrisse* and from Rosa Luxemburg. Another influence was American studies of race in terms of a political economy.

32 For a criticism of this position, see Political Economy of Women Group, *On the Political Economy of Women*, p. 7.

33 See Delphy, *The Main Enemy*; and Christine Delphy, 'Continuities and Discontinuities in Marriage and Divorce', in Diana Leonard Barker and Sheila Allen

(eds.), *Sexual Divisions and Society: Process and Change*, Tavistock, London, 1976. For a criticism of her analysis, see Michèle Barrett and Mary McIntosh, 'Christine Delphy: Towards a Materialist Feminism', *Feminist Review*, 1, 1979.

34 Olivia Harris, 'Households as Natural Units', in Young *et al.*, *Of Marriage and the Market*, p. 58.

35 Anne Phillips, *Hidden Hands: Women and Economic Policies*, Pluto, London, 1983, p. 19.

36 See Sue Sharpe, *Double Identity: The Lives of Working Mothers*, Penguin, Harmondsworth, 1984.

37 Himmelweit, 'Production Rules OK?', in Segal, *What is to be Done about the Family?*, p. 111.

38 Maureen Mackintosh, 'Domestic Labour in the Household', in Sandra Burnam (ed.), *Fit Work for Women*, Croom Helm, London, 1979, p. 187.

39 See, for example, Nadia H. Youssef, 'The Interrelationship between the Division of Labour in the Household, Women's Roles and Their Impact on Fertility'; Carmen Diana Deere, Jane Humphries and Magdalena Léon de Leal, 'Class and Historical Analysis for the Study of Women and Economic Change'; and Eva Mueller, 'The Allocation of Women's Time and Its Relation to Fertility', all in Richard Anker, Mayra Buvinic and Nadia H. Youssef (eds.), *Women's Roles and Population Trends in the Third World*, Croom Helm, London, 1982.

40 Elizabeth Jelin, 'Women and the Urban Labour Markets', in ibid., p. 240.

41 Pat V. T. West, 'intimations of a sweet past never had', *Enough* (journal of Bristol Women's Liberation Group), 3, 1971.

42 Barbara Marsh, McCrindle and Rowbotham, *Dutiful Daughters*, p. 261. See also Sharpe, *Double Identity*, pp. 179–96.

43 Joy Marston, 'Mrs Mable', *Spare Rib*, 55, February 1977.

44 Wendy Whitfield, 'His and Her Housework', *Spare Rib*, 45, April 1976.

45 ibid.

46 ibid.

47 Stef Pixner, 'The pain that I find in dust and disorder', in *Sawdust and White Spirit*, Virago, London, 1985, p. 36.

48 'M.R.', 'Contact'.

49 Jenefer Coates, 'Shared Housework', *Spare Rib*, 25, n.d.

50 Anja Bostock, 'In the Shit No More', *Spare Rib*, 43, February 1976.

51 See Meg Luxton, *More than a Labour of Love*, Women's Press, Toronto, 1980, pp. 209–10.

52 Anon., *People's Food Co-op, Lincoln Estate, Bow*, Big Flame Pamphlet, n.d. (c. 1975).

53 ibid.

54 Barbara Castle, 'Coming Alive Hurts', *Beyond the Fragments Bulletin*, 3, Spring 1982; reprinted in Ann Curno *et al.* (eds.), *Women in Collective Action*, Association of Community Workers in the UK, London, 1982, pp. 13–31.

55 ibid.

56 Barnsley Women, *Women Against Pit Closures*, Barnsley, 1984, p. 23.

57 Malos, *The Politics of Housework*, p. 36.

58 Quoted in Anon., 'Underachievement or Oppression?', *Spare Rib*, 73, August 1978.

59 Rosie Parker, 'The Word for Embroidery was Work', *Spare Rib*, 37, July 1975.

60 Anny Brackx, 'Subverting Sweetness', *Spare Rib*, 67, February 1978.

61 See, for example, 'Hazards of Housework' column, *Women's Struggle Notes* (Big

Flame women's publication), 1, n.d.; Anon., 'The Technology of the Home: A Practical Insulation Guide' ('Women at Home' series of articles), *Undercurrents*, 29, August–September 1978; Malos, *The Politics of Housework*, pp. 36–7.

62 See 'Domestic Work and Childcare', in *London Industrial Strategy*.

63 Jean Gardiner, 'The Economic Roots of Women's Liberation'.

64 Himmelweit, 'Production Rules OK?', in Segal, *What is to be Done about the Family?*, pp. 125–6.

65 Luxton, *More than a Labour of Love*, p. 207.

66 Himmelweit, 'Production Rules OK?', in Segal, *What is to be Done about the Family?*, pp. 125–6.

Chapter 4

1 Jill Rakusen, 'Depo-Provera: Still for Sale', *Spare Rib*, 47, June 1976.

2 Juliet Mitchell, 'Women: The Longest Revolution', *New Left Review*, 40, November–December 1966; reprinted in Edith Hoshino Altbach (ed.), *From Feminism to Liberation*, Schenkman, Cambridge, Mass., 1971, p. 105.

3 ibid.

4 Monica Sjoo, *Contraception Free to All Women and Abortion on Demand*, Bristol Women's Liberation Group, *c.* 1971.

5 Anon., 'Contraception', *Women's Newspaper*, 1, 6 March 1971.

6 Ann Oakley, *Subject Women*, Martin Robertson, Oxford, 1981, p. 193.

7 See Linda Gordon, *Woman's Body, Woman's Right* (Grossman, New York, 1976), on the traditional methods of contraception.

8 See, for example, Roszika Parker, 'If the Cap Fits', *Spare Rib*, 57, April 1977; Marianne Godfrey, 'Commenting on the Cervical Cap', *Spare Rib*, 107, June 1981; Oakley, *Subject Women*, p. 193; Tessa Weare, 'Was the Pill the Answer to Our Needs?', *Women's Voice*, 37, January 1980; and Kate and Janet, 'If the Cap Fits, Wear It', *Shocking Pink*, 3, n.d.

9 Jill Rakusen, 'Depo-Provera: The extent of the problem', in Helen Roberts (ed.), *Women, Health and Reproduction*, Routledge & Kegan Paul, London, 1981, p. 98. The plea to balance the arguments for and against has had some effect: see 'Depo-Provera', Women's Reproductive Rights Information Centre, n.d.; reprinted in *Seven Days*, 31 May 1986.

10 'Depo-Provera', *Fowaad* (newsletter of the Organization of Women of Asian and African Descent [OWAAD]), 3, n.d. On the impact of multinationals on the structure of health provision in the Third World, see Lesley Doyal and Imogen Pennell, *The Political Economy of Health*, Pluto Press, London, 1979, p. 283. On black women's control over fertility in relation to health, see OWAAD, 'Black Women and Health', in *Black Women in Britain Speak Out* (March 1979 OWAAD conference papers); reprinted in Feminist Anthology Collective (eds.), *No Turning Back: Writings from the Women's Liberation Movement, 1975–80*, Women's Press, London, 1981, pp. 145–9.

11 Northern Women's Conference at Sheffield, reported on by the Women's Liberation Front in *Women's Struggle* (bulletin of Women's National Co-ordinating Committee), 1:2.

12 Connie Harris, 'Anti-Abortion Problems', *Women's Liberation Workshop Newsletter*, November 1970.

13 'Information' Column, *Spare Rib*, 37, July 1975.

14 Women's Abortion and Contraception Campaign, report in *WACC Newsletter*, 2:2, April–May 1973.

15 ibid.

16 Jenny Collard, Jill Walker and Mary Ann Hildrew (Manchester Women's Liberation Centre), 'Pro-Abortionists Counter-Demonstrate', *WACC Newsletter*, April–May 1973.

17 Anna Coote and Beatrix Campbell, *Sweet Freedom: The Struggle for Women's Liberation*, Picador, London, 1982, p. 147.

18 Liz Warren, 'Abortion Act Threat',*Spare Rib*, 35, May 1975.

19 National Abortion Campaign, 'Proposals for Local Action' (leaflet), 1975. 'Local Action: Bristol, Cambridge, Chippenham, Liverpool, London, Nottingham, Oxford', *Spare Rib*, 37, July 1975.

20 Coote and Campbell, *Sweet Freedom*, p. 147.

21 Report in *Spare Rib*, 43, February 1976. On the relation to trade unions, see Anne Phillips, *Divided Loyalties: Dilemmas of Sex and Class*, Virago, London, 1987, pp. 117–19.

22 See Ruth Petrie and Anna Livingstone, 'Out of the Back Streets', *Red Rag*, 11, Autumn 1976; Al Garthwaite and Valerie Sinclair, 'The TUC's Right to Choose', *Wires*, December 1979 (reprinted in Feminist Anthology Collective, *No Turning Back*, pp. 36–41); Jane Noble and Ann Scott, 'Hackney Abortion Campaign', *Spare Rib*, 43, December 1975; Roberta Hunter Henderson, 'Feminism is Not for Burning: Speculations', *Cat-Call*, 2, April 1976; Sheila Rowbotham, 'The Women's Movement and Organizing for Socialism', in Sheila Rowbotham, Lynne Segal and Hilary Wainwright, *Beyond the Fragments*, Merlin, London, 1979, pp. 142–3.

23 Anon., 'Abortion on Demand', *Women's Struggle Notes* (Big Flame women's publication), 4, March–May 1975.

24 ibid.

25 See Lynne Segal, 'A Local Experience', in Rowbotham *et al.*, *Beyond the Fragments*, pp. 174–5.

26 Jane Noble and Ann Scott, 'Abortion Conference: Structure and Feminism', *Spare Rib*, 42, December 1975.

27 ibid.

28 Segal, 'A Local Experience', in Rowbotham *et al.*, *Beyond the Fragments*, p. 175.

29 Sheila Rowbotham, 'Women: How Far Have We Come?', *Hackney People's Press*, November 1979; reprinted in Sheila Rowbotham, *Dreams and Dilemmas*, Virago, London, 1983.

30 Petrie and Livingstone, 'Out of the Back Streets'.

31 Hilary Wainwright, Introduction to Rowbotham *et al.*, *Beyond the Fragments*, p. 7. See also Sheila Ernst and Lucy Goodison, *In Our Own Hands*, Women's Press, London, 1981, pp. 302–3 and 320 n.

32 Catherine Rose, *The Female Experience: The Story of the Woman Movement in Ireland*, Arlen House, Galway, Ireland, 1975, pp. 82–3.

33 Eileen Fairweather, 'The Feelings behind the Slogans', *Spare Rib*, 87, October 1979; reprinted in Marsha Rowe (ed.), *Spare Rib Reader*, Penguin, Harmondsworth, 1982, p. 342.

34 Ann Scott, quoted in Marsha Rowe, unpublished notes for a socialist and feminist day school, Leeds, 23 April 1977.

35 See Doyal and Pennell, *Political Economy of Health*, p. 229.

36 Juliet Ash (ed.), *Abortion: Where we stand*, London NAC, March 1976, p. 16.

37 Marie Arnold, 'One Woman's Abortion', *Spare Rib*, 45, April 1976.

38 Sheila Abdullah, speech at International Women's Day rally, London, March 1973; published in *WACC Newsletter*, 2:2, April–May 1973.

39 Hilda Bartle, speech at Counter-demonstration to anti-abortion rally, Manchester, March 1973; published in ibid.

40 ibid.

41 Doyal and Pennell, *Political Economy of Health*, p. 229. See also Clare Ungerson (ed.), *Women and Social Policy: A Reader*, Macmillan, 1985, London, p. 150.

42 Mitchell, 'Women: The Longest Revolution', in Altbach, *From Feminism to Liberation*, p. 105.

43 London Women's Liberation Workshop leaflet, 1970.

44 Caroline Smith, 'Formation of Medical and Biological Group', *Women's Liberation Workshop Newsletter*, 26, 4 April 1971.

45 Anon., 'Why Do We Emphasize Small Group Discussion?', *Shrew*, 6, October 1969.

46 Rakusen, 'Depo-Provera', in Roberts, *Women, Health and Reproduction*, p. 97.

47 See Christina Larner, *Witchcraft and Religion: The Politics of Popular Belief*, Basil Blackwell, Oxford, 1984, pp. 149–52.

48 Sandra McNeill, paper at workshop on reproduction, National Socialist Feminist Conference, January 1978; reprinted in *Scarlet Women*, 6–7, January 1978.

49 See Lesley Doyal, 'Women and the Crisis in the National Health Service', in Ungerson, *Women and Social Policy*, pp. 158–9; Gordon, *Woman's Body, Woman's Right*; and Olivia Harris, 'A Family Affair', *Socialist Review*, 5, September 1978.

50 Anon., 'A Woman's Right to Choose', *Big Flame*, October 1979.

51 Helen Roberts, 'Male Hegemony in Family Planning', in Roberts, *Women, Health and Reproduction*, p. 14.

52 See Doyal, 'Women and the Crisis in the NHS', in Ungerson, *Women and Social Policy*, pp. 158–9.

53 Sue Thomas, 'Abolish Classes – No Choice', *Women's Voice*, January 1975.

54 Anon., in *Fowaad*, February 1980.

55 Black Women's Action Committee of the Black Unity and Freedom Party, in *Black Woman*, August 1971; reprinted in Michelene Wandor (ed.), *The Body Politic: Writings from the Women's Liberation Movement in Britain*, Stage 1, 1978, p. 86.

56 ibid.

57 Emma Lewis, 'Abortion: A Black Woman's View', *Women Now*, October 1975.

58 ibid.

59 See, for example, 'Contraception', *Woman's Newspaper*, 1, 6 March 1971; Jane Kenrick, Peri Moltahedeh and Kate Young, 'Bucharest: What *Kind* of Victory?', paper at Women's Liberation Conference, c. 1974; and 'Women and Science Collective, 'The Politics of Contraception', paper at Women's Liberation Conference, 1977.

60 Bartle, Manchester speech published in *WACC Newsletter*, 2:2, April–May 1973.

61 Gordon, *Woman's Body, Woman's Right*, pp. 391–402.

62 This argument was put in the early 1970s by the Nottingham Women's Liberation Group in a leaflet, 'We Need an Abortion Campaign'.

63 See 'Women and Health', in *Health and Wealth: Belfast and the Six Counties* (Workers' Research Bulletin), Belfast, n.d; and Eileen Fairweather, Roisin McDonough and Melanie McFadyean, *Only the Rivers Run Free: Northern Ireland – The Women's War*, Pluto, London, 1984. For an account of the Irish campaign, see Mary Gordon, 'Fighting for Control', *Irish Feminist Review*, November 1984. More recent articles are Ursula Barry, 'Abortion in the Republic of Ireland', and Irish Women's Abortion Support Group, 'Across the Water', both in *Feminist Review*, 29, Spring 1988.

64 See Petrie and Livingstone, 'Out of the Back Streets'.

65 Segal, 'A Local Experience', in Rowbotham, Segal and Wainwright, *Beyond the*

314   *The Past is Before Us*

Fragments, p. 171. See also Dinny, 'Feeling Sick with Doctors', *York Feminist News*, 7 October 1978; reprinted in Feminist Anthology Collective, *No Turning Back*, p. 142.

66   Report in *Shrew*, Autumn 1976.

67   'Our Lives, Our Children, Our Choice', *West London National Abortion Campaign Newsletter*, Spring 1976.

68   Report in *Spare Rib*, 43, February 1976.

69   Doyal, 'Women and the Crisis in the NHS', in Ungerson, *Women and Social Policy*, pp. 155–6. See also OWAAD, *Black Women and Health*, in Feminist Anthology Collective, *No Turning Back*, p. 145.

70   Report in NAC News, March 1976.

71   ibid.

72   Doyal, 'Women and the Crisis in the NHS', in Ungerson, *Women and Social Policy*, p. 156.

73   Mitchell, 'Women: The Longest Revolution', in Altbach, *From Feminism to Liberation*, p. 105.

74   Petrie and Livingstone, 'Out of the Back Streets'. See also Sue Fawcus, 'Abortion and the Cuts', in Feminist Anthology Collective, *No Turning Back*, pp. 42–5.

75   Gordon, *Woman's Body, Woman's Right*, p. 418.

76   Sue O'Sullivan, 'Capping the Cervix', *Spare Rib*, 105, April 1981.

77   Sheila Rowbotham, 'Revolt in Roundhay', in Liz Heron (ed.), *Truth, Dare or Promise: Girls Growing Up in the Fifties*, Virago, London, 1985, p. 204.

78   ibid.

79   Gail Lewis, 'From Deepest Kilburn', in Heron, *Truth, Dare or Promise*, p. 219.

80   ibid.

81   ibid.

82   O'Sullivan, 'Capping the Cervix'.

83   Abdullah, International Women's Day speech; reported in *WACC Newsletter*, 2:2, April–May 1973.

84   Anon., 'True Life Romance' (Women's Liberation leaflet), n.d. (early 1970s).

85   Marion Dain and Fran McLean, 'An Egg is Not a Chicken', *Red Rag*, 10, Winter 1975–6.

86   Anon., 'A New Look at Contraception', *Ilford Shrew*, c. 1973.

87   Women and Science Collective, 'The Politics of Contraception'.

88   National Abortion Campaign paper at Socialist Feminist Conference, March 1979.

89   ibid.

90   ibid.

91   ibid

92   See Coote and Campbell, *Sweet Freedom*, pp. 224–5.

93   Jan O'Malley, 'My Child, My Choice', *NAC News*, 3 April 1976.

94   'Debbie', quoted in Fairweather, 'The Feelings behind the Slogans'; reprinted in Rowe, *Spare Rib Reader*, p. 342.

95   Brent Against Corrie Pamphlet Group, *Mixed Feelings*, January 1980, p. 30.

96   ibid.

97   See Fairweather, 'The Feelings behind the Slogans'; reprinted in Rowe, *Spare Rib Reader*, pp. 338–45.

98   Bristol International Socialism Group, 'Abortion and Contraception' (leaflet), early 1970s. Since this chapter was written the question of the relationship between mother and foetus has been more fully explored by Sue Himmelweit in 'More than "A Woman's Right to Choose"?', *Feminist Review*, 29, Spring 1988.

99 Anon., 'Questions and Answers on Abortion', *Red Weekly*, 19 June 1975.

100 'Why NAC Does Not Support ALRA's Bill', paper at Socialist Feminist Workshop, Women's Liberation Conference, April 1977.

101 See ibid.

102 Judy Watson and Rose Knight, 'Viability Views', *Socialist Woman*, 6:4, October 1978.

103 Lucy Arnold, 'Abortion: Unjustified Repression', *Spare Rib*, 43, February 1976.

104 ibid.

105 Fairweather, 'The Feelings behind the Slogans'; reprinted in Rowe, *Spare Rib Reader*, p. 343.

106 ibid.

107 Rosalind Pollack Petchesky, 'Reproductive Freedom: Beyond "A Woman's Right to Choose" ', in Catherine R. Stimpson and Ethel Spector Person (eds.), *Women – Sex and Sexuality*, University of Chicago Press, Chicago and London, 1980, p. 100.

108 Kathleen McDonnell, *Not an Easy Choice: A Feminist Re-examines Abortion*, Women's Press, Toronto, 1984; quoted in Angela Neustatter and Gina Newson, *Mixed Feelings: The Experience of Abortion*, Pluto, London, 1986, p. 12. For an interesting comparison with the French women's movement debates on abortion, see Claire Duchen, *Feminism in France: From May '68 to Mitterand*, Routledge & Kegan Paul, London, 1986, pp. 49–60.

Chapter 5

1 For a longer discussion of this, see Sheila Rowbotham, 'What Do Women Want?', *Feminist Review*, 20, Summer 1985.

2 Rosalind Pollack Petchesky, 'Reproductive Freedom: Beyond "A Woman's Right to Choose" ', in Catherine Stimpson and Ethel Spector Person (eds.), *Women – Sex and Sexuality*, University of Chicago Press, Chicago and London, 1980, p. 100. See also Rosalind Pollack Petchesky, *Abortion and Woman's Choice: The State, Sexuality and Reproductive Freedom*, Longman, New York and London, 1984; Verso, London, 1986.

3 See Juliet Mitchell, 'Women and Equality', in Juliet Mitchell and Ann Oakley, *The Rights and Wrongs of Women*, Penguin, Harmondsworth, 1976.

4 Petchesky, 'Reproductive Freedom', in Stimpson and Spector Person, *Women – Sex and Sexuality*, p. 101.

5 Carol Smart, 'Law and the Control of Women's Sexuality: The case of the 1950s', in Bridget Hutter and Gillian Williams, *Controlling Women*, Croom Helm, London, 1981, pp. 40–65.

6 Quoted in Jill Nicholls, 'Abortion: More than a Conventional Meeting', *Spare Rib*, 36, June 1975.

7 A Woman's Right to Choose Campaign, paper at Newcastle Women's Liberation Conference, 24–25 April 1976.

8 See Sheila Rowbotham, *Hidden from History*, Pluto Press, London, 1985, pp. 36–46.

9 Nina Woodcock, 'The fight against Corrie', *MsPrint* (Scottish feminist publication), 4, p. 12.

10 See Petchesky, 'Reproductive Freedom', in Stimpson and Spector Person, *Women – Sex and Sexuality*; Linda Gordon, *Woman's Body, Woman's Right*, Grossman, New York, 1976; Attina Grossman, 'Abortion and the Economic Crisis', *New German*

Critique (University of Wisconsin [Madison]), 14, Spring 1978; Sheila Rowbotham, *A New World for Women: Stella Browne, Socialist Feminist*, Pluto, London, 1977; Parveen Adams and Beverley Brown, 'The Politics of Control of Our Bodies', paper at Socialist Feminist Conference, London, March 1979; and Beverley Brown and Parveen Adams, 'The Feminine Body and Feminist Politics', *M/F*, 3, 1979.

11 Frederick Engels (ed. Eleanor Burke Leacock), *The Origin of the Family, Private Property and the State*, Lawrence & Wishart, London, 1973, p. 71.

12 See Adams and Brown, 'The Politics of Control of our Bodies'.

13 See, for example, Rayna Rapp Reiter, *Toward an Anthropology of Women*, Monthly Review Press, New York, 1975.

14 Petchesky, 'Reproductive Freedom', in Stimpson and Spector Person, *Women – Sex and Sexuality*, pp. 96–7.

15 See Sue Himmelweit, 'Abortion: Individual Choice and Social Control', *Feminist Review*, 5, 1980.

16 See Petchesky, 'Reproductive Freedom', in Stimpson and Spector Person, *Women – Sex and Sexuality*, pp. 115–16.

17 Susan Sherwin, 'A Feminist Approach to Ethics', *Dalhousie Review* (Dalhousie University, Halifax, Nova Scotia), 64:4, Winter 1984–5.

18 Eileen Fairweather, 'The Feelings behind the Slogans', *Spare Rib*, 87, October 1979; reprinted in Marsha Rowe (ed.), *Spare Rib Reader*, Penguin, Harmondsworth, 1982, p. 340.

19 Joyce Lister, 'Saturday Night was Abortion Night', *Spare Rib*, 90, January 1980.

20 Angela Neustatter and Gina Newson, *Mixed Feelings: The Experience of Abortion*, Pluto, London, 1986, p. 2.

21 Kathleen McDonnell, *Not an Easy Choice: A Feminist Re-examines Abortion*, Women's Press, Toronto, 1984; quoted in Neustatter and Newson, *Mixed Feelings*, p. 38.

Chapter 6

1 Michelene Wandor, in Stephanie Dowrick and Sibyl Grundberg (eds.), *Why Children?*, Women's Press, 1980, p. 133.

2 Nemone Lethbridge, 'Postscript to *Baby Blues*', *Spare Rib*, 21, March 1974.

3 Annette Muir, 'On Having Children', *Shrew*, January 1970.

4 Liz Heron, 'The Mystique of Motherhood', in Feminist Anthology Collective (eds.), *No Turning Back: Writings from the Women's Liberation Movement, 1975–80*, Women's Press, 1981, p. 139.

5 ibid.

6 Claire Duchen, *Feminism in France: From May '68 to Mitterrand*, Routledge & Kegan Paul, London, 1986, p. 60.

7 ibid.

8 Terry Slater, 'Why I Decided to Have a Baby', *Spare Rib*, 63, October 1977.

9 Duchen, *Feminism in France*, p. 61.

10 ibid.

11 ibid.

12 ibid.

13 Nell Myers, 'Sometimes a Sad Adventure', *Morning Star*, 28 June 1977.

14 For an analysis of these ideas, see Hester Eisenstein, *Contemporary Feminist Thought*, Unwin, London, 1984, pp. 69–95; and Lynne Segal, *Is the Future Female?*

Troubled Thoughts on Contemporary Feminism, Virago, London, 1987.

15 Heron, 'The Mystique of Motherhood', in Feminist Anthology Collective, *No Turning Back*, p. 139.

16 See ibid., p. 140.

17 Anon., 'Having a Child', *Shrew*, September 1970.

18 Eileen Fairweather, Roisin McDonough and Melanie McFadyean, *Only the Rivers Run Free: Northern Ireland – The Women's War*, Pluto, London, 1984, p. 161.

19 ibid., pp. 161–2.

20 Heron, 'The Mystique of Motherhood', in Feminist Anthology Collective, *No Turning Back*, p. 139.

21 ibid., p. 138.

22 ibid.

23 Tessa Weare, 'Was the Pill the Answer to Our Needs?', *Women's Voice*, 27 January 1980. For a discussion of the medical model of pregnancy, see Ann Oakley, *Women Confined: Towards a Sociology of Childbirth*, Martin Robertson, Oxford, 1980, pp. 34-42.

24 Mary Kelly, 'Sexual Politics', in Brandon Taylor (ed.), *Art and Politics* (proceedings of a 1977 conference on art and politics), Winchester School of Arts Press, 1980, p. 68.

25 Laura Mulvey's film *Riddles of the Sphinx* sought to give expression to women's specific problems and oppression. See 'Women and Representation: A Discussion with Laura Mulvey', *Wedge*, 2, Spring 1978.

26 Ann Oakley, *Subject Women*, Martin Robertson, Oxford, 1981, pp. 206–7.

27 See Ann Oakley, *Women Confined, pp. 34–42*.

28 Rosie Parker, review of Susan Hillier exhibition, *Spare Rib*, 92, March 1980.

29 Dana Breen, 'The Mother and the Hospital', in Susan Lipshitz (ed.), *Tearing the Veil*, Routledge & Kegan Paul, London, 1978, p. 18.

30 For a discussion of biology and sexual politics, see Janet Sayers, *Biological Politics: Feminist and Anti-Feminist Perspectives*, Tavistock Publications, London, 1982.

31 A fascinating, imaginative science-fiction exploration of this idea, published more than a decade before the feminist theory was developed, is Naomi Mitchison, *Memoirs of a Spacewoman*, Pan, London, 1962; Women's Press, London, 1986. The spacewoman in the story acts as a host for grafts of life-forms from other planets.

32 See, for example, M. Z. Rosaldo and L. Lamphere (eds.), *Woman, Culture, and Society*, Stanford University Press, Stanford, California, 1974.

33 Carol D. MacCormack, 'Nature, Culture and Gender: A Critique', in Carol MacCormack and Marilyn Strathern (eds.), *Nature, Culture and Gender*, Cambridge University Press, 1980, p. 10.

34 Gillian Gillison, 'Images of Nature in Gimi Thought', in ibid., p. 172. On the question of nature in relation to European thought and women's liberation, see Sheila Rowbotham, *Women, Resistance and Revolution*, Allen Lane, London, 1972, pp. 37-45.

35 Marilyn Strathern, 'No Nature, No Culture: The Haga Case', in MacCormack and Strathern, *Nature, Culture and Gender*, p. 219.

36 Anon., 'Dragons', *Shrew*, 5:2 (Radical Feminist issue), April 1973.

Chapter 7

1 Rochelle Wortis, paper at Oxford Women's Liberation Conference, 1970.

2 ibid.

3   ibid.

4   Anon., 'Charity Begins at Home', *Shrew*, 3:2, March 1971.

5   A *Dwarf* reader, 'Some More Advice', *Black Dwarf*, 10, January 1969.

6   See Chapters 10–13 on women's pay and employment for a longer discussion of these interconnections.

7   See Sue Sharpe, *Double Identity: The Lives of Working Mothers*, Penguin, Harmondsworth, 1984, pp. 87–93, 100–103, 106–8, 173–87 and 194-8.

8   Diane Ehrenshaft, 'Shared Parenting', *Politics and Power*, 3, 1981.

9   Linda Blandford, 'A Little Less Ecstasy, a Lot More Fun', *Guardian*, 4 February 1981.

10 ibid.

11 Ehrenshaft, 'Shared Parenting'.

12 Lynne Segal, 'Daily Life', *Revolutionary Socialism* (Big Flame journal), 4, 1979–80. See also Marsha Rowe, 'Changing Child Care', *Spare Rib*, 68, March 1978.

13 Marilyn Archer, 'Gay Wives and Mothers', *Spare Rib*, 31, January 1975.

14 Rowe, 'Changing Child Care'.

15 Barbara Charles, 'Lesbian Mums OK: Taking Over the News', *Spare Rib*, 67, 1978.

16 See Sally, interviewed by Helen Hewland, 'If You Think You've Got Problems', *Morning Star*, 12 February 1977.

17 Bernice Humphreys, 'Lesbians and Child Custody', paper at Socialist Feminist Conference, March 1979.

18 See Lynne Segal, *Is the Future Female? Troubled Thoughts on Contemporary Feminism* (Virago, London, 1987), for a fuller discussion of these issues in feminism. See also Hester Eisenstein, *Contemporary Feminist Thought*, Unwin, London, 1984 pp. 48–101.

19 Anon., 'Are Fathers Really Necessary?', *Shrew*, 5:2 (Radical Feminist issue), April 1973.

20 Amanda Sebestyen, 'Thinking about Men', *Spare Rib*, 94, May 1980.

21 ibid.

22 Katya Frishauer and Martha Osamor (United Black Women's Action Group), interviewed in *Socialist Woman*, 6:4, October 1978; reprinted in Feminist Anthology Collective (eds.), *No Turning Back: Writings from the Women's Liberation Movement, 1975–80*, Women's Press, London, 1981, pp. 46–55.

23 Beverley Bryan, Stella Dadzie and Suzanne Scafe, *The Heart of the Race*, Virago, London, 1985, pp. 220–21.

24 Anon., 'The Womanly Art of Breast Feeding', *Sheffield Women's Paper*, 2, May–June 1979.

25 ibid.

26 Zelda Curtis, 'The Baby Killer Scandal', *Scarlet Woman*, 12, Spring 1981.

27 Constance Whippman, 'Trains, Buses, Escalators and a Baby', *Spare Rib*, 30 December 1974.

28 See Jane Lazarre, *The Mother Knot*, McGraw-Hill, New York, 1976; Virago, London, 1987.

29 For a discussion of motherhood and utopia, see Sheila Rowbotham, 'Hopes, Dreams and Dirty Nappies', *Marxism Today*, December 1984.

30 Angela Phillips, 'The Generation Game', *Time Out*, 7–13 November 1980.

31 Gill Hague, 'Mothers and the Movement', *Spare Rib*, 66, January 1978.

32 Blandford, 'A Little Less Ecstasy, a Lot More Fun'.

33 ibid.

34 Ann Mitchell and Nell Myers, 'We are mothers', *Cat-Call*, 5, n.d.

35 Eve Fitzpatrick, 'To My Father', *Spare Rib*, 55, February 1977. The full-length version is reprinted in Sheila Rowbotham, *Dreams and Dilemmas*, Virago, London, 1983, pp. 159–160.

Chapter 8

1 Leeds members of the women's movement, Introduction to *Leeds Pregnancy Handbook*, Leeds Community Press, n.d., p. 1.

2 The Health Education Council's campaign to encourage early ante-natal care led *Spare Rib* to ask: what about diet, working environment and hours? (Newsshorts, *Spare Rib*, 92, March 1980.) At a meeting of the Liverpool Labour Party Women's Council Renée Short linked Britain's high infant-mortality rate to low incomes and bad housing and diets. She also pointed out that inadequate transport made visits to clinics difficult for rural women. (*Militant*, 14, November 1980.)

3 Joyce Lister, 'Underwomanned Wards', *Spare Rib*, 100, November 1980.

4 Anon., 'Ante-Natal Care in Sheffield', *Sheffield Women's Paper*, 2, May–June 1979.

5 ibid.

6 Gilly Westley, 'Childbirth the Way We Want It', *Women's Voice*, 3, February 1978.

7 Jo Robinson, *Health in Homerton: Report on the First Year* (pamphlet), Homerton Health Centre Project, London, September 1981, p. 11.

8 ibid., p. 12.

9 Jo Robinson, quoted in Anon., 'Caring Counts', *Jobs for a Change* (Greater London Council publication), 15.

10 Robinson, *Health in Homerton*, p. 14.

11 ibid.

12 Nell Myers, 'Sometimes a Sad Adventure', *Morning Star*, 28 June 1977.

13 See, for example, Anna Briggs interviewed by Barbara Charles, 'Reproductive Rights', *Spare Rib*, 71, June 1978; and Valerie Charlton and Annette Muir, 'Childbirth', *Spare Rib*, 36, June 1975.

14 See, for example, Marianne Scruggs, 'Castor Oil, Epidurals and Home Birth', *Spare Rib*, 38, August 1975; Sue O'Sullivan, 'Chinese Birth Control: Eating the Calendar', *Spare Rib*, 38, August 1975; and Kathleen Tynan, 'Epidurals', *Spare Rib*, 6, December 1972.

15 See, for example, Valerie Charlton and Annette Muir, 'Childbirth'; Danaë Brook, 'Natural Childbirth', *Spare Rib*, 25, July 1974; and Lynne Saunders, 'Save Our Hospitals', *Women's Voice*, 21, September 1978.

16 Myra Garrett interviewed by Sheila Rowbotham on Tower Hamlets Health Emergency Campaign (1986), in GLC Archives, History Workshop Centre, London.

17 Gilly Westley, 'Childbirth the Way We Want It'.

18 ibid.

19 *Does Anyone Out There Care? Women's Views on Tower Hamlets Maternity Services*, Tower Hamlets National Childbirth Trust Group and Health Campaign, London, 1986, p. 12.

20 Information from interview by Sheila Rowbotham with representative of the Maternity Services Liaison Scheme, Tower Hamlets (1986), in GLC Archives, History Workshop Centre, London. See also Sheila Rowbotham, 'Our Health in Whose Hands?', in Maureen Mackintosh and Hilary Wainwright (eds.), *A Taste of Power: The Politics of Local Economics*, Verso, London, 1987.

21 Women's Liberation Co-ordinating Committee, duplicated newsletter, Spring 1970.

22 An Authors' Collective, Introduction to extract from Vera Schmidt, *Psychoanalytic Education in the Soviet Union: Report of the Moscow Child Care Laboratory* (c. 1921), in An Authors' Collective (eds.), *Storefront Day Care Centres*, Beacon Books, Boston, Mass., 1973, p. 19.

23 Sue Cowley, 'The Tufnell Park Crèche', *Shrew*, Summer 1969.

24 Tufnell Park Women's Liberation Workshop Group, 'More than Minding', in Michelene Wandor (ed.), *The Body Politic: Writings from the Women's Liberation Movement in Britain*, Stage 1, London, 1978, p. 137.

25 Audrey Wise, 'Community Control', *Socialist Woman*, 2:5, November–December 1970.

26 ibid.

27 See Sue Cowley, 'Thatcher's Nurseries: Expansion or Containment', *Red Rag*, 4, July 1973. For a contrasting, employment-oriented, view of child care, see 'Child Care, Every Woman's Right', *Women's Report*, 1:4, May–June 1973.

28 Valerie Charlton, 'The Patter of Tiny Contradictions', *Red Rag*, 5; reprinted in Sandra Allen, Lee Sanders and Jan Wallis (eds.), *Conditions of Illusion*, Feminist Books, Leeds, 1974, p. 170.

29 Angela Rodaway, 'Two, Four, Six, Eight, Who Should We Accommodate?', *Enough* (publication of Bristol Women's Liberation Group), 3, 1971.

30 Charlton, 'The Patter of Tiny Contradictions'.

31 See Anon., 'Child Care, Every Woman's Right'.

32 Sue Freshwater, report from Edinburgh, *Scottish Women's Liberation Newsletter*, 3, 1973.

33 Women and Socialism: One-day Workshop on Day-care Provision for the Under-5s, North London Polytechnic, 6 July 1974; One-day Workshop on Day Care for the Under-5s, Notting Hill Ecumenical Centre, 9 November 1974.

34 See Myra Garrett, 'Girls and Boys Come Out to Play', *Red Rag*, 8, February 1975.

35 ibid.

36 See Esther Breitman, 'We are Watching', *MsPrint* (Scottish feminist publication), 4, 1979.

37 Quoted in 'Shortlist', *Spare Rib*, 48, July 1976.

38 Brenda Freeman, 'Child Care Put Down', letter in *Spare Rib*, 49, August 1976.

39 Spare Rib Collective reply, in ibid.

40 See Valerie Charlton *et al.*, *Children's Community Centre* (pamphlet), 1972; and Dartmouth Park Hill Group, *Children's Community Centre: Our Experience of Collective Child Care* (pamphlet), n.d.

41 'Powis Square Playgroups', report in *Nell Gate* (Notting Hill Gate community newspaper), 6, August–September 1973.

42 Cowley, 'Thatcher's Nurseries'.

43 See reports in *Women's Struggle Notes* (Big Flame women's publication), issues from mid-March to May 1975.

44 Islington Nursery Action Group, 'Why Nurseries Now?', Islington Working Women's Charter Group *Newsletter*, 1975.

45 See Sheila Rowbotham, 'Who's Holding the Baby', *Leveller*, 29, August 1979; reprinted in *Dreams and Dilemmas*, Virago, London, 1983, pp. 125–6.

46 Bradford Under-5s Group, *A Better Deal for Mothers and Pre-school Children* (leaflet), 1980.

47   For a discussion of the connections between child care and local government, see Sheila Rowbotham. 'Sharing the Caring', *New Statesman*, 21 September 1984. On the Greater London Council's policy, see 'Domestic Work and Childcare', in *The London Industrial Strategy*, GLC, London, 1985. The background to the adoption and development of this policy is described in an interview by Liz Heron with Hilary Wainwright, Sheila Rowbotham and Kath Falcon on domestic work and child care (1986), in GLC Archives, History Workshop Centre, London. See also Liz Heron, 'Women's Work', in Maureen Mackintosh and Hilary Wainwright, *A Taste of Power*. The GLC Economic Policy Unit's newspaper, *Jobs for a Change* (1983–6), covered the range of innovations in child-care provision stimulated by the link with local government; see, for example, the following articles: 'Earning a Living, Making a Life' (*JFAC*, 1); 'Who's Minding the Kids?' (*JFAC*, 3); 'Women Plan Transport' (*JFAC*, 7); 'New Ideas in Child Care' (*JFAC*, 9); 'Dads Should Mind Babies Too' (*JFAC*, 14); 'Care Not Cuts' (*JFAC*, 20). On child care for children with special needs, see Jennie Gudgeon, 'Children under Five with Special Needs', *London Childcare Network Newsletter*, 1, Summer 1985. The GLC tried to connect the resources of the local state to needs. The contrasting ideological approach of the central state under Thatcher is discussed in Marion Kozak, 'Family Centres – the Family Cementers?', *National Child Care Campaign Newsletter*, June–July 1986.

48   Parliamentary report, *National Child Care Campaign Newsletter*, December–January 1985.

49   Reported in *National Child Care Campaign Newsletter*, September 1982.

50   Anon., 'Playgroup Against Prejudice', *Spare Rib*, 53, December 1976.

51   Kum-Kum Bhavnani, 'Racist Acts', *Spare Rib*, 117, April 1982.

52   *A Flowering of Ideas* (report of London Childcare Network conference to celebrate new achievements in child care, March 1986), London Childcare Network, 1987.

53   Cowley, 'Thatcher's Nurseries'.

54   See, for example, Anon., 'A Playgroup Called Freedom', *Spare Rib*, 41, November 1975.

55   Anon., *Out of the Pumpkin Shell: Running a Women's Liberation Playgroup* (pamphlet), Women's Liberation Playgroup, Calthorpe Park, Birmingham, n.d. (*c.* 1976).

56   Anon., 'Playgroup Against Prejudice'.

57   See Market Nursery group, *Not So Much a Nursery* (pamphlet), London, n.d., p. 25.

58   I owe this point to Sue Finch, lecture on Market Nursery, Hackney Workers' Educational Association, January 1982.

59   For an international perspective, see Centre for Education, Research and Innovation, *Caring for Young Children: An Analysis of Educational and Social Services*, Organization for Economic Co-Operation and Development, Paris, 1982.

60   See the debate on state aid in *Pavement*, the Wandsworth alternative newspaper: Anon., 'Child Care not State Care', June 1981; Anon., 'Feminism Against State Nurseries: Child Hand-over', June 1981; and Judy Secker, 'Child Care Critic Answered', July 1981.

61   Suzy Beresford, 'Community Needs and Community Control' (workshop report, National Child Care Campaign Conference Papers, July 1980, p. 2.

62   Sue Himmelweit, 'Employment – the Community's Needs – Nurseries', unpublished MS notes for GLC Industry and Employment Committee Child Care Group, December 1982, p. 2; in GLC Archives, History Workshop Centre, London.

63   See, for example, Lynne Segal, 'No Turning Back – Thatcherism, the Family and the Future', in Lynne Segal (ed.), *What is to be Done about the Family?*, Penguin,

Harmondsworth, 1983, pp. 213–31; 'Domestic Work and Childcare', in *London Industrial Strategy*; and Rowbotham, 'Sharing the Caring'.

64 Julia Phillips, 'A very preliminary draft of the main points to be raised in a report to the GLC Industry and Employment Committee', unpublished MS, n.d. (*c.* 1983); in GLC Archives, History Workshop Centre, London.

65 Ken Livingstone, 'Leader's Report on Domestic Labour', 23 March 1982; in GLC Archive kept by London Residuary Body at the History Library, Clerkenwell, London. See also 'Domestic Work and Childcare', in *London Industrial Strategy*; and GLC Women's Committee, *Chance or Choice: Community Care and Women as Carers*, GLC, London, n.d. (*c.* 1985).

66 Sue Wallis, Report of Working Party on Employment Policy in Planning, Wandsworth Council, London 1979.

67 Anna Coote, 'The Sexual Division of Labour and Relations in the Family', paper at Conference on Alternative Strategies for the Labour Movement, October 1981; extracts in *Beyond the Fragments Bulletin*, 3, January 1982.

68 Gillian Pinkerton, 'Values in Child Care: Hidden and Explicit', in Socialist Child Care Collective (eds.), *Changing Child Care: Cuba, China, and the Challenging of Our Own Values*, Writers and Readers Publishing Cooperative, London, 1975, pp. 21–3.

69 'Domestic Work and Child Care', in *London Industrial Strategy*, p. 23.

70 Barnsley Women, *Women Against Pit Closures* (pamphlet), Barnsley, 1984, pp. 28–9.

Chapter 9

1 Anon., *Housing in Crisis: Women's Offensive* (pamphlet), n.d. (*c.* 1973). See also Anon., *We Won't Pay: Women's Struggle in Tower Hill* (pamphlet), Big Flame Women's Commission, 1975.

2 Anon., *Housing in Crisis*.

3 Cambridge Women's Liberation Group, 'Social Insecurity and Ann Baxter', in Michelene Wandor (ed.), *The Body Politic: Writings from the Women's Liberation Movement in Britain*, Stage 1, London, 1978, p. 243.

4 Anon., 'On the Spot', *Power of Women*, 1:1, March–April 1974.

5 Mary McIntosh, 'The State and the Oppression of Women', in Annette Kuhn and Ann Marie Wolpe (eds.), *Feminism and Materialism*, Routledge & Kegan Paul, London, 1978, p. 256.

6 ibid., pp. 256 and 257.

7 Pratibha Parmar, introduction to Ch. 8, 'A Revolutionary Anger', in Ann Curno *et al.* (eds.), *Women in Collective Action*, Association of Community Workers in the UK, London, 1982, pp. 92 and 93.

8 See Curno *et al.*, *Women in Collective Action*, pp. 96 and 100.

9 ibid., p. 100.

10 See Amina Mama, 'Black Women, the Economic Crisis and the British State', *Feminist Review*, 17, Autumn 1984, pp. 29 and 32.

11 McIntosh, 'The State and the Oppression of Women', in Kuhn and Wolpe, *Feminism and Materialism*, p. 256.

12 Eileen Fairweather, 'Don't You Know There's a War Going On?', *Spare Rib*, 78, January 1979.

13 Eileen Fairweather, Roisin McDonough and Melanie McFadyean, *Only the Rivers Run Free: Northern Ireland – The Women's War*, Pluto, London, 1984, p. 210.

14 ibid.

15 McIntosh, 'The State and the Oppression of Women', in Kuhn and Wolpe, *Feminism and Materialism*, p. 257.

16 Women's Liberation Campaign for Independence, *The Demand for Independence* (pamphlet), 2nd edn, Women's Liberation Campaign for Legal and Financial Independence, London, 1975, p. 1.

17 Denise Riley, 'Pronatalism and Working Women', *History Workshop Journal*, 11, Spring 1981.

18 Zoë Fairbairns, 'The Cohabitation Rule: Why It Makes Sense', *Spare Rib*, 104, March 1981.

19 Women's Liberation Campaign for Independence, *Demand for Independence*, pp. 6–7.

20 See ibid.; Katherine Gieve *et al.*, 'The Independence Demand', in Sandra Allen, Lee Sanders and Jan Wallis (eds.), *Conditions of Illusion: Papers from the Women's Movement*, Feminist Books, Leeds, 1974, pp. 269–77; and Angela Weir, 'The Family, Social Work and the Welfare State', in Allen *et al.*, *Conditions of Illusion*, pp. 217–28.

21 Gieve *et al.*, 'The Independence Demand', in Allen *et al.*, *Conditions of Illusion*, p. 270.

22 Women's Liberation Campaign for Independence, *Demand for Independence*.

23 See Lynne Segal, *Is the Future Female? Troubled Thoughts on Contemporary Feminism*, Virago, London, 1987, pp. 105–16.

24 For differing emphases on the state, see, for example, Angela Weir and Elizabeth Wilson, 'Why be a Wife?', *Link* (Communist Party women's journal), Spring 1978; Diana Leonard Barker, 'The Regulation of Marriage: Repressive Benevolence', in G. Littlejohn *et al.* (eds.), *Power and the State*, Croom Helm, London, 1978; Amrit Wilson, 'Why are You Marrying Her?', *Spare Rib*, 67, June 1976; and Beatrix Campbell and Valerie Charlton, 'Work to Rule', *Red Rag*, 14, 1978 (reprinted in Feminist Anthology Collective (eds.), *No Turning Back: Writings from the Women's Liberation Movement, 1975–80*, Women's Press, London, 1981).

25 See Sheila Rowbotham, 'The Trouble with "Patriarchy" ', in Raphael Samuel (ed.), *People's History and Socialist Theory*, Routledge & Kegan Paul, London, 1981, p. 365.

26 Penny Summerfield, *Women Workers in the Second World War*, Croom Helm, London, 1984.

27 Carol Smart, 'Law and the Control of Women's Sexuality: The Case of the 1950s', in Bridget Hutter and Gillian Williams (eds.), *Controlling Women: The Normal and the Deviant*, Croom Helm, London, 1981, pp. 42-58.

28 ibid., p. 42.

29 ibid.

30 See, for example, Denise Riley, 'War in the Nursery', *Feminist Review*, 2, 1979; Riley, 'Pronatalism and Working Women'; Hilary Land, 'The Family Wage', *Feminist Review*, 6, 1980; and Miriam David, 'Day Care Policies and Parenting', *Journal of Social Policy*, January 1982.

31 Riley, 'Pronatalism and Working Women'.

32 Linda Challis, 'The Great Under-Fives Muddle: Options for Day Care Policy', quoted in David, 'Day Care Policies and Parenting'.

33 See, for example, Suzie Fleming, Introductory Essay in Eleanor Rathbone, *The Disinherited Family*, Falling Wall Press, Bristol, 1986.

34 Smart, 'Law and the Control of Women's Sexuality', in Hutter and Williams, *Controlling Women*, p. 43.

35 Beatrix Campbell and Anna Coote, *Sweet Freedom*, Picador, 1982, pp. 106–7.

36 Hilary Wainwright, Introduction to Sheila Rowbotham, Lynne Segal and Hilary Wainwright, *Beyond the Fragments*, Merlin, London, 1979, pp. 16–17.

37 See, for example, Fleming, Introductory Essay in Rathbone, *Disinherited Family*.

38 Anon., 'Thoughts on the Family Allowance Campaign', *Red Rag*, 4, n.d.

39 Jean Coussins and Anna Coote, *The Family in the Firing Line: A Discussion Document on Family Policy*, Poverty Pamphlet 51, NCCL/CPAG, London, 1981, p. 37.

40 See, for example, Lesley Doyal, 'Women and the Welfare State', *Spare Rib*, 63, October 1977; Barbara Charles, 'Thatcher and the Tories', *Spare Rib*, 71, June 1978; Lucy Whitman, 'Policing the Family', *Spare Rib*, 77, December 1978; Anna Coote, 'Burying a Family Policy', *New Statesman*, 20 April 1979; Coussins and Coote, *Family in the Firing Line*; and Julia Mainwaring, 'Social Security Clamping Down', *Spare Rib*, 94, May 1980.

41 Anti-statism did not disappear entirely: see, for example, Anon., 'Feminism Against State Nurseries: Child Hand-over, *Pavement* (Wandsworth alternative newspaper), June 1981.

42 Audrey Wise, 'The Debate of the Decade', in Peter Hain (ed.), *The Crisis and Future of the Left*, Pluto, London, 1980, p. 75.

43 Claimants' Union, *Unsupported Mothers' Handbook*, London, n.d., p. 33.

44 London to Edinburgh Weekend Return Group, *In and Against the State*, Pluto, London, 1980, pp. 14–15.

45 Viv Dufill interviewed by Pam Corr, 'Parents Win', *Women's Voice*, 51, April 1981.

46 Anna Briggs, 'Social Security: Playing to Win', *Spare Rib*, 94, May 1980, p. 25.

47 See London to Edinburgh Weekend Return Group, *In and Against the State*, p. 16.

48 Nicola Murray, Cynthia Cockburn and Jeannette Mitchell, 'The State as We Know It', *Spare Rib*, 107, June 1981.

49 See Chapters 8 and 14.

50 See Eileen McLeod, 'Manmade Laws for Man? The Street Prostitutes' Campaign Against Control', in Hutter and Williams, *Controlling Women*, p. 70.

51 Helen Ewers, 'Care or Custody? The Experiences of Women Patients in Long-stay Geriatric Wards', in Hutter and Williams, *Controlling Women*, p. 124.

52 Kate, 'Elders', *Shrew*, Autumn 1976.

53 Anon., 'Eat the Earth by All Means but Don't Touch the Flowers', *Shrew*, Autumn 1976.

54 ibid.

55 Vanessa Stilwell, 'Women in White Collar Unions', *Case Con*, 15 (Women's Issue), Spring 1974.

56 Lesley Gilbert, 'Women Together: Edinburgh', *Spare Rib*, 27 September 1974.

57 Women's Health Information Collective leaflet, n.d. (mid-1970s).

58 Weir, 'The Family, Social Work and the Welfare State', in Allen *et al.*, *Conditions of Illusion*, p. 227.

59 See Gill Doust, Jill Hughes and Myra Garrett, 'Nursery Nurses: Changing Course', *Spare Rib*, 75, October 1978.

60 See Stilwell, 'Women in White Collar Unions'.

61 Reported in *Islington Gutter Press*, 32, October 1976.

62 London to Edinburgh Weekend Return Group, *In and Against the State*, p. 145.

63 See Sue Goss, 'Women's Initiatives in Local Government', in Martin Boddy and Colin Fudge (eds.), *Local Socialism*, Macmillan, London, 1984, p. 114.

64 ibid., p. 130.

65   Michèle Barrett, *Women's Oppression Today: Problems in Marxist Feminist Analysis*, Verso, London, 1980, p. 245.

66   See Sarah Perrigo, 'Socialist-Feminism and the Labour Party', *Feminist Review*, 23, Summer 1986; and Hilary Wainwright, *Labour: A Tale of Two Parties*, Hogarth Press, London, 1987, pp. 165–88. On black women in the Labour Party, see interview with Merle Amory, 'Labour's New Women', *Spare Rib*, 171, October 1986. On influencing political parties, see Barbara Rogers, *Fifty-two Per Cent: Getting Women's Power into Politics*, Women's Press, London, 1983.

67   Anna McGonigle, speaking at Irish labour history meeting, Autumn 1983; quoted in Sheila Rowbotham, 'What Do Women Want?', *Feminist Review*, 20, Summer 1985.

Chapter 10

1   Peggy Seeger, 'I'm Gonna Be an Engineer', 1972; reprinted in Kathy Henderson, Frankie Armstrong and Sandra Kerr (eds.), *My Song is My Own*, Pluto, London, 1979, pp. 159–62.

2   Miss J. O'Connell, quoted in Sheila Rowbotham, *Woman's Consciousness, Man's World*, Penguin, Harmondsworth, 1973, p. 96.

3   ibid.

4   Mrs M. Turner, quoted in Rowbotham, *Woman's Consciousness, Man's World*, p. 97.

5   ibid.

6   See Sheila Rowbotham, 'The Beginnings of Women's Liberation in Britain', in *Dreams and Dilemmas*, Virago, London, 1983, pp. 32–44.

7   Barbara Wilson, leaflet on National Joint Action Campaign for Women's Equal Rights, Surrey NJACWER, 1969.

8   Sue Pascoe, report of Conference of the Cities of London and Westminster Trades Council on Equal Pay for Women (16 March 1969), *Socialist Woman*, 1:3, May–June 1969.

9   Kath Fincham and Sabina Roberts, 'The Struggle for Democracy', *Socialist Woman*, 1:3, May–June 1969.

10   Audrey Wise, quoted in *Morning Star*, 11 January 1971.

11   ibid.

12   See Fincham and Roberts, 'Struggle for Democracy'.

13   Janet Hadley, 'Pusillanimous Promises', *Bird* (London Women's Liberation Workshop newsletter), 4, April 1969.

14   ibid.

15   Sarah Boston, 'Where Do I Stand?', *Spare Rib*, 23, May 1974, pp. 39–40. See also Pat Turner, 'Job Evaluation', *Women Speaking*, October–December 1973; and Oonagh Hartnett, 'Protection Legislation and Women's Rights', *Women Speaking*, October–December 1974.

16   See Anna Coote and Tess Gill, *Women's Rights: A Practical Guide*, Penguin, Harmondsworth, 1974.

17   Anna Coote, 'Putting Britain to Rights', *Guardian* 24 October 1974.

18   Anon., 'Laws Don't Bring Women Equality', *Women's Voice*, January 1975.

19   Anon., 'New Legislation: Is It Worth the Paper It's Written On?', *Islington Gutter Press*, 33, November 1976.

20   Anon., 'Equal Pay, No Delay', *Women's Struggle Notes* (Big Flame women's publication), 7, January–March 1975.

21 On equal pay, see Anon., 'Striking Progress, 1972–73', *Red Rag*, 5, n.d.; Marsha Rowe, 'Is Weinstock a Male Chauvinist Pig?', *Spare Rib*, 35, May 1975; Anon., 'Workplace Struggles', *Women's Struggle Notes*, 7, January–March, 1975; Beatrix Campbell and Sheila Rowbotham, 'Women Workers and Class Struggle', *Radical America*, 18:5, September–October 1974 (reprinted in Rowbotham, *Dreams and Dilemmas*, pp. 99–115); Patricia Hewitt (ed.), *Danger! Women at Work* (report of conference organized by National Council for Civil Liberties, 16 February 1974), NCCL, London, 1974; Mary Corbishley, *Trico: A Struggle for Equal Pay* (Women's Action pamphlet), London, n.d. (*c*. 1976); and Anon., 'Trico Women's Strike', *Shrew*, 1976.

22 See 'The Nightcleaners', special issue of *Shrew*, 13:9, December 1971; Michelene Wandor (ed.), *The Body Politic: Writings from the Women's Liberation Movement in Britain*, Stage 1, London, 1978. See also Sally Alexander, 'The Nightcleaners: An Assessment of the Campaign', *Red Rag*, 6 (reprinted in Sandra Allen, Lee Sanders and Jan Wallis, eds., *Conditions of Illusion*, Feminist Books, Leeds, 1974, pp. 309–25); and *The Nightcleaners' Campaign* (Socialist Woman pamphlet), London, 1971. On low pay, see for example Anon., 'Equal is as Equal Does', *Shrew*, 4:5, October 1972; Betty Lazarus interviewed by Alison Fell and Christine Peters, 'Strike: Whittington Hospital, April 1973', *Red Rag*, 4, July 1973; Anon., 'We are the Low Paid', *Women's Voice*, 21, September 1975; Sue James, 'The Shopworker is Never Right', *Women's Voice*, 11, n.d. (*c*. 1974); Anon., 'Outworkers Organize and Farmworkers Fight Downgrading', *Spare Rib*, 47, May 1976; Eileen Fairweather, interview with ancillary workers at a North London school, *Spare Rib*, 80, March 1979; Emma Maclennan, 'Contracting Poverty', in 'Back to the Sweat Shops? Fair Wages and Private Contractors', special issue of *Low Pay Review*, 11, November 1982; National Steering Group on Homeworking, *Report of the National Homeworking Conference, 1985*, Greater London Council, London, 1985; and Jane Paul, *Where There's Muck There's Money: A Report on Cleaning in London*, Greater London Council, London, 1986. On work, a bibliography of articles up to 1978 was published in *Spare Rib*, 69, April 1978.

23 Anon., 'Essex University Caterers Down Tools', *Colchester Women's Liberation Journal*, n.d. (*c*. 1974).

24 Anon., 'Workplace Struggles', *Women's Struggle Notes*, 7, January–March 1975.

25 Manchester Women's Liberation Group, 'Comments on the Government's Green Paper on Equal Opportunities', paper at Women's Liberation Conference, 1975.

26 ibid.

27 ibid.

28 On the Working Women's Charter, see for example Anon., 'Working Women's Charter: Not Just a Paper Document', *Spare Rib*, 41, November 1975.

29 Report of Hackney Trades Council Conference on Women (23 November 1974), London, 1974.

30 See Patricia Hewitt (ed.), *Danger! Women at Work*.

31 See Chapters 4 and 5.

32 Michèle Ryan, 'Equality: Just Fill in the Form', *Leveller*, pilot issue, 1976.

33 Mandy Snell, 'Equal Pay and Sex Discrimination', in Feminist Review (ed.), *Waged Work: A Reader*, Virago, London, 1986, p. 34.

34 ibid., p. 12.

35 *Equal Pay is Not Enough*, Women's Liberation Group leaflet, London, n.d. (*c*. 1970).

36 See Ruth Milkman, 'Female Factory Labour and Industrial Structure: Control and Conflict over "Women's Place" in Auto and Electrical Manufacturing, *Politics and*

Society, 12:2, 1983; and Veronica Beechey, 'Women's Employment in Contemporary Britain', in Veronica Beechey and Elizabeth Whitelegg, *Women in Britain Today*, Open University Press, Milton Keynes, 1986, pp. 108–23.

37 Ruth Milkman, *Gender at Work*, University of Illinois Press, Champaign, Illinois, 1987, p. 6.

38 Janet Hadley, 'Pusillanimous Promises'.

39 Audrey Wise, 'Equal Pay is Not Enough', *Black Dwarf*, 10 January 1969.

40 ibid.

41 ibid.

42 See Chapter 6.

43 See Sheila Rowbotham, *Woman's Consciousness, Man's World*, Penguin, Harmondsworth, 1973, pp. 96–7.

44 Kathleen Ennis, 'The Price of Being Female', *Women's Voice*, 3, November–December 1972.

45 Audrey Wise, *Women and Workers' Control* (pamphlet), Spokesman, Nottingham, n.d. (early 1970s), p. 6.

46 Audrey Wise, 'Equal Pay is Not Enough'.

47 Manchester Women's Liberation Group, 'Comments on the Government Green Paper on Equal Opportunities'. See also Anon., 'Twentieth Century Secretary', *Black Dwarf*, 5 September 1970; Anon., 'The Secretary', *Shrew*, 4:5, October 1972; Anny Brackx, 'The Cinderella Industry', *Spare Rib*, 67, February 1978; Anon., 'State Mums: the Work Nobody Wants', *Spare Rib*, 65, December 1977; Anon., 'Childminding', *Spare Rib*, 28, October 1974; Sue Zimmerman, 'High Rise Employment', *Spare Rib*, no number, April 1973; Anon., 'Prostitution', *Spare Rib*, 47, June 1976.

48 Letter to *Spare Rib*, 35, May 1975.

49 Milkman, 'Female Factory Labour and Industrial Structure'.

50 Selma James, *Women, the Unions and Work: What is Not to be Done*, Notting Hill Women's Liberation Group, London, 1972; reprinted by Falling Wall Press, Bristol, 1976. See also Chapter 13.

51 Beatrix Campbell and Valerie Charlton, 'Work to Rule', *Red Rag*, 14, 1978; reprinted in Feminist Anthology Collective (eds.), *No Turning Back: Writings from the Women's Liberation Movement, 1975–80*, Women's Press, London, 1981, p. 111. For a good historical account of the differing meanings of the family wage in the US context, see Martha May, 'Bread before Roses', in Ruth Milkman (ed.), *Woman's Work and Protest*, Routledge & Kegan Paul, London, 1985, pp. 1–21.

52 Heidi Hartman, 'Capitalism, Patriarchy and Job Segregation by Sex', in Zillah Eisenstein (ed.), *Capitalist Patriarchy and the Case for Socialist Feminism*, Monthly Review Press, New York and London, 1979, pp. 206–47.

53 Milkman, 'Female Factory Labour and Industrial Structure'. For an account of exclusionary practices, see Cynthia Cockburn, *Brothers: Male Dominance and Technological Change*, Pluto, London, 1983.

54 See Chapter 13.

55 Irene Bruegel, 'Notes on Sexual Divisions and Labour Market Processes', unpublished paper for the Sex and Class Group of the Conference of Socialist Economists, January 1980.

56 ibid.

57 Charlene Gannagé, *Double Day, Double Bind*, Women's Press, Toronto, 1986, p. 16.

58 North Tyneside Community Development Programme, Final Report, vol. 5, *North Shields: Women's Work*, Newcastle-upon-Tyne Polytechnic, 1978. The attempt

328   *The Past is Before Us*

to understand the contemporary subordination of women by studying early societies is discussed in Sheila Rowbotham, 'When Adam Delved and Eve Span...', *New Society*, 4 January 1979; reprinted in *Dreams and Dilemmas*, pp. 199–207.

59 Milkman, 'Female Factory Labour and Industrial Structure'. See also Milkman, *Gender and Work*, pp. 7–11.

60 Beechey, 'Women's Employment in Contemporary Britain', in Beechey and Whitelegg, *Women in Britain Today*, p. 127. See also, for example, OWAAD [Organization of Women of African and Asian Descent], 'Black Women and Employment', in *Black Women in Britain Speak Out* (March 1979 OWAAD conference papers), pp. 16–17; 'Many Voices, One Chant: Black Feminist Perspectives', special issue of *Feminist Review*, 17, Autumn 1984; A. Phizaklea, *One Way Ticket: Migration and Female Labour in London*, Routledge & Kegan Paul, London, 1983; Clara Moreno, Carmen Pedrosa, Jenny Stiles and Anne Lamming, 'Resident Domestics' Campaign', in Ann Curno *et al.* (eds.), *Women in Collective Action*, Association of Community Workers in the UK, London, 1982, pp. 81–8. Rae Dowds, 'Conference of Irish Women in London, 1984', *Irish Feminist Review*, 1984. For further discussion of race and the economy, see Hermione Harris, 'The Location of Black Women in the Labour Force', paper at Working Convention on Racism in the Political Economy of Britain, Institute of Race Relations, 13–16 December 1971; Anon., 'Black Women and Work', *Shrew*, 4:5, October 1972; and Amina Mama, 'Black Women, the Economic Crisis and the British State', *Feminist Review*, 17, July 1984.

61 See Judy Wajcman, 'Working Women', *Capital and Class*, 18, Winter 1982; and Veronica Beechey, 'Studies of Women's Employment', in Feminist Review (ed.), *Waged Work: A Reader*, pp. 130–59.

62 Wajcman, 'Working Women'.

63 Beechey, 'Studies of Women's Employment', in Feminist Review (ed.), *Waged Work: A Reader*, p. 153.

64 Audrey Wise, 'Trying to Stay Human', talk at Women's Liberation Workshop meeting, 1972; published in *Red Rag*, 3, n.d.; reprinted in Allen *et al.*, *Conditions of Illusion*, pp. 278–88.

65 Anne Showstack-Sassoon, 'Dual Role: Women and Britain's Crisis', *Marxism Today*, December 1982.

66 ibid. See also Hilary Wainwright, *Labour: A Tale of Two Parties*, Hogarth Press, London, 1987, pp. 165–88.

67 Swasti Mitter in National Steering Group on Homeworking, Report of the 1985 National Homeworking Conference, Greater London Council, 1985. See also Swasti Mitter, *Common Fate, Common Bond*, Pluto, London, 1986; Diane Elson and Ruth Pearson, 'Third World Manufacturing' in Feminist Review (ed.), *Waged Work: A Reader*, pp. 67–92; and 'Looking at Appropriate Technology', special issue of *Women's World* (journal of Isis–Women's International Cross-Cultural Exchange, Geneva), 10, June 1986.

68 Sally Alexander, Introduction to Marianne Herzog, *From Hand to Mouth: Women and Piecework*, Penguin, Harmondsworth, 1980, p 25. (Originally published in Germany as *Von der Hand in den Mund*, Rotbuch Verlag, 1976.)

69 Jean Gardiner, 'Women and Unemployment', *Red Rag*, 10, Winter 1975–6, p. 15.

70 Cynthia Cockburn, 'The Material of Male Power', in Feminist Review (ed.), *Waged Work: A Reader*, p. 94.

71 ibid.

72 ibid.

73 See Cockburn, 'The Material of Male Power', in Feminist Review (ed.), *Waged*

Work: A Reader, pp. 95–6.

74 Alexander, Introduction to Herzog, *From Hand to Mouth*, p. 22. See also Veronica Beechey, *Unequal Work: Questions for Feminism*, Verso, London, 1987. Published after this chapter was written, it provides an overview of feminist approaches to women's inequality at work.

Chapter 11

1 Veronica Beechey, 'Women's Employment in Contemporary Britain', in Veronica Beechey and Elizabeth Whitelegg, *Women in Britain Today*, Open University Press, Milton Keynes, 1986, pp. 104–7.

2 See Sheila Rowbotham, 'Women's Liberation and the New Politics', in *Dreams and Dilemmas*, Virago, London, 1983, pp. 17–20.

3 Leonora Lloyd, *Women Workers in Britain* (Socialist Woman pamphlet), London, n.d. (*c.* 1972), pp. 1–2.

4 ibid., pp. 33–4.

5 Anna Paczuska, 'The Right to Work and Equal Pay', paper at Skegness Women's Liberation Conference, October 1971.

6 Anny Brackx, 'Work: A Right to Fight For?', *Spare Rib*, 52, November 1972.

7 ibid.

8 ibid.

9 Anon., 'A Story of Love and Tenderness', paper at Oxford Women's Liberation Conference, 1970.

10 ibid.

11 Claimants' Union, 'Work, Women and Unemployment', paper at Claimants' Union Conference on Unemployment, n.d. (early 1970s). See also 'Women Claimants Unite' (report from the Women's Claimants' Conference), *Libertarian Women's Network Newssheet* (Notting Hill Women's Action Group publication), 15, n.d. (early 1970s); and Liverpool Women's Action Group, 'Guaranteed Independent Income for *All* Women', paper at Socialist Feminist Conference, 1978.

12 Selma James, *Women, the Unions and Work: What is Not to be Done*, Notting Hill Women's Liberation Group, London, 1972, p. 15; reprinted by Falling Wall Press, Bristol, 1976.

13 ibid.

14 Women's Liberation Mouvement, France, *Women and Waged Labour* (*Les Femmes et le salariat*) (pamphlet), n.d. (early 1970s).

15 Marina Lewycka, 'Poverty Old and New' (review of Jeremy Seabrook, *Unemployment: A Question of Power*, Quartet, 1982), *Beyond the Fragments Bulletin*, 4, Winter 1982–3. See also Anne Phillips, *Divided Loyalties: Dilemmas of Sex and Class*, Virago, London, 1987, pp. 113–17.

16 Quoted in Zoë Fairbairns, 'About Time' (review article), *Spare Rib*, 58, May 1977.

17 Frances Cairncross, *Guardian*, 28 March 1981.

18 Sandra Peers, Report on a TUC Weekend School for Equal Pay, *IS Women's Newsletter*, 4, 1971.

19 Mal Varley, letter to *Women's Voice*, 7, July 1977.

20 Audrey Wise, 'Trying to Stay Human', talk at Women's Liberation Workshop meeting, 1972; published in *Red Rag*, 3, n.d.; reprinted in Sandra Allen, Lee Sanders and Jan Wallis (eds.), *Conditions of Illusion*, Feminist Books, Leeds, 1974; pp. 278–88.

21 See, for example, Eveline Hunter, 'On Protective Legislation', *MsPrint* (Scottish feminist publication), 4, n.d. (mid-1970s).

22   ibid.

23   See Val Clarke, 'When Did You Last See Your Wife?', *Socialist Worker*, 10 October 1970; Oonagh Hartnett, 'Protective Legislation and Women's Rights', *Women Speaking*, October–December 1974; 'Mining Communities: The Experience' (interview by Margaret Edney and Ann Scott with women from Betteshanger), *Spare Rib*, 22, April 1974; and interview by Marina Lewycka with the wife of a train driver, in *Flexible Rostering*, a newssheet of the Work Hazard Group, British Society for Social Responsibility in Science, n.d.

24   Notting Hill Women's Liberation Group, *Chesebrough Ponds* (pamphlet), London, n.d. (early 1970s), pp. 3–5.

25   See, for example, Jill Nicholls and Angela Phillips, 'Nursing in Factories', *Spare Rib*, 45, April 1976.

26   Sheila Brown, 'Go to Work on an Ovary', *Red Rag*, 1978.

27   Women and Work Hazards Group, 'Danger: Women's Work', *Spare Rib*, 78, January 1979; reprinted in Marsha Rowe (ed.), *Spare Rib Reader*, Penguin, Harmondsworth, 1987, pp. 188–91.

28   See Sue Sharpe, 'Cleaning Up Asbestos', *Spare Rib*, 54, January 1977.

29   Women and Work Hazards Group, 'Danger: Women's Work', in Rowe (ed.), *Spare Rib Reader*, pp. 188–91.

30   Beverley Bryan, Stella Dadzie and Suzanne Scafe, *The Heart of the Race*, Virago, London, 1985, p. 92.

31   ibid.

32   See Cynthia Cockburn, *Machinery of Dominance: Women, Men and Technical Know-how*, Pluto, London, 1985, pp. 28–9.

33   Anon., 'Working in Islington', *Islington Gutter Press*, 30, July 1976.

34   ibid.

35   See, for example, Vebeka, a Norwegian building worker, interviewed in *Shrew*, Autumn 1976.

36   See Anne Phillips and Barbara Taylor, 'Sex and Skill', in Feminist Review (ed.), *Waged Work: A Reader*, Virago, London, 1986; Sarah Benton, *Patterns of Discrimination*, Association of Cinematograph and Television Technicians Committee of Equality, London, 1975; Cynthia Cockburn, *Brothers: Male Dominance and Technological Change*, Pluto, London, 1983.

37   Cockburn, *Machinery of Dominance*, p. 168.

38   Jackey Morgan, 'A Farming Career', *Cat-Call*, 11, June 1980.

39   Benton, *Patterns of Discrimination*, p. 11.

40   Vebeka, interview in *Shrew*, Autumn 1976.

41   See Veronica Beechey, 'Studies of Women's Employment', in Feminist Review (ed.), *Waged Work: A Reader*, p. 142.

42   See, for example, Amrit Wilson, *Finding a Voice: Asian Women in Britain*, Virago, London, 1978, pp. 56–71; Anon., 'Lower Depths: A Life as a Ward Maid, Gray's Inn Road Variety', *Germ's Eye View*, n.d. (early 1970s); and Karim Sandu, 'Airport 79: A Free Ticket to a Dirty Job', *Women's Voice*, 3, July 1979.

43   Jenny Beale, *Getting It Together: Women as Trade Unionists*, Pluto, London, 1982, p. 15.

44   Clare Cherrington, 'Are You a Typewriter?', *Spare Rib*, 69, April 1978. See also, for example, J. Barker and H. Downing, 'Word Processing and the Transformation of the Patriarchal Relation of Control in the Office', *Capital and Class*, 10, 1980; and Marion Fudger, interview with Bridget St John, 'Women in Music' series, *Spare Rib*, 28, October 1976.

45 Joyce Betries, 'Waitress du Jour', *Spare Rib*, June 1973.
46 Sarah Benton, *Patterns of Discrimination*, p. 31.
47 Betries, 'Waitress du Jour'.
48 Anon., 'Lewis Fisherwoman', *Spare Rib*, 77, December 1978.
49 Amrit Wilson, 'Nursing and Racism', *Spare Rib*, 70, May 1978.
50 ibid.
51 Jenny Golden, 'Conditions of Service', *Jobs for a Change* (Greater London Council publication), 15, 1985.
52 Marisa Casares-Roach, 'Knowledge Brings Confidence', *Women's Voice*, 51, April 1981.
53 Helen, a bus conductor, quoted in Anon., 'Off the Boat', *Spare Rib*, 94, May 1980.
54 Angela Stewart-Park and Jules Cassidy (eds.), *We're Here: Conversations with Lesbian Women*, Quartet, London, 1977, pp. 21–6. See also Sarah Benton, 'Gay Workers Acknowledge Debts to Women's Movement', *Spare Rib*, 37, July 1975.
55 Anny Brackx, 'But Not in the Office', *Spare Rib*, 54, January 1977.
56 ibid.
57 ibid.
58 Greater London Council Industry and Employment Branch, *Danger: Heterosexism at Work* (pamphlet), GLC, 1986, p. 37.
59 ibid.
60 Bryan *et al.*, *The Heart of the Race*, p. 94.
61 Florence Keyworth, 'Invisible Struggles: The Politics of Ageing', in Rosalind Brunt and Caroline Rowan (eds.), *Feminism, Culture and Politics*, Lawrence & Wishart, London, 1982, p. 134.
62 ibid.
63 See Cynthia Cockburn, 'The Material of Male Power', in Feminist Review (ed.), *Waged Work: A Reader*, p. 95.
64 Anon., 'Conditions in a Northern Factory as Described to Me by My Mother', *Shrew*, 3:5, June 1971.
65 Bryan, *et al.*, *The Heart of the Race*, p. 40.
66 Hilary Stafford, letter to *Spare Rib*, 41, June 1976.
67 See, for example, Audrey Wise, *Women and Workers' Control* (pamphlet), Spokesman, Nottingham, n.d. (early 1970s), pp. 6–7.
68 Jackey Morgan, 'A Farming Career'.
69 Muriel Dimen, *Surviving Sexual Contradictions*, Collier Macmillan, London, 1986, p. 178.
70 Ros Carne, 'On the Bench', *Spare Rib*, 29, November 1974.
71 ibid.
72 Marianne Herzog, *From Hand to Mouth*, Penguin, Harmondsworth, 1980, p. 53. (Originally published in Germany as *Von der Hand in den Mund*, Rotbuch Verlag, 1976.)
73 Judy Wajcman, 'Working Women', *Capital and Class*, 18, Winter 1982.

Chapter 12

1 Val, in Eden Grove Women's Literacy Group (eds.), *Our Lives: Working Women*, Islington Adult Education Institute, London, 1984, pp. 62–3.
2 Pauline, in ibid., p. 80.
3 Sue Shapiro and Tessa van Gelderen, 'Fakenham: Danger, Women at Work', *Socialist Woman*, Summer 1972.
4 ibid.

5 Unpublished account of meeting of Hilary Wainwright and Sheila Rowbotham with Lee Jeans women, 1983.

6 Janet Payne, 'Building without Man' (interview with all-women building group), *Undercurrents*, 46, June–July 1981.

7 Marianne Herzog, *From Hand to Mouth*, Penguin, Harmondsworth, 1980, p. 140. (Originally published in Germany as *Von der Hand in den Mund*, Rotbuch Verlag, 1976.)

8 ibid.

9 ibid.

10 ibid.

11 ibid., p. 139.

12 See Adrienne Boyle, 'Job Sharing', *Spare Rib*, 71, June 1978; Adrienne Boyle, 'Job Sharing: A New Pattern of Employment', in Ann Curno *et al.* (eds.), *Women in Collective Action*, Association of Community Workers in the UK, London, 1982; and Veronica Beechey, 'The Shape of the Workforce to Come', *Marxism Today*, August 1985.

13 Helen Hewland, 'Less Work, Same Pay', *Spare Rib*, 91, February 1980.

14 Interview by Liz Heron with Margery Bane (1985), in GLC Archives, History Workshop Centre, London. See also Sheila Rowbotham, 'Our Health in Whose Hands?', in Maureen Mackintosh and Hilary Wainwright (eds.), *A Taste of Power: The Politics of Local Economics*, Verso, London, 1987.

15 Claire Fazan *et al.*, 'Why Should *We* Raise the Money? Women Talk about Why They Marched', *Spare Rib*, 54, January 1978.

16 ibid.

17 Jane Clarke, 'Gwenda's Garage', *Spare Rib*, 161, December 1985.

18 ibid.

19 Jean Sargeant, 'Welcome to Wapping', *Spare Rib*, 165, April 1986. On the social relations embodied in technology, see J. Barker and H. Downing, 'Word Processing and the Transformation of the Patriarchal Relations of Control in the Office', *Capital and Class*, 10, 1980.

20 Billie Hunter (of Association of Radical Midwives), paper at Socialist Feminist Conference, March 1979.

21 ibid.

22 Trisha Ziff, 'Hairdressing' (interview with Kitty Zalsberg), *Spare Rib*, 94, May 1980.

23 Mary McCann, 'A Singularity', *Spare Rib*, 93, April 1980.

24 ibid.

25 ibid.

26 ibid.

27 ibid.

28 Anon., 'It's about the Pattern of Repression', *Bloody Women* (publication of Cambridge Women's Liberation Group), n.d. (early 1970s).

29 Janet Sass, 'Workers Control: Short Cut Profit Crisis', *Spare Rib*, 18, December 1973.

30 Audrey Wise, *Women and Workers' Control* (pamphlet), Spokesman, Nottingham, n.d. (early 1970s).

31 Beverley Bryan, Stella Dadzie and Suzanne Scafe, *The Heart of the Race*, Virago, London, 1985, p. 56.

32 Interview by Angela Phillips with Anne Day, *Spare Rib*, 29, n.d.

33 See Kate Purcell, 'Militancy and Acquiescence among Women Workers', in Sandra Burman (ed.), *Fit Work for Women*, Croom Helm, London, 1979.

34 Jill Tweedie, 'Money Will Not Buy What Women Want', *Guardian*, 29 January 1981.

35 See Judy Wajcman, *Women in Control: Dilemmas of a Workers' Co-operative*, Open University Press, Milton Keynes, 1983, pp. 156–82.

36 See Clare Cherrington, 'Are You a Typewriter?', *Spare Rib*, 69, April 1978.

37 Anon., 'Down on Strippers', *Spare Rib*, 46, May 1976.

38 Joy Mallert, letter to *Spare Rib*, 78, January 1979.

39 Janet Feindel, letter to *Spare Rib*, 76, November 1978.

40 Susan Read, letter to *Spare Rib*, 78, January 1979.

41 Clare Cherrington, 'What Went On at the Frog and Nightgown?', *Spare Rib*, 51, October 1976.

42 Ruth Wallsgrove, 'Prostitutes Organize', *Spare Rib*, 69, April 1978.

43 ibid.

44 Tricia Dearden, 'Prostitution', *Leveller*, 31, April 1980.

45 Helen Buckingham, 'Sexual Self-Determination', paper at Women's Liberation Conference, late 1970s.

46 Mary Gibson and Eveline Garston, 'Prostitution: A Particular Kind of Job', *Women's Voice*, 25, January 1979.

47 Dearden, 'Prostitution'.

48 Feminism and Non-Violence Study Group, 'Women Against War', *Spare Rib*, 94, May 1980.

49 Hilary Wainwright, 'The Women Who Wire Up the Weapons', in Dorothy Thompson (ed.), *Over Our Dead Bodies*, Virago, London, 1983, p. 144.

50 See Lynne Segal, 'A Question of Choice', *Marxism Today*, January 1981.

51 See Beechey, 'The Shape of the Workforce to Come'.

52 Clarke, 'Gwenda's Garage'.

53 See Jessica Benjamin, 'Authority and the Family Revisited or a World without Fathers?', *New German Critique* (University of Wisconsin [Madison]), 13, Winter 1978.

54 Cynthia Cockburn, *Brothers: Male Dominance and Technological Change*, Pluto, London, 1983.

55 See, for example, Anon., 'Women Artists Take Action', *Spare Rib*, 13, July 1973; Anon., 'Women's Workshop, Artists' Union', *Spare Rib*, 29, November 1974; interview by Marion Fudger with Anne Nightingale, 'Women in Music' series, *Spare Rib*, 18, December 1973; and Mary Kelly, 'Sexual Politics', in Brandon Taylor (ed.), *Art and Politics* (proceedings of a 1977 conference on art and politics), Winchester School of Art Press, 1980.

56 Ursula Huws, 'Challenging Commoditization: Producing Usefulness outside the Factory', in Collective Design Projects (eds.), *Very Nice Work If You Can Get It*, Spokesman, Nottingham, 1985, p. 166.

57 Irene Dankelman and Joan Davidson, *Women and Environment in the Third World*, Earthscan, London, 1988, pp. 172–3.

58 On the Greater London Council, see *Jobs for a Change* (GLC publication), 1–20; *The London Industrial Strategy*, GLC, London, 1985; and Mackintosh and Wainwright, *A Taste of Power*.

59 North Yorkshire Women Against Pit Closures, *Strike, 84–85* (pamphlet), Leeds, 1985.

60 Cynthia Cockburn, *Machinery of Dominance: Women, Men and Technical Know-how*, Pluto, London, 1985, p. 257.

Chapter 13

1   Judy Wajcman, 'Working Women', _Capital and Class_, 18, Winter 1982.

2   Joanna de Groot, 'Women and Unions', _Beyond the Fragments Bulletin_, 4, Winter 1982-3.

3   Arsenal Women's Liberation Group, 'Notes on Class and the Women's Movement', paper at second Socialist Women's Conference, September 1973.

4   ibid.

5   Sandy Kondos and Lucy Draper, 'Feminism and Work', paper at Socialist Feminist Conference, March 1979.

6   ibid.

7   Liz Heron, Introduction to Liz Heron (ed.), _Truth, Dare or Promise: Girls Growing Up in the Fifties_, Virago, London, 1985, p. 7.

8   ibid.

9   Valerie Walkerdine, 'Dreams from an Ordinary Childhood', in Heron, _Truth, Dare or Promise_, p. 74.

10   ibid., p. 75.

11   Barbara, Carole and Sue, paper for workshop on working-class jobs, Women's Liberation Conference, mid-1970s.

12   For further discussion, see Anne Phillips, _Divided Loyalties: Dilemmas of Sex and Class_, Virago, London, 1987, pp. 29–79 and 102–48.

13   Beatrix Campbell, 'United We Fall', _Red Rag_, Summer 1980.

14   Amina Mama, 'Black Women and the Economic Crisis', in Feminist Review (ed.), _Waged Work: A Reader_, Virago, London, 1986, pp. 186–7.

15   ibid.

16   Campbell, 'United We Fall'.

17   ibid.

18   ibid.

19   Selma James, _Women, the Unions and Work: What is Not to be Done_, Notting Hill Women's Liberation Group, London, 1972, p. 3; reprinted by Falling Wall Press, Bristol, 1976.

20   ibid.

21   See Angela Weir and Mary McIntosh, 'Towards a Wages Strategy for Women', _Feminist Review_, Spring 1982.

22   ibid.

23   Anna Coote and Beatrix Campbell, _Sweet Freedom: The Struggle for Women's Liberation_, Picador, London, 1982, pp. 144–9.

24   Jill Brown, Pamela Trevithick and Carol Metters, 'The Forward Face of Feminism', _Marxism Today_, January 1981.

25   ibid.

26   Quoted in Claire Fazan _et al._, 'Why Should _We_ Raise the Money? Women Talk about Why They Marched', _Spare Rib_, 54, January 1977.

27   ibid.

28   Beatrix Campbell, 'Equal Pay: The Results of an Action', _Link_ (Communist Party women's journal), 4, Winter 1973. See also 'Equal Pay Victory at Havant, Portsmouth', _Spare Rib_, 2, September–October 1972.

29   Marsha Rowe, 'Is Weinstock a Male Chauvinist?', _Spare Rib_, 35, May 1975.

30   See Beatrix Campbell and Sheila Rowbotham, 'Women Workers and Class Struggle', in Sheila Rowbotham, _Dreams and Dilemmas_, Virago, London, 1983, p. 105.

31   Ann Scott, 'Equal Pay and the Crisis', _Spare Rib_, 44, March 1976. See also

Women's Struggle Notes (Big Flame women's publication), 7, January–March 1975.

32 See Campbell and Rowbotham, 'Women Workers and Class Struggle', in Rowbotham, *Dreams and Dilemmas*, p. 107.

33 See Amrit Wilson, *Finding a Voice: Asian Women in Britain*, Virago, London, 1978, pp. 56–8.

34 ibid., p. 56.

35 ibid., p. 58.

36 Jenny Beale, *Getting It Together: Women as Trade Unionists*, Pluto, London 1982.

37 Beatrix Campbell and Valerie Charlton, 'Grunwick Women', *Spare Rib*, 61, August 1977; reprinted in Marsha Rowe (ed.), *Spare Rib Reader*, Penguin, Harmondsworth, 1982, pp. 210–16.

38 Catherine Hoskyns, 'Equality and the European Community', in Feminist Review (ed.), *Waged Work: A Reader*, pp. 219–20.

39 Swasti Mitter, *Common Fate, Common Bond: Women in the Global Economy*, Pluto, London, 1986, p. 146.

40 Kathleen Fincham and Sabina Roberts, 'The Struggle for Democracy', *Socialist Woman*, 1:3, May–June 1969.

41 'Upstairs Downstairs 100 Times a Day' (interview with Kathleen Fincham), *Spare Rib*, April 1974.

42 Jean Wright, in *Cleaners' Voice*, n.d.

43 Wilson, *Finding a Voice*, p. 56.

44 ibid., p. 58.

45 Campbell and Charlton, 'Grunwick Women'; reprinted in Rowe, *Spare Rib Reader*, pp. 210–16.

46 Pratibha Parmar, 'Gender, Race and Class: Asian Women in Resistance', in Centre for Contemporary Cultural Studies (ed.), *The Empire Strikes Back: Race and Racism in '70s Britain*, Hutchinson, London, 1983, p. 267.

47 Clara Moreno *et al.*, 'Resident Domestics' Campaign', in Ann Curno *et al.*, *Women in Collective Action*, Association of Community Workers in the UK, London, 1982, pp. 86–7.

48 Quoted in Jane Hewland, 'Women's Industrial Union', *Spare Rib*, 3, September 1972.

49 ibid.

50 Quoted in Campbell and Rowbotham, 'Women Workers and Class Struggle', in Rowbotham, *Dreams and Dilemmas*, p. 102.

51 Campbell and Charlton, 'Grunwick Women'; reprinted in Rowe, *Spare Rib Reader*, pp. 210–16.

52 'More than Just a Memory: Some Political Implications of Women's Involvement in the Miners' Strike, 1984–5' (interview by Sheila Rowbotham with Jean McCrindle), *Feminist Review*, 23, Summer 1986.

53 ibid.

54 For a discussion of class, feminism and the labour movement, see Phillips, *Divided Loyalties*, pp. 121–61.

55 De Groot, 'Women and Unions'.

56 Beatrix Campbell, *Wigan Pier Revisited*, Virago, London, 1984, p. 234.

57 Both criticism and an elaborated defence of this phrase can be found in 'Feminism and Class Politics: A Round-Table Discussion' (in which Clara Connolly and Lynne Segal, representing *Feminist Review*, talk with Michèle Barrett, Beatrix Campbell, Anne Phillips, Angela Weir and Elizabeth Wilson), *Feminist Review*, 23, Summer 1986.

58 Quoted in Jenny Beale, *Getting It Together*, p. 94.

59   Joan Bohanna, 'Women Shop Stewards in Industry', *Beyond the Fragments Bulletin*, 4, Winter 1982–3.

60   De Groot, 'Women and Unions'.

61   Hilary Wainwright, 'A New Trade Unionism in the Making?', *Beyond the Fragments Bulletin*, 2, 1981.

62   See Beatrix Campbell and Valerie Charlton, 'Work to Rule', in Feminist Anthology Collective (eds.), *No Turning Back: Writings from the Women's Liberation Movement, 1975–80*, Women's Press, London, 1981, pp. 110–20.

63   Campbell, 'United We Fall'.

64   Weir and McIntosh, 'Towards a Wages Strategy for Women'.

65   Lindsey German, 'Lee Jeans', *Women's Voice*, 51, April 1981.

66   See Maureen Mackintosh and Hilary Wainwright (eds.), *A Taste of Power: The Politics of Local Economics*, Verso, London, 1987, pp. 6–8 and 426–33; and Hilary Wainwright, *Labour: A Tale of Two Parties*, Hogarth Press, London, 1987, pp. 205–6.

67   Swasti Mitter, *Common Fate, Common Bond*, p. 163.

Chapter 14

1   'The Borning Struggle: The Civil Rights Movement' (interview with Bernice Reagon), in Dick Cluster (ed.), *They Should Have Served That Cup of Coffee*, Southend Press, Boston, Mass., 1979, p. 38.

2   See Richard Gombin, *The Origins of Modern Leftism*, Penguin, Harmondsworth, 1975, p. 63. (Originally published as *Les Origines du gauchisme*, Seuil, Paris, 1971.)

3   See Wini Breines, *The Great Refusal: Community and Organisation in the New Left, 1962–1968*, Praeger, New York, 1982.

4   Sara Evans, *Personal Politics: The Roots of Women's Liberation in the Civil Rights Movement and the New Left*, Knopf, New York, 1979, p. 214.

5   ibid.

6   Helke Sander quoted in Sheila Rowbotham, 'Storefront Day Care Centres, the Radical Berlin Experiment', in *Dreams and Dilemmas*, Virago, London, 1983, p. 96.

7   Herbert Marcuse, 'On Revolution', in Alexander Cockburn and Robin Blackburn (eds.), *Student Power*, Penguin, Harmondsworth, 1969, p. 371.

8   Sue O'Sullivan, 'Passionate Beginnings: Ideological Politics, 1969–72', *Feminist Review*, 11, 1982.

9   Anon., *Why Miss World?* (pamphlet), London, n.d.

10   O'Sullivan, 'Passionate Beginnings.

11   ibid.

12   ibid.

13   Big Flame Women and Friends, *Walking a Tightrope* (pamphlet), London, n.d. (c. 1980), p. 3.

14   Rosalind Coward, 'Sexual Violence and Sexuality', *Feminist Review*, 11, Summer 1982.

15   See Michèle Barrett, *Women's Oppression Today: Problems in Marxist Feminist Analysis*, Verso, London, 1980, pp. 60–2; and Lynne Segal, *Is the Future Female? Troubled Thoughts on Contemporary Feminism*, Virago, London, 1987, pp. 126–34.

16   See, for example, from the United States, Jessica Benjamin, 'The Bonds of Love: Rational Violence and Erotic Domination', *Feminist Studies*, 6:1, Spring 1980; Ellen Willis, 'Feminism, Moralism and Pornography', in *Beginning to See the Light: Pieces of a Decade*, Knopf, New York, 1981; and Ellen Willis, 'Radical Feminism and Feminist

Radicalism', in Sohnya Sayers *et al.* (eds.), *The 60s Without Apology*, University of Minnesota Press in cooperation with Social Text, Minneapolis, 1984.

17 Leeds Revolutionary Feminist Group, *Love Your Enemy? The Debate Between Heterosexual Feminism and Political Lesbianism* (pamphlet), Onlywomen Press, London, 1981.

18 Jalna Hanmer, 'Male Violence and the Social Control of Women', in Feminist Anthology Collective (eds.), *No Turning Back: Writings from the Women's Liberation Movement, 1975–80*, Women's Press, 1981, p. 190.

19 Coward, 'Sexual Violence and Sexuality'. For a critical discussion of this strand of feminism, see Hester Eisenstein, *Contemporary Feminist Thought*, Unwin, London, 1984, p. 31.

20 Coward, 'Sexual Violence and Sexuality'.

21 On direct action, see Lesley Merryfinch and Jill Sutcliffe, 'Street Hassles', *Shrew*, Summer 1978 (Women and Violence Study Group Issue). On the use of the law and the problems this can present, see Anon., 'Domestic Violence, Women and Policing in London', *Policing London* (publication of Police Monitoring and Research Group of London Strategic Policy Unit), 24, November–December 1986; Heather Brown, 'A Day in the City: Women, Policing and Violence', *Trouble and Strife*, 8, n.d.; Jane Calvert, 'Protecting Men from Women', *Trouble and Strife*, 8, n.d.; and Carol Smart, 'Law and the Control of Women's Sexuality: The Case of the 1950s', in Bridget Hutter and Gillian Williams (eds.), *Controlling Women: The Normal and the Deviant*, Croom Helm, London, 1981, pp. 41–5.

22 See Segal, *Is the Future Female?*, pp. 112–14.

23 Melissa Benn, 'Adventures in the Soho Skin Trade', *New Statesman*, 11 December 1987.

24 ibid.

25 Interview by A. Gottlieb with Joan Nestle, *Cayenne: A Socialist Feminist Bulletin* (Toronto), 2:1, March 1986.

26 Mandy Rose quoted in Benn, 'Adventures in the Soho Skin Trade'.

27 ibid.

28 Muriel Dimen, *Surviving Sexual Contradictions*, Collier Macmillan, London, 1986, p. 182.

29 Angela Carter, 'The Company of Wolves', in *The Bloody Chamber and Other Stories*, Gollancz, 1979; paperback edn, Penguin, 1981.

30 Sue Ardill and Sue O'Sullivan, 'Upsetting an Applecart: Difference, Desire and Lesbian Sado-Masochism', *Feminist Review*, 23, Summer 1986.

31 Elizabeth Wilson, *Adorned in Dreams: Fashion and Modernity*, Virago, London, 1985, pp. 234–43.

32 ibid., p. 242.

33 Letter to *Spare Rib*, 139, November 1983; quoted in Wilson, *Adorned in Dreams*, p. 236.

34 Wilson, *Adorned in Dreams*, p. 246.

35 ibid.

36 ibid., p. 247.

37 Beverley Bryan, Stella Dadzie and Suzanne Scafe, *The Heart of the Race*, Virago, London, 1985, p. 2.

38 ibid.

39 Hutter and Williams, *Controlling Women*, p. 34.

40 Wendy Holloway, ' "I Just Wanted to Kill a Woman." Why? The Ripper and Male Sexuality', *Feminist Review*, 9, Autumn 1981.

41   ibid.

42   Eileen McLeod, 'Prostitutes Organize', *Spare Rib*, 56, March 1977.

43   Merry Cross, 'Feminism and the Disability Movement: A Personal View', in Joy Holland (ed.), *Feminist Action*, Battle Axe Books, London, 1984, p. 29.

44   ibid.

45   ibid.

46   ibid.

47   Ardill and O'Sullivan, 'Upsetting an Applecart'.

48   Alison Fell, 'Rannoch Moor', in *Kisses for Mayakovsky*, Virago, London, 1984, p. 12.

Chapter 15

1   Meg Luxton, *More Than a Labour of Love*, Women's Press, Toronto, 1980, p. 228.

2   Temma Kaplan, 'Female Consciousness and Collective Action: The Case of Barcelona, 1910–1918', *Signs* (Chicago), 7, 1982.

3   Judy Aulette and Trudy Mills, 'Two Spheres, One World: Understanding Women's Contribution to the 1983–1986 Arizona Copper Strike' (unpublished paper), Departments of Sociology, University of North Carolina and University of Arizona, 1987.

4   Liz Heron, 'Sisterhood Re-examined', *New Statesman*, 1 April 1983.

5   Birmingham International Socialists, paper at Women's Liberation Conference, early 1970s.

6   Valerie Clarke and Kathy Sims, 'Fight the Tory Rent Robbery', *Women's Voice*, 1, 1972.

7   Rosie Boycott and Christine Aziz, 'Women Alone', *Spare Rib*, 17, November 1973.

8   Quoted in Anon., 'Squatters and the Housing Crisis', *Islington Gutter Press*, 22, July–August 1975.

9   Alison Fell, 'Women and Housing', *Spare Rib*, 40, October 1975.

10   See Anon., 'There was a Young Woman Who Lived in a Shoe', *Islington Gutter Press*, 8, n.d.

11   Sophie Watson and Helen Austerberry, 'Home Woman', *Spare Rib*, 91, February 1980.

12   ibid.

13   ibid.

14   ibid.

15   Florence Keyworth, 'Women's Role in the Labour Movement', *Red Rag*, 1, n.d.

16   See, for example, Birmingham International Socialists, paper at Women's Liberation Conference, early 1970s; Tower Hill Women's Group, *Libertarian Women's Newsletter* (Merseyside Issue), 4, 16 July 1973; and Big Flame Women and Friends, *Walking a Tightrope* (pamphlet), London, n.d. (c. 1980), p. 13.

17   'Hazards of Housework' column, *Women's Struggle Notes* (Big Flame women's publication), 3, 1977.

18   Katya Frishauer and Martha Osamor (United Black Women's Action Group), interviewed in *Socialist Woman*, 6:4, October 1978; reprinted in Feminist Anthology Collective (eds.), *No Turning Back: Writings from the Women's Liberation Movement, 1975–80*, Women's Press, London, 1981, pp. 46–55.

19 Heather Brown, 'A Day in the City: Women, Policing and Violence', *Trouble and Strife*, 8, n.d.

20 Quoted in Merseyside Big Flame Women's Group, 'High Rise, High Rents', *Spare Rib*, 42, December 1975.

21 Val, 'Stroppy Women', in Big Flame Women and Friends, *Walking a Tightrope*, p. 13.

22 Maria O'Reilly, 'Netherley United: Women Take On the Housing Corporation', *Spare Rib*, 56, March 1977.

23 Barbara Castle and South Wales Tenants, 'Coming Alive Hurts', in Ann Curno *et al.* (eds.), *Women in Collective Action*, Association of Community Workers in the UK, London, 1982, p. 139.

24 Marie Mulholland, quoted in Loretta Loach, 'Victims and Survivors', *Spare Rib*, 163, February 1986.

25 ibid.

26 See Lliane Phillips, 'Docklands', in Maureen Mackintosh and Hilary Wainwright (eds.), *A Taste of Power: The Politics of Local Economics*, Verso, London, 1987; and The People's Plan Centre and Newham Docklands Forum, *The People's Plan for the Royal Docks* (pamphlet), Greater London Council, 1983.

27 Fell, 'Women and Housing'.

28 ibid.

29 ibid.

30 Big Flame Women, 'Organizing in the East London Dockside Area' (interview with Pat Olley), *Women's Struggle Notes*, 6, August–November, c.1976.

31 ibid.

32 ibid.

33 Sue Crockford and Nan Fromer, 'When is a House Not a Home?', *Shrew*, 4:3, May 1971.

34 Emma Charles, 'Building Blocks', *Spare Rib*, 18, December 1973.

35 Denise Arnold, 'Feminism and Architecture: A Mathematical View', *Slate*, 8, July–August 1978.

36 See, for example, Roberta Hunter Henderson and Liz Cooper, 'Don't Break Down, Break Out', *Shrew*, Autumn 1976.

37 Anon., 'Concrete Forms of Sexism', *Women's Report*, 6:3, September–October 1975.

38 ibid.

39 See Irene Bruegel and Adah Kay, 'Women and Planning', *Architectural Design*, August 1975.

40 Charles, 'Building Blocks'.

41 Islington Borough Council Women's Committee, 'A Borough Plan for Islington Women', Islington Borough Council, London, 1986.

42 Quoted in Helen Berenger, 'Kramer *vs.* Kramer: Myth *vs.* Reality', *Spare Rib*, 94, May 1980.

43 Anon., 'Concrete Forms of Sexism'.

44 Islington Borough Council Women's Committee, 'A Borough Plan for Islington Women'.

45 Friends of the Earth, *Women and Transport* (leaflet), London, 1987.

46 Anon., 'Scotland: Oil Rigs, Violence and Women in Revolt', *Spare Rib*, 95, June 1980.

47 Anna Briggs, 'Who Drives the Family Car?', *Spare Rib*, 57, April 1977.

48 Anna Briggs, ' "RAFT" ', *Spare Rib*, 70, May 1978.

49　See, for example, Greater London Council Women's Committee, *Chance or Choice: Community Care and Women as Carers*, GLC, London, 1984.

50　See Sheila Rowbotham, 'Travelling Public', *New Society*, 28 November 1986; and Sheila Rowbotham, 'Stress at Work', *Zeta* (Boston, Mass.), May 1988.

51　Constance Whippman, 'Trains, Buses, Escalators and a Baby', *Spare Rib*, 30, December 1974.

52　ibid.

53　ibid.

54　See Sheila Rowbotham, 'Travelling Public'; Sheila Rowbotham, 'Stress at Work'; and Maureen Mackintosh, 'Jobs and People's Lives: One Person Operation on Buses and Tubes', in Mackintosh and Wainwright, *A Taste of Power*.

55　Carol Gorney, 'Things That Mother Never Told Us', *Spare Rib*, 87, October 1979.

56　Marina Lewycka, 'Wages and Housework', unpublished paper for Big Flame Women, 1975.

57　See Mariarosa Dalla Costa, *The Power of Women and the Subversion of the Community*, Falling Wall Press, Bristol, 1973.

58　Barbara Moses, 'The End of a Community', *Spare Rib*, 19, January 1974.

59　See Jan O'Malley, *The Politics of Community Action*, Spokesman, Nottingham, 1977, pp. 177–9.

60　Simon Burton, 'Waste Not, Want Not: Energy Savings for Community Laundries', *Jobs for a Change* (Greater London Council publication), 15, 1985; and Anon., 'Technets', *Jobs for a Change*, 11, 1984.

61　See Anon., *People's Food Co-op, Lincoln Estate, Bow* (Big Flame pamphlet), n.d. (c. 1975).

62　Nottingham Women's Group, 'The Implications of a Prices Campaign: The Nottingham Experience', paper at Women's Liberation Conference, early 1970s.

63　ibid.

64　Jane Brown, 'Defend Living Standards: Freeze Prices, Not Wages', *Socialist Woman*, Summer 1974.

65　Mary Crane, 'Unions and Housewives: The Road from Cowley', *Socialist Woman*, Summer 1974.

66　See Lynne Segal and Alison Fell, 'They Call Us Militants', *Spare Rib*, 37, July 1975.

67　Rachel Wilson, 'Wildt Mellor Wives Support Sit-in', *Spare Rib*, 57, April 1977.

68　Anon., *Housing in Crisis: Women's Offensive* (pamphlet), London, n.d. (c. 1973).

69　ibid.

70　ibid.

71　'More than Just a Memory: Some Political Implications of Women's Involvement in the Miners' Strike, 1984–5' (interview by Sheila Rowbotham with Jean McCrindle), *Feminist Review*, 23, Summer 1986.

72　On women's involvement in the miners' strike, see Vicky Seddon, *The Cutting Edge*, Lawrence & Wishart, London, 1986; Joan Witham, *Hearts and Minds*, Canary Press, London, 1986; Barbara Bloomfield, 'Women's Support Groups at Maerdy', in Raphael Samuel, Barbara Bloomfield and Guy Boanas, *The Enemy Within: Pit Villages and the Miners' Strike of 1984–5*, Routledge & Kegan Paul, London, 1986, pp. 154–6; Jill Millar, *You Can't Kill the Spirit*, Women's Press, London, 1987; and Norma Dolby, *Norma Dolby's Diary*, Verso, London, 1987.

73　'More than Just a Memory'.

74　Ann Suddick, 'Making the Links: Women Against Pit Closures' in Raphael

Samuel and Hilary Wainwright (eds.), *A Nuclear Future?* (pamphlet), The Socialist Society, London, 1986, p. 26.

75 ibid., pp. 26–9.
76 ibid., p. 27.
77 ibid., p. 29.
78 Amrit Wilson, 'Women Against the Dust', *Spare Rib*, 44, August 1976.
79 Elizabeth Wynhausen, 'A Union for Prisoners' Wives', *Spare Rib*, 19, January 1974.
80 'Derry Relatives' Action' (interview by member of London Women's Armagh Co-ordinating Committee with Mary Nelis and Nina Hutchison), in Curno *et al.*, *Women in Collective Action*, pp. 32–40.
81 ibid., p. 37.
82 Wilson, 'Wildt Mellor Wives Support Sit-in'.
83 Wilson, 'Women Against the Dust'.
84 Pragna Patel, Smita Bhide and Rita Dia, ' "Masses of Women, but Where is the Movement?" Southall Black Sisters', *Outwrite*, 47, May 1986.
85 See Christina Loughran, 'Armagh and Feminist Strategy: Campaigns around Republican Women Prisoners in Armagh Jail', *Feminist Review*, 23, Summer 1986.
86 ibid. Also on this theme, see *A Difficult Dangerous Honesty: 10 Years of Feminism in Northern Ireland* (pamphlet: transcript of March 1986 symposium entitled 'Feminism: Our Early Years'), Belfast, 1987. (Available from *Women's News*, 7 Winetavern St, Belfast, BT1, 1986.)
87 For a longer discussion of this point, see Sheila Rowbotham, 'What Do Women Want?', *Feminist Review*, 20, Summer 1985.
88 Pratibha Parmar, 'A Revolutionary Anger' in Curno *et al.* (eds.), *Women in Collective Action*, p. 92. See also Anon., 'Black Women Together', *Spare Rib*, 87, October 1979; Anon., 'Harassment at Heathrow', *Spare Rib*, 80, March 1979; Anon., 'Virginity Tests – Stop This Vile Racism', *Women's Voice*, 21, March 1979; Anon., 'British Racism Institutionalized', *Scarlet Women*, 12, Spring 1981; pp. 10–17; Brixton Black Women's Group, 'The Brixton Uprising', *Spare Rib*, 107, June 1981; and Parita Trivedi, 'Black Women and the State', *Socialist Woman*, 10, December 1979.
89 Patel *et al.*, ' "Masses of Women, but Where is the Movement?" '
90 Bell Hooks, 'Sisterhood: Political Solidarity between Women', *Feminist Review*, 43, Summer 1986.
91 Suddick, 'Making the Links', in Samuel and Wainwright, *A Nuclear Future?*, p. 28.
92 Hunter Henderson and Cooper, 'Don't Break Down, Break Out'.
93 Barbara Harford and Sarah Hopkins (eds.), *Greenham Common: Women and the Wire*, Women's Press, London, 1984; quoted in Lynne Segal, *Is the Future Female? Troubled Thoughts on Contemporary Feminism*, Virago, London, 1987, p. 165.
94 Segal, *Is the Future Female?*, p. 164.
95 Sue Finch *et al.*, 'Socialist Feminists and Greenham', *Feminist Review*, 23, Summer 1986.
96 See Feminism and Non-Violence Study Group, *Piecing It Together: Feminism and Non-Violence* (pamphlet), London, 1983, p. 18.
97 Mary Coghill and Sheila Redmond, 'Feminism and Spirituality', in Joy Holland (ed.), *Feminist Action*, Battle Axe Books, London, 1984, p. 92.
98 Sarah Green, quoted in Alice Cook and Gwyn Kirk, *Greenham Women Everywhere*, Pluto, London, 1983, pp. 87–8.
99 Quoted in Finch *et al.*, 'Socialist Feminists and Greenham'.

100   ibid.

101   Stephanie Leland, 'Greenham Women are Everywhere', in Holland, *Feminist Action*, p. 123.

102   See Feminism and Non-Violence Study Group, *Piecing It Together*.

103   Interview with Mary Brewer, recorded at Sowerby Bridge near Halifax by Jill Liddington for 'Feminism and Anti-Militarism', an oral history talk, Northern College, 13 February 1987. I am grateful to Jill Liddington and Mary Brewer for permission to quote.

104   See Dorothy Thompson (ed.), *Over Our Dead Bodies*, Virago, London, 1983.

105   For a fuller account of these issues, see Segal, *Is the Future Female?*, pp. 162–203.

106   Suddick, 'Making the Links', in Samuel and Wainwright, *A Nuclear Future?*, p. 27.

107   ibid.

108   Heron, 'Sisterhood Re-examined'.

Conclusion

1   For example, see Hester Eisenstein, *Contemporary Feminist Thought*, Unwin, London, 1984; Lynne Segal, *Is the Future Female? Troubled Thoughts on Contemporary Feminism*, Virago, London, 1987; Elizabeth Wilson and Angela Weir, *Hidden Agendas: Theory, Politics and Experience in the Women's Liberation Movement*, Tavistock, London, 1986; Juliet Mitchell and Ann Oakley, *What is Feminism?*, Blackwell, Oxford, 1986; and Anne Phillips, *Divided Loyalties: Dilemmas of Sex and Class*, Virago, London, 1987.

2   Liz Heron, *Changes of Heart*, Pandora, London, 1986, p. 110.

3   Ante Ciliga, *The Russian Enigma*, Inklinks, London, 1979, p. 92.

4   ibid.

Sources for Ephemeral Material Cited in the References

The Fawcett Library at the City of London Polytechnic has a large collection of periodicals, leaflets and other documents from the women's liberation movement. It is the main source for the material cited in these references. I have deposited cuttings from various feminist magazines referred to in this book with the Polytechnic of North London Library (Women's Studies Department).

Index